California's

Great Outdoor Events

❖ ❖ ❖ ❖

1995·96 EDITION

by Ken McKowen

ISBN 0-935701-50-8

51695

Foghorn
Press
BOOKS BUILDING COMMUNITY™

9 780935 701500

Foghorn Press
555 DeHaro Street #220
San Francisco, CA 94107
415-241-9550

Foghorn Press titles are distributed to the book trade by
Publishers Group West, Emeryville, California. To contact
your local sales representative, call 1-800-788-3123.

To order individual books, please call Foghorn Press at
1-800-FOGHORN (364-4676).

Printed in the United States of America.

California's

Great Outdoor Events

❦ ❦ ❦ ❦

1995·96 EDITION

by Ken McKowen

Foghorn Press

BOOKS BUILDING COMMUNITY™

Credits

Managing Editor/Book Design—*Ann-Marie Brown*
Editor—*Howard Rabinowitz*
Maps—*Michele Thomas*
Cover Illustration—*Kirk McInroy*

Dedication

This book is dedicated to my wife Denise, for her understanding, love and support during my long hours of late-night work and aborted weekend holidays attempting to meet a very short deadline. She provided me with able assistance, occasional humor, much needed snacks of marginal nutritional value and was a companion willing to attend an extraordinary number of hikes and events to gather the first-hand knowledge that helped me create these written words.

—*Ken McKowen*

Foghorn Press is committed to preservation of the environment. All Foghorn Press outdoors titles are printed on the California standard for recycled paper, which is 50% recycled paper and 10% post-consumer waste.

Contents

Foreword

Just as Mark Twain assured his readers a century ago that the report of his death was greatly exaggerated, I'm happy to say that today's reports about California's demise are just as premature. For untold thousands of years, California was shaped by glaciers, earthquakes, floods, fires and mud slides. The only thing that's changed today is that 32 million people now call California their home, and those people and their homes sometimes find themselves in the path of Mother Nature's never-ending work.

Can we fight Mother Nature? Sure, but we won't win, at least not in the long haul. So what's the answer? From my perspective and experience, the best thing we can do is to learn to understand the natural world around us—the power of that world—and then work within guidelines that allow for our coexistence with nature. Certainly, early native Californians understood their world. While they did not possess the power to move mountains, eliminate entire wetland ecosystems or turn mighty rivers into quiet, backwater reservoirs, they knew that even with their limited technologies they had to live within nature's rules if their peoples were to survive.

So what does all this philosophy have to do with California and the people who live here today? Well, it's pretty simple, actually. During the last several years, ecotourism has become the thing to do, at least for those who can afford multi-thousand-dollar trips to climb the Andes, paddle the Amazon or dogsled to the North Pole. What far too many Californians don't realize is that there are literally thousands of mini-ecotourism opportunities right in our own backyards that are affordable to all.

California's diversity, both in its natural wonders and in its cultural variety, offers opportunities that can be found nowhere else in the world. State, national, regional and local parks, along with other federal lands and local city and county community organizations, offer a multitude of programs, hikes, tours and mini-seminars designed to introduce neophytes to nature's wonders or provide outdoor veterans with new insights and adventures. And it all happens here in California.

California's foothills and forests, its deserts and seashores, its marshes and meadows all offer us more than just an opportunity to explore the wonders of nature. Here, we can escape the hassles and pressures of everyday life. Even in a place as frenetic as Los Angeles we are not very far from places to enjoy the solitude and quiet of a cool, bubbling mountain stream, the chatter of birds and the rustle of an afternoon breeze fluttering through a forest of leaves.

Renewing the human spirit is not just a pursuit for bearded Grizzly Adams-types escaping our modern and less-than-Utopian world. We all possess a spirit that is in occasional need of rekindling. Sometimes all we need is the proper invitation, the knowledge that there are incredible numbers of opportunities for meeting nature on nature's terms and coming away with a sense of self-renewal. This book is your invitation to explore California's natural world. It will serve as a guide to many of the opportunities that abound in the Golden State to learn about nature, to experience first-hand her power, her beauty, her bounty and her open arms that welcome all those who wish to understand more about this wonderful world in which we are merely visitors.

Donald W. Murphy
Director
California State Parks

Introduction

California's natural wonders have attracted millions of people from all walks of life, with varying cultures, beliefs and attitudes. And as Californians notoriously differ in most of their pursuits, so too do they differ in the ways they explore and celebrate the geographic beauty that surrounds them. In celebrating California, that diversity has created a cornucopia of outdoor events and festivals unparalleled in the other 49 states of the Union—or anywhere else in the world, for that matter.

In writing this book, I wanted to help lots of people discover the events and programs that are offered each year in our parks, forests, deserts and other public lands. Unlike most folks who now call California home, I was fortunate enough to have been born in the Golden State several decades ago; I've spent most of my years here traveling, camping, hiking, watching and photographing all the stuff that makes California, well, California. I suppose it was my wanderings in the Sierra every summer as a kid that led to my spending 10 years as a ranger working in a dozen different state parks, from Lake Perris in Southern California to Lake Tahoe in the north. During those 10 years, I had a great time sharing, teaching and exploring with thousands of people the natural beauty and historical and cultural treasures of California.

What you will find in this book is a shortcut to discovering many outdoor activities and downright best fun events that California has to offer. The book doesn't tell all, but it does house the wisdom and wanderings of many, many years of exploration and discovery. The only problem for you, the reader, will be deciding how best to spend your precious little free time out there with so much going on in California's great outdoors. But then, that's the fun part, too, so enjoy!

Here are some words of caution:

Weather: As any television weather person knows, weather is never entirely predictable. Expect what is normal for any particular place and season, but anticipate and plan for uncommon weather.

Difficulty: Many of the hikes, programs, festivals and other activities that I have listed here are appropriate for everybody. Others are designed only for those individuals who possess the strength, skills and proper equipment to participate safely. What is moderately difficult for one person can be back-breaking, muscle-aching torture for others. Know your limitations, and the limitations of those who go with you, and don't exceed them.

Directions: The directions to the starting places for each of the activities and programs listed are as specific as possible, but bringing along a good road map is always advisable.

Scheduling: Some of the events are accompanied by scheduled and telephone symbols, **S**𝓞 which means the event's date, time and location were tentative as this book went to press. Where you see these symbols, always call ahead to confirm dates, times and locations. But also be aware that some events that are *not* listed with the **S**𝓞 symbol may be canceled or rescheduled. It is strongly recommended that you always call ahead to confirm that an event is still being offered and that the date, time, location and fees have not changed. A quick telephone call may save wasted travel time, money and frustration.

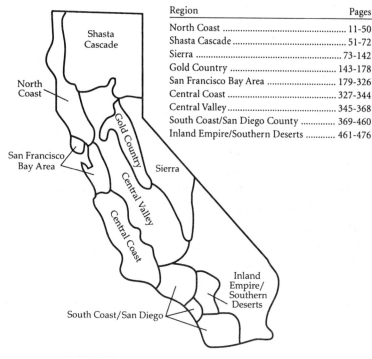

How To Use This Book

You can find the outdoor event you want to attend in three ways:

1) If you know the name of the event or the type of event you want to attend (such as birdwatching or March for Parks), use the index beginning on page 539 to locate it and turn to the corresponding page. Also use the index if you are looking for events in a specific town or city.

2) If you'd like to attend an outdoor event in a particular geographical region of California, use the California state map on page 9. Find the regional chapter containing the area in which you'd like to attend an event, then turn to the corresponding pages in the book.

3) If you'd like to find an event held at a particular time of year, flip through the facing pages in each regional chapter, which are marked with shaded tabs indicating the month of that page's events. Seasonal and ongoing events, also indicated by shaded tabs, are listed at the end of each chapter.

For greater detail, we have divided California into eight geographical regions, which are: North Coast, Shasta Cascade, Sierra, Gold Country, San Francisco Bay Area, Central Coast, South Coast/ San Diego County and Inland Empire/Southern Deserts.

Each event listing has a map location number and map page reference listed underneath it, so you can see on the corresponding regional map approximately where the event will be held. Many locations host more than one event throughout the year.

The scheduled and telephone symbols **S** _(_ indicate that the date and time listed for an event are tentative. Readers *must* call to confirm these events in advance.

As events may be cancelled or rescheduled at any time and for any reason, Foghorn Press strongly suggests you call ahead to confirm *all* events, whether the scheduled symbol appears with the listing or not.

Chapter 1

✤ ✤ ✤ ✤

Great Outdoor Events
of
California's North Coast

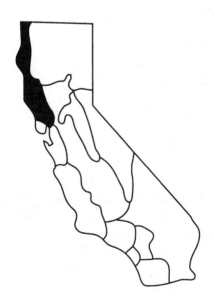

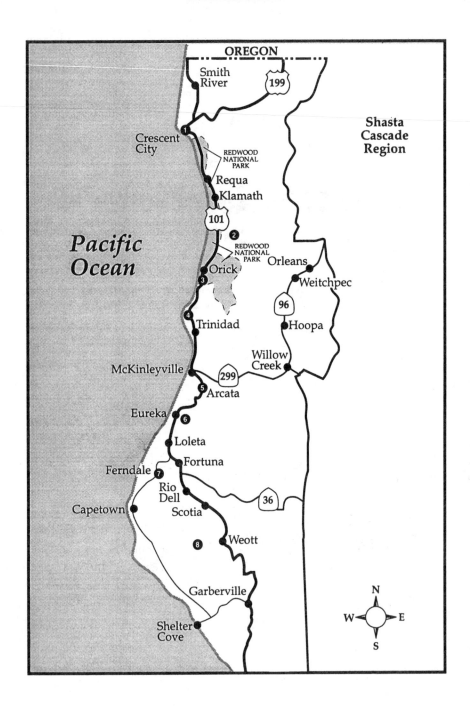

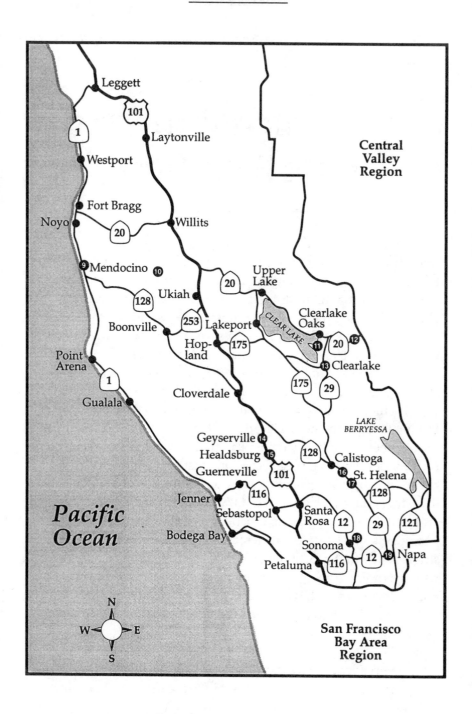

✤ ✤ ✤ ✤

Introduction to the North Coast

In some ways, little has changed along California's North Coast since the Russians first settled here in the early 1800s, building Fort Ross as their wilderness outpost. It still rains dozens of inches each year, summer fog still feeds life-giving moisture to giant, century-old redwoods and there's still that Russian fort sitting on the bluffs overlooking the Pacific. But Fort Ross has been a state park for many years, and it is state and national parks that protect the last remaining five to ten percent of old growth redwoods that have managed to elude the gaping jaws of famished sawmills.

It's more than redwoods that bring people to the North Coast. Fishing for salmon and steelhead is still remarkably good, in spite of the impact that human activities have had and continue to have on the fisheries. There's a rugged coastline that beckons low-tide exploration by hikers and backpackers. The Avenue of the Giants is a drive that everyone should take at least once to see how this entire area once looked, cloaked and shaded by 300-foot-tall redwoods. The quaint towns that are scattered inland and along the coastal strand testify to the fortitude of early settlers in this land, and to the staying power of present-day folks heavily impacted by the economic downturn of the timber and fishing industries.

Explore the charming shops and beautiful views at Mendocino, take a whale-watching trip from Noyo Bay at Fort Bragg, hike up a fern-covered canyon at Gold Bluff Beach, get lost for days in Sinkyone Wilderness, gaze upward at the tallest tree in the world or enjoy the Victorian homes and shops in Ferndale or the charming old town of Eureka.

While the area is notorious for its rain, there are times, for example much of July and August, that are pretty much rain-free. And the morning fog generally burns off by lunch, letting the warming rays of the sun cascade across the beaches and redwood forests. Come prepared for all types of weather and you can enjoy all that California's North Coast has to offer.

World Championship Crab Races

February 19, 1995 • 10 a.m. to 4 p.m.
(see #1 on map page 12)

Gray skies and cold, wet rain is not the kind of weather that attracts most people. It's not always cold and wet here, but you shouldn't worry too much if you happen to forget your sunscreen. Add a whole bunch of crabs, the six-legged kind, running around and suddenly there's a big change in a lot of people's attitudes. What these folks do is convince a bunch of Dungeness crabs to hightail it down raceways in an effort to see which one is the quickest. Little do these crustaceans suspect that the grand prize for all their work is a quick swim in a pot of boiling water. Their loss is your gain, so come on up to the North Coast of California and enjoy the races and the final gastronomically fantastic results.

Crescent City is located in far northern California, along US 101. The entrance fee to the races will probably be about $2. There's an additional fee for the crab feed. After all, you wouldn't want those little crabs to think that their lives were worth only two bucks, would you? Plan on cool weather with an excellent chance of rain.

For more information, contact the Crescent City Chamber of Commerce, 1001 Front Street, Crescent City, CA 95531; (707) 464-3174 or (800) 343-8300.

Foggy Bottoms Milk Run

March 5, 1995 • 10:30 a.m. to 3 p.m.
(see #7 on map page 12)

If you've never been to Ferndale, then you've missed out on California's best-preserved Victorian town. Want a unique way to visit the town and the beautiful farmland that surrounds it? If you're a runner, then join hundreds of others in this family affair held each year. There are three different running courses that wind through the scenic, pastoral setting of this unique coastal village. Each course ends on Ferndale's Main Street. For those not particularly interested in touring the surrounding cattle and farmland on foot, Ferndale offers plenty to see and do, including a nearly inexhaustible supply of gift and curio shops.

Ferndale is not close to any major metropolitan area, so you really have to want to go there. From Eureka, take US 101 south about 17 miles to the Ferndale/Ferndale bridge exit. Cross the narrow Ferndale bridge, then drive five miles into Ferndale and Main Street. The cost of the milk run is $12 per person and family rates are available if you bring the entire brood. As long as the rain and drizzle holds off, it should be a nice cool day for running.

For information, contact the Six Rivers Running Club; (707) 677-3655.

✤ ✤ ✤ ✤

Cache Creek Wildflower Walks

Saturdays & Sundays in April [S] ☎ • 10 a.m. to 2 p.m.

(see #12 on map page 13)

Wildflowers cover the coastal mountains with a blanket of bright and cheerful color each spring. While most people just whiz by in their cars taking casual notice of the flowers, you'll gain much more pleasure from nature's bounty if you stop to sniff the roses, so to speak. Join a naturalist from the Bureau of Land Management who leads this leisurely, four-mile hike along the hillsides and through the gullies of the coastal mountains. There will be many stops to look at flowers, both for identification purposes and so that those who bring cameras can take time to photograph nature's canvas. The hike more or less follows the meandering of Cache Creek, so there's a 600-foot elevation gain, most of it within the first mile. You need to be in reasonably good physical condition. Bring water, lunch, a wildflower field guide if you happen to have one, and a camera. Each hike is limited to just 25 people, so you should call ahead to make a reservation. The meeting place for the hike is at the Redbud Trailhead parking lot, eight miles east of Clearlake Oaks on Highway 20, just west of the North Fork Cache Creek bridge. All hikes are free.

For information and reservations, contact the Bureau of Land Management, 2550 North State Street, Ukiah, CA 95482; (707) 468-4000.

✤ ✤ ✤ ✤

School Days at Fort Humboldt
April 26, 1995 ⑤🄒 · 10 a.m. to 4 p.m.
(see #6 on map page 12)

School Days is really pretty similar to Donkey Days, which is usually held one week later. The biggest difference is that the focus of School Days is on taking school classes on tours of Fort Humboldt's outdoor and indoor logging displays, which include axes, saws and dioramas. And of course, the old, historic steam donkey is fired up and there are steam train rides available. If you have a school group you'd like to take to the fort, or simply like kids and just want to see maybe 1,000 of them having a good time, this is a great day to visit the fort. If a little more peace and quiet is your cup of tea, then try another day. But if you want to witness the steam-spewing, smoke-belching steam donkey in all its glory, you must come on a special event day like this one, because the donkey generally stays put on non-special event days. Oh, by the way, a steam donkey looks slightly reminiscent of an old, giant tractor. In days of old, it was used to drag logs from the woods to the mill or somewhere in between.

Fort Humboldt State Historic Park is located on the south side of Eureka, just off Highland Avenue, which intersects with US 101. Late April is a good time of year to visit the area, because unless there's a storm blowing in from the Pacific, it should be a pretty pleasant spring day. The program is free.

For information, contact Fort Humboldt State Historic Park, 3431 Fort Avenue, Eureka, CA 95501; (707) 445-6567.

✤ ✤ ✤ ✤

Donkey Days
April 29 & 30, 1995 ⑤🄒 · 10 a.m. to 4 p.m.
(see #6 on map page 12)

Logging has a long and fascinating history and the story is told no better than at a Donkey Days event, when a steam donkey is brought out of retirement to perform again. What's a steam donkey, you ask? It's a huge, tractor-like, steam-powered iron and steel monster that was once used to move giant logs from the forests to the mills. Today, the few that remain are relegated to museums, such as the one at Fort Humboldt in Eureka. The annual weekend event features displays of historic logging equipment, steam train rides, hit-and-miss engines, snorting steam donkeys and a logging events competition. This is a really fun weekend in a beautiful part of the North Coast. And if you tire of the logging events, take the short drive to the other side of Eureka where the historic waterfront area's Victorian homes and businesses have been renovated into stores, bed and breakfasts and restaurants. About 1,400 people usually pass through the fort during Donkey Days weekend.

Fort Humboldt State Historic Park is located on Highland Avenue, just off US 101, near the southern side of Eureka. The event is free to the public. The weather could be anywhere from warm and sunny to foggy, cold and rainy.

For information, contact Fort Humboldt State Historic Park, 3431 Fort Avenue, Eureka, CA 95501; (707) 445-6567.

Annual Bicycle Tour of the Unknown Coast

May 6 & 7, 1995 [S] ☎ • Call for start times

(see #7 on map page 12)

While this race, sanctioned by the United States Cycling Federation (USCF), is billed as the toughest century or 100-mile road course in California, shorter and more easily traveled rides are also scheduled for those with less energy and lower endurance levels. Saturday is set aside for skills workshops, bicycle clinics, a pasta feed and early registration. On Sunday, you can join either an easy 10-mile ride over level roads through the local farm country, a 20-miler, which has one small hill, or a 50-mile tour that includes more hills as you follow the Avenue of the Giants through mile after mile of ancient, towering redwoods. The 100-mile century is a tour along the Unknown Coast where you must be an experienced rider in order to handle the seemingly endless hills and weather conditions that can change from inland heat to coastal wind and fog or rain. The rides will take place whether there's sun, wind or rain, so come prepared. Food and beverages will be available to participants at each of the stops. Bike helmets are required of all riders. You must have a multi-geared bike for all but the 10-mile ride. Registration is from 1 p.m. to 6 p.m. on Saturday and begins at 5:30 a.m. on Sunday. To get there, take US 101 to about 12 miles south of Eureka to the Ferndale/Ferndale bridge exit, then cross the old, narrow, concrete Ferndale Bridge and continue on for five miles to Ferndale's Main Street. Follow the signs to the fairgrounds. The cost varies, but plan on about $12 to $20 per person, with special family rates available. Depending on your tour choice, you'll be traveling through a variety of microclimates, some of which will be cool or cold, some wet and some hot and dry, so come prepared for whatever climate Mother Nature chooses.

For information, contact Redwood Sports Velo Promotions, P.O. Box 275, Eureka, CA 95502; (800) 995-8356.

⚜ ⚜ ⚜ ⚜

Mendocino Whale Festival

March 11 & 12, 1995 • 11 a.m. to 5 p.m.
(see #9 on map page 13)

Dozens of towns along California's thousand or so miles of coast have an annual whale festival. So what makes this one any different or better? If you've ever been to the quaint little village of Mendocino and wandered the streets and shops, you wouldn't need to ask such a crazy question. While it's guaranteed the town will charm you, there's never any guarantee that the whales will cooperate. Generally they're so far offshore that all you can see is the occasional water spout, but just getting that little glimpse of these great creatures is a thrill. If you want a close-up view of the migrating whales, you can go on up US 101 a few miles to Fort Bragg and catch a whale-watching boat. Be forewarned, though: If the ocean is doing its normal winter thing, take a good supply of motion sickness remedies, because the idea is to see 'em, not feed 'em, as I did the last time I was up here. Anyway, back in Mendocino the celebration is still fun and so is the shopping. Mendocino is located along Highway 1, about 11 miles south of Fort Bragg. Unless you drop in by parachute, you're going to have to drive some pretty curvy roads, but you can't beat the scenery. The event is free, but whale-watching trips run about $25 per person. If you catch the weather between storms, it should be pleasant but cool. Take some warm, water-repellent clothes if you're going out on a boat.

For more information, contact the Fort Bragg-Mendocino Chamber of Commerce, P.O. Box 1141, Fort Bragg, CA 95437; (707) 961-6300 or (800) 726-2780.

❖ ❖ ❖ ❖

Avenue of the Giants Marathon
May 7, 1995 **S** 🏃 • 8:30 a.m. to 2 p.m.
(see #8 on map page 12)

MAY

This isn't the New York Marathon, but then you won't have to fight your way through quite so many people or breathe so much smog. Instead of block after block of skyscrapers to stare at, there's mile after mile of giant redwoods, meandering rivers and soaring hawks and eagles. The race course winds along much of the Avenue of the Giants and through the ancient redwoods of Humboldt Redwoods State Park's Rockefeller Forest. Actually, the entire race is through redwoods or along the Eel River. Even if you don't win the race, the long jog through the cool forest is said to be both inspiring and relaxing. The starting point for the race is on the Dyerville Bridge at the junction of the Avenue of the Giants and Mattole Road, about 40 miles south of Eureka. There's a $20 entrance fee, although the amount may change by the time race day arrives. The weather is really variable, but it's pretty safe to expect fog in the morning with sun by noon or earlier.

For information, contact the Six Rivers Running Club; (707) 443-1226.

❖ ❖ ❖ ❖

Annual Bountiful Barn Sale

May 20 & 21, 1995 • 10 a.m. to 5 p.m.

(see #15 on map page 13)

While the word "sale" excites a certain segment of the population, this is more than a garage sale in a barn. The sale actually takes place on a working farm, so this is an experience that most of us have never had an opportunity to enjoy. There are plenty of animals for the kids to enjoy, including a pot-bellied pig, a miniature donkey, a pygmy goat and newborn lambs. Kids also get to take home their own free veggie and herb starter kits. There are tractor-pulled hayrides that tour the farm, as well as spinning and weaving demonstrations. Oh, and there actually is a barn sale. You'll find household goods, garden tools, farm odds 'n' ends, old farm junk that may be just the thing for your outdoor decorating, and lots of plants, trees, fresh fruits and vegetables, flowers, fresh-baked pies, and colorful handmade aprons and potholders. There'll even be a picnic lunch available of sausages, potato salad, juices and pie. This event began in 1994 and about 600 people attended each day. There was plenty of parking, and since the hayride tours left every half hour, there was never really a feeling of being a part of the madding crowd.

The event is held at West Side Farms, which is located at 7097 Westside Road, Healdsburg. Take Highway 101 north from Santa Rosa to the Central Healdsburg exit. Turn left at the first stop light onto Westside Road and drive for about six miles to the farm entrance. There is no admission fee; the weather should be sunny and warm.

For information, contact Sonoma County Farm Trails, P.O. Box 6032, Santa Rosa, CA 95406; (707) 996-2154.

World Championship Great Arcata to Ferndale Cross-Country Kinetic Sculpture Race

May 27 to 29, 1995 • Saturday noon till Monday evening
(see #5 on map page 12)

If you can remember the wild and crazy name of this race, then you're well on your way to becoming one of its dozens of participants or thousands of spectators. Now what are kinetic sculptures, you ask? They are human-powered works of art, designed to travel over any and all terrain including roads, sand, mud and even water. Power must be provided by human motion, and the size of your creation is limited only by your imagination, a marginal amount of common sense and the California Highway Patrol's rules for what they'll allow on public roads. Some are relatively simple inventions, holding one or two human engines on top of a floating bicycle of sorts, while others look more like giant snakes or monster crabs powered by numerous people. The race formally begins on Saturday, but there's usually much partying and brake testing on Friday. The first leg of the three-day race begins in Arcata, travels at amazing speed over the dunes of North Spit, ending in Eureka. The second day sees the racers heading out from Eureka and making a two-mile crossing of Humboldt Bay's man-eating, clam-infested waters to Camp Calistoga for a campout. Monday begins with a trip across Cock Robin Island and the mouth of the Eel River, onto Slippery Slimy Slope, then onward for the final sprint to the finish line on Main Street in Ferndale. The competition ends with a special early dinner in Ferndale and everyone is invited. And the grand prize for the winner? The glory, just the glory, and a few prizes for categories such as art, engineering, speed, costumes and sound effects emitted by these creatures. There's also the coveted Medeocar Award for the sculpture that finishes dead middle.

Arcata/Eureka is located about 240 miles north of San Francisco on US 101. The price of competition is $15 per pilot, and it's free to spectate. Count on coastal fog and mist and hope for sun.

For information, contact the Ferndale Chamber of Commerce, P.O. Box 325, Ferndale, CA 95536; phone them at (707) 786-4477 or Kinetic Sculpture Race Inc. at (707) 725-3851.

A Bird In Hand

Late May (rain can delay till June or July)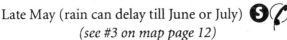
(see #3 on map page 12)

California's redwoods provide a unique environment for the plants and animals that make the groves of ancient giants their homes. Most birds we see in the redwood forests are only visitors, many traveling thousands of miles from Mexico and Central America each year to visit for a few days, weeks or months. Rather than using time-tested binoculars and scopes to spot many of these small songbirds, the leaders of this seminar will capture the traveling passerines with mist nets. You'll then have a chance to see the birds up close while assisting the wildlife managers in banding them for future capture studies as part of the MAPS (Monitoring Avian Production and Survival) program. Capturing and handling the birds successfully and safely depends upon good weather, so stormy skies can postpone the seminar until the following month. Be sure to register well in advance. The fee is $25. This seminar will be held at a yet-to-be-determined site within the Redwoods National and State Parks, which encompasses Jedediah Smith State Park, Del Norte Coast Redwoods State Park, Prairie Creek Redwoods State Park and Redwood National Park. You'll learn the meeting place and the exact date and time when you register.

For information, contact Redwood National and State Field Seminar Coordinator, 1111 Second Street, Crescent City, CA 95531; (707) 465-4113.

❖ ❖ ❖ ❖

Family Tide Pool Day

Late May
(see #3 on map page 12)

This walk through the tide pools is designed as a family outing, so everyone gets the opportunity to learn about the secrets of sea stars, hermit crabs, anemones and the other creatures that call this rocky, waved-washed world their home. As the tides rise and fall, an incredibly rich variety of tidal zone creatures cling tenaciously to the rocks as swift currents and crashing waves replenish their plankton food sources with oxygen and nutrients. If you raise your eyes up to the horizon, you may even catch a glimpse of migrating whales. The exact weekend for this trip will be dictated by the lowest anticipated tide in order to allow the best possible look at the tide pools. A special art project will complete this family day on the beach. There's a fee of $10 for an individual or $20 for a family. Tide Pool Day will be held at a yet-to-be-determined site within the Redwoods National and State Parks. Call ahead for the meeting place and the exact date and time when you register.

For information, contact Redwood National and State Field Seminar Coordinator, 1111 Second Street, Crescent City, CA 95531; (707) 465-4113.

❖ ❖ ❖ ❖

Wildflowers and Weeds
Late May **$** 🌿
(see #3 on map page 12)

Many of the plants and flowers we see along highways and while hiking backcountry trails are not native to this land. They were transported here from Europe and Asia, often accidentally, sometimes purposely. In either case, they have taken hold, often at the expense of native grasses, flowers, shrubs and trees. This seminar is designed to point out the native plants that may have been used by the local Yuroks and Chilula Indians for basket making and food and the nonnative plants that have relocated from other continents. Bring your camera or sketchbook for this six-mile hike through fields and forests filled with the blazing colors of wildflowers and wild weeds. You'll discover park management programs, such as introduced fire, that are designed to restore native vegetation while protecting the forests and meadows from destructive wildfires and wild pests. There's a $25 fee. This seminar will be held at a yet-to-be-determined site within the Redwoods National and State Parks, which encompasses Jedediah Smith State Park, Del Norte Coast Redwoods State Park, Prairie Creek Redwoods State Park and Redwood National Park. You'll learn the meeting place and the exact date and time when you register. Call well in advance to reserve a space.

For information, contact Redwood National and State Field Seminar Coordinator, 1111 Second Street, Crescent City, CA 95531; (707) 465-4113.

✤ ✤ ✤ ✤

 Basic Birds of the Redwood Forest
Early June 🟢🖊
(see #3 on map page 12)

If you've ever wondered what a northern spotted owl looks like, considering all the political and economic unrest it has created in the forests of the Pacific Northwest, then this is the seminar for you. Besides having an opportunity to maybe see a spotted owl—along with another endangered species of old growth forests, the marbeled murrelet—you'll learn the tricks of identifying numerous other birds of the northern redwood forests. Whether you're a birding novice or have been at it for years, this is the perfect chance to see some of our rarer feathered friends, and of course, the more common creatures that help control the bug populations in the forest. The fee for the program is $25. This seminar will be held at a yet-to-be-determined site within the Redwoods National and State Parks, which encompasses Jedediah Smith State Park, Del Norte Coast Redwoods State Park, Prairie Creek Redwoods State Park and Redwood National Park. You'll learn the meeting place and the exact date and time when you register. Call well in advance to reserve a space.

For information, contact Redwood National and State Field Seminar Coordinator, 1111 Second Street, Crescent City, CA 95531; (707) 465-4113.

✤ ✤ ✤ ✤

Fort Humboldt Civil War Day

June 9, 1995 Ⓢ☎ • 10 a.m. to 3 p.m.

(see #6 on map page 12)

Although California didn't play an active role in the battles of the Civil War, the state's support of the Union was crucial, and western forts were maintained by the Union Army. This is a day when you can see demonstrations of Civil War-era weapons and artillery, as well as a recreation of what life was like in military camps for thousands of Civil War combatants. Join the 1,000 or more people who come to witness history being retold. It's even more fun and interesting than Ken Burns' PBS miniseries on the subject. Fort Humboldt is located on the south side of Eureka, just off US 101 on Highland Avenue. The program is free to the public. The weather actually might be pretty nice after the morning fog burns off.

For information, contact Fort Humboldt State Historic Park, (707) 445-6567 or (707) 445-6547, or Eureka/Humboldt County Convention & Visitors Bureau, (800) 338-7352.

From Redwoods to Ridgetops, an Auto Tour

Mid-June Ⓢ☎

(see #3 on map page 12)

The patchwork quilt of redwood state and national parks that covers much of California's North Coast is much too large to explore in a short period of time, at least on foot. Maybe the best way to see a lot of these magnificent parklands in a short period of time is from your car, but with a twist. This traveling automobile seminar also features short walks to the hidden corners of Redwood National Park. The short and easy strolls take you out of your car and into the forests and wildflower-covered prairies. The program fee is $20 for individuals and $35 for two people. This seminar will be held throughout the Redwoods National and State Parks, which encompasses Jedediah Smith State Park, Del Norte Coast Redwoods State

Park, Prairie Creek Redwoods State Park and Redwood National Park. You'll learn the meeting place and the exact date and time when you register. Sign up well in advance.

For information, contact Redwood National and State Field Seminar Coordinator, 1111 Second Street, Crescent City, CA 95531; (707) 465-4113.

✤ ✤ ✤ ✤

Flora of the Redwood Parks
Mid-June $ 📞
(see #3 on map page 12)

While most people come here to stand beneath the towering redwoods and gaze upward, in this seminar you'll find another unique environment beneath and beyond the giant trees. The best place to begin to understand why the redwoods exist in only a very narrow strip of coastal mountains in California, with a few trees just across the border in Oregon, is at the ocean's edge. From the beach, you'll hike inland and ascend through coastal dunes, oak woodlands, the prairies of Bald Hills and finally into redwood forest. The instructor will use the new edition of the Jepson manual to aid in plant identification. If you don't own the rather expensive and technical (but excellent) book, any plant field guide that deals with North Coast redwoods will do. Part of the seminar will focus on Native Americans' uses of local plants. The fee is $25 for the program. This seminar will be held at a yet-to-be-determined site within the Redwoods National and State Parks, which encompasses Jedediah Smith State Park, Del Norte Coast Redwoods State Park, Prairie Creek Redwoods State Park and Redwood National Park. You'll learn the meeting place and the exact date and time when you register, which you should do well in advance.

For information, contact Redwood National and State Field Seminar Coordinator, 1111 Second Street, Crescent City, CA 95531; (707) 465-4113.

✤ ✤ ✤ ✤

Sumeg Village Days

June 22 & 25, 1995 S $\not{C}$ · 10 a.m. to 6 p.m.
(see #4 on map page 12)

Several years ago a Native American village was reconstructed at Patrick's Point State Park and its grand opening was marked by several days of celebration and sacred dances. Today, the annual celebration continues with the healing dance that begins Thursday at dusk and ends temporarily at midnight, then begins again on Saturday evening, lasting all night Saturday. In addition to the sacred healing dance, there are other demonstrations and tours of the village throughout the weekend. You may see one of the local Native Americans carving and burning out the contents of a log to create a new dugout canoe, or another weaving baskets. There's plenty of food and beverages available, as well as booths of Native American crafts so you can take some very special gifts home with you. The nearest hotels are a fair drive away, but the best place to stay is in the park's campground so you can spend as much time as possible at Sumeg Village.

Patrick's Point State Park is located about a half mile off US 101, five miles north of Trinidad. If you walk in or are already staying in the park's campground ($14 per night), there's no fee; otherwise, entrance to the festival will set you back $5 per carload of people. The weather's usually pretty nice this time of year, except perhaps for some morning fog.

For information, contact Patrick's Point State Park; (707) 677-3570.

❖ ❖ ❖ ❖

Scandinavian Mid-Summer Festival

June 24 & 25, 1995 S $\not{C}$ · Afternoon
(see #7 on map page 12)

If you've ever thought about taking a liking to a Viking, here's your chance. As hundreds of people have done for each of the past 44 years, come celebrate Summer Solstice as it was celebrated in old Scandinavia, with traditional music, authentic foods, dances and costumes. There will be a Grand March down Main Street. When your enthusiasm for Vikings wears thin, there's always Ferndale's old Victorian homes to admire in between the festival activities.

Ferndale is a bit off the beaten track, although not difficult to find. Take US 101 about 17 miles south of Eureka to the Ferndale/ Ferndale bridge exit, then cross the old, narrow, concrete Fernbridge and continue on for five miles to Main Street. The festival is free and the weather should be wonderful, except maybe for some morning fog.

For information, contact the Ferndale Chamber of Commerce, P.O. Box 325, Ferndale, CA 95536; (707) 786-4477.

Kayaking the Smith River

Late June [S] ☎

(see #3 on map page 12)

Get wet, get wild and have a great time kayaking the beautiful Smith River that winds through the great redwood and Douglas fir forests of Northern California. This river holds many stories and secrets, both ancient and contemporary, that will be unlocked by an accompanying geologist and fishery biologist. Learn how a century of logging and dam building have changed the river's seasonal flow and the habitat that salmon and steelhead depend upon for spawning. You'll get a firsthand, close-up look at the river and how it continues to change. Kayaks and life jackets are provided. You need not be an expert kayaker to participate. The trip may be canceled if the river is running too high and fast. There will be a $25 fee for the program. Register with the Redwoods National and State Parks well in advance; when you do, they'll tell you the meeting place and the exact date and time of the trip.

For information, contact Redwood National and State Field Seminar Coordinator, 1111 Second Street, Crescent City, CA 95531; (707) 465-4113.

Living in a Well-Ordered World: The Tolowa People

Late June [S] ☎

(see #3 on map page 12)

Each day, thousands of cars stream along Highway 1, where the Tolowa, Yurok and Chilula tribes once made their homes. The Tolowa lived farthest north, along the Chetco and Smith rivers, and this seminar is an opportunity to learn about these fascinating people, how they lived and flourished in the rich lands of the North Coast redwoods, and why their numbers suddenly dwindled to near extinction in a relatively short period of time. You'll spend Saturday learning about traditional aspects of Tolowa culture, including their daily life experiences, social structure, trading economy, religion, basketry, regalia and implementalia. On Sunday, you'll get out of the classroom and spend the day along the Smith River, where you'll hear Native American stories about the river, wander among the plants and see firsthand how the Native Americans used the natural world around them for everything from boats to baskets. This program is wheelchair accessible. The fee for the seminar is $50. It will be held at a yet-to-be-determined site within the Redwoods National and State Parks, which encompasses Jedediah Smith State Park, Del Norte Coast Redwoods State Park, Prairie Creek Redwoods State Park and Redwood National Park. You'll learn the meeting place and the exact date and time when you register.

For information, contact Redwood National and State Field Seminar Coordinator, 1111 Second Street, Crescent City, CA 95531; (707) 465-4113.

JUNE

Clearlake International Worm Races

July 1, 1995 • Noon

(see #13 on map page 13)

Not to be outdone by the jumping frog escapades of his ancestor Mark Twain, C.C. Schoenenberger originated Clearlake's worm races in 1966. The event has now attained worldwide attention and has become the main event of Clearlake's Fourth of July weekend celebration. Rules for the event are few and easy to understand. You can bring your own worm; either red worms or night crawlers are eligible and all are treated as equals here. If you're not into taking the time and spending the money to dig, train and maintain your own worm, you can rent a ready-to-go race worm at the event for just 25 cents. Be advised that if your personal worm is suspected of taking performance-enhancing drugs such as steroids, pre-competition testing may be required. The races are held on a special board with a bull's-eye painted inside a two-foot circle. Four or five worms compete in each race, starting from the bull's-eye. The first to reach the outside of the circle is declared the winner. Worm handlers are not allowed to prod their entries during the race, but may yell encouragement. Before the worm races, there is a parade, then in the evening, fireworks over Clear Lake mark the finish to a long and exciting day.

Redbud Park, in the town of Clearlake, is located off Highway 53, at the southeast end of Clear Lake, between highways 20 and 29. There's a $2 race entry fee and it costs 25 cents to rent a worm. Count on the weather being hot, which worms aren't really fond of.

For information, contact the Clear Lake Chamber of Commerce, P.O. Box 629, Clearlake, CA 95422; (707) 994-3600.

�֎ ✤ ✤ ✤

A Sketchbook Journal: Discovering the Redwoods
Early July
(see #3 on map page 12)

Lewis and Clark kept journal records of their early travels in the wilds of the Northwest, providing the meat for many movies and books a couple hundred years later. Journals have been the bedside companions of untold thousands of settlers and pioneers, recording their travels, their heartaches, their successes, their failures. Come join this seminar and learn the joys of journal drawing and writing, creating your own personal poetry, sketches and prose under the tutelage of a master artist and journal keeper. You'll be taking a series of short walks, meandering through Redwood National and

State Parks, recording your reactions to this beautiful environment with entries in your own journal. Who knows—maybe a hundred years from now someone will read your journal entries and decide your life is worth a book or a movie. There will be a fee of $50 for the program and you must register in advance. This seminar will be held at a yet-to-be-determined site within the Redwoods National and State Parks, which encompasses Jedediah Smith State Park, Del Norte Coast Redwoods State Park, Prairie Creek Redwoods State Park and Redwood National Park. You'll learn the meeting place and the exact date and time when you register.

For information, contact Redwood National and State Field Seminar Coordinator, 1111 Second Street, Crescent City, CA 95531; (707) 465-4113.

✿ ✿ ✿ ✿

Predators
Mid-July ❺ 🐾
(see #3 on map page 12)

We fear them, we admire them, but most of all we misunderstand them. Predators—the bears, mountain lions, coyotes, bobcats, weasels, hawks and owls that have been part of the redwood forests for eons—play a pivotal role in maintaining the balance of nature within these vast lands of redwood and oak woodlands, rivers, lakes and streams. In this seminar, naturalists will take you on a personal exploration of the natural distribution of predators, explaining their social systems and reproductive habits. During visits to local predator habitats, you'll have an opportunity to try your hand at calling predators into view and personally experience the wildlife manager's work using radio telemetry strategy in their ongoing conservation and management programs. There's a $25 fee and you must register in advance. This seminar will be held at a yet-to-be-determined site within the Redwoods National and State Parks, which encompasses Jedediah Smith State Park, Del Norte Coast Redwoods State Park, Prairie Creek Redwoods State Park and Redwood National Park. You'll learn the meeting place and the exact date and time when you register.

JULY

For information, contact Redwood National and State Field Seminar Coordinator, 1111 Second Street, Crescent City, CA 95531; (707) 465-4113.

❖ ❖ ❖ ❖

Logging History Days
July 29 & 30, 1995 **S** Ⓐ
(see #10 on map page 13)

Join this history hike through displays of early logging equipment and tools. Learn about the lives and lore of old loggers and discover how these rugged folks from the Northwest managed to cut down, move and saw into lumber some of the world's oldest and largest trees. Spend time on the logging history tour, then wander some of the trails that will take you through groves of redwoods that still remain. Bring a picnic lunch and spend the day. The event is held at Van Damme State Park, which is located three miles south of the town of Mendocino, off US 101. There's a $5 per vehicle day-use entry fee into the park. For weather, count on morning fog with afternoon sunshine.

For information, contact Van Damme State Park; (707) 937-5804.

❖ ❖ ❖ ❖

In Cold Blood
Late July **S** Ⓐ
(see #3 on map page 12)

This is not a seminar on Truman Capote's blood-chilling book, but a look at the fascinating world of frogs, snakes and salamanders, the cold-blooded creatures of the redwood forests. Explore the world of these little understood and too often misunderstood reptiles and amphibians and learn how they came to be creatures of land rather than of the sea. You'll find out where they find food, their mating habits and how they identify and protect their territories. An expert on the subject will lead you through the forest and along streams where the cold-blooded live. You'll learn how to identify the subtle differences found in some of the species through the use of field guides and other techniques. The fee is $25 and you must register in advance. This seminar will be held at a yet-to-be-determined site within the Redwoods National and State Parks, which encompasses Jedediah Smith State Park, Del Norte Coast Redwoods State Park, Prairie Creek Redwoods State Park and Redwood National Park. You'll learn the meeting place and the exact date and time when you register.

For information, contact Redwood National and State Field Seminar Coordinator, 1111 Second Street, Crescent City, CA 95531; (707) 465-4113.

❄ ❄ ❄ ❄

Bald Hills Mountain Biking
Late July ❺ 🚲
(see #3 on map page 12)

Join in the fun of this 17-mile bike ride that starts near the eastern boundary of Redwood National Park at Schoolhouse Peak. Beginning in the higher elevations of oak woodlands and prairies, you'll descend through some spectacular scenery to the deep, dark depths of the redwood forest, finally ending at Lady Bird Johnson Grove. There will be stops to inspect restoration efforts in the Redwood Creek Basin, and maybe you'll even catch a rare glimpse of a mountain lion, a spotted owl or other wild creatures of the forest. For those not crazy enough to want to bike back up the mountain, shuttle transportation will be provided. The fee is $15. Call the Redwoods National and State Parks to register in advance; you'll learn the meeting place and the exact date and time when you register.

For information, contact Redwood National and State Field Seminar Coordinator, 1111 Second Street, Crescent City, CA 95531; (707) 465-4113.

❄ ❄ ❄ ❄

JULY

Basket-Making Traditions and Techniques
Early August **S** 🖊
(see #3 on map page 12)

In Native American cultures, baskets were more than vehicles for storing acorns and wild bulbs or carrying infants. They served as artistic expressions of the individual basket-maker's view of the world and California's basket-makers were among the best in the land. This is a one-day field seminar where you will learn how to gather and prepare natural materials for basketry, a year-round effort for the Native Americans. You'll see a large collection of baskets and regalia, providing a deeper sense of the variety of patterns, colors and materials used in Native American designs. The fee is $25 and you must register in advance. This seminar will be held at a yet-to-be-determined site within the Redwoods National and State Parks, which encompasses Jedediah Smith State Park, Del Norte Coast Redwoods State Park, Prairie Creek Redwoods State Park and Redwood National Park. You'll learn the meeting place and the exact date and time when you register.

For information, contact Redwood National and State Field Seminar Coordinator, 1111 Second Street, Crescent City, CA 95531; (707) 465-4113.

❖ ❖ ❖ ❖

Fort Humboldt Days
August 5 & 6, 1995 **S** 🖊 • 10 a.m. to 5 p.m.
ee #6 on map page 12)

For preserving California's military heritage and passing that history on to future generations, there's no place better than Fort Humboldt to see and experience what life was like in the last century. Fort Humboldt Days brings all the action of its past history to life in this preserved 1800s military camp, complete with hand weapons, artillery pieces and wagons that would have been here over a hundred years ago. You'll also be able to see how far we've come in making domestic chores easier. Blacksmithing and other old-time crafts will be demonstrated throughout the weekend event.

Fort Humboldt is located near the south side of Eureka, on Highland Avenue, just off US 101. There's no cost for the event; the weather will probably bring morning fog and afternoon sunshine.

For information, contact Fort Humboldt State Historic Park; (707) 445-6567 or (707) 445-6547.

Humboldt Kite Days

August 12, 1995 [S] ☎ • 10 a.m. to 3 p.m.

(see #6 on map page 12)

With its nearly constant winds, California's North Coast is an ideal place to fly kites and that's what this day is all about. Bring your favorite kite or just come and watch the magic of these soaring wind wings. There will be flights of big kites and little kites and demonstrations of skill by kite flyers who are gripping the ground with their toes while trying to steer some really fancy creations into all sorts of aerial acrobatics. There will also be various competitions and just plain, ordinary kite-flying opportunities. If you haven't tried flying a kite since those old 10-cent paper kites of a few decades ago, you've missed out on what technology and the eyes of artists have done to a centuries-old tradition. If you don't carry a kite and string around in the trunk of your car, there will certainly be kites available for sale nearby.

Fort Humboldt is located near the south end of Eureka, on Highland Avenue, just off US 101. The event is free to the public. Expect the weather to be foggy in the morning and sunny in the afternoon.

For information, contact Fort Humboldt State Historic Park; (707) 445-6567 or (707) 445-6547.

Blackberry Festival

August 12, 1995 • 10 a.m. to 5 p.m.
(see #11 on map page 13)

If you've ever tried to pick wild blackberries and suffered the scars of prickly thorns, then you'll really appreciate this turn-of-the-century pie and ice cream social. The main course, of course, is blackberry pie, blackberry cobbler, blackberry ice cream and just plain blackberries. And one of the best things about the day of fun and food is that the blackberries have already been picked and someone else's hands and arms have suffered the trauma and scars. Besides lots of blackberry delectables to munch, there's music, dancing, farm work demonstrations, tours of the farm and old-fashioned staged melodramas. Most of the activities start about 10 a.m., but there's an early morning breakfast hike that begins at 7:30 a.m. The Blackberry Festival is held at Anderson Marsh State Historic Park which is located near Clear Lake. Take Highway 29 north to the town of Lower Lake, then turn onto Highway 53 and go north one-half mile to the Anderson Ranch Parkway. Turn left (west) and follow the signs. This is an understandably popular event with more than 8,000 people coming for the blackberry surprises. The fee hadn't been set at press time, but it shouldn't cost any more than $5 per vehicle. Count on some hot weather and hope for some cooling breezes. Failing that, just be sure to cover your blackberry pie with lots of ice cream.

For information, contact Anderson Marsh State Historic Park; (707) 994-0688 or (707) 279-4293.

A Horseback Ride Through History

Mid-August 🟢 🔆
(see #3 on map page 12)

Most of the people who visit Redwood National and State Parks spend very little time seeing anything more than the trees and forests closest to the paved parking lots. Hop on your (rented) horse for a much closer look, not only at the tall trees in the backcountry, but to experience the story of the North Coast's first settlers, who created small outposts of civilization in the middle of an ancient wilderness. Travel by horseback up the Redwood Creek Basin where you'll hear stories about the miners who traveled the old Trinidad Trail between the coastal settlement of Trinidad and the Klamath gold fields. Logging has played an important part in the Northwest's history and remains, even in today's battles of owls and loggers, vital to the local economies. Follow the history of the area, from early logging and mining through land-fraud schemes and the early efforts of Californians determined to save the venerable giants from the ax and saw. Even after the establishment of the Redwood State Parks in the 1920s and 1930s, and the subsequent creation of Redwood National Park, the story is still not over. The horseback ride is interrupted at lunch time for a hearty steak cookout and beverages. The fee is $90, which includes horse rental and lunch. Advance registration with the Redwoods National and State Parks is a must. You'll learn the meeting place and the exact date and time when you register.

For information, contact Redwood National and State Field Seminar Coordinator, 1111 Second Street, Crescent City, CA 95531; (707) 465-4113.

✤ ✤ ✤ ✤

The Bear Facts
Mid-August **S** 🖊
(see #3 on map page 12)

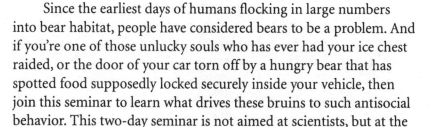

Since the earliest days of humans flocking in large numbers into bear habitat, people have considered bears to be a problem. And if you're one of those unlucky souls who has ever had your ice chest raided, or the door of your car torn off by a hungry bear that has spotted food supposedly locked securely inside your vehicle, then join this seminar to learn what drives these bruins to such antisocial behavior. This two-day seminar is not aimed at scientists, but at the people who come to parks to spend relaxing vacations with their families. Learn about black bear life history, their habitat, their preferred food and its sources, and their denning habits. You'll have an opportunity to head into the field and examine dens, look for bear signs and actually locate radio-collared bears. You'll also learn about avoiding bears in the wild and how unavoidable contacts can affect a bear's behavior. The fee is $50 and you must register in advance. This seminar will be held at a yet-to-be-determined site within the Redwoods National and State Parks, which encompasses Jedediah Smith State Park, Del Norte Coast Redwoods State Park, Prairie Creek Redwoods State Park and Redwood National Park. You'll learn the meeting place and the exact date and time when you register.

For information, contact Redwood National and State Field Seminar Coordinator, 1111 Second Street, Crescent City, CA 95531; (707) 465-4113.

Who Is Eating Your Garbage? Or, Worms are Fun!

Mid-August [S] ☎

(see #3 on map page 12)

You can use those brown and red wiggling worms for more than fish bait. Join this seminar and learn how worms can reduce the amount of garbage that you put in your can, while creating a rich and luxurious growth medium for your garden. In this seminar, you'll learn how to construct a complete and inexpensive composting system. It starts with a box that you can build yourself, shredded newspapers, a little moist soil and some worms. Add your kitchen fruit and vegetable leftovers and you're in the composting business. You'll never have to buy fishing worms again. There's a fee of $15 for the quick course in garbage gardening. This seminar will be held at a yet-to-be-determined site within the Redwoods National and State Parks, which encompasses Jedediah Smith State Park, Del Norte Coast Redwoods State Park, Prairie Creek Redwoods State Park and Redwood National Park. You'll learn the meeting place and the exact date and time when you preregister.

For information, contact Redwood National and State Field Seminar Coordinator, 1111 Second Street, Crescent City, CA 95531; (707) 465-4113.

Bats of the Redwood Forest

Mid-August **S**⏚

(see #3 on map page 12)

If you've ever spent much time camping out in the wilds of the forests, you may have fearfully wondered if all those dark little creatures zipping around above your head at dusk were bats chasing bugs. Old wives' tales and confusion send fear up and down the spines of far too many people when confronted by bats for the first time or the tenth time. Stories about bats getting stuck in your hair or vampire bats that suck human blood are, well, old wives' tales. This seminar gives you a chance to learn why bats are beneficial members of the natural community and why in China they are seen as symbols of family happiness and good luck. You'll spend the early evening watching bats flying their erratic flight patterns in pursuit of dinner. There's a $30 fee for the course that includes materials for constructing a bat box to take home. This seminar will be held at a yet-to-be-determined site within the Redwoods National and State Parks, which encompasses Jedediah Smith State Park, Del Norte Coast Redwoods State Park, Prairie Creek Redwoods State Park and Redwood National Park. You'll learn the meeting place and the exact date and time when you preregister.

For information, contact Redwood National and State Field Seminar Coordinator, 1111 Second Street, Crescent City, CA 95531; (707) 465-4113.

✤ ✤ ✤ ✤

Banana Slug Derby

August 19, 1995 **S**⏚ • Noon to 3 p.m.

(see #2 on map page 12)

This is a time-honored event that brings out the slimier things of the forest. Banana slugs are important creatures that slowly crawl around the redwood forest floor and trees, munching down old dead things. The slug derby brings the fastest of the thoroughbred slugs out for an afternoon of rip-tearing racing thrills and spills. So, gather up your friendly banana slug—both males and females are treated equally in this non-handicapped race. The winning slug gets a ribbon. The event is held at Prairie Creek Redwoods State Park which is located adjacent to US 101, six miles north of Orick. There's a $5 per vehicle day-use fee if you aren't already camped in the park. The weather should be sunny and warm, unless the early morning fog hangs in longer.

For information, contact Prairie Creek Redwoods State Park; (707) 488-2171.

❖ ❖ ❖ ❖

Shorebird Heaven

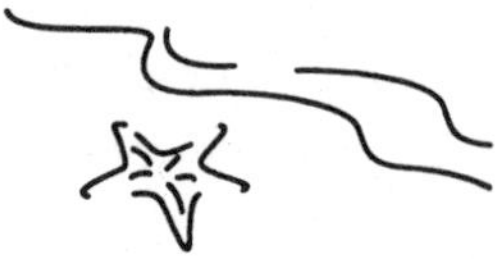

Late August [S] ☎

(see #1 on map page 12)

The shoreline near Crescent City has always been a hot spot for shoreline birders. In this seminar, you'll explore rocky outcrops, sandy beaches and coastal estuaries on foot, with the expectation of seeing dozens of species of shorebirds who flock here as the winter migration begins. There will be a slide show to start the event that will be a tremendous aid in helping you identify the myriad shorebirds, many of which appear nearly identical to the novice birder's eye. Bring binoculars or spotting scopes to help you see these fascinating creatures. The fee is $25 and you must register in advance with the Redwoods National and State Parks. You'll learn the meeting place and the exact date and time when you register.

For information, contact Redwood National and State Field Seminar Coordinator, 1111 Second Street, Crescent City, CA 95531; (707) 465-4113.

❖ ❖ ❖ ❖

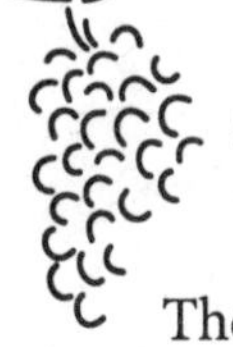

Sonoma Vintage Festival

September 22 to 24, 1995 [S] ☎ • 10 a.m. to 5 p.m.

(see #18 on map page 13)

The modern part of this festival features wine tasting, and the old-world part features the reenactment of a historic wedding. Just to add a bit more history, there will be a re-raising of the bear flag, recreating the short-lived victory of the Bear Flag Revolt and the 22 days of the California Republic. If you didn't realize that California was once, briefly, its own nation just before becoming a state in the Union, why not come on over and learn a little history? It's kind of a strange story about people with names like Ide and Vallejo, but it's worth telling again. The wine tasting is great, the shops are fun and the weather should be warm and sunny. The event is held in Sonoma Plaza and in Sonoma State Historic Park, which are adjacent to each other. The town of Sonoma is located on Highway 12, between Napa and Petaluma. There's no cost to attend the festival.

For information, contact Sonoma State Historic Park; (707) 938-1578.

✤ ✤ ✤ ✤

Annual Weekend Along the Farm Trails

September 23 & 24, 1995 • 7:30 a.m. to 5 p.m.
(various locations)

This is really a different kind of outdoor event, one that more people should try, especially since most of us live in cities. It shouldn't come as any surprise to anyone not living in a cave that California is world-renowned for its agriculture. With that in mind, and knowing that few people have ever spent any time on a real farm, the sponsors of this program choose 10 farms in western Sonoma County to participate in a weekend-long open house for 600 or more special guests. And anyone can become one of those special guests simply by registering and paying a rather reasonable admission fee. What you get are directions to all the participating farms and a list of all the activities that are offered at each. You'll be able to go on behind-the-scenes tours of farms and dairies, take hayrides, do lots of fresh fruit and veggie tasting, have a chance to milk goats and cows, spend some quality time with llamas, and go on horse and carriage rides. And since this is wine country, there'll be ample opportunities for wine tasting. You drive your own car and set your own pace; you can even spend all day at one farm, if it happens to strike your fancy. Directions to the farms are mailed with

SEPTEMBER

your tickets. The cost of the weekend farm tour is $10 for adults, seniors are $8, kids ages 5 to 15 are $5 and everyone else is free. As far as the weather is concerned, you can pretty much plan on it being sunny and hot, but there's plenty of shade relief available.

For information, contact Sonoma County Farm Trails, P.O. Box 6032, Santa Rosa, CA 95406; (707) 996-2154.

Old Mill Days

October 15 & 16, 1995 [S] ☎

(see #16 on map page 13)

Where did people get their flour back in the 1800s? Well, spend a day at the historic Bale Grist Mill and you'll get to see and taste firsthand how wheat, corn, oats and barley were ground into flour. The original mill was built in the 1840s by Edward Bale, an itinerant drunk who landed in Monterey when his ship ran aground. He often got into trouble with the local powers—it's possible his position as a physician for the Mexican Army was all that kept him from suffering their wrath more than he did. In 1839, Bale married into 9,000 acres of land in the Napa Valley. He built his first grist mill, which, over the years, was improved upon several times, the last time when a steam engine replaced the large water wheel. The original water-powered mill has been restored to working condition and Old Mill Days will see everything up and working for your enjoyment and education. Count on hot corn bread and chili to soothe the savage appetite. Usually over 1,000 people show up for this event, so you may want to get there early. It's also an opportunity to visit a few of the wineries in the area and sample the end product of the grape industry. Bale Grist Mill State Historic Park is located about four miles north of St. Helena, on Highway 29. There will probably be a $1 charge per person. Expect clear and mild weather.

For information, contact Bale Grist Mill State Historic Park; (707) 942-4575 or (707) 963-2236.

Geyserville Fall Color Tour

October 28 & 29, 1995 • 9 a.m. to 6 p.m.
(see #14 on map page 13)

This is not your typical tour of autumn-tinged maple and oak leaves fringed with a white crown of frost. This is a chance to see the brilliant golds and reds of grapevine leaves still clinging to the branches, long after the grapes are well on their way to becoming what all good grapes become—wine. Actually, while the leaves are beautiful, the wine tasting is even better. There are a few other events going on, like a pancake breakfast and crafts displays and exhibits, so if you're not a wine fanatic, there is more to see and do. The event is held in the famed Sonoma wine country town of Geyserville which is located on Highway 128, about three miles east of US 101. Most everything is free, unless, of course, you decide to head home with several bottles of wine. For photographers, the scenery should be wonderful with lots of blue sky contrasting quite nicely with the reds, yellows and golds of the withering grape vines. The weather should be beautiful, if maybe a little cool.

For more information, contact the Guerneville–Sonoma County Convention and Visitors Bureau, 5000 Roberts Lake Road, Suite A, Rohnert Park, CA 94928; (707) 586-8100 or (800) 326-7666.

Hometown Harvest Festival

Last Saturday in October • 7 a.m. to 5 p.m.
(see #17 on map page 13)

Any time of the year is a great time to visit California's famed Napa and Sonoma wine country, but the best time may be when the last of the grapes have been harvested and crushed. The Hometown Harvest Festival is that special time of year when up to 5,000 people get together in celebration of the end of another banner wine-making year. They start the day with a pancake breakfast, then quickly move on to a 10K race. For those more inclined to wander aimlessly through arts and crafts booths than run races, over 100

OCTOBER

vendors will be on hand, along with the excitement of a children's carnival, lots of food and, of course, wine. An added attraction is the Winery Olympics where representatives of area wineries compete in typical winery jobs-with-a-twist, such as the forklift rodeo and a wine barrel-rolling competition.

Every dog has his day, so they say, and the harvest festival is one of those days. For dog lovers, this is one of those few events where dog owners are not frowned upon for bringing their pets. In fact, there is a pet parade and a Frisbee-catching contest for dogs.

To get to the Harvest Festival, head to Adams Street between Oak and Stockton in the town of St. Helena on Highway 29, about 17 miles north of Napa. Everything is free, except the food and craft vendors' merchandise. Expect generally warm and pleasant weather, a rare, late October rainstorm notwithstanding.

For information, contact the Upper Valley Community Center, 1480 Main Street, St. Helena, CA 94574; (707) 963-5706.

Old Fashioned Christmas Open House

December 9 & 10, 1995 [S] ☎ • 10 a.m. to 4 p.m.

(see #11 on map page 13)

Anderson Ranch is a throwback to another time and the Christmas season celebration here is a trip back to that age before plastic trees and shopping center Santas. Still, modern kids won't be disappointed, because Santa will be at the ranch, as well as plenty of music filling the air and cakes and other baked goodies to fill the tummies. Anderson Marsh, which sits near the ranch house, is a great place to take a short hike, if you have a little extra time and the weather will allow it. The marsh serves as a home to significant numbers of waterfowl and other birdlife. Anderson Marsh State Historic Park is located near Clear Lake. From Highway 29 heading toward Lower Lake, take the Highway 53 turnoff north about one-half mile to Anderson Ranch Parkway, then turn left and follow the signs. There's no cost for the program, although donations to help in restoration and interpretive efforts are always welcome. It's going to be a little cold and maybe raining, so dress warmly.

For information, contact Anderson Marsh State Historic Park; (707) 994-0688.

North Coast Seasonal Hikes & Programs

Bald Eagle Hikes

Saturdays • Late January through February $\mathbf{S}$ 🖉
10 a.m. to 2 p.m.
(see #12 on map page 13)

Bureau of Land Management resource specialists will lead these hikes to view the wintering bald eagles of Cache Creek. If television is the only place you've ever seen the majesty of a bald eagle soaring overhead, or diving to snag fish from a lake or stream, then here's the perfect opportunity to catch the action up close. Actually, there are quite a few bald eagle wintering sites within California. Some are easily accessible, others aren't, and a few are strictly off-limits to people. The hike will take from three to four hours and cover four miles, with a 600-foot elevation gain. Wear good hiking boots, bring water and lunch, and be prepared for cold weather. If it rains, the hikes are canceled, so if the weather looks threatening, you should call ahead. You'll need to call ahead anyway, because the hikes are limited to 25 people and advance reservations are required. There's no fee for the hikes. The meeting place will be the Redbud Trailhead parking lot, eight miles east of Clearlake Oaks on Highway 20.

For information, contact the Bureau of Land Management, Clear Lake Resource Area, 2550 North State Street, Ukiah, CA 95482; (707) 468-4000.

Healdsburg Summer International Concert Series

Sundays • May 14 through September 24 • 2 p.m. to 4 p.m.
(see #15 on map page 13)

The summer concert series brings an international flair to historic Healdsburg Plaza each Sunday afternoon. The musical groups change each year, but to give you an idea of the range, the music in 1994 included flamenco, Caribbean, Brazilian, Haitian, '40s and '50s swing, Cajun, ragtime, marching bands, rhythm and blues, and opera. You can expect pretty much the same eclectic mix in the future. In conjunction with the music, a series of mini-festivals is also part of the Sunday celebrations, including Shakespearean theater, an antique fair and a Russian River wine festival, which is always held on the first weekend of the concert series. This is a good time for the entire family, so bring a picnic lunch or try one of the local restaurants. To reach Healdsburg Plaza, from US 101 North, take the Central Healdsburg exit. Drive three blocks; the plaza is on the right. The concerts are free, but some of the other associated festival activities have fees. Call or write in the spring for a complete concert schedule. The weather should be fair and sunny.

For information, contact the Healdsburg Downtown Business District, P.O. Box 578, Healdsburg, CA 95448; (707) 431-3301.

❖ ❖ ❖ ❖

Napa Nature Awareness Programs

Summer **S** ⟨⟩
(see #19 on map page 13)

A series of kids' nature programs is offered each year by the city of Napa in conjunction with the Carolyn Parr Nature Museum. The programs change slightly from year to year, but all are aimed at creating a lifelong appreciation of nature in younger children. A nature awareness session for pre-schoolers is for youngsters ages three to five, exploring a new aspect of nature each week through crafts, hikes, books and games. Creativity in nature is the focus of another session that uses pieces of nature to explore crafts, music, games and poetry; it culminates in a nature walk integrating all the activities. Additional programs include: a walk to chase and learn about the creepy-crawly bugs that bug many kids (and adults), at least until they learn why most bugs are friendly and important parts of nature; a look at how nature is a recycler without the help of a garbage collector; a look at the importance of trees, plants and animals in relation to people; and a look at the wild animals that live all around us and how to read signs of their presence, even when we can't see the critters themselves. Most of the programs run from one to two hours, one day a week for a week or two, while some are held on just one Saturday. Advance sign-ups are required. Contact the park for specific schedules and costs. Most of the programs are held at the Carolyn Parr Nature Museum in Westwood Hills Park, which is located on Browns Valley Road in Napa. Prices range from $8 for a one-day program to $26 for programs that meet for several sessions over several weeks. The weather is usually quite warm during summer.

For information, contact the Napa Community Resources Department, 1100 West Street, Napa, CA 94559; (707) 257-9529.

Chapter 2

Great Outdoor Events of California's Shasta Cascade

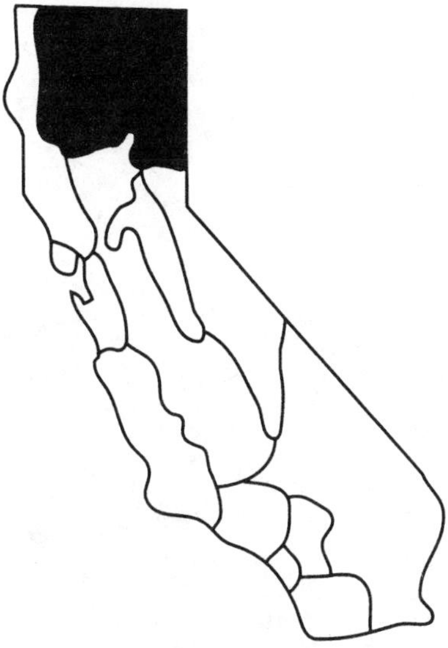

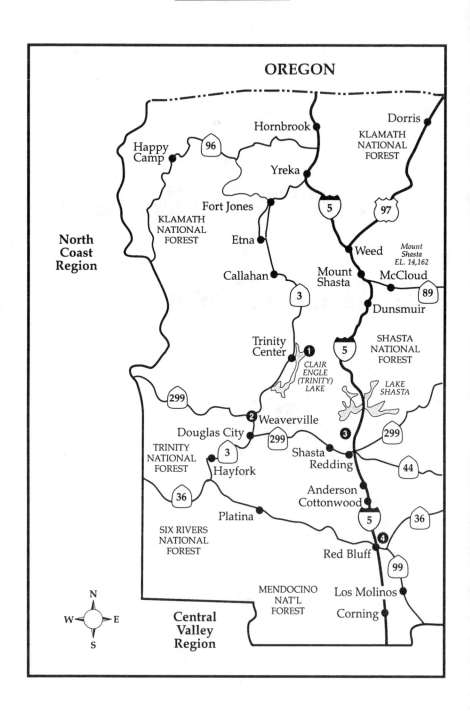

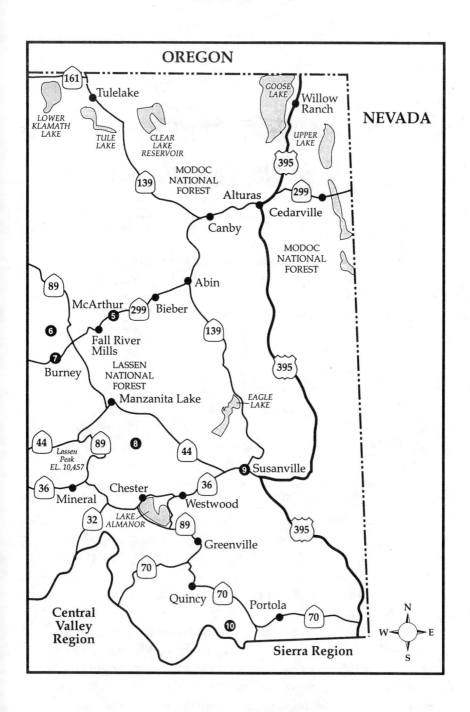

✤ ✤ ✤ ✤

Introduction to
Shasta Cascade

Enter California's remotely populated northern interior, where volcanoes fume and eagles soar. This is a land that few people choose to explore, perhaps because it is too far removed from all major population centers of the state, which is exactly why you should take the extra time needed to get up here. While cattle raising and timber harvesting appear to be the primary source of income for many people who have chosen to settle here, the endless range of outdoor recreation possibilities is probably what keeps them here.

Driving north on Interstate 5, you'll reach Redding and take either a hard left or right turn onto Highway 299 and keep driving. If it's a typical summer day, the temperature will have crested 105 degrees for the sixth consecutive day. What you'll notice is that whichever direction you head, the road will climb upward, quickly leaving behind the dry valley floor and entering the domain of oaks and pines. Once you've ventured into the Trinity country to the west or the Lassen volcanic range to the east, the temperature will drop and cooling breezes kick up in the afternoon to fade the memories of stifling valley heat.

Instead of taking that same old refreshingly boring summer vacation, this year take a winter trip up to where Oregon shares a border with California, to the land of the Lower Klamath National Wildlife Reserve and Tule Lake. Here, winter's cold transforms the lakes into vast sheets of ice, with ducks and geese by the thousands coming here each evening, circling, looking for a break in the ice where they can settle down for the night. While most find safe refuge, some fall prey to the hundreds of hawks and bald eagles that also spend their winters here.

On the western side of California's Shasta Cascade region, rugged mountains, wild rivers, giant Clair Engle Lake and many thousands of acres of public forest land beckon backpackers, hunters, anglers and campers. History buffs will also find much to enjoy as they explore the role this area played in the Gold Rush and in the early history of California's logging industry.

Throughout Shasta Cascade, there are more places to discover than you can imagine, and most of the parks, whether national or state, offer summer hike programs on well-marked trails for your exploring pleasure. Lava Beds National Monument, Lassen Volcanic National Park, McArthur-Burney Falls Memorial State Park, Whiskeytown-Shasta-Trinity National Recreation Area, not to mention the numerous national forests, lakes and rivers—the recreational opportunities abound, both in winter and summer.

Chinese New Year Lion Dance

Late January or February [S] ☎

(see #2 on map page 52)

While Chinese people have lived for a period of time in most of California's Gold Rush towns, Weaverville has special significance because of the large Chinese population that came, many stayed. Weaverville Joss House State Historic Park houses California's oldest continually active Chinese place of worship, or joss house (the name translates into English as "Amongst the Forest Beneath the Clouds"). As you might expect, Chinese celebrations have become an important part of the community life here. Witnessing the colorful Chinese Lion Dance with its accompanying drum-banging and exploding firecrackers—always a very special part of the celebration—is a chance to experience firsthand this unique facet of California's history. While you're in town, take time to tour the joss house. It's a mysterious and magical place that remains sacred as a house of worship for many Californians. Weaverville is located on Highway 299, about 46 miles west of Redding. The dance and street festival are free. There's a fee of $2 for adults and $1 for kids (ages 6 to 17) to tour Joss House—and it's a tour you really should not miss. The weather should be cold, possibly with rain and maybe even snow.

For more information, contact Weaverville Joss House State Historic Park, P.O. Box 1217, Weaverville, CA 96093; (916) 243-8194.

When Snowshoes Were King

January 14 & 28, 1995 and February 11 & 25, 1995

1 p.m. to 2 p.m.

(see #10 on map page 53)

In the 19th century, skis were 10-foot-long slats of wood most often referred to as snowshoes. That little tidbit of information goes a long way in explaining the moniker that Snowshoe Thompson picked up for his gallant and crazy exploits transporting mail over the Sierra all winter long more than a hundred years ago. His snowshoes were really extra-long wood skis. This seminar is a 45-minute talk about the "longboards" that used to rule the mountains and the secret ski-dope concoctions that were applied to the bottoms of the skis to make them go forward and not backward. After the talk, take time to tour the rest of the historic mining buildings in the park, or try your own, more modern cross-country skis on some of the snow-covered park roads. Meet at the small museum at the entrance to Plumas Eureka State Park, located five miles west of Blairsden on County Road A-14, which begins at the intersection of highways 70 and 89.

For information, contact Plumas Eureka State Park, 310 Johnsville Road, Blairsden, CA 96103; (916) 836-2380.

❊ ❊ ❊ ❊

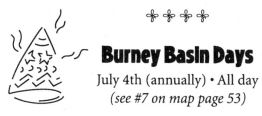

Burney Basin Days

July 4th (annually) • All day
(see #7 on map page 53)

If you happen to be camping up in the Burney Falls area or fishing in any of its many productive trout steams and lakes, you ought to take a break and join in Burney's Fourth of July celebration. The day's activities begin early with a pancake breakfast and end with fireworks after dark. In between, there is a parade, a barbecue and a lot of fun. Essentially, this is just a mountain community's good-time celebration. Burney is located on Highway 299, about 51 miles east of Redding. The event is free, except for the food booths, of course. The weather should be warm and comfortable.

For more information, contact the Burney Chamber of Commerce, P.O. Box 1103, Burney, CA 96013; (916) 335-4994.

❊ ❊ ❊ ❊

Chinese 4th of July Lion Dance

Weekend nearest July 4 **S**𝒞 • 1 p.m.
(see #2 on map page 52)

The colorful Chinese Lion Dance has become a Fourth of July favorite in this small, mountain community. For more on Joss House and the Chinese community in Weaverville, see the listing on page 56. Weaverville is located on Highway 299, about 46 miles west of Redding. The dance is free, but the fee to tour the joss house is $2 for adults and $1 for kids (ages 6 to 17). The weather should be warm and sunny.

For more information, contact Weaverville Joss House State Historic Park, P.O. Box 1217, Weaverville, CA 96093; (916) 243-8194.

❖ ❖ ❖ ❖

Susanville Main Cruise

August 2 & 3, 1995 • All day
(see #9 on map page 53)

The emphasis for two full days is on cars, old cars mostly. Scheduled to coincide with Reno's Hot August Nights, the aim here is to divert many of those old classic cars traveling toward Reno for the weekend into Susanville for Sizzling August Nights, mountain-style. And they have been sizzlingly successful at it for the past three years. There is a car show, a special spotlight cruise and a Main Street cruise that is certain to bring back fond memories of how it used to be when men were men, cars were cars and air-conditioning was for rich wimps. For those whose minds remain alert enough to remember, and whose bodies remain agile enough to do the twist, there will be a hula hoop contest, a bubble-gum bubble-blowing competition, a dance and, of course, the limbo. There will be food booths, T-shirts for sale and free dash plaques. Susanville's Main Street is easy enough to find. The town is located on Highway 36, 109 miles east of Red Bluff and about four miles from Highway 395. It's all free, so enjoy. The weather should be warm and sunny, although there's not a lot of sunshine during the night part of

Sizzling August Nights.

For information, contact the Lassen County Chamber of Commerce, P.O. Box 338, Susanville, CA 96130; (916) 257-4323.

✤ ✤ ✤ ✤

16th Adobe Day

August 19, 1995 • Noon to 4 p.m.
(see # 4 on map page 52)

One of those short side trips off Interstate 5, this little adobe is popular with local school teachers who are teaching their young students about the area's history. Old-time Central Valley life is revived during this annual event at William B. Ide Adobe State Historic Park. Lots of hands-on activities are part of the day, including log sawing, blacksmithing, dipping candles, spinning and weaving cloth, using old woodworking tools, quilting and, of course, making adobe bricks. They try to keep everything in the period, even some of the food that is served; the jerked beef from the smokehouse is the same stuff the pioneers would have prepared and eaten, only a lot fresher. There is plenty of other food, too, including some newfangled concoction recently introduced from the East— they're calling it ice cream. The Ide Adobe Players will perform live 1850s music to accompany period dances. Oh, and in case you wondered who William Ide was, back in late 1840s, he arrived in California about eight months prior to the short-lived Bear Flag Revolt, and for the 22 days of the new republic's existence, Ide served as president. After the revolution folded, he spent many of his remaining days as a judge in Red Bluff.

William B. Ide Adobe State Historic Park is located two miles northeast of Red Bluff on Adobe Road. There will be an entry fee of $2 for adults and $1 for children ages 4 to 11; those under four are free. It should be quite hot, so bring the sunscreen.

For information, contact William B. Ide Adobe State Historic Park, (916) 527-5927 or (916) 529-8599.

✤ ✤ ✤ ✤

Intermountain Fair

September 1 to September 4, 1995 • All day
(see #5 on map page 53)

For more than 75 years, the folks of the Shasta Cascade community of McArthur have had their own country fair. Come up to the mountains and enjoy the day wandering through exhibits and eating great fair food. There are rides for the kids and a demolition derby for those who have ever fantasized about what they'd really like to do with that last lemon vehicle they bought.

McArthur is located on Highway 299, about 67 miles east of Redding. Entry into the fair should be about $3 for adults and $2 for kids and seniors. There should be some great fair-going weather.

For more information, contact the Intermountain Fair, P.O. Box 10, McArthur, CA 96056; (916) 335-5695.

❖ ❖ ❖ ❖

Burney Classic Marathon

Second Sunday in September ❺ 🌙 • All day
(see #7 on map page 53)

For runners, there are many great places in California to race, but the clean air, forests and mountains surrounding Burney are much preferable to the brown summer air found in far too many cities these days. If you like running marathons lost in crowds of hundreds of other runners, then this is not the race for you. The Burney Classic Marathon will probably see fewer than 50 runners, and a bunch of those will only be here to attempt a half marathon, or maybe even the 10K or 5K portion of the complete course. For spectators who get bored with watching, there will be a kite-flying exhibition, health screening booths and book sales. Give the Burney Chamber of Commerce a call for the exact starting time and location. Burney is located on Highway 299, about 51 miles east of Redding. The cost for participants wasn't set at press time, so you'll need to call ahead. The weather should be warm and comfortable.

For more information, contact the Burney Classic Marathon, 37477 Main Street, Burney, CA 96013; (916) 325-2835.

13th Annual Ide Adobe Ferry Champion Horseshoe Pitchers' Contest

October 7, 1995 **S** *Ø* • 11 a.m. to 4 p.m.
(see #4 on map page 52)

Back in the 1850s, two of the biggest sporting events in many communities were horse racing and horseshoe pitching. Since today, horse racing is strictly regulated in California and pitching horses' shoes isn't, here is your chance to make sporting history by winning this recreation of an 1850s pitch-off. You'll have to abide by the 140-year-old rules and use No. 8 draft shoes straight from the hoof. As a contestant in this double-elimination doubles tournament, you'll be required to wear period clothing which will be provided by park personnel should you arrive not suitably attired. An official will record all the pit scores on slates, then report them to the scorekeeper's table, where the permanent numbers are recorded using quill pens, written in copperplate script on parchment, of course! Champions are awarded gold-filled pocket watches or other similar 1850s-period prizes. Runners-up will receive a pair of inscribed reproduction horseshoes. Competitors who have competed in National Horse Pitchers Association-sanctioned tournaments are not permitted; it's backyarders only in this event.

William B. Ide Adobe State Historic Park is located two miles northeast of Red Bluff on Adobe Road. There will be a fee of $3 per vehicle with a nominal competitor's entry fee. It should be a pretty nice day, as far as the weather is concerned.

For information, contact California State Parks, 21659 Adobe Road, Red Bluff, CA 96080; (916) 529-8599.

❖ ❖ ❖ ❖

McArthur-Burney Heritage Days

October 7 & 8, 1995 **S** *Ø* • 10 a.m. to 4 p.m.
(see #6 on map page 53)

The Burney Valley is a beautiful part of California that most people have never had an opportunity to visit, mostly because the

OCTOBER

area is so far away from anything that even resembles a major population center. But people settled this area in the last century, depending upon farming, ranching and logging to support themselves. Many of the skills and crafts those early pioneers practiced are brought back in this heritage weekend. There will be candlemaking, wood crafts and black powder guns filling the air with their explosions and smoke. Before the coming of the pioneers, Native Americans claimed this land as their own and, to honor them, there will be Native American dancing, displays and crafts. And there's always the waterfall in the park, which is actually hundreds of minifalls, many of which pour directly from the rocks to join the water coming from the stream. McArthur-Burney Falls Memorial State Park is located about an hour's drive northeast of Redding. Take Highway 299 and turn north onto Highway 89. Drive about six miles to the park. The event is free. The weather should be cool, but comfortable.

For information, contact McArthur-Burney Falls Memorial State Park; (916) 335-2777.

Christmas at Shasta State Historic Park

December 3, 1995 • 11 a.m. to 4 p.m.
(see #3 on map page 52)

Christmas was always a special time in early California and the Shasta Christmas Open House recreates that special 19th century feeling. Stop in and enjoy Victorian Christmas music, the colorful traditional decorations and maybe do a little holiday gift shopping. The small community of Shasta is one of California's towns that saw its beginnings with the Gold Rush. Today, many of the original stone buildings are merely shells of yesteryear, while others have been restored to their 1800s appearance. Wander through the old general store and bakery, or see some of the historic transportation equipment on display in the old town. Art connoisseurs will enjoy the Williamson Lyncoy Smith Gallery and its fine, often overlooked, collection of historic California paintings.

Shasta is located on Highway 299, about six miles west of Redding. Admission is free for the event. The weather can be cold and rainy, but the activities are indoors, so it really doesn't matter.

For information, contact Shasta State Historic Park, P.O. Box 2430, Shasta, CA 96087; (916) 243-8194.

18th Annual Pioneer Christmas Party
December 16, 1995 • 1 p.m. to 4 p.m.
(see #4 on map page 52)

Welcome to a recreation of a 19th-century Christmas celebration in the northern Central Valley at William B. Ide Adobe State Historic Park. Christmas caroling will provide the appropriate background music for candle dipping, toy making and cookie decorating. Create your own Christmas cards using a quill pen and ink on parchment, or if you have a hankering, slip outside to one of the outbuildings and sneak in a game of Monte with an itinerant gambler. See the lighting of a traditional Plumb Pudding. ("Plumb" is correct, by the way, because there are no plums in this pudding!) Help break the Christmas bag, a Yankee tradition that bears a very close resemblance to the Mexican piñata tradition. The Ide Adobe Interpretive Association will hold a drawing for a Christmas quilt, a beautiful, queen-size reproduction of a pioneer quilt pattern.

William B. Ide Adobe State Historic Park is located two miles northeast of Red Bluff on Adobe Road. There will be a charge of $2 for adults and $1 for children ages 4 to 11; kids under four are free. The weather will probably be cold with a potential for rain.

For information, contact William B. Ide Adobe State Historic Park, (916) 527-5927 or (916) 529-8599.

DECEMBER

Shasta Cascade Seasonal Hikes & Programs

Lassen Volcanic National Park Summer Hikes

Ongoing during summer • Times vary • See listings that follow
(see #8 on map page 53)

If you've never experienced the geysers and bubbling mud pots of Yellowstone National Park, then you're in for a surprise. You don't have to drive for 16 to 20 hours across a desert, several mountain ranges and two states to smell the acrid aroma of boiling sulfur lakes and wander in the wild landscape of a very active volcanic field. In the northeastern reaches of California, Lassen Volcanic National Park is a little slice of Yellowstone, right at our own doorstep. The recent (geologically speaking) volcanic activity began in the Lassen area about two million years ago and has moved through successive episodes that built up volcanic cones of huge dimensions, only to explode or collapse onto themselves as a new center began to rise. In any event, the activity continues, but now, humans have entered the picture and tagged areas of the park with such names as Bumpass Hell, Chaos Jumbles, Devastated Area and the Sulfur Works.

While there are hundreds of miles of trails that you can explore on your own, traveling with a park ranger or naturalist offers an opportunity to really understand what you're seeing. And believe me, there's an incredible number of things to see. After you've spent some time with a ranger, then go explore on your own. Your enjoyment will be even greater. When you first enter the park, assuming it's during daylight hours, you'll be given a colorful map of Lassen which will become your guide along the road that winds through much of the park. You'll also see mileage markers on the road to help you get your bearings.

As at most local, state and national parks, hike schedules are seldom planned more than a couple of months in advance, much too late to be included here. So, to give you an idea of all the ranger-led hikes available, many of which will probably be offered again, here is a list of the offerings from 1994.

For information, contact Lassen Volcanic National Park, P.O. Box 100, Mineral, CA 96063-0100; (916) 595-4444.

Lassen Crater Hike

This hike meets at 12:30 p.m. on Saturdays during summer, but the meeting time is a little deceptive because the meeting place is very near the top of the 10,457-foot peak. And since the only way to get to the meeting place is to hike from the parking lot, you need to hit the trail at about 10 a.m. The trail is kind of easy, although it is also pretty much up, up, up, with occasional resting places. You begin at 8,500 feet and climb up a steady, 15-percent grade. The views along the trail are almost as spectacular as the views from the summit. If it happens to be early in the season and there was a pretty good winter, you're likely to run into snow across a few areas of the trail and some muddy walking where the snow melt is running. Once you make it to the first broad summit area, just a couple hundred feet below the very top, you'll meet up with a ranger for a hike along Lassen's craters and crags and a talk about its most recent eruptions. Geologically speaking, especially using people time (1914-15), it wasn't all that long ago that the mountain last oozed hot goo from its gaping mouth. Wear good hiking boots or sturdy shoes and bring your lunch, water, a windbreaker, a hat and sunscreen. The entire hike will take approximately five to six hours and is five miles from top to bottom, but the park ranger-led program will probably only take an hour.

Trail to Paradise

This is a half-day hike that meets at 9:30 a.m. mid-week in summer. It is relatively short, just three miles round-trip, and it's well worth the time and effort. You'll be hiking up about 600 feet from your starting point and will be greeted by a wildflower-covered meadow. Paradise Meadows was carved out during the last glacier period and it's one of the first meadows to burst into a palette of midsummer color. Bring your camera and lots of film, along with lunch, water and some bug repellent. Your reward will be great.

Flower Walk

This is a one-hour walk along areas of the park known for their wildflower displays. In summer, it meets several times each week. During July, the meeting place is at the Hat Lake Parking Area, at road marker 42. During August, the meeting place shifts to the Kings Creek Picnic Area, at road marker 30.

Manzanita Lake Nature Walk

Manzanita Lake is one of the most popular destinations in Lassen National Park, mostly because it's not only beautiful, but you can drive right to it. Join the ranger for an easy two-hour, 1.5-mile walk around the lake and learn about its role in the evolving landscape of Lassen. You'll also learn the best strategy for catching fish in Manzanita Lake. (Be sure to check fishing regulations carefully, however; special restrictions sometimes apply to park lakes like Manzanita, allowing only fishing of the catch-and-release, barbless-hook variety.) This nature walk meets several times each week.

Mudflows, Hot Rocks & Pyroclasts

This is an easy, 45-minute walk through the Hot Rock area where you and your ranger will explore the geological forces that transformed this area during Lassen Peak's last eruption. This walk is usually offered two or three times each week. The meeting place is at Hot Rock, which is at road marker 48.

Wet & Wild

This is one hike where you don't have to worry about having the proper foot gear. Toss your shoes and jump into a mountain pond, letting the goo and mud ooze between your toes. Then let your feet feel the icy cold of a mountain spring and the grasses and sedges that creep up along its shallow edges. The ranger will help your feet feel their way into understanding how a mountain lake transforms itself into a mountain meadow. The hike meets at various times and days, several days a week, at the Hat Lake Parking Area, which is at road marker 42.

Walk In the Devastated

The Devastated Area, that is. The 1915 eruption of Mount Lassen created some amazing demonstrations of Mother Nature's power and fury. Pyroclastic mudflows ran down from the mountain, changing the land forever. Here is a chance to spend an hour with a knowledgeable ranger wandering through the devastation. The Devastated Area Parking Lot is at road marker 44. This nature walk meets several times each week.

Indian Ways

This is a really special, 45-minute program about the culture of the Atsugewi Indians, presented by a member of the Atsugewi tribe. It's held at the Loomis Museum, which is located near Manzanita Lake.

Rock Talk

You think rocks can't talk? Well, think again. The rocks of Lassen can tell you about two million years of volcanic history. All you have to know is how to listen. The meeting place is behind the Manzanita Lake camper store. This nature walk meets several times each week.

Skins & Bones

While you're bound to see squirrels and some of the other smaller birds and animals of Lassen, and maybe an occasional black bear (especially if you leave an ice chest out at night), this talk is a unique way to see the wild creatures of Lassen. A ranger will pull skulls, jaw bones, teeth, hair and hides out of his bag of tricks for your close-up inspection. This is where you will really begin to understand how different animals have developed varying ways of surviving in the wilds of Lassen. The 45-minute program is held outdoors behind the camper store at Manzanita Lake, several times each week.

Special Evening Programs

Campfire programs, with their fun songs, skits and, of course, a campfire, are a tradition in most every state and national park in

SEASONAL

the country. Lassen National Park's programs are offered every summer evening at either the Manzanita Lake Amphitheater or the Summit Lake Amphitheater, beginning at 9 p.m. during July and 8:30 p.m. in August. The subjects change each night, so there's always something new to experience. Check the campground bulletin boards for the night's subject.

Junior Ranger Programs

This is one of those few programs designed for the younger crowd, ages 7 to 12 years old. It's also used as a babysitting service by some parents looking for time away from Junior. The programs are usually offered several times each week and meet at the Manzanita Lake Amphitheater for two hours. Or at least that's where they begin. Where they ultimately lead is up to the ranger and the program he or she has planned for the day. Kids learn their way toward a Junior Ranger patch by having fun exploring the secrets of Mount Lassen and the surrounding parklands.

Night Prowl

This is such a fun hike that it's a shame it's limited to just 15 people; to ensure a spot, you have to sign up in advance at the Loomis Museum. Turn off your eyes and suddenly your other senses come alive to explore all the things that go bump in the night. The walk begins at twilight and continues until the ranger or the participants decide it's time to go home. This nature walk meets several times each week.

Pioneers

There weren't always paved roads and visitor services available to the people who came to Mount Lassen. Several modern-day pioneers will join you to tell their own stories about life in the early pioneer days in this wild land. The program is held at the Manzanita Lake Amphitheater and meets several times each week.

Sense of Wonder

This is for the little kids, those too young to be Junior Rangers. Bring your four-, five- and six-year-olds to meet the ranger at the

Manzanita Lake camper store for a fun exploration of sensory awareness. Parents are welcome, but aren't required to attend, as long as you come back for your kids on time. This program meets several times each week.

Weaverville Ranger District Hikes and Programs

Ongoing during summer • Times vary • See listings that follow
(see #2 on map page 52)

In the high and rugged Trinity country, access is somewhat limited unless you enjoy backpacking, in which case you may feel as though you're in heaven. If you'd rather hike it with an experienced guide, there are a number of programs that the Weaverville Ranger District naturalists hold each year. Most of the hikes begin in various locations near Clair Engle Lake (Trinity). We've listed the days and times the hikes and programs met in 1994, but please call to confirm as they could change in 1995.

For information about the following events, contact the Weaverville Ranger District at P.O. Box 1190, Weaverville, CA 96093; (916) 623-2121.

Bowerman Barn Tour

The historic barn, originally built in 1878 by Jacob Bowerman, is a fantastic two-story wood building constructed with wooden pegs and square nails hit with real hammers, not stapled with the power nailers used by modern carpenters. The barn is the last of the structures on the original 160 acres purchased by Jacob's brother John in 1861. The old farm was passed down through succeeding family members and finally purchased by the U.S. Forest Service in 1974. A few minor changes have been made to stabilize the old building, but otherwise it remains much as it was 100 years ago. Tours take place at 10 a.m. and 2 p.m. on Mondays and Wednesdays during summer. The barn is located 24 miles north of Weaverville, off Highway 3, on Guy Covington Drive.

SEASONAL

Fishing Pole Success

If you've not had particularly good luck fishing Clair Engle Lake, then join a fishing guide for a special two-hour program where you'll learn some of the secrets of successfully fishing both Clair Engle and Lewiston lakes. You'll probably come away with something besides excuses and fishy fish tales. If you're age 16 or older, you'll need a fishing license. No matter your age, bring your poles, tackle, sunscreen, a hat, sunglasses and anything else you think you may need, like maybe water and a snack. The program is aimed at first-time and beginning anglers, and happens from 9 a.m. to 11 a.m. on Fridays and Sundays in summer. On Fridays, meet at the Stuart Fork boat ramp located about 13 miles north of Weaverville, off Highway 3, along Clair Engle Lake. The Sunday program is held at the Pine Cove boat ramp, located on Clair Engle Lake, about 15 miles north of Weaverville, just off Highway 3.

Lake Eleanor Picnic Hike

This is an easy two-mile round-trip hike that heads west from Clair Engle Lake. There are usually plenty of wildflowers along the way that you can photograph or just admire. The naturalist leading the hike will also spend some time talking about the ecology and plant life of mountain meadows, their transition from lake to meadow to forest. Bring a sack lunch, water and sunscreen and wear comfortable shoes or hiking boots. You'll set off from the Wyntoon Resort Store, which is located on Highway 3 at the north end of Clair Engle Lake. From there, carpools will be formed for the short drive to the Lake Eleanor Trailhead. The hike takes place on summer Wednesdays from 10 a.m. to 2 p.m.

Botany Walk

Seasonal and geologic changes affect the ecology of our forests, and the naturalist leading this leisurely walk will explain how. You'll learn the names of the many plants in the forest and also discover what uses Indians and early settlers made of them. Bring water and wear comfortable walking shoes. Meet at the Bridge Camp Campground, which is located up Stuarts Fork from Trinity Alps Resort, about 15 miles north of Weaverville on Highway 3. The walk takes place on summer Thursdays from 10 a.m. to noon.

Discovery Walk

This is an easy two-mile hike with a naturalist along the shore-line of Clair Engle Lake. The idea is to learn to increase the sensitivity of your senses to better enjoy the lakes and forests. You'll be watching, listening to, smelling and touching the natural world around you on this leisurely walk. Meet at the Clark Springs Day-Use Area, which is located off Highway 3, about 18 miles north of Weaverville. The hike takes place on summer Sundays from 10 a.m. to 2 p.m.

Walk on the Wild Side

This hike looks at the Trinity River and the wildlife that depend upon its flow for their survival. You may see an osprey diving from high in the sky to snag an unsuspecting trout from just below the water's surface. There may be a visit to a beaver pond to explore the handiwork of nature's dam builder, or there may be deer and other wildlife to see coming down to the river for a cool drink of water. Bring binoculars if you have them and water to drink. Meet at the Trinity River Hatchery, which is located just north of Lewiston. Take Highway 3 north to County Highway 105 (Trinity Dam Boulevard), also heading north. After roughly a half mile, there's a marked turnoff to the hatchery. The hike takes place on summer Thursdays from 9 a.m. to noon.

SEASONAL

Furs and Skulls

The mammals that inhabit Trinity National Forest are all special, whether they are squirrels, deer, coyotes or bears. Join a naturalist for a closer look at some of the creatures that are seldom seen, but live and thrive in the forests around your campsite. You'll have an opportunity to see a coyote skull and feel the smooth warmth of bear fur. Bring the kids for this one. On Fridays, the program is held at Hayward Flat which is located about 20 miles north of Weaverville just off Highway 3, near Clair Engle Lake. The Saturday program is held at Tannery Gulch, located 13.5 miles north of Weaverville, just off Highway 3, on Clair Engle Lake. The program takes place on summer Fridays and Saturdays at 1 p.m.

Chapter 3

❖ ❖ ❖ ❖

Great Outdoor Events
of
California's Sierra

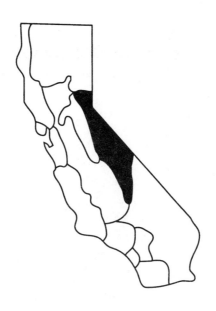

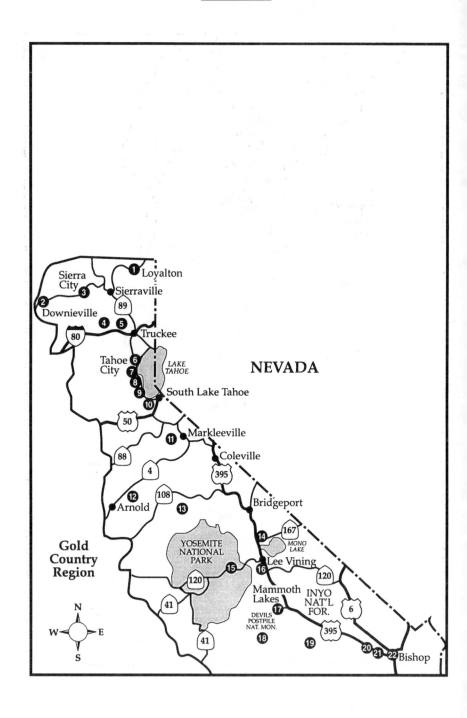

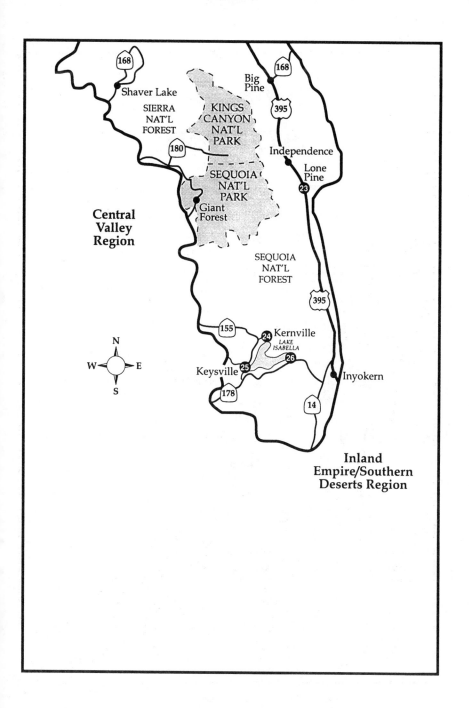

✢ ✢ ✢ ✢

Introduction to the Sierra

Thrust upward in monuments to nature that reach over 14,000 feet above sea level, the magnificent granite spires and monoliths of the Sierra Nevada are testaments to the great forces which have worked nonstop on their exquisite sculpture for millions of years. And nature's efforts continue unabated as avalanches, earthquakes, wind, rain, snow and ice work in perfect harmony to grind these great mountains level with the sea once again.

Fortunately for us, as nature continues working tirelessly seven days a week, 24 hours a day, she has temporarily created a magnificent playground for humans. The Sierra has become a recreation destination for both citified gentlemen and ladies and for rugged outdoor types who should have been born back in the early 19th century, when Jedediah Smith roamed these mountains and valleys in search of beaver.

In the days when the Donner Party attempted to drag their heavily loaded wagons over the crest of the Sierra in a snowstorm, there were no marked trails or roads to guide them. Needless to say, their inexperience, coupled with early snowstorms, made their miserable lives even more miserable. Today, freeways, paved highways and hundreds of miles of dirt roads create innumerable points of access into the Sierra. While heavy winter snow or a rare summer rock slide may temporarily block Sierra roads, getting in for the fishing, hiking, skiing, sightseeing, boating, camping, golf or gambling is hardly a problem.

What comes as a shock to a few people each year is that these mountains can still be deadly, both in summer and winter. Once you get off the popularly traveled roads, knowing where you're going feel for the beauty and power of these mountains you need to get into the backcountry. What could be more fun than getting there with the expert guidance of state park or U.S. Forest Service rangers and naturalists, or accompanying an organized hike led by skilled members of organizations like the Sierra Club, which have been hiking these mountains for years?

Anyone who has ever spent much time hiking in the Sierra Nevada has discovered the magnificence of its granite peaks, cascading streams and wildflower-covered alpine meadows. Millions of people head up the mountains from the valleys each year, especially during summer, in order to escape the sweltering valley temperatures, but also during winter to enjoy the skiing. Actually, the best time of year to hike in the Sierra is during fall. The crowds have gone back to work or school, the daytime weather is almost always comfortable and the leaves are dressing themselves in their autumn colors.

Since weather is always a consideration in the Sierra, especially in fall and winter when a weather forecaster's prediction of partly cloudy skies can turn out to be two feet of snow instead, assume that every hike will go off as planned. Severe weather may change only the planned destination and the length of the hike, assuming you can get to the starting place.

For winter hikes, snowshoes or cross-country skis generally can be rented locally. Sierra veterans know that some winters don't see enough snow early in the season for skiing, so you may want to call and check snow conditions prior to renting equipment, or traveling great distances. Rock skiing, even on someone else's rented skis, isn't much fun.

However you choose to get there, remember to be prepared for anything, from summer snowstorms and winter rainstorms to raging rivers and dry creeks. And please, if you are going hiking or backpacking into the backcountry alone, or even in a small group, tell someone responsible where you are going and when you plan to return.

Introduction to Cross-Country Skiing at Sugar Pine Point State Park

January 7, 1995 **$** $\emptyset$ • 10 a.m. to 1 p.m.
(see #7 on map page 74)

This course is not for those who have done much cross-country skiing. In fact, the focus of this class is teaching first-time skiers the absolute basics of the sport. You'll learn things like: how to turn around and go the opposite direction when you have six-foot skis attached to your feet and you're standing on a hillside; how to stand back up after you fall down, because you are going to fall down; how to shuffle your feet and make yourself move forward; how to scream down a hill at the earth-shattering speed of maybe five miles-per-hour, even though you'd swear you're about to break the land speed record; and how to stop when you want to stop, even though it probably won't work for you. Since everyone is pretty much in the same beginners' boat, this is really a lot of fun and the best chance you'll have for easing into a fantastic sport that almost anyone in even less-than-marginal shape, from 3 to 93 years old, can do, even the first time out. Once the ranger leading this thing gets everyone reasonably accustomed to their skis, he or she will lead you on a short and easy two-mile ski-hike over some pretty level terrain. After completing this three-hour program, you'll be ready to tackle some of the longer, marked trails in the park. You'll have to bring your own cross-country ski equipment which can be rented in any number of shops in Tahoe City, Truckee or South Lake Tahoe, or in your favorite hometown ski shop. As far as clothing goes, dress in light layers and try to find some good wool socks for your feet. Shy away from those insulated downhill ski pants and heavy down jackets, because cross-country skiing makes you sweat a lot in all that padding. Bring water to drink and a snack. Sunscreen is essential as are good sunglasses, otherwise you'll go home semi-blind if it happens to be a sunny day. Call to verify the date and time of the hike, and also to make sure there's enough of the white stuff to ski on. There is a $5 per vehicle day-use fee at the park. The meeting place is next to the General Creek Campground kiosk at Sugar Pine Point State Park on the west shore of Lake Tahoe, about 10 miles south of Tahoe City on Highway 89.

For information, contact Sugar Pine Point State Park, P.O. Box 266, Tahoma, CA 95733, (916) 525-7982; or Sierra District State Parks, (916) 525-7232.

❖ ❖ ❖ ❖

Tex Cushion Memorial Sled Dog Race

January 7 & 8, 1995 [S] ☎

(see #17 on map page 74)

Thanks to novelists like Jack London and Hollywood moviemakers, we associate the cry of "mush, mush," with the dogsleds of Alaskan and Yukon winters. While dogsleds have never been a hot choice for winter transportation in the Sierra, sled racing has caught on as a fun winter event for people looking for a different kind of competition than skiing. If you've got your own sled dogs, you can join in the fun, or just stop by Mammoth on a winter trip and enjoy being a spectator. The dogsled race course covers eight miles of snow-blanketed trails that meander through some of the Sierra's most beautiful winter scenery. Bring your cross-country skis and you can probably get to some pretty good views of the action without sinking to your rear end in snow. Mammoth Lakes is located about 10 miles off US 395 on Highway 203, 31 miles north of Bishop. There will probably be a fee to watch the races, but it wasn't set at press time. This is one of those events where it makes little difference what the weather is like. Since the race is held in the dead of winter, be prepared for heavy snow, but hope for those blue Sierra skies.

For information, contact Sierra Nevada Dog Drivers, Inc., 1272 Balboa Avenue, Burlingame, CA 94010; (800) 367-6572.

❖ ❖ ❖ ❖

Introduction to Cross-Country Skiing at Grover Hot Springs State Park

January 8, 1995 • 10 a.m. to 1 p.m.
(see #11 on map page 74)

A ranger guides you in the basics of cross-country skiing, then leads a short and easy two-mile ski-hike over some pretty level terrain. After completing this three-hour program, you'll be ready to tackle some of the longer, marked trails in the park. (For tips on how to dress and what to bring, see the listing on page 78.) Since the snow is always questionable at Grover, call to make sure there's enough of the white stuff to ski on. Bring your swimsuit for a leisurely dip in the mineral hot springs after your ski tour. You can't rent cross-country skis at the park, so rent them before you get there. There is a $5 day-use fee at the park. There is a fee of $4 for those 18 and older and $2 for everyone else to use the hot springs. The meeting place is Grover Hot Springs State Park, which is located at the end of Hot Springs Road. It's about four miles west of Markleeville, a very small town which is on Highway 89, about 18 miles south of the intersection of highways 89 and 88.

For information, contact Grover Hot Springs State Park, P.O. Box 188, Markleeville, CA 96120, (916) 694-2248; or Sierra District State Parks, (916) 525-7232.

✤ ✤ ✤ ✤

Emerald Bay In Winter

January 14, 1995 • 10 a.m. to 1 p.m.
(see #9 on map page 74)

Emerald Bay's Eagle Point Campground is only open about two months each year and that's during summer. It's a beautiful place, even when the campground is full of people, motor homes and yapping dogs. But if you really want to experience the beauty of Emerald Bay, toss your cross-country skis in your car and come back in winter. A ranger will lead this moderately easy ski tour down the campground road to the edge of the bay, where there's a pretty good chance of spotting one or more of the wintering bald eagles that hang out in the trees and cruise overhead looking for a big, fat trout for dinner. The trip will take about three hours and is for cross-country skiers only. You'll be dropping from about 6,800 feet down to Lake Tahoe's 6,200-foot elevation. That's the good news. The bad news is you've got to ski back up to the top—no ski lifts here. At any rate, the grade back up isn't too bad. Bring lunch and water and be prepared for not-so-good weather. The meeting place is at the Eagle Point Campground entrance, which is on the south side of Emerald Bay, along Highway 89. If you're coming from the north, call about road conditions, because heavy winter storms can close the highway around Emerald Bay for several days or weeks at a time. And it's a long, long drive all the way back around Lake Tahoe.

For information, contact D.L. Bliss State Park, P.O. Box 266, Tahoma, CA 95733, (916) 525-7277; or Sierra District State Parks, (916) 525-7232.

❖ ❖ ❖ ❖

Donner Full Moon Ski Tour
January 14, 1995 • 6:30 p.m. to 9:30 p.m.
(see #4 on map page 74)

If you've never had an opportunity to see Donner Lake under a full moon, then you're in for a real treat, assuming of course that the weather cooperates. Grab your cross-country skis, or your snow-shoes if you're not quite up to the long boards, and join a ranger for this easy two-mile trek from the Donner Museum parking lot out to historic China Cove on the shore of Donner Lake. With no cloud cover, the moon should rise big and full, casting its bright reflection across a frozen, or partially frozen, snow-covered lake. Be sure to dress according to the weather. You might want to toss a flashlight into your pack, just in case clouds decide to obscure the moon. Bring some snacks to enjoy next to the lakeside campfire at China Cove. If the weather happens to be too ugly, you may want to call the park and be sure the hike is still being held, especially if you're planning to rent cross-country skis or snowshoes. Meet at the Donner Memorial State Park Museum parking lot, which is at the east end of Donner Lake, just off Interstate 80, near the Truckee agricultural check station.

For information, contact Donner Memorial State Park, (916) 582-7892; or Sugar Pine Point State Park, P.O. Box 266, Tahoma, CA 95733, (916) 582-7982.

Donner Party Escape

January 15, 1995 • 10 a.m. to 1 p.m.
(see #4 on map page 74)

Here's a chance to put yourself in the footsteps of the ill-fated Donner Party, the westward-bound pioneers who unsuccessfully tried to cross the Sierra nearly 150 years ago. Unlike the Donner expedition, though, your group will drive from the meeting place at the Donner Memorial State Park parking lot to the stretch of rock and cliffs that separated the Donners from the downhill side of the mountain. Rent snowshoes if you don't own a pair, because after driving to where the snow is no longer plowed on the old pass, assuming it's a reasonably snowy winter, everyone will put on their oversized, clubby footwear and re-enact one of the Donner Party's escape attempts. The major differences are that you'll bring along plenty of water and something to nibble on, other than your partner's arm. You can also return to your car at the end of the hike and drive to the nearest restaurant or hotel. A ranger will relate the history of the Donner Party and their many attempts to escape their snow-bound fate. This is a moderately easy hike that will meet at the Donner Memorial State Park Museum parking lot, which is located about two miles west of Truckee, just off Interstate 80.

For information, contact Donner Memorial State Park, (916) 582-7892; or Sierra District State Parks, (916) 525-7232.

Moonlight Tour to Olympic Meadow

January 15, 1995 • 6 p.m. to 10 p.m.
(see #7 on map page 74)

Moonlight tours always work better when winter clouds don't interfere, so you might want to call and check out the weather. Assuming Mother Nature is cooperating, snowing only during the week and leaving the weekends clear and cold, the ski trek out to Olympic Meadow is a relatively easy, level tour. Part of your trail actually served as the cross-country skiing race course back in 1960, when Squaw Valley hosted the Winter Olympics. You'll be skiing, initially, through the fir and pine forest of Sugar Pine Point and crossing General Creek, fortunately across a small bridge. Once you reach the meadow, the more adventurous and advanced skiers might want to do a little off-trail skiing on the adjacent hillside, all under a big and bright full moon. Bring adequate clothing, as the temperatures could easily plummet into the teens or below during the ski-hike, although that's not real likely. You may also want to tuck some snacks and something to drink into your daypack. Snowshoes won't work on this trip, because it's a little tough keeping up with cross-country skiers over the five-mile trek. The meeting place is the Cross-Country Ski Trail parking lot in Sugar Pine Point State Park, about 10 miles south of Tahoe City on Highway 89. Drive into the General Creek Campground and park in the lot near the entry kiosk.

For information, contact Sugar Pine Point State Park, P.O. Box 266, Tahoma, CA 95733, (916) 525-7982; or Sierra District State Parks, (916) 525-7232.

✤ ✤ ✤ ✤

Animals in Winter: Sugar Pine Point State Park

January 21, 1995 • 10 a.m. to 1 p.m.
(see #7 on map page 74)

When you wander through Sierra forests during summer, wildlife is fairly abundant, even though you may not see everything that lives near where you trample. During summer, the weather is nice and there's plenty of food available, especially near campgrounds where too many human animals have a strange proclivity for feeding junk food to wild animals, or where human animals get sloppy and leave leftovers out for stellar jays and squirrels. So where do all these animals go during the dead of winter, when most anything edible is either dead and rotted, or frozen and buried under 10 feet of snow and ice? Obviously, birds can fly south, or at least down to the Central Valley, but what about the smaller animals like Douglas tree squirrels, ground squirrels, deer, raccoons, black bears, coyotes and chipmunks? On this intriguing hike, you'll discover which animals remain active all winter and what they do to survive, where deer and bears disappear to and what all those ground squirrels and chipmunks do during long, cold winter nights and short winter days. And if you've ever noticed animal tracks in the snow, the ranger who leads this hike will help you learn to identify which critters they belong to and give you an idea of what the particular animal was doing, like foraging for food or sprinting frantically to escape becoming food for something bigger. There's a $5 per vehicle day-use fee. The meeting place will be the Cross-Country Ski Trail parking lot near the General Creek Campground entry kiosk in Sugar Pine Point State Park, located about 10 miles south of Tahoe City, just off Highway 89.

For information, contact D.L. Bliss State Park, P.O. Box 266, Tahoma, CA 95733, (916) 525-7277; or Sierra District State Parks, (916) 525-7232.

✤ ✤ ✤ ✤

Introduction to Cross-Country Skiing at Donner Lake

January 21, 1995 • 10 a.m. to 1 p.m.
(see #4 on map page 74)

A ranger guides you in the basics of cross-country skiing, then leads a short and easy 1.5-mile ski-hike over some pretty level terrain. After completing this three-hour program, you'll be ready to tackle some of the longer, marked trails in the park. (For tips on how to dress and what to bring, see the listing on page 78.) This introductory course will meet at the Donner Memorial State Park Museum parking lot, which is located at the east end of Donner Lake, just off Interstate 80, about two miles west of Truckee.

For information, contact Donner Memorial State Park, (916) 582-7892; or Sierra District State Parks, (916) 525-7232.

✤ ✤ ✤ ✤

Red Lakes Ski Trip

January 22, 1995 • 10 a.m. to 3 p.m.
(see #11 on map page 74)

This is a good ski-hike for strong intermediate cross-country skiers who have learned to make wide sweeping turns on their boards. You must also know how to stop, as you'll need to avoid trees, boulders and cliff faces. The terrain around Red Lakes is varied, so you'll have an opportunity to ski up and down hills of different angles and across wide open meadows. There will be plenty of time to practice your telemark turns or just go bonzo down hills for the thrill of it. Bring your own skis, water, lunch, sunscreen and clothes to handle changing weather conditions. This seven-mile trip will last about five or six hours. Meet at the Red Lakes parking area off Highway 88, about a mile east of Carson Pass Summit.

For information, contact Grover Hot Springs State Park, P.O. Box 188, Markleeville, CA 96120; (916) 694-2248.

✤ ✤ ✤ ✤

Intermediate Cross-Country Ski Clinic

January 28, 1995 • 10 a.m. to 1 p.m.
(see #7 on map page 74)

For those of you who have developed a good working relationship between your skis and varied winter terrain, it's time to learn some of the more advanced methods of propelling yourself farther and faster along the trail, with less effort. This clinic is not meant for someone who has only been out a few times on skis. You must have a good command of the basics of kick, glide and pole, and be capable of covering the seven to ten kilometers (six miles) of up and down terrain in two hours without too much difficulty. Bring your skis, water and lunch and be prepared for a good time and bad weather. There is a $5 per vehicle day-use fee. This hike meets at the Cross-Country Ski Trail parking lot in Sugar Pine Point State Park, about 10 miles south of Tahoe City on Highway 89.

For information, contact Sugar Pine Point State Park, P.O. Box 266, Tahoma, CA 95733, (916) 525-7982; or Sierra District State Parks, (916) 525-7232.

✤ ✤ ✤ ✤

Meiss Meadows Ski Trip

January 29, 1995 • 10 a.m. to 4 p.m.
(see #11 on map page 74)

Meiss Meadows is located north of Carson Pass and this trip to explore the meadow is rated as an intermediate-to-advanced ski-hike. There should be some good off-trail trekking and wonderful views of Lake Tahoe from the ridge tops. The entire trip should only take about five or six hours. The meeting place is the parking lot just west of Carson Pass Summit on Highway 88. A Sno-Park permit is required to use the parking lot and the fine is significant if you don't display one. One-day permits are available from most shops that rent cross-country ski equipment, or you can contact the California Sno-Park Program, P.O. Box 942895, Sacramento, CA 95846-0001; (916) 653-4000.

For information, contact Grover Hot Springs State Park, P.O. Box 188, Markleeville, CA 96120; (916) 694-2248.

Introduction to Cross-Country Skiing at Grover Hot Spings State Park

February 4, 1995 • 10 a.m. to 1 p.m.

(see #11 on map page 74)

FEBRUARY

A ranger guides you in the basics of cross-country skiing, then leads a short and easy 1.5-mile ski-hike over some pretty level terrain. After completing this three-hour program, you'll be ready to tackle some of the longer, marked trails in the park. (For tips on how to dress and what to bring, see the listing on page 78.) Since the snow is always questionable at Grover, call to make sure there's enough of the white stuff to ski on. Bring your swimsuit for a leisurely dip in the mineral hot springs after your ski tour. There is a fee of $4 for those 18 and older and $2 for everyone else to use the hot springs. The meeting place is Grover Hot Springs State Park, which is located at the end of Hot Springs Road. It's about four miles west of Markleeville, a very small town which is on Highway 89, about 18 miles south of the intersection of highways 89 and 88.

For information, contact Grover Hot Springs State Park, P.O. Box 188, Markleeville, CA 96120, (916) 694-2248; or Sierra District State Parks, (916) 525-7232.

Beginning Snowshoe Clinic

February 4, 1995 • 10 a.m. to noon

(see #4 on map page 74)

For those not inclined to snap on the cross-country skis, but still inclined to explore the Sierra's winter wonderland, why not try it on snowshoes? This is an introduction to snowshoeing for the real beginner. If you don't happen to have a pair of showshoes hanging in your garage, call some of your local cross-country ski rental shops. Many also rent snowshoes. If you're really new at this snow travel stuff, you also may wish to rent cross-country ski poles to help with your balance. Once you get over having to take slightly strange steps with the floppy shoes attached to your snow boots, you'll soon discover the fun that snowshoes can be, especially if you've ever tried to walk through deep snow without them. Bring your camera if you have one, but since you'll probably fall once or twice, make sure you won't mind if anything you bring gets a little wet. Wear loose fitting, comfortable clothing and dress in several light layers, rather than wearing a heavy winter coat. You may also want to bring water and a light snack. An important note: You'll need reservations for this hike, because it's limited to just 15 people. The hike will leave from the Donner Memorial State Park Museum, located about two miles west of Truckee on Donner Pass Road, just off Interstate 80.

For information, contact Donner Memorial State Park, (916) 582-7892; or Sierra District State Parks, P.O. Box 266, Tahoma, CA 95733, (916) 525-7232.

Winter Survival Clinic

February 4, 1995 • 10 a.m. to 1 p.m.
(see #7 on map page 74)

Three hours spent in this clinic is three hours well spent for anyone thinking about off-trail skiing or for people heading out for overnight cross-country skiing tours. Weather in the Sierra can change from warm sunshine one hour to a raging blizzard the next. Being caught out in one is no big deal if you're prepared and know what to do. This clinic will offer instruction and practice in building provisional shelters, starting emergency fires when every stick of wood you see around you is wet with snow, fixing broken skis and finding your way in the forest, preferably with a compass, but without one if that's the situation you find yourself in. The rangers will also discuss the bare-minimum items you should carry with you on any daytime ski outing and how to fix broken and injured bodies with some basic first-aid instruction. You'll also learn about the hazards of hypothermia, how to identify the early signs of this potentially deadly condition and what to do to counter them. There is a $5 per vehicle day-use fee. Meet at the Sugar Pine Point State Park day-use parking area, which is located about 10 miles south of Tahoe City on Highway 89. Bring your cross-country skis, water, lunch and warm clothes.

For information, contact Sugar Pine Point State Park, P.O. Box 266, Tahoma, CA 95733, (916) 525-7982; or Sierra District State Parks, (916) 525-7232.

✢ ✢ ✢ ✢

Animals in Winter: Grover Hot Springs State Park

February 5, 1995 • 10 a.m. to 2 p.m.
(see #11 on map page 74)

For a description of this intriguing hike and talk about animals' winter survival strategies, see the listing on page 84. There is a fee of $4 for those 18 and older and $2 for everyone else to use the hot springs. Grover Hot Springs State Park is at the end of Hot Springs Road, about four miles west of Markleeville, which is on Highway 89, about 18 miles south of the intersection of highways 88 and 89. Call ahead to confirm the date.

For information, contact Grover Hot Springs State Park, P.O. Box 188, Markleeville, CA 96120; (916) 694-2248.

✢ ✢ ✢ ✢

Moonlight at Grover

February 11, 1995 • 5:30 p.m. to 9:30 p.m.
(see #11 on map page 74)

Like the feel of a warm, outdoor soak? Then it's best if you get here a few hours before the scheduled 5:30 p.m. start time of this hike. Grover Hot Springs is home to natural mineral hot springs that have been diverted into a pool for your soaking pleasure. Bring your bathing suit and a towel and enjoy soaking in the hot pool for an hour or two, or until you've turned purplish, prunish and the lifeguard has to haul you out. Afterward, the moonlight evening starts with stories and a hot dog roast around an open campfire. After such an All-American dinner, it's time to snap on your skis and take a leisurely ski-hike around Hot Springs Meadow. If the weather cooperates and there's snow on the ground and clear skies above, perhaps the coyotes will provide a chorus of howling in the background. You'll also have an opportunity to see stars like you've never seen stars before, if, of course, Mother Nature decides not to blow a storm through on this particular evening. There is a fee of $4 for those 18 and older and $2 for everyone else to use the hot springs. Grover Hot Springs State Park is at the end of Hot Springs Road, about four miles west of Markleeville, which is on Highway 89, about 18 miles south of the intersection with Highway 88. Call ahead, not only to confirm the date, but to see if there is enough snow in the meadow to ski on, especially if you plan on renting your skis.

For information, contact Grover Hot Springs State Park, P.O. Box 188, Markleeville, CA 96120; (916) 694-2248.

✤ ✤ ✤ ✤

Animals in Winter: Sugar Pine Point State Park

February 11, 1995 • 10 a.m. to 1 p.m.
(see #7 on map page 74)

For a description of this intriguing hike and talk about animals' winter survival strategies, see the listing on page 84. The meeting place will be the Cross-Country Ski Trail parking lot adjacent to the General Creek Campground entry kiosk at Sugar Pine Point State Park. The park is located about 10 miles south of Tahoe City, just off Highway 89.

For information, contact D.L. Bliss State Park, P.O. Box 266, Tahoma, CA 95733, (916) 525-7277; or Sierra District State Parks, (916) 525-7232.

✤ ✤ ✤ ✤

Donner Full Moon Ski Tour

February 11, 1995 • 6:30 p.m. to 9:30 p.m.
(see #4 on map page 74)

If you've never had an opportunity to see Donner Lake under a full moon, then you're in for a real treat, assuming of course that the weather cooperates. For a full description of this cross-country ski-hike, see page 81. Meet at the Donner Memorial State Park Museum parking lot, which is at the east end of Donner Lake, just off Interstate 80, near the Truckee bug station (or agricultural check station).

For information, contact Donner Memorial State Park, (916) 582-7892; or Sugar Pine Point State Park, P.O. Box 266, Tahoma, CA 95733, (916) 582-7982.

✤ ✤ ✤ ✤

Washoe Meadows Ski Tour

February 12, 1995 • 10 a.m. to 2 p.m.
(see #11 on map page 74)

This is one of the Tahoe area's newest state parks, one that few people visit. The ski-hike is a pretty, leisurely tour that offers good views of the surrounding mountain landmarks like Freel Peak and Mount Tallac. You'll ski over a fairly level trail leading through tall trees and open meadow lands. Actually, part of the tour is over land that serves as a golf course during the greener months of the year. Meet at the Lake Tahoe Golf Course, which is located adjacent to Highway 50 in Meyers, a couple miles west of South Lake Tahoe. Bring snacks, clothing for changeable weather and water.

For information, contact Grover Hot Springs State Park, P.O. Box 188, Markleeville, CA 96120; (916) 694-2248.

✤ ✤ ✤ ✤

Introduction to Cross-Country Skiing at Sugar Pine Point State Park

February 12, 1995 • 10 a.m. to 1 p.m.
(see #7 on map page 74)

A ranger guides you in the basics of cross-country skiing, then leads a short and easy 1.5-mile ski-hike over some pretty level terrain. After completing this three-hour program, you'll be ready to tackle some of the longer, marked trails in the park. (For tips on how to dress and what to bring, see the listing on page 78.) Call to verify the date and time of the hike, and also to make sure there's enough of the white stuff to ski on. There is a $5 per vehicle day-use fee. The meeting place is the parking lot near the General Creek Campground kiosk at Sugar Pine Point State Park on the west shore of Lake Tahoe, about 10 miles south of Tahoe City on Highway 89.

For information, contact Sugar Pine Point State Park, P.O. Box 266, Tahoma, CA 95733, (916) 525-7982; or Sierra District State Parks, (916) 525-7232.

❋ ❋ ❋ ❋

Whiskey Flat Days

February 17 to 20, 1995 • 10 a.m. to dusk
(see #24 on map page 75)

During the heady Gold Rush days of the 1860s, hundreds of wishful 49ers trudged their way to Whiskey Flat, looking to strike it rich. Today the mountain town calls itself Kernville, but the community still celebrates its Gold Rush heritage each year with Whiskey Flat Days. This 40th annual celebration will turn back the clock 130 years during four fun-filled days of guided mine tours, crafts booths, puppet shows, a costume contest, a carnival, a petting zoo and pony rides. There will be a grand parade on Saturday, February 18, and a Wild West rodeo on both Saturday and Sunday. The wilder bunch can enter the Whiskerino Beard and Mustache Contest, bring along their favorite amphibian to compete in the Frog Races or test their verbal spewing ability in the Epitaph Contest. In other words, there's something for everyone. Kernville, a.k.a. Whiskey Flat, is located near Lake Isabella. Head about 43 miles east of Bakersfield along Highway 178, then north another couple miles on Highway 155. Most of the long weekend is free, except for some of the special events. Remember: This is winter in the high Sierra, so be prepared for any weather, including snow.

For information, contact Whisky Flat Days, P.O. Box 397, Kernville, CA 93238; (619) 376-2629.

❋ ❋ ❋ ❋

Off-Track Skiing Clinic

February 18, 1995 • 10 a.m. to 2 p.m.
(see #7 on map page 74)

FEBRUARY

If you're tired of skiing in those chewed-up parallel tracks on the same trails as everyone else, then maybe it's time to try a little off-track skiing. There's nothing like skiing down a small, open or tree-covered hillside, your skis blasting through fresh, untracked powder. This clinic is designed for intermediate and advanced skiers who want to further develop wilderness and off-track skiing skills. The rangers will teach you the basics of handling difficult snow, like some of the lumpy, icy, slushy spring cement the Sierra is so well known for. You'll also learn about speed control, what climbing skins are and when to use them, skiing the steep stuff and avalanche awareness. The ranger will toss in some instruction about first aid and winter survival, just in case things ever get out of your control. This is a moderately difficult hike designed for reasonably proficient cross-country skiers. If you don't already own cross-country skis, try to rent some of the heavier, metal-edged models and the matching heavy boots. You'll also need to bring a little food and water for this four-hour outing. There is a $5 per vehicle day-use fee. It meets at the General Creek Ski Trail parking area at Sugar Pine Point State Park, just off Highway 89, about 10 miles south of Tahoe City.

For information, contact Sugar Pine Point State Park, P.O. Box 266, Tahoma, CA 95733, (916) 525-7982; or Sierra District State Parks, (916) 525-7232.

Carson Pass Ski Trek

February 19, 1995 • 10 a.m. to 3 p.m.
(see #11 on map page 74)

This cross-country ski-hike will require that you have one of those Sno-Park permits to park in the Carson Pass Summit parking area, but the couple of bucks for the permit are well worth the scenery you'll enjoy on this trip. A ranger will lead you from the summit out to Lake Winnemucca and to lands beyond, depending upon weather, time and the group's ability and willingness. You really won't see much of the small lake, because it lies on the downhill side of a 10,000-feet-above-sea-level mountain, so it is sure to be frozen and covered with snow. But that means you can ski across it. This is a relatively easy intermediate ski trip that should take about five hours, with the traditional lunch break tossed in. Bring food, water, adequate clothing for variable weather conditions and a camera for the views. Sno-Park permits are available at most shops that rent cross-country ski equipment, or you can contact the California Sno-Park Program, P.O. Box 942895, Sacramento, CA 95846-0001; (916) 653-4000.

For information, contact Grover Hot Springs State Park, P.O. Box 188, Markleeville, CA 96120; (916) 694-2248.

Donner Party Survival Hike

February 19, 1995 • 10 a.m. to 1 p.m.

(see #4 on map page 74)

If you have any interest in the early history of the first settlers crossing the Sierra, or attempting to cross the Sierra, then this short winter hike will introduce you to the most famous and ill-fated wagon train ever to attempt the crossing. The Donner Party didn't fair particularly well, getting stuck in snow, running out of food and generally having a pretty tough time. Many of the Donner people didn't survive, but you've got some better leaders on your trek, so your reenactment of being stuck in the snow with little food should be a lot easier. Besides, you can sneak some snacks into your daypack. This hike is for snowshoes only and will cover only about one mile during the three hours. Meet at the Donner Memorial State Park Museum parking lot, two miles west of Truckee on Donner Pass Road.

For information, contact Donner Memorial State Park at (916) 582-7892; or Sierra District State Parks, P.O. Box 266, Tahoma, CA 95733, (916) 525-7232.

Avalanche Clinic

February 25, 1995 • 10 a.m. to 1 p.m.
(see #7 on map page 74)

This is an easy, relatively level three-mile cross-country ski tour that will highlight the important aspects of avalanche awareness. You'll learn how to evaluate slopes, weather and snow-pack stability, all of which can influence the potential for avalanches. Three hours here could easily save your life or the life of someone you know, if you are skiing off-trail in some of the more remote and beautiful parts of the winter Sierra. Rangers will demonstrate techniques for rescuing people buried by an avalanche and how to get your own rear end out of one, should you suddenly find yourself in the wrong place at the wrong time. Bring your cross-country skis, lunch, water and, if you happen to have one in your back pocket, an avalanche beacon. There is a $5 per vehicle day-use fee. Meet at the Cross-Country Ski Trail parking lot at Sugar Pine Point State Park, just off Highway 89, about 10 miles south of Tahoe City and one mile south of Tahoma.

For information, contact Sugar Pine Point State Park, P.O. Box 266, Tahoma, CA 95733, (916) 525-7982; or Sierra District State Parks, (916) 525-7232.

✤ ✤ ✤ ✤

Schallenberger Ridge Ski-Hike

February 25, 1995 • 10 a.m. to 3 p.m.
(see #4 on map page 74)

This is one of those hikes meant for good cross-country skiers, not beginners. If you've got your act together as far as skiing goes, this hike is well worth the sweat that you're going to lose climbing the ridge line. Seems like every year more people start this trek than ever finish it. There's a flat stretch that leads from the meeting place at the Donner Memorial State Park parking lot, about two miles west of Truckee. Following this short, flat stretch, the trail suddenly heads up, fairly steeply for a couple hundred yards. About the time you think you can catch your breath, the group turns off the snow-covered road and heads up an even steeper mountainside, with no trail, no guidance markers, just a ranger in the lead. You have to know how to do a little maneuver called a herringbone in order to get up the really steep parts. Once you finally emerge above the treeline, you'll follow the ridge up and up to the top, where everyone will stop for lunch. From the top of Schallenberger Ridge, there are great views of Donner Lake, and to the south, Granite Chief Wilderness and Squaw Valley, although you can't actually see the valley. What makes this outing really fun is the trip back. Assuming there's enough snow, and you don't freak out when confronting speed, the back side of the ridge is a big, wide open bowl where you can go really fast or swoop down with the style and elegance of an accomplished telemarker. This hike will go, no matter the weather, assuming there's enough snow coverage—so dress accordingly and hope for the best. If the snow coverage isn't all that great, the hike will simply head off in a different direction. The trip will take about five hours, cover a couple miles and gain 1,100 feet, topping out at about 7,000 feet in elevation. You need to call in advance and register for this particular hike.

For information, contact Sugar Pine Point State Park, P.O. Box 266, Tahoma, CA 95733, (916) 525-7982; or Sierra District State Parks, (916) 525-7232.

Red Lakes Ski Trip

February 26, 1995 • 10 a.m. to 3 p.m.
(see #11 on map page 74)

Geared toward strong intermediate cross-country skiers, this seven-mile trip will last between five and six hours. For more about the Red Lakes area, see page 85. Meet at the Red Lakes parking area off Highway 88, about a mile east of Carson Pass Summit.

For information, contact Grover Hot Springs State Park, P.O. Box 188, Markleeville, CA 96120; (916) 694-2248.

Kern Canyon & Walker Pass Tour

March 4, 1995 $

(see #26 on map page 75)

Geology and ecology are the focus of this trip through the southern Sierra Nevada Mountains. The day-long tour will explore Kern Canyon and the river that carved its way through the mountains on its way to the sea, with a stop at Lake Isabella. Mining, initially for gold and later for other minerals, is what brought the first large numbers of settlers into the Sierra. This is an opportunity to visit the Keysville, Kernville and Weldon mining districts for a look at both the past and present-day operations to extract tungsten and gold from the mountains. You'll stop at archaeological sites around 5,250-feet-above-sea-level Walker Pass, as well as at other Native American sites such as Solstice Rock and Birthing Stone. This geology tour will begin at Lake Isabella; contact the trip leader for the specific meeting place and time.

The cost is $20 per person which includes transportation. You'll need a field guide; the trip leader can give you information on which would be best. This is winter in the Sierra, so hope for sunny and dry, but dress for cold and wet.

For information, contact the Bureau of Land Management, 3801 Pegasus Drive, Bakersfield, CA 93308-6837; (805) 391-6081.

Cross-Country Ski Waxing Clinic

March 4, 1995 • 10 a.m. to noon

(see #7 on map page 74)

This clinic isn't for everyone. But if you want to take a step back in time, before the advent of plastic skis with fish-scale bottoms, then stop by for this two-hour class. If you happen to have your own wooden or more modern plastic skis with waxable bases, bring them along. For old wooden skis, you'll get to enjoy the smell of pine tar as it oozes over the bases and experience the thrill of trying to spread sticky klisters to meet spring snow conditions. By

---

the time you leave, you'll have a good understanding of ski-base preparation and how and when to apply kick and glide waxes, how to do field waxing and how to wax for races. A ranger will also explain how different waxes, depending upon the outside temperature and the texture of the snow, allow your skis to easily slide forward, but grip as you push them backward to propel you up the trail. Bring your own favorite waxing system if you have one. Definitely wait until after the clinic before you go out and spend money on waxing systems that might not work all that well for you. This is an indoor program held at Sugar Pine Point State Park's Ehrman Mansion complex, about 11 miles south of Tahoe City off Highway 89. There is a $5 per vehicle day-use fee.

For information, contact Sugar Pine Point State Park, P.O. Box 266, Tahoma, CA 95733, (916) 525-7982; or Sierra District State Parks, (916) 525-7232.

Snowfest

Early March [S] ☎

(see #6 on map page 74)

For years, this has been a favorite annual event for the locals, especially for Tahoe City kids, because a lot of them are out of school for the week. While snow and skiing are the main attractions for tens of thousands of tourists each winter, Snowfest offers lots more for anyone willing to brave a possible winter storm in getting here. There is almost always a wild assortment of contests, most of which have nothing to do with speeding down a snow-covered mountain at death-defying velocities. Ice sculpting, snowpeople-making, dog sled races, snow golf and a weird game of softsnow ball (a game loosely rooted in baseball), will keep your days active and never boring. Of course, there's always the dozen or so nearby ski resorts and mile after mile of cross-country ski trails to explore if Snowfest isn't your cup of warm brandy. Tahoe City is at the intersection of highways 89 and 28, about 14 miles south of Truckee and Interstate 80. Most everything is free, but there may be fees for a few of the events. If no storms are blowing through, you'll probably be greeted with relatively warm days and temperatures well below freezing at night.

For more information, contact the Tahoe North Visitor and Convention Bureau, 950 North Lake Boulevard #3, Tahoe City, CA 96145; (800) 824-6348.

❀ ❀ ❀ ❀

Meiss Meadows Ski Trip

March 5, 1995 • 10 a.m. to 4 p.m.
(see #11 on map page 74)

MARCH

Meiss Meadows is located north of Carson Pass and this trip to explore the meadow is rated as an intermediate-to-advanced ski-hike. For more on the trip, the area and how to obtain a necessary Sno-Park permit, see page 86.

For information, contact Grover Hot Springs State Park, P.O. Box 188, Markleeville, CA 96120; (916) 694-2248.

❀ ❀ ❀ ❀

Blake Jones Trout Derby

Second Sunday in March 🟢 🌙 • Sunrise to sunset
(see #20 on map page 74)

Almost any time is fishin' time in the eastern Sierra, so why not try your hand at winning a fishing contest? This is one of those contests, sometimes referred to as a blind bogey, that offers anyone a chance to win, no matter how long, fat or heavy your fish happens to be. The contest organizers catch a fish the day before the event, weigh and measure it, and that's the target you're shooting for. Only nobody knows how much the target fish weighs or how long it is, because that's a secret, at least until it's time to do all the measuring of everybody's fish and announce the winner. There are prizes up to $500, which isn't exactly fish bait. The derby takes place at Pleasant Valley Reservoir, which is just off US 395, seven miles north of Bishop. The weather should be cool and comfortable, although evenings can still be quite chilly.

For more information, contact the Bishop Chamber of Commerce, 690 North Main Street, Bishop, CA 93514; (619) 873-8405.

Introduction to Cross-Country Skiing at Sugar Pine Point State Park

March 11, 1995 • 10 a.m. to 1 p.m.
(see #7 on map page 74)

A ranger guides you in the basics of cross-country skiing, then leads a short and easy 1.5-mile ski-hike over some pretty level terrain. After completing this three-hour program, you'll be ready to tackle some of the longer, marked trails in the park. (For tips on how to dress and what to bring, see the listing on page 78.) Call to verify the date and time of the hike, and also to make sure there's enough of the white stuff to ski on. There is a $5 per vehicle day-use fee. The meeting place is the parking lot near the General Creek Campground kiosk at Sugar Pine Point State Park on the west shore of Lake Tahoe, about 10 miles south of Tahoe City on Highway 89.

For information, contact Sugar Pine Point State Park, P.O. Box 266, Tahoma, CA 95733, (916) 525-7982; or Sierra District State Parks, (916) 525-7232.

Introduction to Cross-Country Skiing at Donner Lake

March 12, 1995 • 10 a.m. to 1 p.m.
(see #4 on map page 74)

Join a ranger for an introduction to the basics of cross-country skiing, then take a short and easy 1.5-mile ski-hike. After completing this three-hour program, you'll be ready to tackle some of the longer, marked trails in the park. (For tips on how to dress and what to bring, see the listing on page 78.) This course will meet at the Donner Memorial State Park Museum parking lot, which is located at the east end of Donner Lake, just off Interstate 80, about two miles west of Truckee.

For information, contact Donner Memorial State Park, (916) 582-7892; or Sierra District State Parks, (916) 525-7232.

✣ ✣ ✣ ✣

Intermediate Cross-Country Ski Clinic

March 18, 1995 • 10 a.m. to 1 p.m.
(see #7 on map page 74)

If you're beyond basics and want to learn some of the more advanced methods of cross-country skiing, this is the clinic for you. You must be able to cover seven to ten kilometers (six miles) of up and down terrain in two hours. Bring your skis, water and lunch and be prepared for a good time and bad weather (just in case). There is a $5 per vehicle day-use fee. This hike meets at the Cross-Country Ski Trail parking lot in Sugar Pine Point State Park, about 10 miles south of Tahoe City on Highway 89.

For information, contact Sugar Pine Point State Park, P.O. Box 266, Tahoma, CA 95733, (916) 525-7982; or Sierra District State Parks, (916) 525-7232.

✣ ✣ ✣ ✣

Carson Pass Ski Trek

March 19, 1995 • 10 a.m. to 3 p.m.
(see #11 on map page 74)

For information about this cross-country ski-hike, the Carson Pass Summit area and how to obtain a prerequisite Sno-Park permit, see page 93.

For information, contact Grover Hot Springs State Park, P.O. Box 188, Markleeville, CA 96120; (916) 694-2248.

✣ ✣ ✣ ✣

Off-Track Skiing

March 25, 1995 • 10 a.m. to 2 p.m.
(see #7 on map page 74)

Tired of skiing the same trails as everyone else? For information about this clinic for intermediate and advanced skiers who want to further develop wilderness and off-track skiing skills, and what you'll need to bring along, see page 93. The four-hour outing meets at the Cross-Country Ski Trail parking area at Sugar Pine Point State Park, just off Highway 89, about 10 miles south of Tahoe City.

For information, contact Sugar Pine Point State Park, P.O. Box 266, Tahoma, CA 95733, (916) 525-7982; or Sierra District State Parks, (916) 525-7232.

Donner Party Escape

March 25, 1995 • 10 a.m. to 1 p.m.
(see #4 on map page 74)

A ranger will relate the history of the Donner Party and their several attempts to escape their snow-bound fate. For more information on this moderately easy hike, and what you should bring along, see page 82. It leaves from the Donner Memorial Museum parking lot, which is located about two miles west of Truckee, just off Interstate 80.

For information, contact Donner Memorial State Park, (916) 582-7892; or Sierra District State Parks, (916) 525-7232.

Keysville Classic Mountain Bike Race

March 25 & 26, 1995 • All day
(see #25 on map page 75)

This annual mountain bike race is actually a series of races sponsored by the South Sierra Fat Tire Association. The individual legs range over several miles of hilly and rugged terrain near Keysville and include uphill, downhill and cross-country bicycle competitions. The race is a sanctioned Off-Road Bicycle Association event; it's staged for all age and skill levels, ranging from children to top professional riders. For the less ambitious, there are plenty of areas for viewing the race. Bring your own bike if you have one and take time out from being a spectator to try your own hand at riding in the mountains, without having to race against anyone.

To get to Keysville, take Highway 178 east from Bakersfield for about 52 miles to the town of Lake Isabella, then turn left onto Highway 155. Drive about one mile and turn left onto Keysville Road, then drive another two miles to Keysville. The races are free for spectators, but there's a small entry fee for competitors. The weather will be warm and sunny, hopefully.

For information, contact the Keysville Classic Mountain Bike Race, 2039 North Baker, Bakersfield, CA 93305; (805) 872-1601.

❧ ❧ ❧ ❧

Railroading in the Sierra
March 26, 1995 • 10 a.m. to 2 p.m.
(see #4 on map page 74)

The morning begins with a short talk and slide show at the Donner Memorial State Park Museum, which will introduce you to some of the history of winter trains in the Sierra. When three feet of snow falls during one night, it takes a pretty good effort and a lot of equipment to keep the tracks clear and the trains moving, and this is a chance to see some of the real stuff. Following the slide show and talk, you'll get back into your car and drive a couple of miles to the train depot in Truckee for a special demonstration of railroading snow removal equipment. If all goes well, there may even be a storm dumping its best stuff on the ground, so there's really something to see. Meet at the Donner Memorial State Park Museum, located about two miles west of Truckee on Donner Pass Road, just off Interstate 80.

For information, contact Donner Memorial State Park, (916) 582-7892; or Sierra District State Parks, P.O. Box 266, Tahoma, CA 95733, (916) 525-7232.

❧ ❧ ❧ ❧

Bishop's Annual Mule Days

Memorial Day weekend • All day
(see #22 on map page 74)

You won't see any fancy, motorized floats in this annual parade, because it's mostly a procession of mules. And if you just can't get enough of seeing, smelling and laughing at mules in the parade, you'll be treated to mule races, pack mule cargo loading and a few other mule-related competitions that are sure to tickle your fancy. For those who tire easily of such muling around, there will be an art show featuring 180 art booths, as well as food, games and some good music. This event has been going on each Memorial Day weekend for more than 25 years and draws about 30,000 people over the weekend, so don't be left out. The mule events are spread between City Park and the city fairgrounds in Bishop, which is on the eastern flank of the Sierra, along Highway 395. The parade and the arts and crafts fair are free, while the fairground events vary in price. The weather should be warm and sunny during the day, perhaps a little chilly in the evening.

For information, contact the Bishop Chamber of Commerce, 690 North Main Street, Bishop, CA 93514; (619) 873-8014.

Whitewater Wednesday

June 21, 1995 • Tours leave every half hour, beginning at 9 a.m.,
ending at 5 p.m.
(see # 24 on map page 75)

If you've ever wanted to put a little excitement in your life, but weren't sure how, here's a great opportunity to brave the cold, wet rapids of the wild and scenic Kern River. For just $17.50, you'll have one hour of wild, lickety-split, exhilarating, screaming, white-knuckled whitewater rafting fun...and they'll even serve you lunch when it's all over. This introductory program has been in existence for about eight years now; these days, they haul 800 people or more down the river on the annual Whitewater Wednesday. Reservations are strongly encouraged, although drop-ins can sometimes be accommodated.

The trips depart the river's edge every half hour beginning at 9 a.m., with the final trip hitting the rapids at 5 p.m. Kernville is located about 153 miles east of Bakersfield on Highway 178.

For reservations and information, contact Kernville Chamber of Commerce, P.O. Box 397, Kernville, CA 93238; (619) 376-2629.

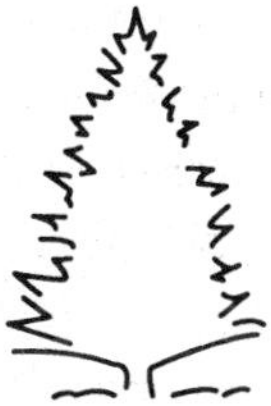

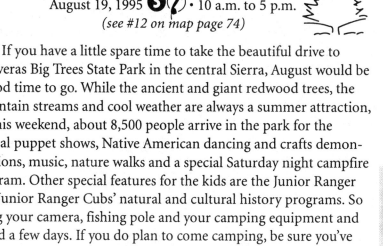

Calaveras Family Day

August 19, 1995 [S] ☎ • 10 a.m. to 5 p.m.

(see #12 on map page 74)

If you have a little spare time to take the beautiful drive to Calaveras Big Trees State Park in the central Sierra, August would be a good time to go. While the ancient and giant redwood trees, the mountain streams and cool weather are always a summer attraction, on this weekend, about 8,500 people arrive in the park for the special puppet shows, Native American dancing and crafts demonstrations, music, nature walks and a special Saturday night campfire program. Other special features for the kids are the Junior Ranger and Junior Ranger Cubs' natural and cultural history programs. So bring your camera, fishing pole and your camping equipment and spend a few days. If you do plan to come camping, be sure you've got reservations first by calling MISTIX at (800) 444-7275. This is a really popular park in summer, so you ought to call the full 56 days in advance to secure a weekend camping spot in Calaveras. Calaveras Big Trees State Park is located four miles northeast of Arnold on Highway 4. If you're not camping, there will be a day-use fee of $5 per vehicle to enter the park. Unless you happen to hit a summer thunderstorm, the weather should be quite warm and pleasant; if it gets a little too warm, you can always soak in the river.

For information, contact Calaveras Big Trees State Park, P.O. Box 151, Columbia, CA 95310; (209) 795-2334.

Downieville Miner's Weekend

First weekend in August **S** ⓒ • All day
(see #2 on map page 74)

Bring your fishing pole and gold pan, because there are lots of things to do in this Gold Rush town that sits near the confluence of the Downie and Yuba rivers. The weekend events include a parade, a flea market and a Saturday night street dance. There are also plenty of historic 19th-century buildings that house gift shops and other businesses. Gold mining is still popular on the rivers and fishing is pretty good if you get bored with everything else.

Downieville's main street is Highway 49, about 45 miles north of Nevada City. Most of the weekend events are free. Expect the weather to be warm and sunny, but with the slight chance of an afternoon thunder shower.

For information, contact the Sierra County Chamber of Commerce, P.O. Box 222, Downieville, CA 95936; (916) 993-6900.

❖ ❖ ❖ ❖

Downieville Septemberfest

Saturday & Sunday of Labor Day weekend • All day
(see #2 on map page 74)

Come to one of the northern Sierra's prettiest little historic Gold Rush towns for their annual end-of-summer celebration. Expect lots of good food, a walk through the flea market and, periodically, standstill traffic. Why does it stand still, you ask? Because of the Great Donkey Race, where speed is less important than getting these beasts of burden to cooperate as their riders vie for local fame, bragging rights and little else. It's all in fun and it's a fun place to spend your last, long weekend of summer.

Downieville's main thoroughfare is Highway 49, about 45 miles north of Nevada City. Most of the events are free and the weather should be quite warm, with a slight possibility of afternoon thunder-showers.

For information, contact the Sierra County Chamber of Commerce, P.O. Box 222, Downieville, CA 95936; (916) 993-6900.

Millpond Traditional Music Festival

September 15, 16 & 17, 1995 • All day
(see #21 on map page 74)

If you needed an excuse for taking a one- or two-day trip to the eastern Sierra, this is it. Here's an event that provides for some family fun, three days of great traditional music, arts and crafts displays to wander through, workshops with musicians and games for kids and adults alike. The kids will have an opportunity to learn how to catch a *pugwi,* which, in the language of the Paiute Indians, means fish. Expect about 2,000 people to show up for this weekend of music. While the acts are subject to change, expect to hear everything from bunkhouse, gold mining, railroad and skid row ballads and stories to some gritty blues, bluegrass and Cajun fiddlin'. With perhaps the exception of rap and hardcore rock, there's probably something for just about everyone's musical tastes. Give the organizers a call well in advance for ticket information and updated prices. The weekend event takes place at Millpond Recreation Area, which is located about five miles north of Bishop, off Highway 395. Advance tickets are in the $30 to $40 range, while it'll cost you $45 at the gate. The weather should be warm during the day, but you'll probably need a jacket during the evenings.

For information, contact the Inyo Council for the Arts, P.O. Box 537, Bishop, CA 93515; (619) 873-8014.

❖ ❖ ❖ ❖

Freel Peak

First Sunday in October **S** 📞 • 9 a.m. to 3 p.m.
(see #11 on map page 74)

If you have a hankering to hike to the highest of all the peaks rimming Lake Tahoe, then you're in for a treat. Rangers will lead the way to the top of Freel Peak, all 10,881 feet of it. While this is only a five- to six-hour hike, it's still rated as pretty tough because of the elevation. Once on top, you'll see some great views of the lake and Nevada. Bring along water, lunch and some warm clothes. Don't

SEPTEMBER

---

forget your hiking boots. Meet at the beginning of Horse Meadows Road, which is located on the east side of Highway 89, about halfway between Luther Pass and the junction of highways 88 and 89. Look around for the park ranger's dark green truck.

For information, contact Grover Hot Springs State Park, P.O. Box 188, Markleeville, CA 96120; (916) 694-2248.

Maggie's Peaks

First or second Saturday in October [S] ☎ • 10 a.m. to 5 p.m.
(see #9 on map page 74)

Without getting into the reasons why a person of ostensibly sound mind would dedicate two nearly identical peaks to some long-forgotten person named Maggie, I'll promised you that this hike can take your breath away. It begins at about 6,500 feet at the Bayview Trailhead on the south side of Emerald Bay, just off Highway 89. From there, you head upward until you reach 8,500 feet. Once on top, you'll have some great views of Emerald Bay, Lake Tahoe, the hundreds of lakes that fill the glaciated potholes of Desolation Wilderness and the surrounding mountains. The hike is meant for people in pretty good condition—you've got to cover seven sometimes steep miles in the seven hours allotted, with a break or three thrown in for snacks. So bring your own lunch and water, wear sturdy hiking boots and bring a little moleskin just in case your feet aren't as tough as the boot leather. You may also wish to take some warm clothes. And since anything can happen, a small flashlight might be advisable just in case the hike gets back after dark, which it shouldn't, but....

For information contact D.L. Bliss State Park, P.O. Box 266, Tahoma, CA 95733, (916) 525-7277 or Sierra District State Parks, (916) 525-7232.

Castle Peak

First or second Sunday in October • 10 a.m. to 4 p.m.
(see #4 on map page 74)

Considering the rugged terrain that surrounds the Pacific Crest Trail, a portion of which this hike happily covers, this trek is only moderately difficult. The seven-mile round-trip still heads up and down hills, but unless the group, or part of the group, decides to climb to the top of the peak above Grubb Meadow, this is a good intermediate trip. The hike will take from four to six hours, depending upon whether or not the mountaintop leg is completed. Meet at the Donner Memorial State Park Museum, which is at the east end of Donner Lake, just off Interstate 80 at the Truckee bug station (or agricultural check station). Since parking is limited at the Castle Peak Trailhead, carpools will be formed for the short drive to the top of the pass at Boreal. Bring food, water, sturdy boots and clothes for cold or wet weather; still, this is early in the fall, so the weather should be pretty nice.

For information, contact Sugar Pine Point State Park, P.O. Box 266, Tahoma, CA 95733, (916) 525-7982; or Sierra District State Parks, (916) 525-7232.

Fontenillis Lake Hike

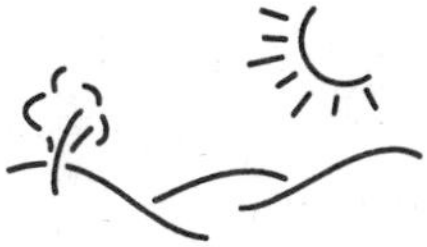

Second Saturday in October • 8:30 a.m. to 6 p.m.
(see #9 on map page 74)

While this isn't the king of the endurance hikes offered each year by the Sierra state park rangers, it's enough to take the wind out of many a pseudo-mountain person's sails. In 10 short hours, you climb from the 6,500-foot Bay View Trailhead at the south side of Emerald Bay, just off Highway 89, up to 8,600 feet for some great views of the bay, Lake Tahoe and many of the lakes that dot Desolation Wilderness. This isn't a hike for beginners nor for those with new hiking boots to break in. The 14-mile trip, half of which is headed continually up for some 2,000 feet, is pushed along at a pretty brisk pace. Bring water, food, good hiking boots and warm clothes. Toss a small flashlight in your pack because the days are getting shorter; if things don't go as briskly as planned, it's nice to have a little light to illuminate the way along the winding and rugged trails on the way back down.

For information, contact D.L. Bliss State Park, P.O. Box 266, Tahoma, CA 95733, (916) 525-7277; or Sierra District State Parks, (916) 525-7232.

✤ ✤ ✤ ✤

The Great Awful Trek

Second Sunday in October ❺⟨⟩ • 8 a.m. to 6 p.m.
(see #7 on map page 74)

This is the Mother of all day hikes, starting from Donner Pass and ending in Squaw Valley. The Awful Trek has been a Sierra state parks tradition for probably 20 years now, maybe longer. Be fore-warned: The awful part of the name refers to the length and eleva-tion gains of this adventure, not to the incredibly spectacular high Sierra scenery that you will traverse. You start at the top of old Donner Pass and hike 15 strenuous, blister-rubbing, thigh-bursting, lung-heaving miles of the rugged, granite-strewn Pacific Crest Trail, crossing peaks and valleys and traversing major ridges. The weather is always questionable, but generally it's cold in the morning and gets pretty warm by afternoon; dress in layers, so you can shed and add clothing as needed. Bring plenty of water, as most streams, with the possible exception of one near the end of the hike, are dry this time of year. Plus, unfiltered or non-purified water is best left to the local wildlife whose stomachs are better adapted to dealing with the strange creatures that sometimes inhabit the clearest of mountain streams. Carry lunch and snacks to keep up your energy level, that is if you hope to keep up with the brisk pace that will be set.

Because of the remoteness and difficulty of this hike, rangers reserve the right to send anyone away whom they feel may not be up to snuff. Age is not a particular factor; a few years ago a 12-year-old girl made the entire hiking group look like they were walking backward on one leg. However, if you or your equipment looks to lack the ability to make the entire trip, you'll be asked to stay behind.

This is not a hike for people wearing running shoes. Good hiking boots are pretty much a must, because portions of the trail are strewn with loose and very sharp chunks of granite—painful stone bruises are not something you want to be saddled with when you've still got seven or eight miles left to hike. If I haven't scared you off yet, and I hope not, you'll have to arrange for your own transportation or car shuttle to get you picked up at the fire station in Squaw Valley, sometime between 5:30 and 6:30 p.m. The rangers can't transport you in their truck. The hike begins at the metal shed at the summit of Donner Pass on Donner Pass Road (old Highway 40 for those folks who have been around long enough), not Interstate 80.

For information, contact Sugar Pine Point State Park, P.O. Box 266, Tahoma, CA 95733, (916) 525-7982; or Sierra District State Parks, (916) 525-7232.

✤ ✤ ✤ ✤

Kokanee Salmon Festival
October 7 & 8, 1995 • 10 a.m. to 4 p.m.
(see #10 on map page 74)

Each autumn, many of Lake Tahoe's tributary streams are filled with kokanee salmon as they leave the lake and head upstream to spawn. The salmon festival is a wonderful opportunity to visit the Taylor Creek Stream Profile Chamber and see the changes that nature has designed into the life of kokanee, landlocked cousins of the seagoing sockeye salmon. The males, who turn a brilliant red and develop long, hooked jaws, fill the creek. The festival includes a dinner of barbecued salmon (the ocean variety), a Tadpole Trot along the Rainbow Trail for kids, 5- and 10-kilometer runs, Sammy Salmon, the official mascot of the festival, and the beautiful fall colors of the aspens that crowd the meadow. Also, there will be T-shirts available and booths with a wide variety of exhibits. The visitor center and Taylor Creek Stream Profile Chamber are located off Highway 89, just north of South Lake Tahoe's Camp Richardson. Most of the day is free, but there is a charge for the salmon dinner.

The weather is always variable during early October, but usually it's pretty nice. Expect sweater-comfortable days and cold nights.

OCTOBER

For information, contact the U.S. Forest Service, Lake Tahoe Basin Management Unit, 870 Emerald Bay Road, Suite #1, South Lake Tahoe, CA 96150; (916) 577-2600.

❖ ❖ ❖ ❖

Third Annual Sierra Timberfest

October 7 & 8, 1995 **$** ⏱ · 10 a.m. to 4 p.m.
(see #1 on map page 74)

Many a lad has had visions of growing up and working in the woods as a lumberjack. Although the timber industry is changing in today's world of new technologies and environmental concerns, the lore and lure of the woods still make the lifestyle fascinating. Come on up to where loggers still work and get a firsthand feel for logging. There will be special shows, demonstrations and contests, sawmill and museum tours and an antique logging train exhibit. You'll also find plenty of food, arts and crafts, and speakers on hand to answer questions. Timberfest is held in Loyalton, which is located on Highway 49, about 14 miles northeast of the intersection of highways 49 and 89, and 25 miles north of Truckee. Much of the event is free. Considering the fires that were sweeping through the Loyalton area just as this was being written in 1994, you probably should call to confirm that Timberfest is still being held in 1995. Assuming that it is, you can also assume that the weather will be variable in October; it's usually mild during the day and cold at night.

For information, contact the Sierra County Chamber of Commerce, P.O. Box 222, Downieville, CA 95936; (800) 200-4949.

❖ ❖ ❖ ❖

Pedal Through Fall

Second Sunday in October **$** ⏱ · 10 a.m. to 3 p.m.
(see #11 on map page 74)

If you own a mountain bike, then you owe it to yourself to join the ranger and a bunch of other outdoor types for this moderate trip over dirt roads around Sierra's Monitor Pass. If the timing is right, and only Mother Nature can make that decision, there will be absolutely beautiful fall colors spreading out among the aspen groves that cover some of the mountains. Whether the colors are present or not, this should be a really great time just touring some of the high mountain terrain for which the Sierra is best known. Bring yourself, your bike and a spare tire and tube to the top of Monitor Pass, which is on Highway 89, about nine miles west of US 395.

For information, contact Grover Hot Springs State Park, P.O. Box 188, Markleeville, CA 96120; (916) 694-2248.

✤ ✤ ✤ ✤

Railroading in the Sierra
Third Sunday in October • 10 a.m. to 2 p.m.
(see #4 on map page 74)

Anyone who has ever crossed the Sierra via Interstate 80 has certainly seen the trains slowly climbing up the steep mountains or disappearing inside the snow sheds. It was the railroad, and the 1860s competition between the California owners of the Central Pacific and the East's Union Pacific, that really opened the West to the world. That same route, carved from the sides of sheer cliffs and drilled, blasted and chipped directly through the great, gray granite walls of the Sierra, is still in use today. The old wooden snow sheds and the smoke- and spark-spewing steam engines of old have been replaced by concrete snow tunnels and diesel-electric locomotives. The day's tour starts in Donner Memorial State Park's Emigrant Museum for a slide show about the equipment used to keep the tracks clear of snow during winter. Then it's time to jump into your car and follow the ranger to the top of Donner Pass to see the Summit Tunnel and the last remaining historic wooden snow sheds still in use. The Summit Tunnel is a marvel of construction with a unique history: The Big Four, during their race eastward against the westward-building Union Pacific, decided that to save time they would drill straight down into the solid granite, then begin tunneling both east and west in order to meet workers tunneling into the

OCTOBER

mountain from both sides. And they did it all with incredible accuracy, considering they had no laser-guided surveying equipment. The entire program takes about four hours and you'll have to cover only about a mile, or perhaps a little more, on foot and over fairly level terrain. Bring your camera and lunch. The Donner Memorial State Park Museum is located on Donner Pass Road, about two miles west of Truckee.

For information, contact Donner Memorial State Park, (916) 582-7892; or Sierra District State Parks, P.O. Box 266, Tahoma, CA 95733, (916) 525-7232.

Mount Tallac Hike

Third Saturday in October [S]☎ • 9 a.m. to 6 p.m.

(see #8 on map page 74)

This is a long, hard hike that will take you to the top of Mount Tallac for some fantastic views of Lake Tahoe and the hundreds of lakes to the west in Desolation Wilderness. This Lake Tahoe landmark peaks out at just under 10,000 feet, so you'll be breathing some pretty thin air during your 3,000-foot climb from the starting point. You'll be covering a total of 12 miles during the nine hours of hiking, with a few breaks tossed in, so bring food, water and your strong legs. Wear some warm clothes because Sierra weather can be really changeable this time of year. You'll also need some good hiking boots; sandals and running shoes won't make it. Meet at the Mount Tallac Trailhead which is located at the far end of the road to Fallen Leaf Lake. Fallen Leaf Lake Road is located off Highway 89 just north of Camp Richardson, a couple of miles north of the intersection of Highway 50 and Highway 89 (South Lake Tahoe "Y").

For information, contact D.L. Bliss State Park, P.O. Box 266, Tahoma, CA 95733, (916) 525-7277; or Sierra District State Parks, (916) 525-7232.

The Almost Great Awful Trek

Third Sunday in October Ⓢ☎ • 9 a.m. to 4 p.m.

(see #11 on map page 74)

If you're into mountain-peak hopping, and aren't quite ready to handle the Great Awful Trek, which is usually held the week prior to this, then the Almost Great Awful Trek is a good alternative. A ranger will lead this six- or seven-hour hike that crosses two mountaintops. You'll have a great time and enjoy even greater views sitting atop Red Lake Peak and Steven's Peak. While not as hard as its near-namesake, this really is a difficult hike, but if you come prepared, both physically and with the right equipment, it should all work out. Bring your lunch and plenty of water. Wear good hiking boots, because nice smooth trails aren't a hallmark of this trip. The initial meeting place is on Highway 88, about one mile west of Blue Lakes Road, or 3.5 miles west of the intersection of highways 88 and 89. Look for the park ranger's green truck. From here, carpools will be formed for the drive to Carson Pass, where the actual hike begins.

For information, contact Grover Hot Springs State Park, P.O. Box 188, Markleeville, CA 96120; (916) 694-2248.

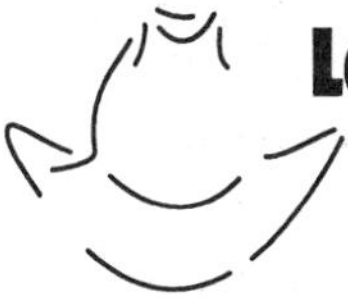

Lone Pine Sierra Film Festival

October 14 & 15, 1995 • All day

(see #23 on map page 75)

Most people have never heard of the Alabama Hills and would probably guess they were anywhere but in California's Owens Valley, within view of Mount Whitney. But decades ago, within the spectacular scenery of these hills, Hollywood found an ideal setting for movie-making, especially Tinsel Town's version of the life and times in the Old West. This weekend festival will feature showings and memorabilia of many old, great (and some not-so-great) movies made in the area. Oldies such as *How the West Was Won*, *The Charge of the Light Brigade* and *Along the Great Divide*, as well as TV westerns including *The Lone Ranger*, *Red Ryder*, *Death Valley Days*, *Rawhide* and *Bonanza*, saw much of their shooting, both bullets and

film, done in these hills. The annual film festival will also include tours of these beautiful and geologically fascinating hills, including a trip along Movie Flat Road, where guides can point out some of the old filming sites and the backdrops for scenes in some of newer movies like *Tremors* and *Star Trek V*. The festival is centered in the Owens Valley town of Lone Pine, along Highway 395. The event is free, but there is a fee for the barbecue and bus tour through the hills. (Of course, public access into the hills is free.) Beyond the main paved road, access into the hills is on dirt roads, and some are not particularly fit for regular passenger cars. Most people pass through this area on their way to begin the hike to the top of Mount Whitney. If all goes well, the weather will be sunny, but cool.

For information, contact the Lone Pine Film Festival, P.O. Box 1120, Lone Pine, CA 93454; (619) 876-4444.

✤ ✤ ✤ ✤

Donner Peak Hike

Third Saturday in October **S**(*) · 10 a.m. to 2 p.m.
(see #4 on map page 74)

This is a scramble to the top of Donner Peak, and although you're only going to about 8,000 feet above sea level, it's a pretty strenuous climb. You head about four miles uphill, part of which is not on a trail because no trail exists. Once you get to the top, you're in for some pretty nice views of Donner Lake, Lake Angela and a whole lot of other lakes, streams and surrounding mountains. You can also see two of the passes that the emigrants used to get across the great mountains in the last century. Bring water, snacks and clothes for changeable weather. Meet at the top of Donner Pass on Donner Pass Road, not Interstate 80's Donner Summit. Drive past the Alpine Skills Institute and park near the marked Pacific Crest Trail trailhead.

For information, contact Donner Memorial State Park, (916) 582-7892; or Sierra District State Parks, P.O. Box 266, Tahoma, CA 95733, (916) 525-7232.

✤ ✤ ✤ ✤

Gilmore Lake Hike

Last Saturday in October [S] ☎ • 10 a.m. to 5 p.m.
(see #8 on map page 74)

It's a difficult, four-mile, 2,000-foot climb to Gilmore Lake, but the lake, Glen Alpine Falls and the scenic views of Lake Tahoe make the hike worth the effort. On this hike, you'll get an idea of the power of the glaciers, most of which last passed through the area about 10,000 years ago, which was not so long ago if you're a rock. Plan on about seven hours to finish the entire trip. It all begins at the Glen Alpine end of Fallen Leaf Lake Road. You can reach the meeting place by driving north on Highway 89 out of South Lake Tahoe. Fallen Leaf Lake Road is just past Camp Richardson. Bring your camera, lunch, water and enough clothes to counter any late fall weather that Mother Nature may throw your way.

For information, contact D.L. Bliss State Park, P.O. Box 266, Tahoma, CA 95733, (916) 525-7277; or Sierra District State Parks, (916) 525-7232.

Markleeville Peak Loop Hike

Last Sunday in October [S] ☎ • 10 a.m. to 4 p.m.
(see #11 on map page 74)

You'll not be spending a lot of time on trails during this cross-country hike to the top of 9,417-foot Markleeville Peak, then down into Charity Valley with its aspen-covered hillsides. If all goes well, the aspens will have begun their fall change from bright green to even brighter gold and red, and you will hike among their splendor. The hike ends back where you originally parked your car. Bring your camera, water and lunch; wear some good boots that will hold up to some rough Sierra hiking. Meet on Blue Lakes Road, about a mile past where the asphalt road turns to dirt. Blue Lakes Road is off Highway 88, about two miles west of the intersection of highways 88 and 89.

For information, contact Grover Hot Springs State Park, P.O. Box 188, Markleeville, CA 96120, (916) 694-2248; or Sierra District State Parks, (916) 525-7232.

Mono Lake Halloween Walk

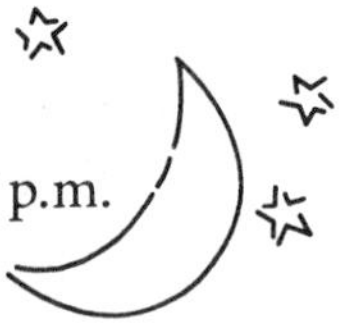

Last Sunday in October [S] ☎ • 5:30 p.m. to 7 p.m.

(see #16 on map page 74)

Now, Mono Lake can be spooky enough just on its own, but add ghosts, goblins, witches and a vivid imagination and you've got all the mixings for a really spooky near-Halloween night. It all begins at the South Tufa Parking Area, which is down a dirt road that heads off Highway 395, just past the town of Lee Vining. Bring any spooky stories you'd like to share with all those freaky beasts that the ranger has lined up to frighten the group. This is also a great chance to wander among the tufa towers, howl at the moon (if there's one shining), and enjoy a cool evening. Bring along warm clothes and something to barbecue. Park staff will provide hot apple cider to warm your insides.

For information, contact Mono Lake Tufa State Reserve, P.O. Box 99, Lee Vining, CA 93541; (619) 647-6331.

❀ ❀ ❀ ❀

Donner Party History

Last Sunday in October [S] ☎ • 10 a.m. to 1 p.m.

(see #4 on map page 74)

Unlike the winter when the infamous Donner Party attempted to cross the Sierra in November, 1846, and got themselves caught in the biggest snowstorm of the 19th century, this is usually a good time to drive up the mountain and tour the three main camps of the ill-fated wagon train. The Donners and other families were spread out over several miles and this easy, three-hour walking-and-driving tour covers all three sites in about three hours. Hear about how the Donner Party made their historically fatal mistake, the efforts they made to escape and the grim cannibalism some of them resorted to in order to survive the winter. There will be a little bit of walking—just short jaunts to the sites of the old camps over level ground and on easy trails near the Emigrant Trail Museum at Donner Memorial State Park, and at Alder Creek, which is north of Truckee on Highway 89. Meet at Donner Memorial State Park, just off Donner Pass Road, two miles west of Truckee.

For information, contact Sugar Pine Point State Park, P.O. Box 266, Tahoma, CA 95733, (916) 525-7982; or Sierra District State Parks, (916) 525-7232.

Carson River Hot Springs

First Sunday in November [S] ☎ • 9:30 a.m. to 3:30 p.m.

(see #11 on map page 74)

If you're into exploring undeveloped hot springs where few people venture, here's a great opportunity. A ranger will guide you to one of those hot-watery places on the East Fork of the Carson River, an area that is obviously volcanically active. Since hot springs can feel really good to a tired body after a long hike, bring your swim suit or some other attire appropriate for getting wet and wild. Since there isn't a paved trail to this place, you are advised to wear good hiking boots so your feet don't suffer too much. Water and a snack would also be good to bring along. Meet at the intersection of Diamond Valley Road and Airport Road. Diamond Valley Road heads east from Highway 89, just a mile or two south of Woodfords, and about 10 miles north of Markleeville.

For information, contact Grover Hot Springs State Park, P.O. Box 188, Markleeville, CA 96120, (916) 694-2248; or Sierra District State Parks, (916) 525-7232.

Stephens Party History Tour

Second Saturday in November [S] ☎ • 8 a.m. to 2 p.m.

(see #7 on map page 74)

This hike was first offered in 1994 and hopefully will be continued in 1995. You'll need to call to check on the date and also to see if there's snow, in which case the hike may be canceled if it's too deep. Your hiking trail will follow part of the route that the first emigrant wagon train used to cross the Sierra. You'll be heading up the McKinney Creek watershed on part of the McKinney-Rubicon Trail. If all goes well, you'll end up at Miller Lake for lunch and a well-deserved break. Meet at Sugar Pine Point State Park's General Creek Campground to arrange for carpools to the starting point. Wear some sturdy hiking boots; bring water, lunch and your camera.

For information, contact Sugar Pine Point State Park, P.O. Box 266, Tahoma, CA 95733, (916) 525-7982; or Sierra District State Parks, (916) 525-7232.

✤ ✤ ✤ ✤

Donner Party History

Second Saturday in November **S** 𝒪 • 10 a.m. to 1 p.m.
(see #4 on map page 74)

For details of this hike exploring the area where the Donner Party found itself tragically snowbound, see page 118. The hike meets at the Donner Memorial State Park Museum, which is located about two miles west of Truckee on Donner Lake Road, just off Interstate 80.

For information, contact Donner Memorial State Park, (916) 582-7892; or Sugar Pine Point State Park, P.O. Box 266, Tahoma, CA 95733, (916) 582-7982.

✤ ✤ ✤ ✤

Cross-Country Ski Equipment Clinic

Last Saturday in November **S** 𝒪 • 10 a.m. to noon
(see #7 on map page 74)

Whether you're a cross-country skiing fanatic or a complete clubfooted novice, this is the place to be for a preseason look at all the newest and best winter equipment. Rangers and ski industry representatives will be on hand to show and tell all about the newest in technologically magnificent cross-country skis, poles, boots, bindings, goggles, clothing and winter camping gear. Things have changed a lot in the last 20 years. Before then, about the only thing you had to think about was the newest development in ski base waxes and klisters. Then came the fish-scale no-wax skis with a dizzying array of bottom designs, all proclaimed to be the best for Sierra power to Sierra cement. Today, you get to choose from among light touring, touring, telemark, racing telemark, racing, skating, backcountry and randonnee skis. And, just in case you thought you were out of the woods because you are able to fake some surface knowledge about all those skis, there are an equal number of boot and binding combinations. Come on up. Ask your questions. See some demonstrations. You should walk away knowing at least as much about cross-country ski equipment as any pimply-faced 18-year-old ski salesperson in your hometown discount ski shop. Actually, a little knowledge about what you should purchase in order to enjoy a little weekend exercise in the Sierra will go a long way to seeing that you really don't waste your money or thrash your body on bogus equipment. The entire thing lasts about two hours and meets in the Cross-Country Ski Trail parking lot at Sugar Pine Point State Park, which is located about 10 miles south of Tahoe City and one mile south of Tahoma on Highway 89, on the west shore of Lake Tahoe.

For information, contact Sugar Pine Point State Park, P.O. Box 266, Tahoma, CA 95733, (916) 525-7982; or Sierra District State Parks, (916) 525-7232.

NOVEMBER

Sierra Seasonal Hikes & Programs

Sierra City Kentucky Mine Concert Series

Friday evenings, Memorial Day through Labor Day
(see #3 on map page 74)

 The Kentucky Mine was one of Sierra City's most profitable gold-mining operations; the story of the efforts and accomplishments of these early miners is celebrated in exhibits in the Kentucky Mine Museum. During the summer season, there's a different celebration going on. A series of concerts highlights a variety of musical styles from the United States and around the world. Jazz, bluegrass, Latin and Celtic music, even an orchestra and the age-old tradition of storytelling take their appropriate places in the museum's open-air amphitheater. Before settling down to enjoy the music, take time to wander the historic buildings of Sierra City and the Kentucky Mine Museum. The Kentucky Mine Museum Amphitheater is located off Highway 49, about one mile east of Sierra City and 15 twisting miles east of Downieville.

For information, contact the Sierra County Chamber of Commerce, P.O. Box 222, Downieville, CA 95936; (800) 200-4949.

❖ ❖ ❖ ❖

Mono Lake Tufa Walks

Saturday & Sundays from mid-September to mid-June
1 p.m. to 2:30 p.m.
(see #16 on map page 74)

Surrounded by the surreal nature of Mono Lake, you tend to wonder if you're still on planet Earth. Join a ranger on an easy, one-mile walk among the strange tufa towers that line the edge of one of

North America's oldest lakes. No fish can live in the lake's super-salty water, but that same clear, briny soup supports a huge population of brine shrimp, which in turn provide breakfast, lunch, dinner and more than a few between-meal snacks for major populations of nesting and migrating birds. Bring your camera, lots of film and plan to allow at least one-and-a-half hours for the hike. Meet at the South Tufa parking area of Mono Lake Tufa State Reserve. Look for the sign and a dirt road that cuts off Highway 395, just south of the town of Lee Vining.

For information, contact Mono Lake Tufa State Reserve, P.O. Box 99, Lee Vining, CA 93541; (619) 647-6331.

Mono Lake Ranger District Hikes

July 1 through Labor Day • Times vary • See listings that follow
(see #14 on map page 74)

A few years ago the U.S. Forest Service finally constructed a visitor center at Mono Lake. It sits on a small ridge, overlooking ancient Mono Lake, one of the oldest lakes in North America. U.S. Forest Service naturalists and state park rangers are here to help interpret the sometimes bizarre natural landmarks of the area.

Each year, the ranger district offers a series of hikes daily from July 1 through Labor Day. Most take less than two hours to complete and are reasonably easy. The following hikes usually are offered several times each week at different times of the day. For their most current hike schedule, contact: U.S.D.A Forest Service, Mammoth Ranger District, P.O. Box 148, Mammoth Lakes, CA 93546; (619) 924-5500.

Bennetville

Here's a chance to learn about the botany of the eastern Sierra, while wandering through an old ghost town. A ranger will be along to talk about the curious history of the area, the roads and tunnels, and also to help you figure out the difference between sage and manzanita, lupine and larkspur. Meet at the Junction Campground

SEASONAL

at the junction of Highway 120 and Saddlebag Lake Road. Highway 120 is about nine miles west of the Lee Vining Ranger Station on US 395. This is about a three-hour walk.

Bird Walk

Mono Lake serves as a stopover point and breeding ground for hundreds of thousands of birds each year. Join a ranger or naturalist for a short walk along the shoreline of Mono Lake to see and learn about the birds that call this saline lake home and how important the creeks are that empty into Mono Lake from the nearby Sierra mountains. This hike meets at Mono Lake County Park, which is five miles north of Lee Vining, just off US 395.

Black Point Hike

It doesn't take a professional geologist to look around Mono Lake and determine that volcanoes played a major role in molding the landscape. Black Point is a great place to explore the deep fissures of an ancient volcano. This is actually a pretty strenuous two-mile, 2.5-hour hike, because you have to climb straight up the side of an ancient volcano to the top where all the fissures are located. Wear hiking boots and bring plenty of water, because it's dry and hot up there. Meet at Mono Lake County Park.

Crater Auto Tour

For those who don't like walking (or who are unable to walk), this three-hour auto tour is the perfect way to gain a better understanding of the history behind the mountains that line much of the area along US 395 near Mono Lake and points south. Meet the ranger at the Oh! Ridge Overlook, about one mile west of the June Lake Junction and US 395.

Junior Naturalist Program

This one hour of discovery is designed for kids. If you have a young one from age 6 to 12, bring him or her to the Mono Lake Visitor Center in Lee Vining for some amazing stories and fun games that are designed to teach youngsters a few of the basic concepts of nature.

Kid's Tufa Tour

Here's another program designed especially for kids. They can meet a ranger at the South Tufa Reserve, which is located on Highway 120 about five miles east of US 395, on the shore of Mono Lake. The kid's hike through the tufa formations takes less than two hours; a separate hike for adults leaves at the same time. Wear good walking shoes and bring some drinking water.

Lundy Canyon

To get to beautiful Lundy Canyon, drive about seven miles north from Lee Vining along US 395 to Lundy Road. Take a left and follow it about five miles to the Lundy store at the west end of Lundy Lake. There, you'll meet a ranger who will lead a short hike that includes a talk on the area's gold mining history, as well as a close-up look at the wildflowers, other plants and geology of the area. Plan on about two hours for the walk and talk.

Nature for Kids

This is a one-hour nature walk for kids who are between the ages of 6 and 12. It departs from the June Lake Loop a couple days each week and from Silver Lake Beach on another couple days each week. Kids usually find this a great adventure.

Panum Crater Hike

Here's your opportunity to explore one of the newer volcanoes to rock and roll the eastern Sierra. This one requires some walking, but you should be back at your car in less than two hours. Meet at Panum Crater, which is a pretty prominent landmark located about four miles east of US 395, just off Highway 120.

Patio Talk

This could almost be considered an informal, round-table discussion about nature, except that it's formally scheduled each day during summer. The topics vary from natural to cultural history. Meet on the east patio of the Mono Lake Visitor Center in Lee Vining.

SEASONAL

South Tufa Walk

There are secrets locked inside those strange, dried mud-like formations that circle parts of Mono Lake. Meet at the South Tufa Reserve parking lot for this one-and-a-half-hour jaunt through the forest of tufas. Bring water and sunscreen.

Stars Over Mono

The stars over Mono Lake are pretty much the same stars you'll find over Sacramento, San Francisco, Los Angeles or San Diego. The big difference is that they appear hundreds of times brighter and more numerous, because they don't have to compete with hundreds of shopping centers and thousands of street lights. Join the ranger for an hour or two for this evening program, where you'll learn to identify some of the constellations, individual stars and maybe even a couple of planets like Mars and Venus. The program is usually held two evenings each week, from July 1 through Labor Day and some-times on through mid-October. Meet at the Navy Beach parking area, about five miles east of US 395 on Highway 120, near the South Tufa Reserve.

Campfire Programs

This is a chance to sit back, relax and enjoy an evening of song, skits, stories, maybe a slide show and just plain fun. The programs are held on different days at either the Oh! Ridge Amphitheater or at the Silver Lake Campground. They begin at 8:30 p.m. in July and at 8 p.m. during August and on Labor Day weekend.

Mono Lake Visitor Center Evening Programs

From July 1 through Labor Day, and sometimes on through mid-October, each Saturday and Sunday evening at 7 p.m. the Visitor Center offers a slide show, storytelling or other programs that deal with the natural or cultural history of the Mono basin. It's free, so stop in and enjoy yourself while learning more about this fascinating area of California.

Mammoth Lakes Ranger District

July 1 through Labor Day • Times vary • See listings that follow
(see #17 on map page 74)

The eastern side of the Sierra is a land of contrasts, even more so than the more heavily visited western side. The Mammoth Ranger District is centered around the Mammoth Lakes area, about 40 miles northwest of Bishop on Highway 395. I'm really not sure how the area acquired the name Mammoth. I doubt it was for the great woolly beasts that roamed the Earth a few million years ago. More likely, the stature of the mountains that rise steeply from the glacier-carved basins had something to do with it.

If you've not been to Mammoth before, or if it's been a very long time since your last visit, the first thing your should think about doing is stopping in at the U.S. Forest Service's Mammoth Visitor Center in the town of Mammoth Lakes. That's where you can pick up a copy of the most recent hike schedule. There's also an excellent orientation slide show offered on Saturday evenings at 8 p.m. that will give you an idea of all that awaits you in the Mammoth area.

What is listed here are the hikes and other programs that were offered last summer, starting with the July 4th weekend and ending Labor Day. Some of the hikes probably won't be offered, while other new ones will be added, in future seasons. The hikes are designed by the rangers and naturalists who lead them, and occasionally those people transfer in and out of the district, and new arrivals sometimes have other interests they wish to focus on during their hikes.

Generally, these or similar hikes are offered once each week, sometimes more frequently, throughout the summer. So grab your hat, hiking boots, water, sunscreen and other essentials, then explore the eastern Sierra with a guide who really knows the area and its cultural and natural history.

For information, contact the Mammoth Ranger District, P.O. Box 148, Mammoth Lakes, CA 93546; (619) 924-5500.

SEASONAL

Are There Bears in the Woods?

You bet there are. If you join the ranger for this program, you'll learn more than you ever wanted to know about bears in the woods. If you've ever had your ice chest or tent raided by a hungry bruin, you weren't doing what you should have done to protect your food, the bear and yourself. Most areas of the Sierra have bears and the bears, much like people, are attracted to free food. When they get out of control, and it's usually in areas where too many people have invaded their homes, they are often trapped and moved to more remote areas of the mountains. The ranger will demonstrate how you can protect your food from the most ambitious freeloading bears, whether you're car camping or backpacking. The program is held at the Pumice Amphitheater, which is located at Shuttle Stop #4 on the road to Devil's Postpile.

Altitude Eleven Thousand

If you've ever looked up at those tall mountains and wondered what the view might be like from the top, stop thinking and grab your camera. What's great about this hike is that, when you reach the top, the only shortness of breath you'll experience will be because of the view. You don't reach the top by huffing and puffing your way up some steep, dusty trail, but by taking a ski gondola to the 11,053-foot summit of Mammoth Mountain. The ranger will meet you on top and provide a personal orientation tour of the 360-degree view. Bring a camera and, since it can get pretty brisk up in that thin air, stuff a windbreaker in your daypack. There is a fee for taking the scenic gondola ride; you'll have to get a ride ticket from the ski area.

Dwellers of the Great Basin

Long before mountain men like Jedediah Smith passed through these mountains, the Piutes called this land their home. Spend about two hours with a ranger on a short hike of less than one mile to visit an old Native American dwelling site. Learn how these people survived in what appears to be, and is, a hostile and unforgiving land, especially during winter. Where did they live? Where did they find food? Where did they go during the long, cold winters? These and many more questions will be answered. This is a very popular tour, so you'll need to call ahead for reservations. The group will form a caravan and drive to the point where the short walk begins.

Emerald Lake Hike

This is more like a walk than a hike—during the two hours the ranger allots for this program, less than one mile will be covered. With such a short distance and so much time, there will be plenty of opportunity to stop and admire the wildflowers along the trail. If you've done little or no hiking and would like to start easy, this is the ideal hike. You'll be meeting at the Emerald Lake Trailhead at the end of Coldwater Campground.

Gold in Them Hills

The Sierra foothills were not the only place in California that saw gold-mining operations. The eastern Sierra also was home to gold-hungry miners. This one-hour hike through the Mammoth Consolidated Gold Mine is a step back in history. Actually, this is the hike where you can learn how Mammoth Lakes really got their name. There's old mining equipment, mine buildings and some great views of Gold Mountain. You'll meet the ranger at the Duck Pass Trail parking lot at the top of Coldwater Campground. Bring water to drink.

SEASONAL

Hot Creek

With all the old volcanoes in the area, you might think that one or two of them would still be active. Well, you're right. This is still pretty volcanically active land and there are bubbling hot springs to prove it. Follow the ranger up Hot Creek to an ancient volcanic caldera and see bubbling, boiling water and steam escaping from beneath the earth. You'll find out about the geologic past of the Mammoth Lakes area and whether or not there's anything to fear in the present volcanic brew. Meet at Hot Creek for this relatively easy hike that covers less than one mile in about an hour.

Hug-A-Tree

If you have young kids and you take them camping and hiking, then your owe it to them and to your own peace of mind to be sure they attend this program. This is an educational program that only lasts about an hour, but it will teach your kids everything they need to know about surviving if they ever get lost in the forest. Search-and-rescue professionals developed the Hug-A-Tree program, and it has already saved children who have accidentally become separated from their parents while camping or hiking. All ages are welcome to attend; parents or guardians are required to attend with their children. Meet at the Mammoth Visitor Center.

Inyo Craters

This is a relatively easy half-mile walk to see a couple of Mammoth's most recently formed volcanic craters. The walk passes through stands of Jeffrey pine and over pumice hills for close-up views of these two steep-sided craters. The bottom of each crater has filled with water, creating two small lakes. While you can drive to the parking area and see these on your own, if you meet the ranger at the visitor center and caravan to the Inyo Crater parking lot, you'll learn much more about the area and how it came to be what it is today.

Junior Rangers

This is more than a one-hour babysitting service provided by the rangers. Kids, ages 6 to 12, will have a really great time learning about the natural world around them. From volcanoes to animals to Native Americans, the subjects that may be covered during any one program are limited only by the imagination of the ranger leading the program. The meeting place for Junior Rangers is at the Mammoth Visitor Center.

Leave It to Beaver

If you're old enough to remember the old television comedy by the same name as this hike, well, this isn't anything even marginally related. This two-hour hike will show you all the fantastic things that happened to what originally was a pretty sterile, glacially carved lake after a family of beavers decided to take up housekeeping. Meet the ranger at Shuttle Stop #7 on the road to Devil's Postpile.

Mammoth City

Gold and the thought of discovering one's own fabulously rich mine has always driven people to extremes, at least into some pretty extreme primitive behavior. Mammoth City learned this well during the Gold Rush era. Before the small mountain town became the summer fishing and winter skiing capital of the eastern Sierra, it was home for some pretty hardy men and women who settled here, trying to capture that golden dream from themselves. A few succeeded, a few died in the attempt and many more simply lived hard and left broke. Join a ranger for an hour of exploring the remains of this once-booming gold town. Meet at the Mammoth City historical site, located about one-half mile past Twin Lakes on Old Mammoth Road.

Natural History Through the Lens

When you explore the natural world of California's forests through the viewfinder of a camera, the bits and pieces of nature that we usually ignore, or at least fail to recognize, suddenly burst into full view. Grab your camera and, if you have one, a macro lens, and join this small group of people to look at the small world of the forest in a whole new light. You'll have an opportunity to explore spider webs and dew droplets, flower petals, lichen and maybe a few bugs. Meet at the Mammoth Visitor Center.

Panorama Dome

Meet at the Tamarack Lodge for a half-mile walk to a point where you can see and photograph panoramic views of the Mammoth Lakes area. There are also wildflowers and maybe even some beautiful cloud formations to see from this viewpoint. This is a relatively short jaunt, taking just one-and-a-half hours.

Range of Light

There are many panoramic vistas in the Mammoth area and the Minaret Vista is one of the best. John Muir, upon seeing the

SEASONAL

Sierra from one of these points, referred to these wondrous mountains as the Range of Light. Bring your camera for this short hike.

Ranger's Choice

This is a couple hours worth of wandering the Red's Meadow area with a ranger who will help you identify all those beautiful wildflowers that spring to life for a few short weeks each summer. Besides learning the names of each of the flowers, you'll also discover what uses the Native Americans and early settlers who lived here made of them, for everything from food to medicine. Bring your wildflower field guide and a magnifying hand lens, if you have them.

Reading Is a Magic Trip

Offered throughout the summer of 1994, and hopefully again in 1995, this is a cooperative effort of McDonald's, the Mammoth Lakes Library and the U.S. Forest Service designed for kids ages five to ten years. Each Thursday, the kids will meet at McDonald's for a storytelling session that will deal with a different topic each week. This is a really fun time for kids, but it's limited to just 25 youngsters for each program, so you'll have to call the ranger station for reservations in advance at (619) 924-5500.

The Starkweather Experience

A ranger or naturalist will lead this 2.5-mile hike along the Starkweather Lake Trail to explore the forest, wildflowers, avalanche paths and open meadows. The hike will take about three or four hours to complete, so remember to bring water, lunch and other mountain essentials like sunscreen and a hat. You'll be leaving from the Minaret Vista Park entrance station.

Three Lakes Hike

There is more to Mammoth Lakes than the drive-to lakes. On this one-mile hike you'll get to see three spots for fishing or exploring. Lake George, Lake Barrett and T.J. Lake are easily reached on this gentle, two-hour walk, which is ideal for the entire family. A ranger will be along who can help you identify the wildflowers you'll encounter. Bring water and a camera for some great pictures of your wilderness experience. Meet at the Lake George parking lot.

The Web of Life

It's been preached by many, but perhaps Chief Seattle explained it best when he said, "Life is like a web which unites all things, like the blood which unites one family. What man does to the web, he does to himself." Here's an opportunity to learn what Chief Seattle and others who have espoused this holistic philosophy, like naturalist John Muir, meant. This is a scenic one-hour tour that begins at the Sotcher Lake Shuttle Stop, which is on the way to Devil's Postpile.

Life in the Meadows

An evening program is the perfect way to cap off a day of fishing, exploring and enjoying the great outdoors in the Mammoth area. Meeting on one set evening each week, this fun and informative program looks at the history and ecology of Mammoth Lakes and the wild critters who call it their home. There is a fee (probably about $6 per person) for this program, which includes hot chocolate, popcorn and marshmallow roasting. It's a lot cheaper than any movie, with popcorn, that you'll find back in the city. The program is scheduled to be held at the Sierra Meadows Ranch.

Old Fashioned Family Campfire

This is old fashioned in a couple of ways. There will be plenty of around-the-campfire singing, games, skits, songs and other program activities. And it's all free. All you have to bring is your own marshmallows for burning in the campfire. This evening program is generally offered in the Shady Rest Amphitheater at 8:30 p.m. one night each week.

Smokey, Wildfires and You!

Wildfires have always been a natural part of the forests and meadows of the Sierra. Now that there is so much human activity in the mountains, what has our role become in this balance of nature and human need? Join a fire prevention ranger for a campfire

SEASONAL

program, slide show and a special visit by Smokey Bear. Bring a flashlight to help you find your way back to your car or campsite after the program. This program usually meets at the Convict Lake Amphitheater at 8:30 p.m., one weekend night each month.

❧ ❧ ❧ ❧

Sequoia and Kings Canyon National Parks

Daily during summer; weekends in winter • Times vary
(various park locations, see listings below)

For anyone venturing into the southern Sierra, Sequoia and Kings Canyon national parks are must-sees. The rugged Sierra, its geography carved by glaciers that receded a mere 10,000 years ago, is showcased in these parks. Throughout the year, rangers and naturalists lead a variety of hikes in the parks, some of which are designed specifically for youngsters, while others are aimed at the entire family. What follows is a tentative listing of what probably will be offered during 1995. It's always difficult for park staff, be they national, state or local, to plan history and nature programs a year or more in advance given the uncertainty of annual budgets. And park personnel, especially state and national, are prone to transfers, sometimes resulting in a park losing its resident expert in a given subject. If any of the following programs grab your interest, it's best to contact the park for a schedule of their current activities before traveling great distances and possibly meeting with disappointment. Generally speaking, most of these hikes are offered one or more times each week during summer.

Unlike Yosemite National Park, automobile access to Sequoia and Kings Canyon national parks is limited. From Fresno, Highway 180 is the one way into Kings Canyon National Park and only penetrates a few miles past Cedar Grove. The primary route into Sequoia is via Highway 198 out of Visalia. Mineral King, located in the southern portion of Sequoia, can be reached from Mineral King Road, which cuts off Highway 198 about three miles east of Three Rivers. Most of the roads are steep and winding; some are closed in winter. Park entry is $5 per vehicle, although the fee may be increased to as much as $5 per person. In summer, expect your typical high Sierra weather which means warm days, cool nights, a chance of thundershowers and even a chance, although not too likely, that in the higher elevations snow could cover your tent or motor home in July. Winter visitors will be greeted with below-freezing temperatures, snowstorms, warm days, wind—you name it and you're likely to find it at one time or another.

For information, contact Sequoia and Kings Canyon national parks, Three Rivers, CA 93271; (209) 565-3134.

Grant Tree Walk

Stroll with a ranger along this wheelchair-accessible trail among the giant sequoias that have made the park famous. While the sight of these monarchs is breathtaking, the story of their survival is even more remarkable. Saved from loggers' saws, the General Grant Tree in Kings Canyon is conceded to be the second largest tree in the world, surpassed only by Sequoia's General Sherman, both of which are probably 4,000 years old.

Tree I.D.

While the giant sequoias are unmistakable, many of the other trees found in the park are not as easy to identify. A ranger with a thorough knowledge of the park's flora will help you understand the difference between Ponderosa pines, lodgepole pines, red and white firs, as well as numerous other species.

Budding Naturalists

This is a wonderful opportunity for kids to learn more about the natural environment that sustains life on Earth. There are two wheelchair-accessible programs, one for kids age five to seven and a second for kids age 8 to 12. The popularity of these walks and talks requires that reservations be made in advance through the parks' visitor centers. Each class is restricted to just 14 kids, lasts about one hour and requires about one-half mile of walking or wheelchairing.

SEASONAL

Circle of Earth and Sky

From most perspectives, the Native Americans who inhabited this region of California before the coming of white settlers had a much different way of looking at the world around them. Nature's abundance wasn't here for them to waste or exploit for personal gain. Instead, their lives were very much a part of the environment around them, dependent upon the benevolence of a sometimes hostile environment for their continued sustenance. Here's a perfect opportunity to learn more about how these people survived for thousands of years without the benefit of modern science or the need to destroy the forests and meadows that surrounded them.

Meadow Meander

Every high Sierra meadow has a story to tell, if you listen carefully. In this case, a ranger will be along on this half-mile, wheelchair-accessible meander through one of the hundreds of meadows that dot these mountains. Listen while the voices of the ages tell about how ancient glaciers carved out large depressions from these solid granite mountains, and how lakes formed and over the ages filled with sediment to become today's meadows. Wildflowers paint their beautiful hues over meadows for a few short weeks each summer; the wildlife that depend upon these high mountain oases might surprise you.

Bear Essentials

Black bears were here long before these mountains became national parkland. Learning to live safely among bears isn't as difficult as it may seem, but knowing how bears think and how they go about finding food and shelter is essential to doing so. While bears are fairly common, if you haven't had an opportunity to see one, join the ranger and learn what to do so as not to accidentally attract a bear to dinner.

The Rocks Begin to Speak

Wind, rain, snow, glaciers and time have joined forces to create the scenery in Sequoia and Kings Canyon national parks. The mountains these forces have shaped over eons contain the geologic history of the Sierra. Learn to understand what these granite walls are telling us and understand where we are going.

Web of Life

While wildlife is reasonably abundant in the parks, sometimes ground squirrels are all we ever get to see. Here's your chance to see a few of the other animals that tend to shy away from direct contact with people, as well as an opportunity to learn how each of these animals plays a vital role in maintaining a healthy forest environment.

Wet and Wild

Rivers, lakes and waterfalls continue to carve their indelible marks on the surrounding mountains. A ranger will, figuratively at least, open your eyes to the aquatic world that forms the basis for much of the life that exists here. This is a fun exploration of the river, so come prepared for getting a bit wet—wear shoes you don't mind doing a little wading in.

Leapin' Lizards

Did you every wonder why you see lizards doing push-ups on rocks, or why they seem to like sunning themselves? Here's your chance to find out everything you ever wanted to know about lizards, such as: Are lizards poisonous? Do lizards have teeth? What do lizards eat? What eats lizards? Spend an hour with a ranger and learn it all.

Other Ranger-Led Hikes

Rangers lead numerous other talks and hikes, some short, some a bit longer, but all fascinating. They might include: a trip to Kanawyer's Camp and Copper Mine to learn a bit more about the history of the area; a look at ants and bugs; a look at the role horses have played in these mountains; a sketch-walk for budding and not-so-budding artists; a look at fishing opportunities in the mountains; a boulder-hopping romp; wildflower viewing; a sunset walk; a night star talk; a hike along scenic ridgetops; a stroll through quiet meadows and a look at the different philosophies for managing the resources of a national park verses managing nearby national forests.

SEASONAL

Campfires

Tradition is sometimes difficult to ignore, and in the case of this time-honored tradition, there is nothing more enjoyable than sitting around a roaring campfire. Singing favorite camp songs, listening to stories about the parks, perhaps seeing a slide show that takes you on an intimate tour of the park to witness the other seasons, or seeing more stars in the heavens above than you thought possible is as much a part of camping in the Sierra as are bugs, sleeping bags and tents. There are campfire programs in one or both of these national parks every night during summer.

Sierra Club's Sierra Outings

Various dates and times • See listings that follow

If there's an organization synonymous with outings in the Sierra Nevada, it has to be the Sierra Club. In addition to the hundreds of hikes and outings offered by local Sierra Club chapters throughout California, the parent organization offers backpacking and lodge trips deep into the Sierra, to many other states and countries around the world.

The Sierra Club Outings annual catalog is generally available well before the beginning of each new year, and it provides significantly more detail about the few hikes that are listed here. While the Sierra Club charges a fee for each of its outings, the fee is set at a level that covers the costs of administering the Outings program and does not help support other Sierra Club activities. So you get a qualified hike leader and a great trip, at a minimum cost.

There are various requirements for participating in an Outing. You must become a Sierra Club member, which costs only $35 per year for a single or $43 for a joint membership. There are a number of member benefits, besides supporting the nation's premier environmental organization, which include a subscription to their magazine and your local chapter's newsletter containing all the local outings, most of them free.

Each Outing is rated for its difficulty and for the accommodations, which can range from a small tent pitched on a lonely mountainside to a comfortable lodge and warm bed. Food is provided, for the most part, and the hiking can range between easy and extremely strenuous.

Call the Sierra Club Outing Department and request their most recent Outings catalog. In 1994, it contained 350 great trips. In the future, it is sure to contain more. When you see an Outing that looks appealing, call the Sierra Club and request a specific trip brochure that will offer significantly more detail designed to help you decide if a particular Outing is right, or wrong, for you.

For information and an Outings catalog, contact the Sierra Club Outing Department, 730 Polk Street, San Francisco, CA 94109; (415) 923-5630 (24-hour voice mail).

Below I've listed a very small sampling of the 25 or more backpacking trips offered just in the Sierra Nevada mountains. There are also many more popular, multi-day, non-backpacking outings held by the Sierra Club in California, many of which will most likely be repeated in the future. The prices listed will probably change slightly.

Clouds Rest and Half Dome

Mid-June 🄢 🄲
(see #15 on map page 74)

This seven-day backpacking adventure begins and ends in Yosemite's Tuolumne Meadows with stops along some of the park's most spectacular scenic views. Since the crowds usually don't show up until July, this is a good time to see few people and lots of water in the rivers and tumbling over the waterfalls. There's a layover day near Clouds Rest and Half Dome in between daily six-to-ten-mile hiking days. You need to be in good physical condition, because of the distances hiked and the elevation, the highest of which will be 10,180 feet above sea level. The cost of the trip is about $285.

SIERRA EVENTS

Above the Clouds, John Muir Wilderness and Kings Canyon
Mid-August **S**

For six days, you and a small group of backpackers will be doing a lot of off-trail hiking to high country basins and numerous glacier-carved lakes. There will be a two-day layover, so you can climb to Mount Sill's 14,125-foot summit, fish one of the nearby high Sierra lakes, or just sit and read a book. There will be five-star food to quell the hungry beast within you and lots of quiet time to relax. This is a moderate backpacking trip, so you need to be in reasonably good physical condition. The cost of the trip is about $320.

Woman's Beginner Backpack
Mid-August **S**
(see #18 on map page 74)

Ansel Adams Wilderness in the southern Sierra is one of the more beautiful and remote areas of the great mountain range. For women who want to learn about backpacking, this seven-day trip is a great way to go. You need to be in good physical condition because you'll be hiking between 7,000 and 10,500 feet above sea level where the air gets pretty thin. During the week, you'll cover about 25 miles total, with a few short-hike days and some off-trail rock scrambling. Most afternoons are left open for your own mini-adventures. The cost is about $295.

Seven Gables and Countless Lakes
Late August **S**
(see #19 on map page 74)

It's hard to beat being in the John Muir Wilderness anytime and late summer is no different. This lake-hopping trek will take you through Humphrey's Basin and onto Bear Lake Basin. The trail is often nonexistent and you will find yourself camping above 11,000 feet. Layover days will give you plenty of time to climb a few summits, fish some of the surrounding lakes or explore some of the nearby high country. This is for experienced backpackers in good physical condition only. The cost is about $405 for the eight-day trip.

Monarch Magic
Early September **S**(⏰)

This is a wild and spectacular trek that will cover 38 miles in its planned eight days. Two of those days will be layovers, giving you ample time to explore the Monarch Divide territory of Kings Canyon National Park. Most of the time will be spent in the mountains above 10,000 feet. The cost is about $390.

Emigrant Wilderness Base Camp
Late August **S**(⏰)
(see #13 on map page 74)

Sierra Club base camp outings let you spend your days as you please, either taking day hikes, fishing or simply relaxing in the spectacular setting of the Emigrant Wilderness in the high Sierra. This particular trip is eight days of pure enjoyment in the mountains northwest of Yosemite. There are dozens of small glacial-carved lakes to visit and plenty of incredible scenery to photograph, if you bring your camera equipment along. The cost is about $785.

History and Hiking Donner Pass from Clair Tappaan Lodge
Late July **S**(⏰)
(see #5 on map page 74)

The Sierra Club's Clair Tappaan Lodge was built in 1934 as a ski lodge for its members. Today, its great meals and warm bunks attract those people who aren't always, or who are never, into backpacking or camping. Various outings are offered year-round, and the lodge is especially popular with winter cross-country skiers. This particular outing will give you a great chance to learn about the ill-fated Donner Party and to see the country where early construction crews carved tunnels through solid granite mountains in order to lay rails of steel for the transcontinental railroad. There will be several day hikes, ranging from three to seven miles, to a lot of historic and beautiful places during the six days of this outing. You'll spend all of your time between 7,000 and 9,100 feet above sea level. The cost is about $415.

SEASONAL

Chapter 4

Great Outdoor Events of California's Gold Country

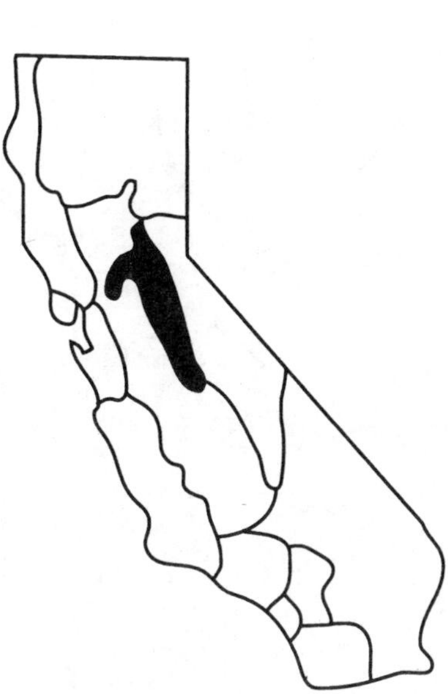

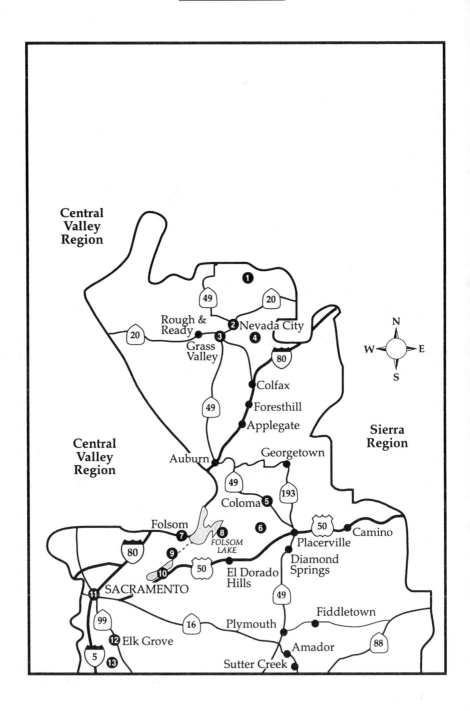

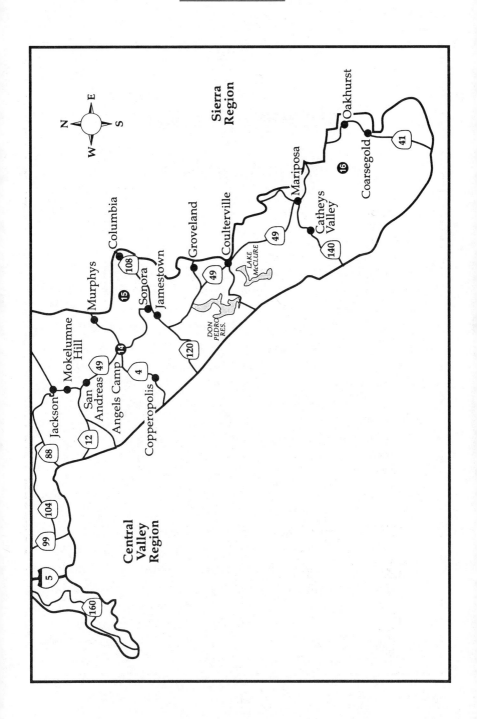

✤ ✤ ✤ ✤

Introduction to Gold Country

It's sometimes called the Mother Lode, the Sierra foothills or the Golden Chain, but whatever the name, it's still the place where James Marshall discovered gold in January of 1848. In spite of his best efforts to keep the whole thing secret, he managed to set the stage for the greatest Gold Rush in history. And the rush for gold has really never ended. People still come to these oak-and pine-studded hillsides to look for gold, and many of them find it, although most only in quantities large enough merely to say they found gold! But the gold is still here. And there are plenty of local business folks who will show you some eye-popping gold nugget specimens, then sell you anything from gold pans to portable suction dredges to help you find your own. And do people still find big gold nuggets? You bet they do! At least the few who are really lucky or really know what they are doing, or both.

Today, most people come to California's Gold Country for an enjoyable day or more wandering through Gold Rush-era towns with their historic old wooden and brick buildings, wooden side-walks, historic steam trains, gold-mining tours and untold numbers of antique shops. The people who are lucky enough to live in towns with names like Placerville (first known as Hangtown), El Dorado, Big Oak Flat, Sonora, Jamestown, Auburn, Grass Valley, Angels Camp and many, many more enjoy celebrating their Gold Rush heritage, and they enjoy their country living.

You'll find that, like the Big Four who built the western half of the transcontinental railroad in the 1860s, I've fibbed a bit about where the Gold Country boundaries lie, choosing to include the Central Valley city of Sacramento as part of it. The Big Four—railroad magnates Huntington, Hopkins, Stanford and Crocker—convinced the federal government that the Sierra foothills began a couple of miles east of downtown Sacramento because the government paid them significantly more taxpayer money for laying track in hill country than in flat valley country. I've included Sacramento in the foothill Gold Country for two much less profitable reasons. First, historically Sacramento served as the gateway to the gold fields and much of its history is tied to the discovery of gold. And second, California's Office of Tourism includes Sacramento in their Gold Country maps, probably for much the same reason.

Ishi Day

March 11, 1995 **$** 🕭 · 10 a.m. to 5 p.m.
(see #11 on map page 144)

Ishi was the last Yahi Indian in Northern California who lived the life of his ancestors, or at least as close to that life as the early 1900s could afford in the hills surrounding the Redding and Red Bluff area of the northern Central Valley. Ishi spent his last days living in relative physical comfort while anthropologists at the University of California studied him. This annual day of remembrance is a look at Ishi's life through the eyes of present-day children who have learned about the man and his way of life. They have crafted poems and created works of art depicting their young visions of Ishi. The essays, poems and art have been previously submitted and judged and are on display. If you've never had an opportunity to visit the California State Indian Museum and view its one-of-a-kind display of baskets, this is a great time to do it. The California State Indian Museum is located next to Sutter's Fort State Historic Park at 2618 K Street in Sacramento, just three blocks west of the Business 80 freeway. The cost for the event is $2 for adults and $1 for kids ages 6 to 12.

For information, contact the California State Indian Museum, 2618 K Street, Sacramento, CA 95816; (916) 324-8112 or (916) 324-0971.

Creek Week

During Earth Week, late April **$** 🕭
(see #11 on map page 144)

Many creeks meander throughout the greater Sacramento area, and, being a part of the urban environment, they tend to serve as convenient dumping grounds for various and nefarious chunks of civilization's cast-off junk. Annually, up to 1,000 people join forces for a week-long clean up of the creeks and rivers, interspersed with nature walks, storytelling sessions and stenciling of storm drains to remind people that what they pour down there ends up in their rivers. There are contests for the best junk found, the most junk collected and other equally unsavory categories of fancy. There is also a contest where kids design and build totem poles that represent the rivers and wildlife in the area, and a junk scavenger hunt. The Saturday that ends the event is a celebration barbecue with free food donated by local businesses and free T-shirts given to participants of the clean-up efforts. Creek Week clean-up sites are located throughout the greater Sacramento area. Call for specific meeting times and places. There's no cost for participation, except your time and energy. The weather should be warm and balmy, but there's always a chance of a spring rainstorm passing through.

For information, contact Sacramento Urban Creeks Council (it's a private residence, so please call or write, but don't stop in), 5225 Atlanta Way, Sacramento, CA 95841; (916) 332-3775.

❊ ❊ ❊ ❊

Camellia Cup Regatta
April 15 & 16, 1995 **S** ⦿
(see #8 on map page 144)

If you have a boat or if you like boats, you shouldn't miss the oldest inland regatta in Northern California. The weekend-long event is open to boats of all classes and to sailors of all levels of experience. After a full day of sailing the open waters of Folsom Lake, there's a barbecue, music and dancing all evening to deplete your last ounce of energy. Folsom Lake, home of the regatta, sits in the picturesque Sierra foothills, so there are some great views and some wonderful coves to explore up the two forks of the American River that flow into the reservoir. Should you become tired of boating, the park offers access to a 32-mile bike trail that follows the American River to its confluence with the Sacramento River.

Folsom Lake is located east of Sacramento, just outside the town of Folsom. From the town of Folsom, cross the American River and turn right at the first traffic light on Folsom-Auburn Road. Drive to Beals Point, which is on the right a mile or so past Dam Road. Entry will cost you $25 per person, but call to confirm the cost and dates. The cost of the barbecue is extra. The weather is usually warm and pleasant this time of year, although a late spring rainstorm can stir things up.

For information, contact the Folsom Yacht Club, (916) 985-3704; or Folsom Lake State Recreation Area, (916) 988-0205.

❀ ❀ ❀ ❀

Elk Grove Creek Week
Last Sunday in April
(see #12 on map page 144)

Elk Grove, historically a farming and ranching town, is quickly becoming a bedroom community for Sacramento, which lies less than a dozen miles to the north. Creeks meander through the Elk Grove area and there is increasingly a need, not only to clean out the year's accumulation of dispossessed junk, but also to educate people about the importance of our natural waterways to wildlife and flood protection. Interpretive walks will accompany the creek clean-up activities and the day ends with ice cream for all. Elk Grove is located just off Highway 99, about 12 miles south of downtown Sacramento. There's no cost to participate. The weather is usually warm and sunny, unless late spring rains pass through.

For information, contact the Elk Grove Community Services District, Parks and Recreation, 10519 East Stockton Boulevard, Suite #100, Elk Grove, CA 95624; (916) 685-1297.

❀ ❀ ❀ ❀

Historic Grass Valley Walking Tour
First Saturday in May
(see #3 on map page 144)

While you can enjoy a walking tour of Grass Valley anytime, having author and Nevada County historian and resident Michel Janicot along as a guide will add significantly to your stroll back through history. While many of the original wooden buildings burned in the fires that frequented most Gold Rush towns, many of the Grass Valley buildings that were constructed between 1860 and 1890 still house businesses and people's homes. Others were rebuilt, sometimes more than once. A reproduction of the home of 19th century international celebrity and stage performer Lola Montez is located on Mill Street. It houses the Grass Valley and Nevada County Chamber of Commerce, a small museum and many artifacts from Lola's original home. The Chamber office is a good place to get a copy of a self-guided tour map if you choose to do this on your own. One of the oldest buildings in town, originally built in 1855, currently houses the Odd Fellows Hall and Grass Valley Hardware. In its 140 years, the three-building complex has served as a newspaper office, hardware store, bakery, grocery and dry goods outlet. The tour is easy and will take less than two hours to complete. It's also limited to the first 20 people who sign up. Grass Valley is located in the lower range of the Sierra Nevada Mountains, about 22 miles north of Auburn on Highway 49. There's a $10 fee per person for the tour. Count on the weather being warm and sunny.

For information, contact the Nevada County Land Trust, P.O. Box 2088, Nevada City, CA 95959; (916) 265-0430.

Deer Creek Fauna and Flora Wade
First Saturday in May • 11 a.m. to 2 p.m.
(see #2 on map page 144)

Most everyone knows that Nevada County's creeks and rivers were once loaded with gold, but these same waters are also home to a large and diverse wildlife population. A naturalist with a background in fisheries biology will lead this adventure through Deer Creek, so bring rubber boots or comfortable shoes that you don't mind wading through water in. This is a great opportunity to learn more about how plants and animals adapt to their environment, the intricacies of food webs and the dispersal of each species to ensure their survival. This is an easy hike, although it takes four hours. In addition to your water shoes, bring a sack lunch, a notebook, drinking water and some bug repellent, just in case the mosquitoes are active. The hike is limited to 15 people and kids are more than welcome, so why not make this a family outing? Call for directions to the meeting place, which will be near Nevada City in Gold Country. There's a $12 fee per person. The weather should be sunny and warm.

For information, contact the Nevada County Land Trust, P.O. Box 2088, Nevada City, CA 95959; (916) 265-0430.

❀ ❀ ❀ ❀

Pacific Coast Rowing Championships

Mid-May

(see #10 on map page 144)

This is one of those non-participatory athletic events that is really quite entertaining just to watch, especially if you've never seen those long, sleek racing shells literally skim across the water, propelled only by teams of in-synch rowers. If you have your own canoe or other such floating device, you can get a little better view of the action, but there's plenty to be seen from the shoreline of Lake Natoma, where the event is held. Each year about 35 college teams fight it out here in preparation for the national competition, which actually may be held on Lake Natoma in the near future. If you have kids, bring them along; if you like to fish, the trout are usually biting in this heavily stocked lake. Lake Natoma is situated on the American River, downstream from Folsom Lake, east of Sacramento. Take the Hazel Avenue exit from Highway 50 and head north. The lake is on the right. The entrance fee into the Lake Natoma area is $5 per vehicle. The weather should be warm or hot.

For information, contact California State University's Sacramento Aquatic Center; (916) 985-7239.

❀ ❀ ❀ ❀

Marshall Gold Art In the Park

May 13 & 14, 1995 **$** *• 10 a.m. to 4 p.m.*
(see #5 on map page 144)

Expect this event to be more than a simple arts and crafts show. First, it's held in the place where James Marshall discovered gold in 1848 and started the Gold Rush. The old town of Coloma, which sprang to life in the wake of Marshall's discovery, is a quaint foothill community filled with historic buildings, reconstructed homes and a sawmill. The sawmill is similar to the one Marshall was operating when he found the yellow metal in its tailrace. During the weekend event, many of the historic buildings are open; docents wearing period attire are on hand to offer information about the buildings and the people who lived and died here. You can enjoy many demonstrations such as bread baking, basket weaving and more. There's lots of food and the crafts program offers some unique pieces of work, most of it for sale. Bring a picnic lunch if you don't want to purchase food on-site, because the park has a beautiful, shaded picnic area.

Marshall Gold Discovery State Historic Park is located on historic Highway 49, about halfway between Auburn and Placerville. There's a $5 fee per vehicle to enter the park. It should be a warm and comfortable day.

For information, contact Marshall Gold Discovery State Historic Park; (916) 622-3470.

❖ ❖ ❖ ❖

Sutter's Fort Trader's Faire and Demonstration Days

May 13 & 14 **$** *• 10 a.m. to 4 p.m.*
(see #11 on map page 144)

When John Sutter first came to California, he built a fort near the confluence of the Sacramento and American rivers. While the fort has been reconstructed and appears much as it did back in 1846, what really brings it back to life are its living history and demonstration days. Trappers and Native Americans fill the old fort with their tents and supplies; the smoke from their campfires fills the air, and occasionally a cannon or musket sends its blast reverberating through the fort. There are barrel makers, weavers, bakers and more to see. If you happen to be standing around the beehive ovens when the bread comes out, you can sometimes get a piece to eat, and there's nothing better than hot, homemade bread smeared with freshly churned butter. At the opposite end of the fort, the blacksmith is usually working on his anvil, creating tools and other useful items for living in the 1840s. Nearby, there should be someone else dipping candles, and there are always plenty of docents in period clothing portraying the people who actually lived in the fort during Sutter's time. Sutter's Fort State Historic Park is located at 2701 L Street in Sacramento, just off the Business 80 freeway. The cost may change, but in past years has been about $3 for adults. The weather should be warm and sunny. There's not much shade inside the fort, but there are lots of big trees and a lawn surrounding the outside, so think about a picnic.

For information, contact Sutter's Fort State Historic Park; (916) 445-4422.

❖ ❖ ❖ ❖

Angels Camp Jumping Frog Jubilee & Calaveras County Fair

May 18 to 21, 1995 • Starts at 8 a.m.
(see #14 on map page 145)

Okay, frog jockeys, here's your opportunity for fame and $5,000 in prize money if you and your favorite frog can beat the current world record of nearly 21.5 feet. If your frog wins but doesn't beat the current world record, you'll walk away with $750. This jubilee began last century when Samuel Clemens (better known by his pen name, Mark Twain) wrote a reasonably innocent and only marginally truthful story called "The Notorious Jumping Frog of Calaveras County," about a gold prospector named Jim Smiley and his frog, Dan'l Webster. In the tale, someone secretly fed the frog lead shot, so its owner couldn't possibly win a frog-jumping contest wager. Twain's story helped shoot him into literary history almost immediately, although it was many years later that Angels Camp, where the original story was set, would begin what would quickly become a world-renowned event. The actual frog jumping contest began in 1928, when 51 folks jockeyed their frogs in the first-ever contest. Today, over 2,000 people will be jumping frogs. There are some things to keep in mind should you choose to compete. You can bring your own frog if you wish, but if you have no luck or desire to go froggin', there are plenty of "community" frogs available for use by amateur frog jockeys. Now, if you're a little squeamish and don't want to handle the wiggling amphibians, there are jockeys on hand willing to represent you and your personal or borrowed frog. Jumping your frog is really pretty easy. Simply place it in the start circle, then without touching it again, jump, yell, make faces, do whatever you like to spook the little green creature into jumping as far as possible in three jumps. The longer jumpers make the finals, and the longest jump in the finals wins it all. Actually, watching what people are willing to do in public just to get a frog to move is plenty of entertainment for most people. But, should you get bored frog-watching, there are plenty of crafts and food booths, farm animals on display, carnival rides and all the rest of the fun stuff that comes with a county fair. The 1994 winner was three-year-old Cody Shilts whose frog Free Willy leaped 19 feet and one-half inch to take it all. Cody, the youngest winner ever, will be back in 1995 as the defending four-year-old champion.

Frog Town is located at the Calaveras County Fairgrounds at the south end of Angels Camp, just off Highway 49. Entry fees range from $7 to $9 (in 1994) for adults, $2 less for kids under 12. Parking is $2 and it costs $3 for each frog entry, be it your own green thing or one of the borrowed critters. You can almost always count on the weather being warm.

For information, contact Calaveras County Fair and Jumping Frog Jubilee, P.O. Box 96, Angels Camp, CA 95222; (209) 736-2561.

❖ ❖ ❖ ❖

Honored Elders Day

May 20 & 21, 1995 **S** 🚶 · 10 a.m. to 4 p.m.
(see #11 on map page 144)

Before the Americans, before the Spanish arrived in California, dozens of Native American tribes inhabited this rich and wild land. Each year, the descendants of those who came first gather at the California State Indian Museum to honor their remaining elders. They are honored for their lifelong contributions to the local Native American communities and to the continuation of the Native American culture. There's always dancing and games, along with native foods and crafts demonstrations and sales. If you've never been to the museum, this is a great opportunity to see the excellent collection of beautiful baskets and other artifacts. And when you're done with the museum, Sutter's Fort is just a few yards away. The California State Indian Museum is located at 2618 K Street in Sacramento, just off the Business 80 freeway. There's no cost for the program. By May, you can count on some pretty warm, if not hot, weather.

For information, contact the California State Indian Museum; (916) 445-4422.

✤ ✤ ✤ ✤

Bed, Breakfast and Blossoms Trek

Late May **S** 🚶
(see #3 on map page 144)

Spend two beautiful, blooming days touring historic bed-and-breakfast inns in the Gold Country towns of Grass Valley and Nevada City. Begin by meeting historian Edie Reihm at the Off Broad Street Playhouse for her personal insight into the history of the area. Within walking distance in Nevada City, you'll find gardens to admire, one special private garden to visit, wildflowers to see and a special look at the inside of some of the more fascinating historic buildings. Master gardeners will be along to share their secrets. The trip concludes with a short drive to nearby Grass Valley for a look at more gardens and historic buildings. Grass Valley is located on Highway 49, about 24 miles north of Auburn and Interstate 80.

Nevada City is another four miles north on Highway 49. The trip will cost about $20 per person and reservations are required. The weather should be really nice and sunny.

For information, contact the Nevada County Land Trust, P.O. Box 2088, Nevada City, CA 95959; (916) 265-0430.

Independence Trail Wildflower Trek

Third Saturday in May • 9 a.m. to noon

(see #2 on map page 144)

Spring in the Sierra foothills provides a spectacular wildflower display. The relatively new, wheelchair-accessible Independence Trail follows an historic flume along the South Fork of the Yuba River. It's also an easy trail for kids, so bring the entire family. Longtime Nevada County residents Lila Schiffner, Ginny Forsman and Beverly Hackett, artist and author of *Wildflowers of the Foothills*, will point out the many different flowers that are sure to be seen along the way. Lupine, Indian paintbrush and perhaps even a few tiger lilies are just of few of the flowers that should be out in full bloom. Depending upon the group, the trip will cover anywhere from four to six miles and take about three hours to complete. The trek will probably leave from Nevada City, which is located about 28 miles north of Auburn on Highway 49. Please call to confirm the date and meeting place. It'll cost you $12 per person to be part of this program. It should be a nice warm day.

For information, contact the Nevada County Land Trust, P.O. Box 2088, Nevada City, CA 95959; (916) 265-0430.

Skillman Gold Country Horse Trek

Third Saturday in May • All day

(see #2 on map page 144)

Join Barbara Reed on this equestrian ride and enjoy her insights into the history of both the local plants and the lands surrounding the Pioneer Trail. The ride is limited to 18 experienced riders and their horses. Camping facilities, plenty of parking for horse trailers and a corral are available at the Skillman Campground, which is located just outside Nevada City. You'll need to reserve your spot on this popular trek. When you call to confirm your reservation, you can also confirm the date and meeting place, which will probably be the Skillman Campground located above Five Mile House, near Nevada City, about 28 miles north of Auburn on Highway 49. There's a $25 fee per person for the horse trek. The weather should be warm and sunny.

For information, contact the Nevada County Land Trust, P.O. Box 2088, Nevada City, CA 95959; (916) 265-0430.

Gold Country Photo Workshop
Third Saturday in May 🟢🗓️ • 9 a.m. to dusk
(see #2 on map page 144)

Here's an opportunity to join professional photographer Wayne Green for a day-long photo excursion into some beautiful areas of Nevada County. If you've never seen or photographed the 225-foot Bridgeport Covered Bridge, completed in 1862, here is the perfect opportunity. The bridge is an adventure just to walk across and even more fun to photograph. As the light changes throughout the course of the day, you can explore and photograph different aspects of the bridge and the surrounding woods, wildflowers and the South Fork of the Yuba River. Bring food and water, along with your photo gear which should probably include a tripod, neutral density and polarizing filters, a few extra lenses if you have them and lots of film. The photo hike and workshop is limited to just 12 people, so call early for reservations and to confirm the date. You'll need a good map because some of the roads around here can be a little confusing. Start at Nevada City, which is located about 28 miles north of Auburn on Highway 49, then head eight miles west on Highway 20 to Pleasant Valley Road, which goes north to the tiny community of Bridgeport and the covered bridge. The excursion will cost only $25, which is cheap if you've ever priced professional photographer-led photo trips. It should be a warm and sunny day.

For information, contact the Nevada County Land Trust, P.O. Box 2088, Nevada City, CA 95959; (916) 265-0430.

✤ ✤ ✤ ✤

Gold Bullion Mountain Bike Run

Saturday & Sunday of Memorial Day weekend • 10 a.m. departure
(see #2 on map page 144)

This 30-mile, two-day bike ride starts on the historic Pioneer Trail, the same trail that once was used to haul millions of dollars in gold bullion from the Gold Country mines to Nevada City. The ride continues across the Yuba River at Missouri Bar, then climbs the dirt roads to Malakoff Diggins State Historic Park. This is where the last of the great monitors in the late 19th century, shooting their powerful streams of water, washed away entire mountains in search of gold. A support vehicle will travel along to carry supplies and camping gear. You've got to be an intermediate or advanced mountain biker and at least 12 years old to take part in this great Gold Country adventure. The trip is limited to the first 20 riders who sign up. The ride begins at the Samurai Bike Shop in Nevada City, which is located about 28 miles north of Auburn on Highway 49. The cost is about $20 per rider, plus food and camping fees. It should be warm during the day, cool at night—in other words, perfect weather for a ride.

For information, contact the Nevada County Land Trust, P.O. Box 2088, Nevada City, CA 95959; (916) 265-0430.

✤ ✤ ✤ ✤

 # Spirit of Coyote Horse Trek

First Saturday in June • 1 p.m. to 5 p.m.
(see #2 on map page 144)

If you're an experienced horseback rider, here's your opportunity to see some really varied Nevada County land. The trail begins at the 978-acre Old Nicolaysen Ranch, continues to secluded Deer Creek Falls, then heads back through the 300-acre Personeni Ranch.

The leaders are quite knowledgeable about the area's flora and fauna and its history, including Native American dwelling sites. The terrain is a bit rough in some areas and the trip includes two creek crossings. The trip will take about three or four hours and is limited to 18 riders, age 15 or older. Call for directions to the meeting place, which will be near Nevada City, located about 26 miles north of Auburn on Highway 49. There will be a fee of about $18 per person. June usually means some hot weather, so both you and your horse should come prepared.

For information, contact the Nevada County Land Trust, P.O. Box 2088, Nevada City, CA 95959; (916) 265-0430.

Sixteen-to-One Mine Tour

First Saturday in June $

(see #2 on map page 144)

This is one of several gold mines that are still active and profitable in California's Gold Country. The mine is located near Alleghany in Sierra County. Here you'll have an opportunity to meet mine owner and operator Michael Miller, who can tell you all about the history of the mine and what his plans are for the future. You'll have a chance to see the workings of the offices and mill and take a tour of the underground operations. This will be a five- to six-hour tour which will begin with a carpool in Nevada City, then head through North San Juan to the mine. Bring a camera and lunch, and be prepared to walk less than a mile on the actual tour. This tour is limited to the first 20 adults to sign up. Call to confirm the date and carpool meeting place, which will be somewhere in Nevada City, which is located about 28 miles north of Auburn on Highway 49. The cost is $50 per person. The weather should be warm and sunny.

For information, contact the Nevada County Land Trust, P.O. Box 2088, Nevada City, CA 95959; (916) 265-0430.

Columbia Diggins

June 1 to 3, 1995 [S] ☎ • 10 a.m. to 5 p.m.

(see #15 on map page 145)

The little historic town of Columbia, sitting in the Sierra foothills, was the site of one of California's richest mining efforts. Today, the recreated Gold Rush town bustles with gold panning, stagecoach rides and lots of shops to explore. During the Diggins, Columbia gets even busier, as the historic discovery of gold is reenacted in a reconstruction of the tent town that first thrived here in 1852. Here's an opportunity to relive the excitement of the old days. Because of its educational value, this is a popular event for school groups; school officials are asked to call the park to make advance reservations for their classes. You can bring a picnic lunch or enjoy one of the restaurants in town. This is really a fun place for a family day away from the hustle and bustle of city life. Columbia State Historic Park is located three miles north of Sonora, just off Highway 49. This is also one of the few state historic parks that won't charge you an entry fee.

For information, contact Columbia State Historic Park, (209) 532-4301 or (209) 532-0150.

Nevada County Adult Gold Panning Trek

First Sunday in June [S] ☎

(see #2 on map page 144)

Nevada County has always been known for its gold, and here's your chance to take some of it home with you. The trip leader is Norm Beckert, who owns Hilltop Mining in Nevada City and has been leading and instructing modern gold seekers for several years. You'll either meet and carpool or take your own truck, if you have one, over about 45 minutes of rather primitive road in order to get close enough to walk the last bit of distance to the claim. You'll be climbing over rocks and crossing water, so dress appropriately. Bring your own gold pan, a shovel and a small glass or plastic medicine-type bottle, preferably with a tight, screw-on top, for collecting your gold. Lunch and drinking water would also be handy as gold panning is hard, back-breaking work that will definitely build up your appetite. Gloves, mosquito repellent, a hat and sunscreen will also prove useful, because it will probably be quite warm and sunny. This trip is limited to just 18 adults, so sign up early. Call to confirm the date and meeting place; it will probably be in Nevada City, located about 28 miles north of Auburn on Highway 49. This one will cost you $25 per person, but it's worth the money, even if you don't find that thumb-sized gold nugget.

For information, contact the Nevada County Land Trust, P.O. Box 2088, Nevada City, CA 95959; (916) 265-0430.

�֍ �֍ ✦ ✦

Malakoff Diggins Homecoming

June 11, 1995 **S** 🖉 • 10 a.m. to 5 p.m.
(see #1 on map page 144)

This celebration has been going on for many, many years in this Gold Rush mining town. The party is supposed to honor the people who used to live here, although most have long since passed on to that gold field in the sky. Without anyone to welcome home, what does that leave to do? There are the tours of North Bloomfield, entertainment, maybe some street square dancing, exhibits, crafts and food. There will also be people in period clothing, from whom you can borrow a gold pan and try your luck in the nearby creek. One of the old monitors that was used to wash away millions of tons of mountain dirt looking for gold is usually started up and shot down Main Street. When you or the kids get tired of celebrating the homecoming, you can head up the road to the pond and go fishing or swimming. Malakoff Diggins State Historic Park is located about 16 miles northeast of Nevada City on North Bloomfield Road, which is gravel and steep in sections. There's a $5 fee per vehicle for day use of the park. It should be a pretty warm day.

For information, contact Malakoff Diggins State Historic Park; (916) 265-2740.

✦ ✦ ✦ ✦

California Railroad Festival

June 16 to 18, 1995 **$**(/) • 10 a.m. to 5 p.m.
(see #11 on map page 144)

Each year, the California State Railroad Museum in Old Sacramento celebrates railroading in the West. And Sacramento seems the appropriate place for such a celebration, since it was here that ground first was broken in the mid-1800s for construction of the western link of the transcontinental railroad. Today, Old Sac boasts the finest museum of railroading history in the country, which displays dozens of restored cars and locomotives. There's also a train operation that picks up passengers at the reconstructed freight depot and steams down the tracks that lie adjacent to the picturesque Sacramento River. There are always special exhibits and activities during the festival each year, plenty to keep anyone busy, even those who are not train fanatics. But just in case you really, really don't like trains and all that technological stuff, there are dozens of shops in Old Sac just waiting for you.

The California State Railroad Museum and Old Sacramento are located near 2nd and J streets in Sacramento, adjacent to the Sacramento River. From Interstate 5, take the J Street exit, then drive back under the freeway. Some of the historic buildings and exhibits are free; there's a $6 fee for adults to enter the museum and an additional fee for the steam train ride. The weather will probably be hot, into the upper 90s.

For information, contact the California State Railroad Museum; (916) 445-7373 or (916) 324-0539.

JUNE

❖ ❖ ❖ ❖

Pony Express Day

June 17, 1995 • All day
(see #7 on map page 144)

It was a dream that began 135 years ago and quickly made folk heroes of the riders who crossed half a continent on horseback in a matter of days, simply to deliver a pouch of U.S. Mail. The Pony Express met an untimely end when costs became too high and competition from the newly invented telegraph too great to continue operations. Reenactment of the historic Pony Express rides begins on June 7, in St. Joseph, Missouri. The riders enter California at Woodsford, and from there, they ride into Folsom on June 17, for a local welcome and celebration, then continue onto Sacramento where the ride ends. The riders will come down Sutter Street in the historic part of Folsom, to the Folsom History Museum and Wells Fargo Assay Office. Each year, about 1,000 people are on hand to welcome the "re-riders," as they are called today. It's just a fun day in a fun historic Gold Rush town.

The historic town of Folsom is located about 25 miles east of Sacramento, off US 50. There's no cost for the event. It'll probably be pretty hot, so dress accordingly.

For information, contact the Folsom Historic Society, 823 Sutter Street, Folsom, CA 95630; (916) 985-2707.

Folsom July Rodeo

July 3 & 4, 1995 [S] ☎ • 8:15 p.m.

(see #7 on map page 144)

The Fourth of July rodeo, with a purse of $60,000, is one of the largest rodeos in the country, and has been held in the historic Gold Rush town of Folsom for 35 years. Only professional cowboys and cowgirls who are members of PRCA, the Professional Cowboys Rodeo Association, are allowed to compete in the nightly, seven-event wrangler rodeo series. Saddle bronc and bareback riding, barrel racing, calf roping, steer wrestling, team roping and the dangerous and exciting bull riding provide thrills, spills and just a heck of a lot of fun for spectators. There's also a full carnival and a spectacular Fourth of July fireworks display. The outdoor arena holds 7,000 people and it fills up, so you should plan to arrive early. And you might want to bring a pad for your seat, because the concrete bleacher-style seats get mighty hard after a couple of hours. The rodeo is held in the Dan Russell Arena, which is in Folsom City Park, near the corner of Natoma and Stafford streets in Folsom.

General Admission is $11 for adults, $6 for kids under 12. Reserved seats are available for $13. The weather is almost always hot, although it generally cools off in the evening.

For information, contact the Folsom Chamber of Commerce, 200 Wool Street, Folsom, CA 95630; (916) 985-2698.

✤ ✤ ✤ ✤

Wassama Gathering Days

July 8, 1995 **S** 𝒫 • 10 a.m. to 4 p.m.
(see #16 on map page 145)

Each year, Native American peoples gather at Wassama Roundhouse State Historic Park to celebrate their cultures. There will be native dancing, music and food, although bringing your own food can be fun and is less expensive. This is a colorful and exciting event, and while photography is allowed in most areas, some of the dances and ceremonies are considered sacred, and the taking of photos is strongly discouraged. Wassama provides the perfect opportunity to see the real thing, as far as California Native American culture is concerned. This is one of the better events to attend because few spectators, at times no more than 250, travel here, as Oakhurst isn't exactly close to anyplace where lots of people live. Food and beverages are available. Wassama Roundhouse State Historic Park is reached by taking Highway 49 to Oakhurst and turning onto Roundhouse Road. There's no cost to attend the program.

For information, contact Wassama Roundhouse State Historic Park; (209) 822-2710.

✤ ✤ ✤ ✤

Historic Folsom Powerhouse Centennial Celebration

July 14 & 15, 1995 • 6:30 to midnight Saturday; all day Sunday
(see #9 on map page 144)

Paris may be the city better known today as the City of Light, but a hundred years ago you'd have gotten a major argument from the residents of Sacramento. On September 9, 1895, the Folsom Powerhouse began sending hydroelectricity 22 miles to Sacramento to light the Grand Electrical Carnival, marking the beginning of the long-distance transmission of electrical power. The old powerhouse still sits above the banks of Lake Natoma, a short dammed section of the American River which winds its way through Sacramento and empties into the Sacramento River. Take a peek inside the power-house—it appears much the same as when it was finally shut down upon the completion of the upstream modern Folsom Dam in the early 1950s. The turbines, electrical generators, massive control panel and penstocks remain in place. It's a beautiful old building and the only 19th-century powerhouse that's still intact and open to the public. The woodland surroundings make a wonderful backdrop for a day of celebration that will include a carnival, boat rides, jazz on the lake and a picnic, all capped off with an evening light show. The two-day celebration begins on Saturday with a banquet and costume ball that runs from 6:30 p.m. to midnight at the Radisson Inn, located just down the street from the powerhouse. The remain-der of the events take place on Sunday. The historic Folsom Power-house is located at the intersection of Scott and Riley streets in the historic Gold Rush town of Folsom. A portion of the event will also be held in the nearby Negro Bar unit of Folsom Lake State Recre-ation Area, which is just across the grand old Rainbow Bridge, on the opposite side of Lake Natoma. There's a $2 parking fee to get into the park. As far as the weather this time of year, count on it being hot, generally in the 90s or higher.

For information, contact Folsom Lake State Recreation Area, 7806 Folsom-Auburn Road, Folsom, CA 95630; (916) 988-0205.

❖ ❖ ❖ ❖

Miners' Picnic
July 16, 1995 **❺** • 11 a.m. to 5 p.m.
(see #4 on map page 144)

In the old days of Empire Mine, located in historic Grass Valley, the miners and their families held an annual picnic to celebrate life.

That was a pretty significant thing, considering that the miners spent much of their lives deep underground chipping and blasting away the gold ore. And, unfortunately, too many of the miners never made it out alive. This Sunday event will reenact the old picnic, so there's fun for everyone. Games, musical entertainment, food and tours of the beautiful Bourne cottage and other mine buildings are all part of the day. To reach Empire Mine State Historic Park, take Highway 49 to Grass Valley and turn off on the Empire Street exit. Follow the signs to the park, which is about one mile from the freeway. There's a $5 fee per vehicle. It should be a very warm day, but there's plenty of shade in the park, which is more like a giant garden.

For information, contact Empire Mine State Historic Park; (916) 273-8522.

❖ ❖ ❖ ❖

15th Annual Folsom Heritage Quilt Show

August 8 to September 4, 1995
Wednesdays through Sundays, 11 a.m. to 4 p.m.
(see #7 on map page 144)

Quilt-making is a time-honored activity, once done out of necessity, now practiced more for pleasure. Each quilt is a masterful piece of art that showcases the skills of its creator. This annual display of heirloom quilts has become a must-attend event for both master and novice modern-day quilt makers. Some 5,000 people will stop by and admire these beautiful creations made of scrap pieces of cloth. It's held at the Folsom History Museum, 823 Sutter Street, Folsom, about 25 miles east of Sacramento, off US 50. There's no cost to get into the quilt show, but after seeing some of the beautiful work, it's liable to cost you a chunk of change to purchase that one thing that you just can't live without. Count on it being really hot, approaching triple digits.

For information, contact the Folsom Historical Society, 823 Sutter Street, Folsom, CA 95630; (916) 985-2707.

AUGUST

❖ ❖ ❖ ❖

Admission Day Celebration

September 9, 1995 • 11:30 a.m. to 1:30 p.m.

(see #11 on map page 144)

What better place to celebrate California's entry into the Union back in 1850 than on the steps of the Capitol? 1995 will mark California's 145th birthday with a giant birthday cake, ice cream, musical entertainment, and let us not forget the politicos who will give a few speeches. The best thing is that all the cake and ice cream are free and the speeches are short. During some years, the event is held on the north steps; on other years, the more popular and visible west steps serve as the stage for the party. It just depends whether or not a more important demonstration has accidentally been booked onto the west steps. California's Capitol is located on 10th Street between L and N streets. Count on it being pretty hot, but the Capitol is air-conditioned, so you can go inside to cool off. And going inside to take a look around is something that you should do anyway. The tours of the restored Capitol are free and the place really is quite impressive and beautiful.

For information, contact the California State Capitol Museum; (916) 324-0312.

U.S. National Handcar Races

September 16 & 17, 1995 **S**🕿

(see #11 on map page 144)

This is a competitive athletic team event that takes little training to participate in, but some real effort and a little luck to win. But even if you don't win, it's a lot of fun for everyone, competitors and audience alike. Teams are made up of five people: one starter who gives the railroad handcar a gigantic heaving push to get it going, then the four people onboard who begin pumping the handle up and down as frantically as they can in order to propel the vehicle down 300-yards of track to the finish line. More than 100 teams compete here in Old Sacramento each year, traveling from as far away as Texas and British Columbia. There are several categories, such as women, old men, and mixed and open classes, all designed to even things up a bit. Since most people don't have a handcar readily accessible for practice, practice days and times are set aside for all the teams. But pumping a railroad handcar isn't brain surgery, so don't despair if you've never tried it before. It's a lot of fun. Call a month or so in advance in order to get your team registered.

Old Sacramento State Historic Park is located on 2nd Street, between J and K streets, just off the Interstate 5 at the J Street exit. The train tracks where the races are held are located between Front Street and the Sacramento River.

For information, contact Gold Rush State Historic Parks; (916) 445-7373.

Marshall Gold Demonstration Day

October 7, 1995 • 10 a.m. to 4 p.m.
(see #6 on map page 144)

If you've ever wondered what it was like to live back in the heady days of the Gold Rush, here's the perfect chance to experience some of the day-to-day activities of those early Californians. There will be numerous demonstrations, from cooking and basket making to blacksmithing and weaving, to give you a glimpse back into the lives of the pioneers. They should have the sawmill working, so you can see what James Marshall was supposed to be doing for John Sutter before he went and found gold in the mill's tailrace, messing up Sutter's plans for expanding his personal empire in this land he called New Helvetia. All in all, the 1850s weren't a particularly fun time, at least if you lived in one of the small mining towns like Coloma. The work was hard, the days long and there were no guarantees that you would see anything even closely resembling retirement. But this event is fun, plus you'll get a chance to tour some of Coloma's historic buildings, which are usually closed to the public.

Coloma and Marshall Gold Discovery State Historic Park are both located on Highway 49, about halfway between Auburn and Placerville. There's a $5 fee to park your car in the park. The weather

OCTOBER

should be cool, but pleasant.

For information, contact Marshall Gold Discovery State Historic Park; (916) 622-3470.

❧ ❧ ❧ ❧

Acorn Day
October 14, 1995   • 10 a.m. to 4 p.m.
(see #11 on map page 144)

The California State Indian Museum becomes the Acorn Museum on this one day. Come and enjoy learning how acorns served as the primary food source for most of California's Native Americans, especially those in the Central Valley and Sierra Nevada foothills. You'll have an opportunity to help shell, grind and sift acorns, then leach the bitter tannin out of the meal before boiling up a basket full of tasty acorn mush. There will be other demonstrations including obsidian knapping, basket-making and storytelling to entertain the entire family. Native American crafts will be for sale, everything from baskets to arrowheads. The exhibits are generally set up adjacent to the museum. The California State Indian Museum is located at 2618 K Street in Sacramento, just off the Business 80 freeway. There's no entrance fee to the museum on Acorn Day. The weather will probably be cool, but comfortable.

For information, contact the California State Indian Museum; (916) 324-8112.

❧ ❧ ❧ ❧

 # Sutter's Fort Candlelight Tour
November 18, 1995
(see #11 on map page 144)

On most days of the year, if you want to tour Sutter's Fort, you must do it during daylight hours. That's fine, but long ago there was a nightlife, of sorts, back at the old fort. On this one night, you can join a docent dressed in 1840s clothing who will take you and a small group of other visitors on an evening lantern and candlelight tour of Sutter's Fort. There will be many historic characters on hand, or at least their docent spirits, who will be demonstrating what these early pioneers did in the evenings. The tour is capped off with coffee, cider and pie. It is expected that only about 150 people will attend, so this should be an intimate and entertaining look at the old fort. Sutter's Fort State Historic Park is located at 2701 L Street in Sacramento, just off the Business 80 freeway. The price of this very special evening program tentatively will be $10 per person, but call to confirm. Considering that winter will be fast approaching, the night could prove to be a real pioneering adventure if it rains.

For information, contact Sutter's Fort State Historic Park, (916) 445-4422.

Empire Mine Holiday Open House

November 24 & 25, 1995 [S] ☎ • Noon to 4 p.m.

(see #4 on map page 144)

Now, for some reason lots of folks insist on calling the Bourne home at Empire Mine a cottage, and by 19th-century San Francisco mansion standards, it probably is. But it's a beautiful home that sits on an expansive lawn, amidst gardens and wildflowers, and it gets a special holiday look this time of year. The cottage is open for tours and there are refreshments served and entertainers on hand to perform. You'll learn something about the history of the incredible underground gold mine next door that supported the lifestyle of the owners of the cottage. You can also walk part way down one of the old mine shafts and see some of the other buildings, such as the place where millions of dollars in gold was melted into ingots for transport to San Francisco and other points.

Empire Mine State Historic Park is located in Grass Valley, off Highway 49. Take the Empire Street exit and head up the hill about one mile to the park. The open house will cost $2 for adults and $1 for kids. The weather can be quite cool, possibly with rain.

For information, contact Empire Mine State Historic Park; (916) 273-8522.

Native American Film Festival and Arts Faire

November 24 to 26, 1995 • 8 a.m. to 4 p.m.
(see #11 on map page 144)

Learn more about the real lives of Native Americans through both historic and contemporary films. These are *not* the typical early Hollywood trash that showed Plains tribes attacking settlers in Northern California or dumb chiefs wandering around muttering "How." There will also be Native American craftspeople here to demonstrate their skills and sell various crafts items. The films are educational and the faire is a fun chance to see some Native Americans working at skills that were perfected a few thousand years ago.

The California State Indian Museum is located at 2618 K Street in Sacramento, just off the Business 80 freeway. There is no cost for the program. The weather will probably be cool, but the films are shown inside the museum, so it doesn't matter what's going on outside.

For information, contact the California State Indian Museum; (916) 324-8112.

❀ ❀ ❀ ❀

Miner's Christmas

December 2, 3, 9 & 10, 1995 • 10 a.m. to 4 p.m.
(see #15 on map page 145)

Santa will be making an early arrival for the kids in Columbia on two weekends, while on a more historic note, a few miners will be sitting around a campfire telling tales about the riches they hope to reap from the gold-filled hills around the old Gold Rush town. The miners will also be selling coffee, cider and hot roasted chestnuts, which you can enjoy while carolers keep you entertained throughout the day. You can sample the results of candy cane-making, ride a stage, and visit some of the town's shops for a little Christmas shopping. And if your hands can stand the cold water, you, or better yet your kids, can try panning for gold. The flume that carries the water is salted with flakes of real gold in the sand, but it also has large chunks of iron pyrite, better known as "fool's gold."

Since most kids haven't mastered gold panning, they almost always end up with hunks of fool's gold and are as excited as you would be if you found the real thing. Columbia State Historic Park is located about three miles north of Sonora, just off Highway 49. There's no cost to get into the park, but it will cost you a few bucks for some of the special programs, like panning for gold. The weather will probably be cold, but tolerable if you bundle up a little.

For information, contact Columbia State Historic Park; (209) 532-4301 or (209) 532-0150.

Governor's Mansion Christmas Memories
December 2 & 4, 1995 • 10 a.m. to 4 p.m.
(see #11 on map page 144)

What was Christmas in the Governor's Mansion like when Ronald Reagan, Pat Brown or any of the state's other governors and their families lived in this beautiful Victorian mansion? Well, since 1903, the mansion has served all the governors and their families as home until Ronald Reagan became Governor and promptly moved himself and Nancy to another residence, thus closing a part of California's history. But now that history is open to the public, and what better time than the Christmas season to see the house with its grand and beautiful Christmas tree and other seasonal spangles. Docents in period costume will be in each of the main rooms, offering intimate looks into the history of the house and the famous people who lived here. There will be choirs singing and continuous walk-through tours, including a stop in the kitchen where fresh-baked Christmas cookies will be served.

Governor's Mansion State Historic Park is located at 16th and H streets in Sacramento. There's a fee of $2 for adults and $1 for kids. The weather will probably be cold, possibly with fog or rain.

For information, contact the Governor's Mansion State Historic Park; (916) 323-3047.

DECEMBER

Stanford Mansion Christmas Fest

December 9, 1995 **$** *(see #11 on map page 144)*

This is a grand gala holiday celebration in an old mansion. There have been plans to restore it to its previous grandeur for years, but nothing has been done yet. Once owned by Leland Stanford, who was partially responsible for building the western half of the transcontinental railroad, the old Victorian is now a state historic park. This is a special pre-Christmas celebration hosted by docents wearing period costumes. It will feature a chance to try your hand at traditional Victorian parlor games. Christmas crafts will be part of the fun, and you'll hear period music while participating in a little ballroom dancing.

The Stanford Mansion State Historic Park is located at 8th and N streets in downtown Sacramento. The Christmas Fest is free. The weather will probably be cold, with fog or rain, but as you're inside, it doesn't matter too much.

For information, contact Stanford Mansion State Historic Park; (916) 323-0575.

✤ ✤ ✤ ✤

Christmas In Coloma

December 10, 1995 **$** · 9 a.m. to 4 p.m. *(see #6 on map page 144)*

Drive over to where James Marshall discovered gold at Sutter's sawmill, located beside the American River, and see how these early pioneers celebrated Christmas. Well, actually, most of this small Gold Rush town, including the reconstructed sawmill, is slightly different than it used to be, but when Mr. and Mrs. Claus arrive, the kids won't care much. There's also an opportunity to experience a real feeling for the Old West with rides on a Wells Fargo stage, buggy rides, and a living history told by docents wearing period costumes and doing the things that people did 140 years ago. There will be music, dancers, a town ball and lots of things for kids to do, including playing in real snow, which will probably have to be imported since it seldom snows much in Coloma. This is a really popular day in the park, with about 7,000 people coming out to enjoy the season. Dress warmly, because it will probably be cold.

Coloma is located on Highway 49, about halfway between Placerville and Auburn. There's a $5 fee per vehicle to enter the park.

For information, contact Marshall Gold Discovery State Historic Park; (916) 622-3470.

Gold Country Seasonal Hikes & Programs

The Acorn Eaters: Tribal Customs in California

February 1 to April 30, 1995 • Wednesdays through Sundays,
11 a.m. to 4 p.m.
(see #7 on map page 144)

This three-month celebration of California Native Americans brings not only an artifact and photographic exhibition, but also features Native American folk artists demonstrating a variety of ancient skills. For thousands of years, California's Native Americans survived each day by using what nature offered. Modern-day Native Americans will entertain you with traditional dances and storytelling sessions, as well as demonstrations of basket weaving, food preparation and clothing design and manufacture. If you're willing, you'll have a chance to try your own hand at basket weaving and acorn grinding. During the three-month stay, there will also be an outreach program to schools which will include many of the same demonstrations that are performed in the museum.

The Folsom History Museum is located at 823 Sutter Street in the historic Gold Rush town of Folsom, about 25 miles east of Sacramento, off US 50. There is no cost for the programs. The weather will range from cold, rainy and foggy in February to warm and sunny in April.

For information, contact Folsom Historic Society, 823 Sutter Street, Folsom, CA 95630; (916) 985-2707.

Lava Cap Mine Tour

Saturdays: third in May, first in June, third in September
and second in October **S**✐ • 10:30 a.m. to noon
(see #2 on map page 144)

If you are a Gold Country historian or a photographer looking
for unique photographic opportunities of a hard-rock gold mine,
then this easy hike is just your ticket. Lava Cap Mine owner Steve
Elder will lead this special hike that covers about two miles. The
mine is currently being restored to its early glory, with most of the
work based on a 1939 documentary about the mine and the men
who made their livings, and sometimes died, in its deep tunnels.
You'll get a chance to see the movie and then wander around the old
mine works, where you can see the only head frame still standing in
Nevada County. The hike is limited to 20 people, so call for reservations. Call for the date and meeting place, which will probably be in
Nevada City, located about 28 miles north of Auburn on Highway
49. The mine tour will cost about $22 per person. The weather
should be warm and sunny for all of the programs.

For information, contact the Nevada County Land Trust, P.O.
Box 2088, Nevada City, CA 95959; (916) 265-0430.

❀ ❀ ❀ ❀

Safari Air Gold Country Flyovers

Generally Saturdays: third in May, first in June, third in September
and second in October **S**✐ • 10:30 a.m. to noon
(see #2 on map page 144)

Take one of these half-hour flights and see the Nevada County
Gold Country from a whole new perspective. Get a bird's-eye view
of the historic old gold mines and the roads and trails that still lead
to them. Considering all the rivers, lakes and streams, you'll undoubtedly discover some new places to prospect for gold, hook a fish
or hike, depending upon your interests. This is a small plane, limited
to just three people on each flight. You really need to call ahead for
reservations on this one. Call to confirm your reservation, date and

SEASONAL

meeting place, which will probably be near Nevada City, located about 28 miles north of Auburn on Highway 49. The flyovers cost $35 per person. The weather should be pretty good, so the flights should all be easy to take, even for those whose stomachs get queasy when little planes start bouncing around too much.

For information, contact the Nevada County Land Trust, P.O. Box 2088, Nevada City, CA 95959; (916) 265-0430.

Consumnes River Preserve Nature Walk

Most Saturdays and Sundays • [S] ☎ Call for the start time

(see #13 on map page 144)

One of the few remaining valley oak, riparian forest and wetland habitats in California is being preserved with the help of the Bureau of Land Management, Ducks Unlimited, The Nature Conservancy, the Wildlife Conservation Board, Sacramento County Parks and Recreation and the Department of Fish and Game. The Consumnes River is the only major river that remains free-flowing into the valley, unrestrained by dams. The surrounding land is a lush and beautiful testament to how the Central Valley appeared before the advent of dams, levees and drained wetlands. Docents lead nature walks through this rare habitat, which is home to wintering waterfowl and some 200 species of birds and other wildlife.

The preserve is located 30 miles south of Sacramento just off Interstate 5. Take the Twin Cities Road exit east to Franklin Boulevard, then go south to the Consumnes River Preserve Trailhead parking area, which is on the left. There's no charge for the hikes. Count on the weather being hot in summer, with cold, rain or fog in winter.

For information, contact Consumnes River Preserve, 13501 Franklin Boulevard, Galt, CA 95632; (916) 684-2816.

Chapter 5

Great Outdoor Events of California's San Francisco Bay Area

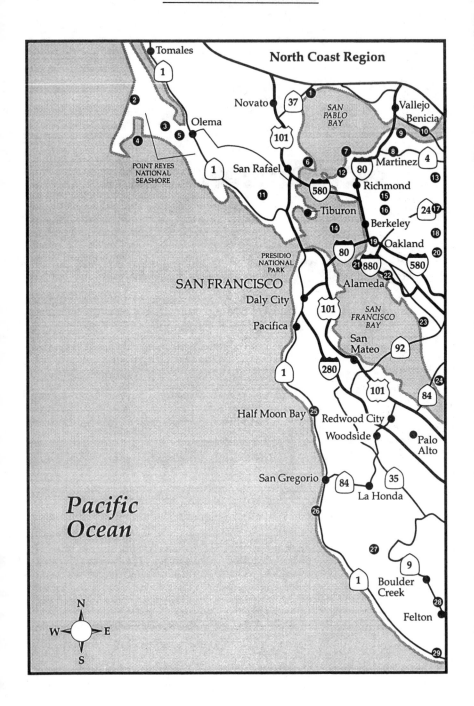

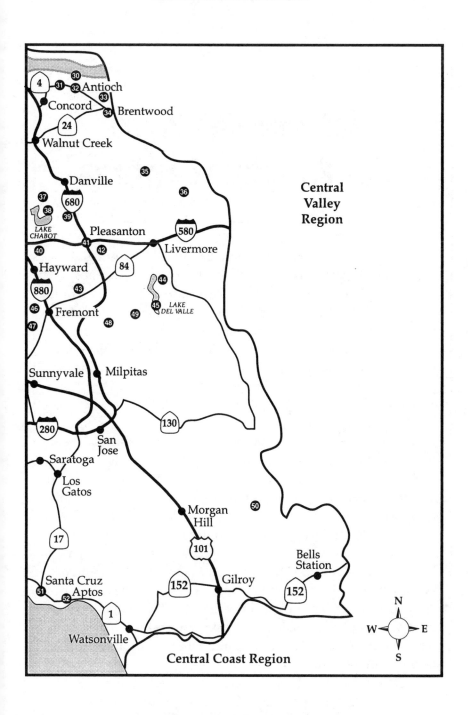

Introduction to the San Francisco Bay Area

Think about San Francisco and the Golden Gate Bridge, Fisherman's Wharf and Alcatraz probably first come to mind. Take a moment and explore a little further—you'll soon discover a world of natural wonders that most people leave blissfully untouched. Actually, many Bay Area residents are very much aware of the natural beauty that surrounds them. They jealously protect the remaining open lands, while spending as much time as possible enjoying the trails, wildlife and fresh air of these state, regional and federal lands.

Come blasting into the Bay Area on one of the many freeways and you really won't see much of the wetlands and mountains, unless, of course, you take your eyes off the road, taking the chance of playing bumper tag with the thousands of vehicles that surround you. Get off the freeway, temporarily skipping downtown Oakland and San Francisco, and head over to Marin County's Mount Tamalpais. Drive to the uppermost parking lot on Mount Tam, get out of your car and hike the remaining short distance to the trail that circumscribes the very top of the mountain. From here, you have the best possible opportunity to see the expansiveness and complexity of the mountains, hills, bays and wetlands that have come together to create the greater San Francisco Bay Area. You'll see huge bridges, giant seagoing tankers and towering skyscrapers rendered tiny and relatively insignificant when compared with the surrounding grandeur of Mother Nature.

Set among natural landmarks such as towering redwoods, isolated bays and teeming wetlands, the San Francisco Bay Area

SAN FRANCISCO BAY AREA EVENTS

includes lands south to Half Moon Bay and Santa Cruz, north to Point Reyes National Seashore and, to the east, East Bay Regional Parks and Mount Diablo and Henry Coe state parks. It's a vast area, one that takes a couple of lifetimes to explore in its entirety. Join some of the guided programs listed here and you'll quickly discover new parks, new trails and new relationships, both with people and with the best nature has to offer.

CALIFORNIA'S GREAT OUTDOOR EVENTS   183

Santa Cruz Fungus Fair

January 7 & 8, 1995 • 10 a.m. to 4 p.m.
(see #51 on map page 181)

This is not your typical fair: There are no wild rides, no obnoxious barking carnies, no overpriced greasy food. Just a bunch of fungi, which your dictionary describes as molds, mildews, mushrooms, rusts and smuts, all of which are parasites making their livings on other living and dead organisms. Sounds really appetizing, right? The Fungus Fair, however, just sticks to showing mushrooms, about 150 different species of them. If you've ever thought about exploring the wooded hills and valleys during spring when wild mushrooms are at their growing peak, then this is an opportunity to see what the good ones look like. You'll also learn the things to look for in order to identify the poisonous spore-puffers in the flesh. The fair is held at the Santa Cruz Museum of Natural History. There's a suggested museum donation of $3 for adults and $2 for children.

For information, contact the Santa Cruz Museum of Natural History, 1305 East Cliff Drive, Santa Cruz, CA 95602; (408) 429-3773.

✤ ✤ ✤ ✤

Sealabration

January 28, 1995 **S** 🖊
(see #26 on map page 180)

Año Nuevo State Reserve is home to a couple thousand elephant seals, magnificently huge beasts that drag themselves out onto the sand for their annual birthing and mating rites. The annual Sealabration is a fundraising event sponsored by the San Mateo Coast Natural History Association, with the proceeds going to further build and develop the interpretive center and ongoing research programs at the reserve. There will be special tours among the elephant seals, which by this time should have begun to give birth. Also, you will witness the ever-present battles between the males to establish and maintain their harems. Their trumpeting is awesome and the battles occasionally bloody. Be ready to move quickly should one of the big bulls decide to head your direction. Usually about 400 people show up for this event, so call early to reserve your space. Regular tours of the elephant seals, which begin in December and end in March, can be booked by calling MISTIX at (800) 444-7275.

Año Nuevo is just off Highway 1, about 27 miles south of Half Moon Bay. Organizers have announced a $5 fee for Sealabration, but it may be more. Expect cold, wet and windy weather and come prepared for it. Of course, you may get lucky and find the sun shining brightly and only light winds.

For information, contact Año Nuevo State Reserve; (415) 879-2025.

✤ ✤ ✤ ✤

Annual Monarch Butterfly Migration Festival

February 11, 1995 • 10 a.m. to 4 p.m.
(see #51 on map page 181)

It's an absolutely incredible feeling to walk among thousands of fluttering, beautiful orange butterflies. There are several areas around California's central coast where monarchs gather in large numbers, but this is one of the better locations to see and photograph these wonderful creatures. If you don't make it on this day, get here soon after, because the monarchs will head out quickly, having already spent about four or five months vacationing here in Santa Cruz. The celebration isn't really just for butterflies, although they are the most obvious reason for it. Out in the ocean, only a couple hundred yards away from the eucalyptus groves favored by the monarchs, gray whales are passing by on their way south. Also, among the trees or out on the beach, you can see many of the birds that migrate through the Santa Cruz area. There are tours led by state park staff and volunteers, skits, music and food.

The festival and the butterflies will be at Natural Bridges State Beach, which is located at the end of West Cliff Drive in Santa Cruz. Entrance to the park is $6 per vehicle, although you can park outside the park for free, which you might have to do anyway if you get here in mid-afternoon; the parking lot tends to fill up. Come prepared for cool weather, and if a winter storm is passing through, be prepared for rain.

For more information, contact the Santa Cruz Visitors Bureau, 701 Front Street, Santa Cruz, CA 95060; (408) 425-1234 or (800) 833-3494. You may also contact Natural Bridges State Beach; (408) 423-4609.

❖ ❖ ❖ ❖

Spring Dog Walk

March 4, 1995 **$**🦮 • 9:30 a.m. to noon

(see #10 on map page 180)

The Spring Dog Walk along Carquinez Strait is the name given to this unique naturalist-led hike. Seldom are dogs allowed on hikes, let alone invited. You do have to keep Bowser on a leash, but you and your dog both will have the chance to enjoy the four-mile hike on the bluffs overlooking the strait. There should be plenty of wildflowers and songbirds, so bring binoculars if you have them. You'll be gone about four hours on this hike. It leaves at 9:30 a.m., so be sure to bring food and water enough for both you and your dog. The walk is usually held on the first Saturday in March and meets at Carquinez Strait Regional Shoreline in Benicia. Registration is required.

For information, contact Carquinez Strait Regional Shoreline; (510) 757-2620.

❖ ❖ ❖ ❖

Railroad History Tour of San Francisco Bay National Wildlife Refuge

Early March Saturday **$**🦮 • 1 p.m. to 4 p.m.

(see #24 on map page 180)

Trace the path of the South Pacific Coast Railroad that once hosted steam locomotives chugging through the salt marshes around San Francisco Bay. This is a van tour limited to 13 people, so you'll need to call in advance for information and reservations. Bring your binoculars if you're interested in birds, because there are plenty to be seen. To reach the San Francisco Bay National Wildlife Refuge Visitor Center, from Interstate 880 or US 101, take Highway 84 toward the east end of the Dumbarton Bridge. Take the Thornton Avenue exit and drive south for one mile. The refuge is on the right side. Follow the road to the stop sign and turn left into the parking lot.

For information, contact the San Francisco Bay Wildlife Society, P.O. Box 524, Newark, CA 94560-0524; (510) 792-4275.

❋ ❋ ❋ ❋

San Francisco Bay Ghost Town

Early March Sunday **S**(📷) • 2:30 p.m. to 3:30 p.m.
(see #24 on map page 180)

Yes, out in the bay's salt marshes, the old town of Drawbridge was once a thriving community. Its exciting history and inevitable decline can be seen in a slide show. Meet at the San Francisco Bay National Wildlife Refuge's Environmental Education Center for this one-hour program. While at the center you'll also be able to learn more about the wildlife refuge and the animals that call this wetland home. To reach the center from Interstate 880 near Milpitas, exit on Highway 237 toward Alviso (Mountain View), then turn north onto Zanker Road. Continue for two miles and make a sharp right turn at Grand Boulevard into the center.

For information, contact the San Francisco Bay Wildlife Society, P.O. Box 524, Newark, CA 94560-0524; (510) 792-4275.

❋ ❋ ❋ ❋

Old Ways Workshop: Edible, Useful and Medicinal Plants

March 4, 1995 **S**(📷) • 9:30 a.m. to 4 p.m.
(see #47 on map page 181)

For thousands of years, the Native Americans who inhabited the hills we now call the East Bay lived on what they found in the wilds of nature. Come learn what California's earliest inhabitants knew, what plants they used, what animals they hunted and what streams they fished. Your day will start in the field searching the hills, valleys and marshes for plants that sustained Native American families and will provide part of your lunch. But these native plants provided more than food. They were used for basket weaving, fire making and building shelters and boats. Near the end of the workshop, you'll spend some time making a soaproot brush. Bring your lunch, a pocket knife and water. You must register in advance for the workshop. It will be held in Coyote Hills Regional Park. You must be at least 12 years of age. The fee is $10. To reach Coyote Hills from Fremont, take Interstate 880 (Nimitz Freeway) to the Decoto Road/ Highway 84 exit and head west to the Thornton Avenue/Paseo Padre Parkway exit. Turn north and go one mile to Patterson Ranch Road, then turn left and drive into the park. There's a $3 parking fee on weekends and holidays.

For information, contact Coyote Hills Regional Park, 8000 Patterson Ranch Road, Fremont, CA 94555; (510) 795-9385.

Trail Maintenance Workshops

March 4, 1995 [S] ☎ • 9 a.m. to 3 p.m.

(see #19 on map page 180)

Trails require constant maintenance if they are to remain safe and usable; that maintenance requires a lot of people power that can't be handled by park staff alone. So come on out and attend one or all of the workshops that will instruct you in techniques for, and the safe and best use of tools in, keeping trails well maintained. You'll learn about trail drainage and erosion control, which includes construction of water bars, low water crossings, how to check dams, culverts and riprap. There'll be trail brushing and plant pruning lessons that show how to keep a trail clear of vegetation. Bring lunch, and wear gloves and sturdy shoes or boots. Call to check on the specific workshops offered, if you have a particular area of interest, whether it be erosion control and drainage, trail brushing or constructing new trails. The workshops are scheduled to meet at the Skyline Training Center in Oakland.

For information, contact the East Bay Regional Parks District, 2950 Peralta Oaks Court, Oakland, CA 94605-0381; (510) 636-1684.

California Least Tern Habitat Restoration

March 4 & 5, 1995 • 9 a.m. to 3 p.m.

(see #23 on map page 180)

California's endangered species can use all the help they can get. The California least tern nests on sandy beaches, some of the most popular people-areas along California's coast. With the competition from builders and bathers, the least terns' opportunities to find undisturbed nesting sites are limited. One of the areas where the terns have a fighting chance for survival is at Hayward Shoreline Regional Park. You can help create additional nesting sites and materials by hauling 20-pound buckets of sand and shells and dumping them in areas above the high-tide line. Anyone is welcome to come on down and help out. The Hayward Shoreline Interpretive Center is located at the end of Breakwater Avenue in Hayward.

For information, contact the Hayward Shoreline Interpretive Center; (510) 783-1066.

Black Diamond Explorers—Flowers

March 10, 1995 • 3:30 p.m. to 5 p.m.

(see #33 on map page 181)

This after-school program is designed to help youngsters ages 9 to 11 explore the trails of the Black Diamond Mines, an old reclaimed coal-mining area. Wildflowers and animals will be the topic of the one-and-a-half-hour program. Learn to tell the differences among the Bay Area's wildflowers and discover a world of wildlife that you may not even have realized existed so close to home. Advance registration is required and there is a small fee. To reach

Black Diamond Mines Regional Preserve, take Highway 4 east into Antioch and take the Somersville Road exit. Drive south about three miles to the park entrance.

For information, contact Black Diamond Mines Regional Preserve, 5175 Somersville Road, Antioch, CA 94509; (510) 757-2620.

✿ ✿ ✿ ✿

Black Diamond Mines Sketch Hike

March 11, 1995 $ ⏱ • 9 a.m. to 2:30 p.m.
(see #33 on map page 181)

No matter what your age, if you've got a talent for drawing or even an interest in trying your hand at drawing, why not spend a spring day in one of the East Bay Regional Parks District's most beautiful parks? You'll join others at all levels of skill for a short hike with plenty of stops for sketching the scenery. While walking and drawing, there will be talks by the accompanying naturalist about the park's natural and cultural history. There's a $5 fee for the hike through Black Diamond Mines Regional Preserve and advance registration is required. To reach Black Diamond Mines, take Highway 4 east into Antioch and take the Somersville Road exit. Drive south about three miles to the park entrance.

For information, contact Black Diamond Mines Regional Preserve, 5175 Somersville Road, Antioch, CA 94509; (510) 757-2620.

✿ ✿ ✿ ✿

Fishing from Antioch Pier

March 11, 1995 $ ⏱ • 1 p.m. to 2:30 p.m.
(see #32 on map page 181)

Grab your fishing pole and learn some of the tricks of successful ocean-pier angling. If you don't have your own fishing gear, there will be some on hand to borrow. You'll learn about the different fish that live in the Delta and how to rig your tackle to catch them. If you're 16 years old or older, bring your fishing license for this East

Bay Regional Parks District program. Preregistration is required before you can attend this early spring program. The cost is only about $3 per angler. It will be held at Antioch Regional Shoreline.

For information, contact Antioch Regional Shoreline; (510) 757-2620.

❖ ❖ ❖ ❖

Black Diamond Explorers—Birds

March 11, 1995 Ⓢ ☎ • 3:30 p.m. to 5 p.m.

(see #33 on map page 181)

Another after-school program for the 9- to 11-year-old crowd is a one-and-a-half-hour exploration of the Black Diamond Mines Regional Preserve. This time, birds are the focus of the program. Everyone gets to make a bird feeder to take home so you can continue the exploration and observation of our feathered friends on your own. There's a small fee and advance registration is required. To reach Black Diamond Mines Regional Preserve, take Highway 4 east into Antioch and take the Somersville Road exit. Drive south about three miles to the park entrance.

For information, contact Black Diamond Mines Regional Preserve, 5175 Somersville Road, Antioch, CA 94509; (510) 757-2620.

❖ ❖ ❖ ❖

Family Fishing and Lake Tour Adventure

March 12, 1995 Ⓢ ☎ • 8 a.m. to noon

(see #38 on map page 181)

This is a great family outing where kids and parents alike can learn more about fish and how to catch them. It's also more than a simple fishing trip. The boat ride will take you through an area rich in both natural and cultural history, and your guide will tell you all about it. But it's not all learning. You'll also get a chance to try all this newfound knowledge by trying to catch a fish or two. Bring your fishing poles, lunch and something to drink. Space is limited, so you must register in advance. The fee will be about $8 for adults and $6 for kids. The program is usually held around the second Sunday in March at Lake Chabot, which is east of San Leandro.

For information, contact Garin Regional Park, 1320 Garin Avenue, Hayward, CA 94544; (510) 795-9385.

❖ ❖ ❖ ❖

Beginners Birdwatching Workshop

Second weekend in March **S** 🖉
Friday 7 p.m. to 9 p.m.; Saturday 8 a.m. to noon
(see #48 on map page 181)

If you're still searching for a non-impact, environmentally safe, inexpensive and relaxing pastime, you might just think about joining the millions of people around the world who go birdwatching regularly. There are thousands of species of birds—some are small and basic brown, while others shine like iridescent rainbows. They have voices as melodious as a symphony orchestra and as raucous as fighting, screaming cats. Join this two-day seminar and learn where to look, how to look and what to listen for when out there trying to identify these flighty creatures. A slide show, handouts and study skins will all be used to get you started on a lifetime of enjoyment. The workshop is designed for complete novices, so don't worry that you'll be the only person here who doesn't know the difference between a scrub jay and a blue bird.

The fee is $12 for adults and $6 for kids. The program will be held at the Coyote Hills Regional Park Visitor Center. To reach Coyote Hills from Fremont, take Interstate 880 (Nimitz Freeway) to the Decoto Road/Highway 84 exit and head west to the Thornton Avenue/Paseo Padre Parkway exit. Turn north and go one mile to Patterson Ranch Road, then turn left and drive into the park. There's a $3 parking fee on weekends and holidays.

For information, contact Coyote Hills Regional Park, 8000 Patterson Ranch Road, Fremont, CA 94555; (510) 795-9385.

❖ ❖ ❖ ❖

Wildlife Stories

Mid-March Saturday [S] ☎ • 2 p.m. to 3 p.m.
(see #24 on map page 180)

This program was held in 1994 and will hopefully be repeated in 1995. If it is, expect it to feature professional wildlife photographers such as Moose Peterson or Joe Galkowski, who will come and share their beautiful images of California's diverse wildlife. Their slide shows will focus on what you can see around the San Francisco Bay. And if you're a budding shutterbug, you'll have an opportunity to see what it takes to be a professional photographer and sell your images to leading magazines.

To reach the San Francisco Bay National Wildlife Refuge Visitor Center, from Interstate 880 or US 101, take Highway 84 toward the east end of the Dumbarton Bridge. Take the Thornton Avenue exit and drive south for one mile. The refuge is on the right side of the road. Follow the road to the stop sign and turn left into the parking lot.

For information, contact the San Francisco Bay Wildlife Society, P.O. Box 524, Newark, CA 94560-0524; (510) 792-4275.

Star Struck

Mid-March Saturday [S] ☎ • 7:30 p.m. to 9:30 p.m.
(see #24 on map page 180)

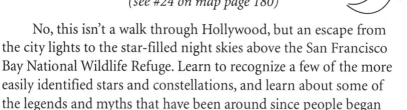

No, this isn't a walk through Hollywood, but an escape from the city lights to the star-filled night skies above the San Francisco Bay National Wildlife Refuge. Learn to recognize a few of the more easily identified stars and constellations, and learn about some of the legends and myths that have been around since people began looking at the night sky. Bring warm clothing and binoculars. To reach the San Francisco Bay National Wildlife Refuge Visitor Center, from Interstate 880 or US 101, take Highway 84 toward the east end of the Dumbarton Bridge. Take the Thornton Avenue exit and drive south for one mile. The refuge is on the right side. Follow the road to the stop sign and turn left into the parking lot.

For information, contact the San Francisco Bay Wildlife Society, P.O. Box 524, Newark, CA 94560-0524; (510) 792-4275.

✤ ✤ ✤ ✤

Go Fly a Kite

March 18, 1995 [S] ☎ • 2 p.m. to 4:30 p.m.

(see #47 on map page 181)

Considering that men and women didn't fly until this century, it seems a little strange that people have known the secrets of flying kites for over 2,000 years. They were used in celebrations, for scientific investigation (remember Ben Franklin's experiments with lightning?), for military reasons and, of course, just for fun. Now, it's unlikely that you'll be flying one of those three-quarter-ton monsters that are launched in a Japanese kite festival each year, but you'll have an opportunity to make and fly something a little more manageable in size. You'll learn a little of the history of kite flying and have a lot of fun. Bring the kids, because this is meant for everyone. The fee is only $5 and the program will be held at Coyote Hills Regional Park. Advance registration is required. To reach Coyote Hills from Fremont, take Interstate 880 (Nimitz Freeway) to the Decoto Road/Highway 84 exit and head west to the Thornton Avenue/Paseo Padre Parkway exit. Turn north and go one mile to Patterson Ranch Road, then turn left and drive into the park. There's a $3 parking fee on weekends and holidays.

For information, contact Coyote Hills Regional Park, 8000 Patterson Ranch Road, Fremont, CA 94555; (510) 795-9385.

✤ ✤ ✤ ✤

Early Welcome-to-Spring Bicycle Ride Around Coyote Hills

March 18, 1995 [S] ☎ • 10 a.m. to 11:30 a.m.

(see #47 on map page 181)

Following a long, cold and dreary winter, it's time to welcome spring back with an invigorating bike ride through the greening hills of the East Bay. Wildflowers, wildlife and an easy wild ride are all to be had on this hour-and-a-half jaunt with family, old friends and maybe some new friends. The meeting place is Coyote Hills Regional Park. This is a free ride and designed for all ages, so bring the kids. To reach Coyote Hills from Fremont, take Interstate 880 (Nimitz Freeway) to the Decoto Road/Highway 84 exit and head west to the Thornton Avenue/Paseo Padre Parkway exit. Turn north and go one mile to Patterson Ranch Road, then turn left and drive into the park. There's a $3 parking fee on weekends and holidays.

For information, contact Coyote Hills Regional Park, 8000 Patterson Ranch Road, Fremont, CA 94555; (510) 795-9385.

❖ ❖ ❖ ❖

Pleasanton Ridge Hike
March 18, 1995 **$** *() · 9:30 a.m. to 5 p.m.*
(see #44 on map page 181)

The hike will cover 15 miles over some pretty steep terrain in Del Valle Regional Park. All ages are welcome to join this all-day hike, as long as you're in pretty good hiking shape. There should be some great scenery and great views from the ridge. Birds and other wildlife are almost always seen, and the first budding wildflowers should be poking their heads out, providing that the spring weather has been cooperative. To get to Del Valle Regional Park, take Interstate 580 to Livermore and exit on North Livermore Road. Go south on North Livermore, which turns into South Livermore and then Tesla Road. After about two miles, turn left onto Mines Road. Continue about four miles, then turn right onto Del Valle Road, which leads to the park entrance and the Rocky Ridge Visitor Center. There's a $4 parking fee.

For information, contact Del Valle Regional Park, 7000 Del Valle Road, Livermore, CA 94550; (510) 373-0332.

MARCH

Wildflower Walk in Morgan Territory

March 19, 1995 **$** 🖊 • 10 a.m. to 3 p.m.
(see #36 on map page 181)

The Wildflower Walk in Morgan Territory is actually a short hike that covers about five miles. While the spring wildflower show is always dependent upon spring rains which are sometimes few and far between, there's always something of color coming up through the green spring grasses on Mount Diablo. Bring water and lunch; don't forget your hiking boots, because you'll be exploring the valley bottoms and the nearby hilltops with an East Bay Regional Parks District naturalist. Call to confirm the date and the meeting place.

For information, contact Black Diamond Mines Regional Preserve, 5175 Somersville Road, Antioch, CA 94509; (510) 757-2620.

❖ ❖ ❖ ❖

Lake Chabot Kids Charity Fishing Derby

March 20 to 24, 1995 **$** 🖊 • 5 a.m. to 3 p.m.
(see #38 on map page 181)

This is a fun way to help raise money for the Haven of Living Water, an East Bay charity that provides food for the area's homeless. The derby is open to all kids, ages 12 and younger. Prizes will be awarded for different categories, such as biggest fish, smallest fish and most fish caught. The entry fee is $2 or two cans of food, which allows you to participate in as much or as little of the event as you desire. You can fish during regular fishing hours, with the last weigh-in finishing up at 3 p.m. at the marina.

For information, contact the East Bay Regional Parks District's Lake Chabot Marina; (510) 582-2198.

❖ ❖ ❖ ❖

Women Enjoying the Great Outdoors Seminar Series

March 24, 1995 **S** *(/)* • 6 p.m. to 9 p.m.

(see #49 on map page 181)

"Women on Common Ground: An Equinox Ramble and Campout Brainstorm" is the real title of this program sponsored by the East Bay Regional Parks District. The program was offered in 1994 and hopefully will be continued in 1995. The program is a series of workshops that explore ways that women can reclaim their right to enjoy open parklands on their own. If fears for your personal safety have kept you away from park trails, either during the day, for late evening strolls or all-night camping trips, then you really should join a couple of these seminars designed for women. The first program will be held in late March and will be an evening walk along Alameda Creek in Sunol-Ohlone Regional Wilderness. If all goes well, a camping trip may be held on or near the spring equinox in April. A third seminar will probably meet again in the fall. While not required, this first program is recommended for any woman wishing to go on the equinox camping trip. It's also for women who can't or don't want to attend the campout, but still want information about what they can do to take back their parklands. Registration is required and there will be a $7.50 fee.

For information, contact the East Bay Regional Parks District; (510) 862-2244.

❖ ❖ ❖ ❖

Marsh Creek Trail on Two Wheels

March 25, 1995 **S** *(/)* • 1 p.m. to 3 p.m.

(see #33 on map page 181)

No, this isn't done on a motorcycle, speeding around corners on two wheels. It's a casual bicycle ride on the quiet side of Contra Costa County's Marsh Creek. There's a good chance that this may be a first-time ride on this trail for most folks, since this a relatively new trail, which runs between Oakley and Brentwood. You must preregister; when you do so, get directions to the Marsh Creek

Regional Trail, where the tour begins.

For information, contact Black Diamond Mines Regional Preserve, 5175 Somersville Road, Antioch, CA 94509; (510) 757-2620.

✤ ✤ ✤ ✤

Rose Hill Cemetery Workday

March 25, 1995 • 9 a.m. to noon
(see #33 on map page 181)

Volunteers are an important part of any park program. Want to help? Bring work gloves and help the park staff at Black Diamond Mines preserve the historic Rose Hill Cemetery. The cemetery served the needs of protestants, mostly Welsh, from several early coal-mining communities that thrived in the Black Diamond Mines area from about 1860 until the turn of the century. Among those who found a final resting place in the cemetery were miners who succumbed to the life-threatening dangers of their profession. The work program is generally held during one Saturday in March and another during April, but call to confirm. Bring water. To reach Black Diamond Mines Regional Preserve, take Highway 4 east into Antioch and take the Somersville Road exit. Drive south about three miles to the park entrance.

For information, contact Black Diamond Mines Regional Preserve, 5175 Somersville Road, Antioch, CA 94509; (510) 757-2620.

✤ ✤ ✤ ✤

Full Moon Prowl at Pleasanton Ridge

March 27, 1995 • 7 p.m. to 9:30 p.m.
(see #44 on map page 181)

A full moon prowl on Pleasanton Ridge at Del Valle Regional Park is a different way to experience the great outdoors. Most wildlife is nocturnal; at the very least, critters stay hidden during the main portion of the day when people are most prone to prowling about. The hike will cover only about three miles and begins with an ascent through the forests to the ridgetops. You'll wander through rocky creek beds and over open land, all the time looking and listening for foxes, coyotes, owls and opossums. It will probably get pretty cool and you might get wet and muddy by the time the hike finishes at about 9:30 p.m., so dress accordingly. Bring a good flashlight with fresh batteries. You must register in advance. This free hike is open to anyone who is eight years old or older. To get to Del Valle Regional Park, take Interstate 580 to Livermore and exit on North Livermore Road. Go south on North Livermore, which turns into South Livermore and then Tesla Road. After about two miles, turn left onto Mines Road. Continue about four miles, then turn right onto Del Valle Road, which leads to the park entrance and the Rocky Ridge Visitor Center. There's a $4 parking fee.

For information, contact Del Valle Regional Park, 7000 Del Valle Road, Livermore, CA 94550, (510) 373-0332; or Sunol-Ohlone Regional Wilderness, (510) 862-2244.

APRIL

❖ ❖ ❖ ❖

Journey to the Mouth of the Salinas River
Early April **S** 🖋 • 10 a.m. to 2 p.m.
(see #24 on map page 180)

Here's an opportunity for those of you who are accustomed to the water traffic, sediment and pollution problems facing San Francisco Bay to explore the relatively pristine Salinas River National Wildlife Refuge. The hike begins with a carpool from the San Francisco Bay National Wildlife Refuge to where the Salinas River empties into Monterey Bay, just north of the community of Marina. Most people pass over the river estuary at 60 miles-per-hour while traveling down US 101 and miss this window on nature. Join the San Francisco Bay Wildlife Society for a slightly slower look at this meeting of fresh and salt water which has created an incredibly rich and diverse wildlife habitat. Reservations are required for this trip. You need to contact the San Francisco Bay Wildlife Society for meeting information. There's no cost to participate. The weather should be cool but comfortable, unless a spring storm is blowing through.

For information, contact the San Francisco Bay Wildlife Society, P.O. Box 524, Newark, CA 94560-0524; (510) 792-4275.

Trall Maintenance Workshops

April 1, 1995 • 9 a.m. to 3 p.m.
(see # 19 on map page 180)

For information about these workshops, which will instruct you in the safe and best use of tools and techniques for keeping trails well maintained, see page 188. They are scheduled to meet at the Skyline Training Center in Oakland.

For information, contact the East Bay Regional Parks District, 2950 Peralta Oaks Court, Oakland, CA 94605-0381; (510) 636-1684.

❖ ❖ ❖ ❖

Post-Aprll Fool's Day Deception Hike

April 2, 1995 • 1 p.m. to 3 p.m.
(see #16 on map page 180)

Nature has its own way of fooling us, especially if we're not expecting to be fooled. Here's a chance to spend two hours with a naturalist uncovering nature's deceptions, the ones designed to help creatures and plants make it in a world where only the strongest, or sneakiest, survive. This is an easy, short hike through the Tilden Nature Area in Berkeley. The hike is designed for all ages and there's no fee. To reach the Tilden Nature Area from Oakland, head east on Highway 24 and pass through the Caldecott Tunnel to the Fish Ranch Road exit. Head west on Fish Ranch to the Grizzly Peak Boulevard intersection, where you'll turn right and enter the park's south entrance. For the nature area, turn left.

For information, contact the Tilden Nature Area, Environmental Education Center, Berkeley, CA 94708; (510) 525-2233.

❖ ❖ ❖ ❖

Botanical Garden Gambol

April 2, 1995 • 10 a.m. to noon
(see #16 on map page 180)

Wildflowers pretty much do their own thing, assuming there is enough winter and spring rain, but the Botanical Garden in Tilden Regional Park in Berkeley doesn't give nature a chance to fail. The garden is a great place to see many of California's beautiful, sometimes spectacular native plants. What's great about this special hike is having a naturalist along to offer insight into the garden's plants, which is much more entertaining and enlightening than simply reading plant identification signs. To reach the Tilden Nature Area from Oakland, head east on Highway 24 and pass through the Caldecott Tunnel to the Fish Ranch Road exit. Head west on Fish Ranch to the Grizzly Peak Boulevard intersection, where you'll turn right and enter the park's south entrance. To reach the botanical garden, turn right once inside.

For information, contact the Tilden Nature Area, Environmental Education Center, Berkeley, CA 94708; (510) 525-2233.

❖ ❖ ❖ ❖

Senior Safari–Springtime in Stewartville

April 4, 1995 • 1:30 p.m. to 3:30 p.m.
(see #33 on map page 181)

This early-April hike is great for older adults who prefer shorter, less demanding outdoor treks. You'll meet a naturalist at the eastern entrance to Black Diamond Mines Regional Preserve and drive as a group to the Star Mine Group Camp. Then it's out of the vehicles for an easy one-mile walk to look at wildflowers, explore the Prospect Tunnel and see what's left of one of California's few coal mining areas. There will be hard hats and flashlights provided when you get there. This hike should catch the early wildflower season, so you may want to bring you camera. There is a very small fee for this seniors-only hike. To reach Black Diamond Mines Regional Preserve, take Highway 4 east into Antioch and take the Somersville

APRIL

Road exit. Drive south about three miles to the park entrance.

For information, contact Black Diamond Mines Regional Preserve, 5175 Somersville Road, Antioch, CA 94509; (510) 757-2620.

Rock Climbing Basics

April 4, 1995 • 9 a.m. to 5 p.m.

(see #49 on map page 181)

If you're a teenager or older, and are looking for a real summer rush, try a little rock climbing. You'll have to call and register in advance, because space is limited in the class, but what a way to get ready for summer fun! You'll join a small group and hike about a mile out to Cave Rocks and then spend the afternoon learning many of the basics that will make your rock climbing endeavors much more fun, safe and successful. The instructors will teach climbing safety, how to tie knots that stay tied, belaying, rappelling and other skills. Here's a chance to impress your friends with your "rock star" status. Bring lunch and water to Sunol-Ohlone Regional Wilderness in Sunol. The program is usually held in April and again in August. There's a $10 fee for the program, although the amount is subject to change. To reach the Sunol-Ohlone Wilderness from the intersection of interstates 580 and 680, drive south on Interstate 680 for about eight miles to the Highway 84/Calaveras Road exit. Head south on Calaveras Road approximately four miles to Geary Road. Turn left on to Geary and drive to the park entrance and the visitor center. There's a $3 parking fee.

For information, contact Sunol-Ohlone Regional Wilderness, P.O. Box 82, Sunol, CA 94586; (510) 862-2244.

Coyote Kids

April 4, 5 & 6, 1995 **S** 🕐 • 10 a.m. to 1 p.m.
(see #47 on map page 181)

This is a day camp that gets a bunch of six to nine year olds together for about four hours each day for three days. The camp will focus on exploring the marsh at Coyote Hills in the East Bay, looking at the special plants and animals that live in this unique environment. In addition to learning how the plants and animals survive and thrive, the kids get to see how the Ohlone tribe made this same land their home and lived in relative comfort. Advance registration is required and there is a fee, which will be about $20.

To reach Coyote Hills Regional Park from Fremont, take Interstate 880 (Nimitz Freeway) to the Decoto Road/Highway 84 exit and head west to the Thornton Avenue/Paseo Padre Parkway exit. Turn north and go one mile to Patterson Ranch Road, then turn left and drive into the park. There's a $3 parking fee on weekends and holidays.

For information, contact Coyote Hills Regional Park, 8000 Patterson Ranch Road, Fremont, CA 94555; (510) 795-9385.

Black Diamond Explorers—Insects

April 6, 1995 **S** 🕐 • 3:30 p.m. to 5 p.m.
(see #33 on map page 181)

If bugs bug you more than your kids, but you want a little respite from your kids anyway, then this is a great after-school program for the youngsters to learn more about the insects that live all around us. The kids, ages 9 to 11, who attend will get a chance to see not only the everyday insects we encounter in the woods, but they'll also see strange critters whose protective camouflage makes them look more like leaves, bark and twigs. There's a small fee and advance registration is required. To reach Black Diamond Mines Regional Preserve, take Highway 4 east into Antioch and take the Somersville Road exit. Drive south about three miles to the park entrance.

For information, contact Black Diamond Mines Regional Preserve, 5175 Somersville Road, Antioch, CA 94509; (510) 757-2620.

❧ ❧ ❧ ❧

Morgan Territory Hike

April 8, 1995 **$** 🕐 • 10 a.m. to 3 p.m.
(see #33 on map page 181)

This one is held in the Black Diamond Mines Regional Preserve, which is located near Antioch. It will be a relatively short, 4.2-mile hike, and will cover some pretty steep terrain. But if you get a chance to see one of the preserve's resident eagles soaring over the ridgetop, the hike will be worth it. Wear some good hiking boots and bring your binoculars, some water and lunch. To reach Black Diamond Mines Regional Preserve, take Highway 4 east into Antioch and take the Somersville Road exit. Drive south about three miles to the park entrance.

For information, contact Black Diamond Mines Regional Preserve, 5175 Somersville Road, Antioch, CA 94509; (510) 757-2620.

❧ ❧ ❧ ❧

Backpacking for Beginners

April 8 & 9, 1995 **$** 🕐
(see #43 on map page 181)

Have you read the magazines and listened to the stories by people who rave about the advantages of backpacking over car camping? Did they convince you that you'd really like to try backpacking, but you don't know where to start? Well then, the East Bay Regional Parks District has got a class for you. Here's your chance to learn about what to take and how to pack it. Then you head off with other novices and a couple of seasoned veterans for two days and one night of exploring the pleasures of carrying your home on your back. The trip will explore the Mission Peak area of Garin Regional Park in Hayward. There is a pre-trip planning meeting held about two weeks before the actual trip. Preregistration is required, and since the size of the group is limited, you really should call a month or so in advance so as not to miss out. The fee for the trip will be about $10 for adults. To reach Garin Regional Park, take Highway 238 south from Hayward about four miles to Garin Road. Turn left and enter the park. There is a $3 parking fee.

For information, contact Coyote Hills Regional Park, 8000 Patterson Ranch Road, Fremont, CA 94555; (510) 795-9385.

Opening Day of the Straits

Second Saturday in April • 10 a.m. to 10 p.m.
(see #10 on map page 181)

APRIL

This is one of those outdoors events that can be almost as fun to watch as it is to participate in. Like Avis, the car rental company that advertises itself as number two, Benicia seems to have always ended up number two in most everything it tried. It tried to be named California's state capital and lost out to Sacramento. It took its best shot at becoming San Francisco Bay's major port and lost out to San Francisco. Finally, in 1979, Benicia started its Opening Day of the Straits celebration, and since nobody else has one, I guess the Bay Area town is finally number one. Actually, best or second best, the opening day celebration is a lot of fun. If you have a boat of any size, you might want to sail, steam or motor along in the boat parade. And if you're prone to seasickness and don't own a boat, just grab your blanket or beach chair and find a comfortable viewing spot on the sand. There's a chicken and steak barbecue if you don't bring your own picnic lunch or dinner.

The event is held at the Benicia Marina and Yacht Club in Benicia, off Interstate 780, about one mile west of Interstate 680 and five miles east of Interstate 80. The event, with the exception of the food, is free. The day should be pretty nice sweater weather, unless a spring rainstorm is passing through.

For information, contact Benicia Chamber of Commerce, P.O. Box 185, Benicia, CA 94510; (800) 559-7377.

Arbor Days Volunteer Work

April 9, 10 & 11 $ ⟳ · 10 a.m. to 1 p.m.
(locations vary)

You can help beautify the East Bay Regional Parks District by bringing yourselves, your family and your friends out to the parks on this annual tree-planting celebration in the parks. Wear your work clothes, bring some good gloves and a shovel and have a great time in the parks selected as most in need of new trees. Each program requires only a certain number of workers, so call in advance to register and to find out which park needs you. The program is usually held during three days in early or mid-April in preparation for the upcoming May Day celebration.

For information, and to register, contact the East Bay Regional Parks District; (510) 636-1684.

✤ ✤ ✤ ✤

California Native Plant Sale Volunteer Recruitment

April 10 to 14, 1995 $ ⟳ · 8:30 a.m. to 5:30 p.m.
(see #16 on map page 180)

Volunteers are needed to help get everything in order for the annual native plant sale held at Tilden Regional Park's Botanical Garden in Berkeley. During the week prior to the sale, which usually occurs during the second weekend in April, help is needed to water plants and lawns, put up barriers to protect gardens and place signs where needed. Wear sturdy shoes and work clothes. All ages of volunteers are needed and will be happily put to work.

To reach the Tilden Nature Area from Oakland, head east on Highway 24 and pass through the Caldecott Tunnel to the Fish Ranch Road exit. Head west on Fish Ranch to the Grizzly Peak Boulevard intersection, where you'll turn right and enter the park's south entrance. To reach the botanical garden, turn right once inside.

For information, contact the Tilden Nature Area, Environmental Education Center, Berkeley, CA 94708; (510) 525-2233.

North Bay Birds

Mid-April Saturday 🅢🖉 • 10 a.m. to 2 p.m.
(see #1 on map page 181)

APRIL

Join members of the San Francisco Bay Wildlife Society as they leave the San Francisco Bay National Wildlife Refuge, near Newark in the East Bay, and visit nearby San Pablo Bay National Wildlife Refuge, to the north, near Sears Point. It will require a bit of stamina to make the seven-mile round-trip hike to Lower Tubs Island. You need to make a reservation in order to attend, which will work out fine since you need to call and confirm the date and get exact directions to the meeting place. Right now, it's scheduled to meet at the gate into San Pablo Bay National Wildlife Refuge, located just off Highway 37, near Sears Point. If a late-spring rainstorm blows into town, the hike will be canceled.

For information, contact the San Francisco Bay Wildlife Society, P.O. Box 524, Newark, CA 94560-0524; (510) 792-4275.

✤ ✤ ✤ ✤

Intermediate Backpacking in Ohlone Wilderness

April 14, 15 & 16, 1995 🅢🖉 • 1 p.m. Friday to 5 p.m. Sunday
(see #49 on map page 181)

If you've done a little backpacking or if you've completed the "Backpacking for Beginners" course offered a week or so earlier in the month of April (see page 204), then why not join this three-day outing during the peak wildflower season? Veteran backpackers and naturalists will lead the way, spending time to show off the best of the hills' wildflowers and identify the birds and other wildlife you're bound to encounter on the trip. You will leave from Sunol around 1 p.m. on Friday and you'll spend Saturday night at Stewart's Camp in Ohlone, then hike to Del Valle on Sunday. Great trip, great fun, great photo opportunities, if a camera is one of those extra pieces of needless weight you decide to carry on your back. There's a pre-trip meeting about two weeks before the trip leaves. You must preregister—the earlier, the better. The cost of the trip is about $38 and it is open to all ages. To reach the Sunol-Ohlone Regional Wilderness from the intersection of interstates 580 and 680, drive south on Interstate 680 for about eight miles to the Highway 84/Calaveras Road exit. Head south on Calaveras Road approximately four miles to Geary Road. Turn left onto Geary and drive to the park entrance and the visitor center. There's a $3 parking fee.

For information, contact Sunol-Ohlone Regional Wilderness, P.O. Box 82, Sunol, CA 94586; (510) 862-2244.

Nature Crafts Workshop for Educators and Group Leaders

April 15, 1995 $ ☎ • 1:30 p.m. to 4:30 p.m.

(see #16 on map page 180)

If you teach kids about nature as an educator or as a volunteer, this workshop will give you some new ideas and new materials to work with. You'll learn nature crafts such as making dinosaur eggs and leaf prints, building monarch butterfly kites, working with animal track stamps and more. East Bay plants, animals and all those bothersome but important bugs will be the subjects of investigation. This program will be held at the Tilden Nature Area's Environmental Education Center in Berkeley. There's a $15 fee for the workshop. Preregistration is required. To reach the nature area from Oakland, head east on Highway 24 and pass through the Caldecott Tunnel to the Fish Ranch Road exit. Head west on Fish Ranch to the Grizzly Peak Boulevard intersection, where you'll turn right and enter the park's south entrance. To reach the nature area, turn left once inside.

For information, contact Tilden Nature Area; (510) 525-2233.

Big Basin Trail Days

April 22, 1995 **S** 🚶 • 9 a.m. to 5 p.m.
(see #27 on map page 180)

Did you know that Big Basin Redwoods was the first state park in California? Did you know that it has miles and miles of hiking trails in its 18,000 acres? Maintaining these trails in a land that gets enough rain each year to support large groves of giant redwoods is a tough, neverending job. With the help of volunteers—and that's where you come in—a significant amount of repair work, along with the building of a few miles of new trails, is accomplished each year on the Saturday closest to Earth Day. The annual Trail Days program in Big Basin is directed by the Santa Cruz Mountain Trail Association. There are generally about 100 people who show up for this, so bring your own shovels, gloves and other implements of hard, manual labor. Toss in a lunch and some water and you're set for a great day of fun work with a great group of people. Meet at Big Basin Redwoods State Park Headquarters before 9 a.m. Big Basin is located about 20 miles north of Santa Cruz via highways 9 and 236. It should be cool and comfortable, unless a late-spring rainstorm passes through. The program is free.

For information, contact Big Basin Redwoods State Park, 101 North Big Trees Road #5, Felton, CA 95018; (408) 338-6132.

APRIL

❖ ❖ ❖ ❖

Wilderness Weekend

April 22 & 23, 1995 **S** 🚶
(see #50 on map page 181)

Henry W. Coe State Park is an 80,000-acre park with 200 miles of trails that meander through open grasslands, oak woodlands and pine forests. What's great about the park is that there's really no development, which means you must bring in everything you're going to need. Wilderness Weekend is the one weekend each year when you can drive into the backcountry camping area. Bring your horses, bicycles and hiking boots so you can get around and see the fabulous spring wildflower displays. About 2,000 people take advantage of this weekend camping opportunity. The weather is usually beautiful for the event, although it rained buckets during the 1994 event, creating a muddy quagmire. Entrance into the park during the special event is usually through a back gate and along a dirt road located off Highway 152, west of San Luis Reservoir. Henry W. Coe State Park is located about 40 minutes from Morgan Hill and US 101 via Dunne Avenue. You need to call the park for special event access information. There will be a $5-per-vehicle entry fee.

For information, contact Henry W. Coe State Park; (408) 779-2728.

❋ ❋ ❋ ❋

California Trail Days

April 22, 1995 **S** 🖊 • 8:30 a.m. to 1:30 p.m.
(various East Bay locations)

Each year, throughout California, Trail Days are opportunities to get out and help repair some old and well-worn East Bay Regional Parks District trails, and maybe build a few new ones. If you come out and help on Trail Days in the parks that have an organized program, you'll receive a California Trail Days T-shirt. In some park locations, you'll get an invitation to a post-workday barbecue. You really need to call for information on this one, because there are usually many different locations where you can help out.

For information, contact the East Bay Regional Parks District; (510) 636-1684.

❋ ❋ ❋ ❋

Sunset Sail on San Francisco Bay

April 22, 1995 **S** 🖊 • 6 p.m. to 8:30 p.m.
(see #22 on map page 180)

Take an evening catamaran ride around San Francisco Bay and see the city from a different perspective. There will be a naturalist from the East Bay Regional Parks District along on the ride who will share some of the cultural and natural history of the West Coast's most famous seaport. And if you get a little hungry, well, dinner is included in the $27 fee for the trip. (Note: The fee may change.) Kids must be at least eight years old in order to accompany an adult on this trip. The cost for kids ages 8 to 12 is $21. Non-East Bay residents will pay a few dollars more. Advance registration is required. The ride will leave from the Alameda Ferry Terminal at 2990 Main Street in Alameda.

For information, contact the East Bay Regional Parks District, 2950 Peralta Oaks Court, Oakland, CA 94605-0381; (510) 636-1684.

✤ ✤ ✤ ✤

Women on Common Ground: Springtime Campout

April 22, 1995 **S**🕐

(see #49 on map page 181)

This weekend campout and nighttime exploration of Sunol-Ohlone Regional Wilderness is geared toward women who want to reclaim their right to hike and camp on their own, especially after dark, without fear for their personal safety. You don't have to be an experienced camper to be part of this outing. There will be a night hike, campfire songs and some quiet time to listen to all those things that go bump in the night. Interested women are encouraged to attend a pre-campout meeting in late March (see page 197), although it is not required. This is for adults only, and the fee will be about $10. Preregistration is required.

To reach the Sunol-Ohlone Wilderness from the intersection of interstates 580 and 680, drive south on Interstate 680 for about eight miles to the Highway 84/Calaveras Road exit. Head south on Calaveras Road approximately four miles to Geary Road. Turn left onto Geary and drive to the park entrance and the visitor center. There's a $3 parking fee.

For information, contact Sunol-Ohlone Regional Wilderness, P.O. Box 82, Sunol, CA 94586; (510) 862-2244.

✤ ✤ ✤ ✤

Earth Day Saturday

April 22, 1995 **$(** · 10 a.m. to 4 p.m.
(see #24 on map page 180)

This San Francisco Bay National Wildlife Refuge program is designed to entertain and educate your kids, but it works equally well for adults. Winners of the Endangered Species Poster Contest will be honored and programs about local endangered species will be offered, as well as a variety of activities and presentations by environmental organizations. Native plants will be available for sale.

To reach the San Francisco Bay National Wildlife Refuge Visitor Center from Interstate 880 or US 101, take Highway 84 toward the east end of the Dumbarton Bridge. Take the Thornton Avenue exit and drive south for one mile. The refuge is on the right side. Follow the road to the stop sign and turn left into the parking lot.

For information, contact the San Francisco Bay Wildlife Society, P.O. Box 524, Newark, CA 94560-0524; (510) 792-4275.

❀ ❀ ❀ ❀

Dynamic Delta

April 23, 1995 **$(** · 2 p.m. to 3 p.m.
(see #32 on map page 181)

This is a library tour of the Sacramento River Delta. Sit back and enjoy a slide program that will show you, in just one hour, more about the backwaters of the Delta than you could see by boat in a week. Although it might not be as much fun, it will teach you about the rich history that surrounds the towns and levees making-up this rich and beautiful water wonderland. Meet in the Antioch Library, located on 18th Street, between G and D streets in the Delta town of Antioch. Kids must be at least seven years old in order to attend this free program.

For information, contact Black Diamond Mines Regional Preserve, 5175 Somersville Road, Antioch, CA 94509; (510) 757-2620.

❀ ❀ ❀ ❀

Lake Chabot Annual Fishing Derby

April 22 & 23, 1995 **S** 🎣
6 a.m. to 5 p.m. Saturday; 6 a.m. to 2 p.m. Sunday
(see #38 on map page 181)

This is the big annual fishing event at Lake Chabot in the East Bay. It's a great opportunity to catch a few of the 5,000 pounds of trout that are usually planted just prior to the event. And if the trout aren't interested in your bait, or you aren't interested in rainbow trout, then there are the resident monster bass and catfish that can run up to 10 and 20 pounds, respectively. But don't be surprised if it happens to be a crappie that grabs your hook. Kids under age 16 pay $3 and don't need a fishing license; adults pay $5 and do need a license. The entry fee is subject to change, but it's good for both days of the derby.

For information, contact Lake Chabot; (510) 582-2198.

❖ ❖ ❖ ❖

Old Ways Workshop: Making Stone Tools

April 23, 1995 **S** 🎣 • 10 a.m. to 4 p.m.
(see #47 on map page 181)

For thousands of years, California's Native Americans fashioned cutting tools from stone. While many types of stone were useful, obsidian was easily the most important. The workshop day begins with an introduction to pecking and grinding, then moves quickly into learning knapping, which is the art of removing all the extra pieces from obsidian until just the sharpened arrow point or knife blade remains. Flaked obsidian is sharper than a surgeon's scalpel, so you need to bring leather work gloves and safety glasses; the East Bay Regional Parks District naturalist will provide the first aid and bandages. There's a $25 fee for the program and you must be at least 12 years old to participate. The workshop is held at the Coyote Hills Regional Park Visitor Center. Advance registration is required. To reach Coyote Hills from Fremont, take Interstate 880 (Nimitz Freeway) to the Decoto Road/Highway 84 exit and head west to the Thornton Avenue/Paseo Padre Parkway exit. Turn north and go one mile to Patterson Ranch Road, then turn left and drive into the park. There's a $3 parking fee on weekends and holidays.

For information, contact the East Bay Regional Parks District, (510) 636-1684; or Coyote Hills Regional Park, 8000 Patterson Ranch Road, Fremont, CA 94555, (510) 795-9385.

Canoe the Slough

Late April Sunday [S] ☎ • 10 a.m. to noon

(see #24 on map page 180)

This is a "BYOB" event—bring your own boat, that is, along with paddles and the mandatory PFDs, or life jackets, as most people call them. This casual paddle exploration trip on Newark Slough is for canoes and small row boats, but please, no inflatable boats. Here's your chance to explore the salty wetlands from a slightly different perspective. Reservations are required for this one, so call ahead to confirm that the paddle trip is still on and that they've still got space for you. You'll be meeting at the Newark Slough boat launch off Thornton Avenue, near the San Francisco Bay National Wildlife Refuge Visitor Center.

For information, contact the San Francisco Bay Wildlife Society, P.O. Box 524, Newark, CA 94560-0524; (510) 792-4275.

Half Moon Bay Pacific Coast Dream Machine

Last Saturday in April [S] ☎ • 10 a.m. to 4 p.m.

(see #25 on map page 180)

If you have a thing for machines, then this is the place to be in late April. You can spend the entire day wandering among some 1,500 exhibits of every type of machine you can imagine, including automobiles, motorcycles, aircraft, both gas and steam-powered tractors, engines, tanks and a few surprises. Helicopter and DC-3 plane rides will be available for your mechanically-inclined pleasures. This event attracts about 12,000 people, so you may want to arrive early in order to beat the midday crush. There will also be lots of food to eat and music to enjoy. The event is held at the Half Moon Bay Airport, which is located in the city of Half Moon Bay, not far from the intersection of highways 92 and 1. The program will cost adults $10, seniors and kids $5; kids under six years old are free. The weather should be cool and breezy.

For information, contact the Coastside Adult Day Health Center, 645 Correas Street, Half Moon Bay, CA 94019; (415) 726-5505.

Full Moon Prowl at Black Diamond

April 24, 1995 [S] ☎ • 7:30 p.m. to 9:30 p.m.

(see #33 on map page 181)

The Full Moon Prowl at Black Diamond is similar to the East Bay Regional Parks District's night hike at Pleasanton Ridge, but in a different location and a month later. Different wildlife wanders in the woods after the sun goes down. With the absence of shopping center lights, the stars shine much brighter and the constellations seem bigger, making for easier identification. Dress for some cool evening temperatures and bring a good flashlight. As with the other hikes, there will be a naturalist along to help find and identify the after-dark wildlife and the stars above. The hike should leave from near the Black Diamond Mines Regional Preserve Visitor Center. Call to confirm the date and to make the required advance reservations. To reach Black Diamond Mines Regional Preserve, take Highway 4 east into Antioch and take the Somersville Road exit. Drive south about three miles to the park entrance.

For information, contact Black Diamond Mines Regional Preserve, 5175 Somersville Road, Antioch, CA 94509; (510) 757-2620.

Fishing Contra Loma

April 26, 1995 **$(** • 9:30 a.m. to 11:30 a.m.
(see #32 on map page 181)

Are you a retired, or unretired, senior who is looking for a fun, relaxing way to spend some of your leisure time? How about fishing? There are several lakes in the East Bay and the fishing can be pretty good, if you know the basics and a few of the tricks. A fishing instructor will join you for a couple of hours in the morning to help you understand how fish think, where they go when they aren't biting your hook and what you have to do to ensure that your fishing license wasn't purchased in vain. Here's your chance to learn how to set up your tackle, as well as where and how to tie hooks, weights and lures onto your line. The course is meant for seniors who want to catch the "big one," and it will be held at Contra Loma Reservoir, just a few miles south of Antioch. You have to register in advance, but the fee for the class is only about $2.

For information, contact Contra Loma; (510) 636-1684 or (510) 757-0404.

❖ ❖ ❖ ❖

Family Camping for Beginners

April 28, 1995 **$(** • 7 p.m. to 9 p.m.
(see #43 on map page 181)

Camping is a great family activity, but if you've never been, how are you going to know what to do? Setting up camp, building the traditional campfire, camp cooking and safety around the campsite are subjects easily learned. This class will provide the basic instruction and then give you a chance to join some other first-time campers for an overnight camp trip. You'll learn some fine recipes and some fun songs during the night at Garin Regional Park's Arroyo Flat Campground, near Hayward. Advance registration is required. There will be a pre-trip meeting near the end of April, so sign up as far in advance as you can. The same class should be offered again in June, just in case you missed it the first time around. To reach Garin Regional Park, take Highway 238 south from Hay-

---

ward about four miles to Garin Road. Turn left and enter the park. There is a $3 parking fee.

For information, contact Garin Regional Park, 1320 Garin Avenue, Hayward, CA 94544; (510) 795-9385.

✤ ✤ ✤ ✤

Teacher Environmental Education Workshop

April 29,1995 **$ ⌀** • 9 a.m. to 3 p.m.
(see #22 on map page 180)

If you are looking for new places to take your students to study nature, then join this East Bay workshop for its two stops in two very different ecosystems. The first stop will be at Crab Cove in Alameda for an exploration of the saltwater shoreline where mud flats and rocky outcrops create a wet and wild environment for plants and animals. You won't find those same living plants and creatures anywhere in a redwood forest, which is the day's second stop. The workshop is for adult educators and the fee is $35. Preregistration is required.

For information, contact the East Bay Regional Parks District, 2950 Peralta Oaks Court, Oakland, CA 94605-0381; (510) 636-1684.

✤ ✤ ✤ ✤

Exploring the California Delta

April 29, 1995 **$ ⌀** • 9:30 a.m. to 11:30 a.m.
(see #33 on map page 181)

Okay, exploring the wetlands around the Ironhouse Sanitary District in Oakley may not sound particular appealing. But the discoveries you'll make on this trip are well worth the harassment you may experience from your friends and family should they discover where you spent your morning. This is really an excellent place to learn about marsh plants, wildlife and their habitats. The two-hour walk is open to all ages and is free. Call to confirm the date, time and meeting place.

For information, contact Black Diamond Mines Regional Preserve, 5175 Somersville Road, Antioch, CA 94509; (510) 757-2620.

❊ ❊ ❊ ❊

May Fête at Ardenwood

May 1, 1995 • 10 a.m. to 4 p.m.
(see #46 on map page 181)

Come welcome the planting season or simply enjoy the day outdoors. For the fifth year, Ardenwood's May Fête does a wonderful job of recreating a May Day celebration from a century ago. Gather your family and come frolic in the park, enjoy the flowers, the dancing and all the activities that are associated with this 2,000-year-old celebration. Of course, there will be the traditional maypole dancing, performances by harpsichordists and the crowning of the May Queen at the gazebo. Kids and adults will have an opportunity to make miniature May baskets, flower garlands and old-time toys. And for those of a competitive nature, old-time games and contests will be held. Ardenwood Regional Preserve is located near the junction of Highway 84 and Ardenwood Boulevard in Fremont. There will be a fee for the event, probably about $6 for adults and $4 for kids and seniors.

For information, contact Ardenwood Regional Preserve; (510) 796-0199 or (510) 796-0663.

❊ ❊ ❊ ❊

Songbird Watching and Listening Workshop

First weekend in May
(see #38 on map page 181)

Once you've mastered birdwatching, or even have a basic understanding of it, you'll want to try this workshop. Many birds are identified by their songs, in addition to their color, size and habitat. And what better season to spend time listening to birds singing than in spring when they are vying for mates and breeding territory?

Here, you'll have an opportunity to learn the songs of local nesting songbirds by listening to tapes. A slide show, study skins, books and handouts will also be used to help you learn the identity of our fine feathered friends. The initial meeting will be held in the evening at Lake Chabot, where your time will be spent learning about bird songs, their behavior, nesting habits and how and where they feed. All of the information comes in handy when you finally make it to the field on Saturday to seek out the real thing. The Saturday meeting will be held at Coyote Hills and Garin Regional Park, both birding bonanzas. On Sunday, the group will explore Sycamore Grove and repeat Saturday's learning experience with some different species. All ages are welcome to attend, but advance registration is required. There's a fee of about $20 for adult residents, $25 for nonresidents.

For information, contact the East Bay Regional Parks District, (510) 636-1684; or Coyote Hills Regional Park, 8000 Patterson Ranch Road, Fremont, CA 94555, (510) 795-9385.

MAY

❖ ❖ ❖ ❖

Pierce Ranch Dairy Day— Point Reyes National Seashore

First Saturday in May ⑤ 🖊 · 11 a.m. to 4 p.m.
(see #3 on map page 180)

For over a century, California's coastal strand of grasslands, including the area that is now Point Reyes National Seashore, was used for cattle ranching. The Pierce Ranch was established here in 1858 and it's one of the oldest dairy ranches on the Point Reyes Peninsula. The ranch has now been renovated and there is a self-guided trail that provides information about the historic structures on the grounds. Each year, a maypole celebration, along with an 1870s schoolhouse, live farm animals and dairy farm activities such as butter churning, transform the ranch back to its past of robust ranch activity. You should use a map to get there, but if you don't have one, turn off Highway 1 at Olema and take the Bear Valley Road to a few miles past Inverness where the road forks. Keep right, heading toward another intersection at the Tomales Bay State Park entrance, where a left turn will get you onto Pierce Point Road. Follow Pierce Point Road several miles until it deadends at the ranch. There's no cost for the program. The weather is really variable this time of year, but you'll probably see fog in the morning with warm sunshine later in the day.

For information, contact Point Reyes National Seashore, Point Reyes, CA 94956; (415) 663-1092.

✤ ✤ ✤ ✤

Senior Safari–
Eastern Alameda County Regional Parks
May 2, 1995 **S**(/ · 10 a.m. to 4 p.m.
(locations vary)

This is an adults-only trip that makes a grand circle of some of the East Bay's most beautiful parks and scenic areas including Pleasanton Ridge, Shadow Cliffs, Sunol and Las Trampas regional parks. You'll be traveling mostly by auto, with stops to get out, stretch your legs and see and talk about some of the geology, plants and wildlife that make these parks so special. There is a fee of about $8 for residents and $10 for nonresidents. Advance registration is required.

For information, contact the East Bay Regional Parks District, 2950 Peralta Oaks Court, Oakland, CA 94605-0381; (510) 636-1684.

✤ ✤ ✤ ✤

Special Kids Fishing Derby
May 3, 1995 **S**(/
(see #42 on map page 181)

Here's another call for volunteers to help out with about 200 kids with emotional and physical disabilities who get to come out and enjoy the outdoors at Shadow Cliffs Regional Recreation Area in

Pleasanton. You can help the kids try to catch the big one on borrowed fishing poles, then celebrate their catches with prizes. All volunteers will need to attend an early-morning orientation session. You must register prior to the derby.

To reach Shadow Cliffs, take Interstate 580 to Pleasanton and the Santa Rita Road exit. Head south on Santa Rita to Valley, turn left, then left again on Stanley. The park is on the right. There is a day-use parking fee of $4.

For information, contact the Tilden Nature Area, Environmental Education Center, Berkeley, CA 94708; (510) 525-2233.

❀ ❀ ❀ ❀

24th Angel Island Guardsmen Race

May 6, 1995 **S** *ℭ* • 11 a.m. to 5 p.m.
(see #14 on map page 180)

If you don't like running marathons or 10K races, how about trotting around the 4.8-mile trail that circles Angel Island? There are some beautiful views of the Golden Gate Bridge and the San Francisco skyline along the way, so your running might be slowed to a snail's pace just to take them in. It's a fun day, so even if you don't want to run you can always wander to the top of the island for an even better view of San Francisco Bay. There's a lot of history on Angel Island, with many Civil War-era buildings still in place, along with an old Nike missile base. The only way to get to Angel Island is by boat. If you don't own one, you can take the Tiburon Ferry from Tiburon, (415) 435-2131, or one of San Francisco's Red and White Fleet, (800) 229-2784. The fee for the event wasn't set at press time, and neither was the weather, which will probably be foggy in the morning, but otherwise warm.

For information, contact Angel Island State Park; (415) 435-1915.

MAY

"We Mean Clean" Week

May 6, 1995 • 9 a.m. to 3 p.m.
(see #21 on map page 180)

Garbage, trash and junk are the nemesis of recreational pursuits on our waterways and along our ocean beaches. Join a bunch of other concerned folks in this program, co-sponsored by East Bay Regional Parks District and the city of Oakland, and work on restoring the beauty along Martin Luther King, Jr. Regional Shoreline. Bring your own gloves and wear work clothes that you don't mind getting a little dirty. Also bring your lunch because this is a long work day. It will probably be held on the first Saturday in May, but call ahead to be sure. To reach the shoreline from downtown Oakland, take Interstate 880 to the Hegenberger Road exit. Head west about one mile to Doolittle Drive and turn right. The park begins just past Swann Way.

For information, contact Martin Luther King, Jr. Regional Shoreline; (510) 430-1783.

❖ ❖ ❖ ❖

Macedo Ranch Hike

May 6, 1995 • 10 a.m. to 3 p.m.
(see #36 on map page 181)

This hike is part of the Mount Diablo Interpretive Association's "April on the Mountain," even though it is held in May. But don't let the confusion of titles and dates bother you. Simply pack a lunch and some water and meet the interpreter-led group for a day exploring the foothills and mountains of Mount Diablo State Park. The hike will cover about six miles in five hours. Plan to cross through oak woodlands and over open meadows with a hike down into Pine Canyon. Bring your camera, because there will be some beautiful views of Castle Rocks up on the mountain. Call for the meeting place and to confirm the date.

For information, contact Black Diamond Mines Regional Preserve, 5175 Somersville Road, Antioch, CA 94509; (510) 757-2620.

❖ ❖ ❖ ❖

A Whale of a Mother's Day Weekend

May 6 & 7, 1995 **S** 🖉

(see #2 on map page 180)

This is a special Moms-seeing-Moms boat ride on the waves. The trip is an overnighter at Point Reyes with accommodations that are more of an adventure than a night at the Hilton. You'll be spending part of the day whale watching from the bluffs during the peak of their yearly northern migration. After a full day of the sights and sounds of Point Reyes National Seashore, grab your sleeping bag because your night will be spent in the bunk-style accommodations of the Point Reyes Historic Lifeboat Station. While this is dubbed as a Mother's Day weekend, all are welcome. The fee is $50 per person and doesn't include food, so you must bring your own. Advance registration is required.

For information, contact the East Bay Regional Parks District, 2950 Peralta Oaks Court, Oakland, CA 94605-0381; (510) 636-1684, ext. 2609.

❀ ❀ ❀ ❀

Senior Safari–Ohlone Regional Wilderness

May 11, 1995 **S** 🖉 • 10 a.m. to 5 p.m.

(see #49 on map page 181)

This hike is designed for older adults who aren't able to get out on most of the other hikes, either because they lack adequate transportation for the auto tours or can't hike long distances because of physical limitations. The group will get together in a van and head out to the top of Alameda's highest peak, with several stops planned along the Ohlone Wilderness Trail. The tour begins at the Pleasanton Senior Center at 5353 Sunol Boulevard. Because space in the van is limited, advance registration by mid-April or earlier is required for this mid-May tour. The cost should be about $20 for the all-day trip.

For information, contact the East Bay Regional Parks District, 2950 Peralta Oaks Court, Oakland, CA 94605-0381; (510) 636-1684.

❀ ❀ ❀ ❀

Briones Regional Park Hike

May 13, 1995 **S** 🅛 • 10 a.m. to 3 p.m.
(see #13 on map page 180)

Briones Regional Park is located a few miles west of Pleasant Hill and its valleys and mountains are the destination for this 5.5-mile hike. The moderate terrain and relatively short distance should make this hike more appealing to those unwilling or unable to tackle the longer, tougher hikes offered throughout many East Bay Regional Parks. This one is open to all ages and everyone who joins the hike to the top of the hills is sure to enjoy the views. Bring a camera, lunch and water to drink.

Briones Regional Park is located in the hills south of Martinez and north of Lafayette. From Lafayette, take Happy Valley Road north from Highway 24 for about four miles, to the intersection with Bear Creek Road. Turn right onto Bear Creek Road and drive about 0.5 miles to Briones Road, which enters the southwest portion of the park.

For information, contact the East Bay Regional Parks District, 2950 Peralta Oaks Court, Oakland, CA 94605-0381; (510) 636-1684, ext. 2609.

✤ ✤ ✤ ✤

Cord Grass Control

May 13, 1995 **S** 🅛 • 9 a.m. to 2 p.m.
(see #2 on map page 180)

This is a call to all volunteers who want to help eradicate an invader that is taking over parts of the marsh habitat near the Hayward Regional Shoreline. Wear old clothes, bring your work gloves and plan to get dirty. You'll be helping the critically important and diminishing wetlands, while making some new friends and having fun. Cord grass removal day is usually held about the first Saturday in May. If the cord grass is under control after 1994's effort, which isn't likely, the park will sponsor other volunteer environmental clean-up programs, so call anyway. The work day is long enough that you'll need to bring water and a lunch. There's no age limit here, so bring the kids. Meet at the Hayward Shoreline Interpretive Center, which is located at the end of Breakwater Avenue in Hayward.

For information, contact the Hayward Shoreline Interpretive Center; (510) 635-0138.

✤ ✤ ✤ ✤

65th Anniversary of the Cement Ship

May 13, 1995 **S** 🖉 • 10 a.m. to 4 p.m.
(see #52 on map page 181)

The *Palo Alto* is the one survivor of only three experimental ships that were constructed of concrete in 1919 in response to World War I-induced steel shortages. In 1930, it was floated to Seacliff State Beach and sunk in hopes of creating a unique and profitable attraction. Unique was about all it succeeded in being. Still, people valiantly sought to make it useful. During its heyday, big bands played on its decks. In the past several decades, untold thousands of fish have been caught from its decks and it has served as a rendezvous for generations of lovers. The anniversary event will feature tours, games and crafts, and there will be food to purchase. Seacliff State Beach is located south of Santa Cruz, just off Highway 1 in Aptos. Take the Seacliff exit and head toward the ocean. There's a fee of $5 per vehicle to get into the park. The weather should be pretty nice, unless the fog rolls in.

For information, contact the California State Parks district office; (408) 688-3241.

✤ ✤ ✤ ✤

Contra Loma Kids Fishing Derby

May 13, 1995 **S** 🖉 • 8 a.m. to 1 p.m.
(see #32 on map page 181)

This is an annual event designed to help kids develop the skills and knowledge for a lifetime of fishing pleasure. The program coordinator will be on hand to offer suggestions and assistance to those who may need some help. There are some big fish in Contra Loma Reservoir and this just might be the fishing trip that gives your kids the thrill of a lifetime, if one of them happens to hook into Moby Fish and win the derby. There is on-site derby registration and no fee charged for kids, except parking fees for their parents' cars. The derby is held at Contra Loma Reservoir, located just south of Antioch.

For information, contact Contra Loma Marina; (510) 636-1684 or (510) 757-0404.

❧ ❧ ❧ ❧

Bike Ride around Lake Chabot

May 14, 1995 **Ⓢ** ⫻ • 10 a.m. to 3 p.m.
(see #38 on map page 181)

This isn't an easy ride, but it's well worth the effort, especially if you've been biking for a while. You'll join other cyclists for a five-hour ride that will take you all the way around Lake Chabot, which is located east of San Leandro. The ride is fairly strenuous; although there is no age limit set for riders, you probably shouldn't bring the real little ones along on this. Bring water and your lunch and maybe some energy snacks. Preregistration is required.

For information, contact the East Bay Regional Parks District; (510) 636-1648.

❧ ❧ ❧ ❧

Mother's Day at Ardenwood

May 14, 1995 **Ⓢ** ⫻ • 2:30 p.m. to 4 p.m.
(see #46 on map page 181)

Rather than taking your favorite mother to brunch like so many people tend to do, why not take her to Ardenwood's Victorian Garden, which should be in full and glorious bloom? Spend the day with Mom strolling the grounds, riding in an elegant carriage or in a down-home hay wagon. You can tour the Patterson Mansion or take Mom on a visit to Lady Blacksmith's shop and see her working on her newest creation. Munch on fresh pastry and sip lemonade or bake a May basket for Mom to take home as a memento of one of the most special Mother's Days she's ever enjoyed. If available, the first 150 Moms will get a single perfect flower as an additional Mom's Day remembrance. Ardenwood Regional Preserve is located near the junction of Highway 84 and Ardenwood Boulevard in Fremont. The preserve is open from 10 a.m. to 4 p.m. The center's seasonal entrance fee is charged.

For information, contact Ardenwood Regional Preserve; (510) 796-0199 or (510) 796-0663.

Educators' Workshop: After the Sun Goes Down

May 19, 1995 [S] ☎ • 7:30 p.m. to 10:30 p.m.

(see #49 on map page 181)

Most teachers have neither the opportunity nor the background to teach their students about nighttime nature. In this workshop, educators will spend three hours with a naturalist studying astronomy and our nearest neighbor, the moon. There'll be a night hike to search for nocturnal wildlife and a chance to learn some sensory games. Wear dark clothes that are quiet when you move, as well as good boots or sturdy shoes. Bring a flashlight that works. The program will be held at Sunol-Ohlone Regional Wilderness and is limited to adults. There's a $20 fee. Preregistration is required.

For information, contact the East Bay Regional Parks District, 2950 Peralta Oaks Court, Oakland, CA 94605-0381; (510) 636-1684.

Wilder Ranch Spring Event

May 20, 1995 [S] ☎ • 10 a.m. to 4 p.m.

(see #29 on map page 180)

If you've ever driven down Highway 1 along California's central coast, then you've undoubtedly noticed all the farms and cattle ranches that line the roadway. Most of them have been there for generations; some began life when Spain and Mexico created their great cattle *ranchos*. Wilder Ranch, one of those early cattle and farming operations, is now preserved for its historic significance.

This spring event turns back the clock, something most of us would no doubt like to do, and recreates life at the old turn-of-the-century ranch. There will be special tours, demonstrations of blacksmithing, horse-drawn-carriage rides, cow milking, a fashion show, music, food and drinks. This is a great family event, so bring the kids. They'll love it.

Wilder Ranch State Park is located right off Highway 1, three miles north of Santa Cruz. There will be an entry fee of $6 per vehicle into the park, so it's cheaper than going to a movie. It should be a beautiful day, weather-wise.

For information, contact Wilder Ranch State Park; (408) 688-3141.

✤ ✤ ✤ ✤

Garin Park Hike

May 20, 1995 **S** 🖉 • 10 a.m. to 2 p.m.
(see #43 on map page 181)

Here is a great place to view songbirds of the coastal mountains. Along with the lingering spring migrants, you might have a chance to see some early summer arrivals. This is an easy four-mile hike and it should be a great birding day. Bring your bird books, water and lunch. To reach Garin Regional Park, take Highway 238 south from Hayward about four miles to Garin Road. Turn left and enter the park. There is a $3 parking fee.

For information, contact the East Bay Regional Parks District, 2950 Peralta Oaks Court, Oakland, CA 94605-0381; (510) 636-1684, ext. 2609.

✤ ✤ ✤ ✤

10th Annual Bay Area Storytelling Festival

May 20 & 21, 1995 **S** 🖉 • 9 a.m. to 7:30 p.m.
(see #15 on map page 180)

Be part of the 10th annual meeting of some of the best tall-tale tellers in the land. From heartfelt love stories to ghastly ghostly tales, legends from yesteryear and contemporary times are the focus of two full days of storytelling. The festival is held at the East Bay

Regional Parks District's Kennedy Grove Regional Recreation Area. Space is limited, so advance reservations are required for this program. The cost will be somewhere in the neighborhood of $40 for the entire weekend, with less charged for individual storytelling concerts. To reach Kennedy Grove, take Interstate 80 to the San Pablo Dam Road exit and drive east for two miles, turning left onto Orinda Road, which deadends after about one mile in the park.

For information, contact the East Bay Regional Parks District, 2950 Peralta Oaks Court, Oakland, CA 94605-0381; (510) 636-1684, ext. 2609.

Points for Fishing Point Pinole

May 28, 1995 [S] ☎ • 2:30 p.m. to 4:30 p.m.
(see #7 on map page 180)

This is one of the times you don't need a fishing license to wet your line. If the $20-plus needed for a license, and even more money for a fishing pole, reel, tackle and bait, has kept you from trying fishing just to see if you like it, then come on down to Point Pinole on San Pablo Bay. There will be an expert angler on hand to talk about the fish that live beneath the pier you'll be casting from, as well as some fishing poles available for loan. The weather should be great, but it may be a little foggy. The program will only cost you about $3. You need to call in order to verify the time and date and preregister for the program.

For information, contact the East Bay Regional Parks District, 2950 Peralta Oaks Court, Oakland, CA 94605-0381; (510) 636-1684, ext. 2609.

Boating by Moonlight

Fourth week in May [S] ☎ • 7:30 p.m. to 9:30 p.m.
(see #45 on map page 181)

Join a naturalist for this evening boat cruise on Lake Del Valle. You'll motor through quiet coves and open water as the sun drops behind the surrounding mountains and you'll witness thousands of stars as they begin to flicker in the darkening sky. You'll learn something about the lake's natural history and the animals that call the shoreline their home. Kids must be at least seven years old to participate and must wear life jackets while on the boat. Advance registration is required. To reach Lake Del Valle, take Interstate 580 east to the North Livermore Avenue exit. Head through town. After eight miles, North Livermore Avenue turns into Tesla Road. Turn right onto Mines Road, which will take you to the lake.

For information, contact the East Bay Regional Parks District, 2950 Peralta Oaks Court, Oakland, CA 94605-0381; (510) 636-1684, ext. 2609.

❖ ❖ ❖ ❖

Old Ways Workshop: Cordage and Nets

May 27 & 28, 1995 • 10 a.m. to 3 p.m.
(see #47 on map page 181)

The series of Old Ways Workshops continues with this session focusing on the production of string and rope from the plants that grow in the hills around the park. The morning will be spent working with native plants such as dog bone, nettle and cattails to fashion cordage. You'll spend the afternoon with store-bought string to learn the basics of net making, something Native Americans used extensively for catching fish in the ocean and streams. There's a $15 fee and you must be at least 10 years old to participate. The workshop is held at the Coyote Hills Regional Park Visitor Center. Preregistration is required. To reach Coyote Hills from Fremont, take Interstate 880 (Nimitz Freeway) to the Decoto Road/Highway 84 exit and head west to the Thornton Avenue/Paseo Padre Parkway exit. Turn north and go one mile to Patterson Ranch Road, then turn left and drive into the park. There's a $3 parking fee on weekends and holidays.

For information, contact the East Bay Regional Parks District, (510) 636-1684; or Coyote Hills Regional Park, 8000 Patterson Ranch Road, Fremont, CA 94555, (510) 795-9385.

❖ ❖ ❖ ❖

Anthony Chabot Campfire Programs

May 27 & 28, 1995 Ⓢ☎ • 7:30 p.m. to 8:30 p.m.
(see #37 on map page 181)

Naturalists from the Crab Cove Visitor Center will be on hand to answer your most puzzling questions about Anthony Chabot Regional Park and nearby Lake Chabot. If you're curious about the natural and cultural history of the park, or of any of the East Bay regional parks, join the crowd heading to the evening campfire programs. Non-campers are invited and there's no fee, so it's a lot cheaper than going to see a movie. You can bring your own popcorn if you like. The programs are held in the campfire center at Anthony Chabot Campground.

To reach the park from downtown Oakland, take Interstate 580 to the 35th Avenue exit. Continue up the hill; 35th Avenue turns into Redwood Road, which leads into the park and to the campground.

For information, contact Crab Cove Visitor Center, 1252 McKay Avenue, Alameda, CA 94501; (510) 521-6887.

Basic Outdoor Skills: Knots, Splices and Lashings

May 29, 1995 Ⓢ☎ • 9:30 a.m. to 1:30 p.m.
(see #47 on map page 181)

If you've ever tried to tie anything and it refused to stay tied, this is a good opportunity to become as proficient in knot-tying as any Boy Scout. You'll learn to tie several knots, some that slip when they're supposed to, as well as some that shouldn't slip and won't. And along with the knots, you'll also learn hitches and bends for some of those special times when square knots and bowlines just won't do the job. Following lunch, which you have to provide for yourself, the group will explore basic lashings and splices used by pioneers. Preregistration is required for this free class. It will be held at the Coyote Hills Regional Park Visitor Center in Fremont. To reach Coyote Hills from Fremont, take Interstate 880 (Nimitz Freeway) to the Decoto Road/Highway 84 exit and head west to the

Thornton Avenue/Paseo Padre Parkway exit. Turn north and go one mile to Patterson Ranch Road, then turn left and drive into the park. There's a $3 parking fee on weekends and holidays.

For information, contact the East Bay Regional Parks District, (510) 636-1684; or Coyote Hills Regional Park, 8000 Patterson Ranch Road, Fremont, CA 94555, (510) 795-9385.

✤ ✤ ✤ ✤

Memorial Day at Rose Hill Cemetery

May 29, 1995 • 1 p.m. to 4 p.m.

(see #33 on map page 181)

The traditional Memorial Day focuses on the country's veterans who served and died in our wars. This is a remembrance of Mount Diablo's many coal miners and their families who are buried in Rose Hill Cemetery. A display of historic photographs helps recapture the lives of the people who came here as their final resting place. You can ride the free shuttle bus to the cemetery. The shuttle should run between 1 p.m. to 4 p.m. on the day of the event, but call to confirm the date and times. Meet at Black Diamond Mines Regional Preserve. To reach the preserve, take Highway 4 east into Antioch and take the Somersville Road exit. Drive south about three miles to the park entrance.

For information, contact Black Diamond Mines Regional Preserve, 5175 Somersville Road, Antioch, CA 94509; (510) 757-2620.

✤ ✤ ✤ ✤

Thursday Morning Bird Walk

June 1, 1995 • 7 a.m. to 9 a.m.

(see #18 on map page 180)

Join a naturalist for a bird walk and geology talk at Robert Sibley Volcanic Regional Preserve. If you've lived in the Bay Area for long, you've undoubtedly felt a few earthquakes. Those shakers are still changing the area's geology. Learn more about what shakes, what doesn't and how well birds handle all the geologic diversity found here. The preserve is located in the East Bay, off Highway 24 and Skyline Boulevard. Bring you binoculars and bird field guides, if you have them.

For information, contact the Tilden Nature Area, Environmental Education Center, Berkeley, CA 94708; (510) 525-2233.

✳ ✳ ✳ ✳

Flyfishing Basics Workshop
June 2 & 3, 1995 Ⓢ 🎣
7 p.m. to 9:30 p.m. on Friday; times vary on Saturday
(see #47 on map page 181)

Flyfishing is one of those so-called pure forms of fishing that far too many people have come to believe is only for the rich, snobby elite. Not true. You'll run into all kinds of people who enjoy flyfishing. This class will be held at Coyote Hills and is designed for those who are interested in stripping away all the mystique of the sport and learning the basics of this time-honored pastime. The Friday evening class will explore the basics through a series of slides, handouts and some hands-on practice. You'll begin to understand the knots, the tackle and the difference between floating and sinking lines. To be successful at flyfishing, you need to know something about the natural history of streams, lakes and rivers, the fish you're trying to entice and the critters that inhabit the streams. Those subjects will also be covered. The instructor will schedule a one-on-one, 45-minute casting session with each participant for Saturday during the session. Fly rods and reels will be available for loan. You must be at least seven years old to participate. Advance registration is required.

To reach Coyote Hills from Fremont, take Interstate 880 (Nimitz Freeway) to the Decoto Road/Highway 84 exit and head west to the Thornton Avenue/Paseo Padre Parkway exit. Turn north and go one mile to Patterson Ranch Road, then turn left and drive into the park. There's a $3 parking fee on weekends and holidays.

For information, contact the East Bay Regional Parks District, 2950 Peralta Oaks Court, Oakland, CA 94605-0381; (510) 636-1684, ext. 2609.

National Trail Day at Redwood Regional Park

June 3, 1995 **S** • 9 a.m. to 4 p.m.

(see #20 on map page 180)

Throughout the nation, people in parks everywhere grab their work gloves, pull on old work clothes and spend a day rehabilitating old trails or building new trails on this day. Spending part of your day in the redwoods, helping to rehabilitate the park's public facilities is a great thing to do. And it's fun, too. Contact the park to find out exactly where to meet, since the trails that need the most work change from year to year, sometimes from month to month. Bring water and lunch. You must be at least 13 years old to participate.

For information, contact Redwood Regional Park; (510) 527-4140.

❖ ❖ ❖ ❖

Breeding Bird Survey

June 4, 1995 **S** • 6 a.m. to 10 a.m.

(see #47 on map page 181)

On this exploration of Coyote Hills, you will try to find as many nesting marsh birds as possible. You and a naturalist will look for nesting pied-billed grebes, common moorhens, maybe a few hovering white-tailed kites, some Bewick's wrens and more. You'll also have an opportunity to learn about the lives of these feathered creatures. This hike isn't meant for kids any younger than seven years of age.

To reach Coyote Hills from Fremont, take Interstate 880 (Nimitz Freeway) to the Decoto Road/Highway 84 exit and head west to the Thornton Avenue/Paseo Padre Parkway exit. Turn north and go one mile to Patterson Ranch Road, then turn left and drive into the park. There's a $3 parking fee on weekends and holidays.

For information, contact Coyote Hills Regional Park, 8000 Patterson Ranch Road, Fremont, CA 94555; (510) 795-9385.

Lake Del Valle Shoreline Nature Ride

June 4, 1995 $ ℓ • 10 a.m. to 11:30 a.m.
(see #45 on map page 181)

If you own a horse, or if you want to rent one, this should be a good morning to join a naturalist for a leisurely ride along Lake Del Valle's eastern shore. There's more to the beautiful scenery than meets the eye and the naturalist will help you discover those little secrets that you might not notice on your own. You should see terns diving into the lake waters and emerging with small fish, as well as the always busy and beautiful swallows buzzing around in their constant hunt for bugs. You need to register in advance for the program. There's a $5 fee for those who bring their own horse and it will cost about $25 if a horse must be provided.

To reach Lake Del Valle, take Interstate 580 east to the North Livermore Avenue exit. Head through town. After eight miles, North Livermore Avenue turns into Tesla Road. Turn right onto Mines Road, which will take you to the lake.

For information, contact the East Bay Regional Parks District, 2950 Peralta Oaks Court, Oakland, CA 94605-0381; (510) 636-1684, ext. 2609.

❀ ❀ ❀ ❀

Ardenwood Tuesday Twilight

June 6, 1995 $ ℓ • 7 p.m. to 9 p.m.
(see #46 on map page 181)

Bring the entire family to this exploration of the secrets of evening on a farm. Most people have heard roosters crowing at dawn, but do you know what happens just before the sun sets each evening? How do animals like chickens get ready for the night, when they have no home security systems to protect them from predators like foxes and coyotes? Here's a chance for you and your kids to find out. Ardenwood Regional Preserve is located near the junction of Highway 84 and Ardenwood Boulevard in Fremont.

For information, contact Ardenwood Regional Preserve; (510) 796-0199 or (510) 796-0663.

❀ ❀ ❀ ❀

Thursday Morning Bird Walk

June 8, 1995 • 7 a.m. to 9 a.m.
(see #46 on map page 181)

Birders of all ages are invited to Ardenwood Regional Preserve in the East Bay to explore the role that birds play down on the farm. Farms create special environments, attracting rodents for owls and bugs for smaller birds. Have you ever noticed all the blackbirds and gulls gathered in a freshly plowed field? Besides learning about how birds adapt to people and their activities, you can learn something about their wild world at this really special place in the East Bay. Ardenwood Regional Preserve is located near the junction of Highway 84 and Ardenwood Boulevard in Fremont.

For information, contact Ardenwood Regional Preserve; (510) 796-0199 or (510) 796-0663.

Family Fishing Festival

June 10, 1995 • 8 a.m. to 10 a.m. & 10:30 a.m. to 12:30 p.m.
(see #42 on map page 181)

There's a first time for everything. While fishing is the most popular participatory sport in the country, there are undoubtedly a few souls who have never learned the few simple things you need to know in order to go chasing those lunkers. This class is always given in conjunction with the Department of Fish and Game's free fishing day, one of the two days each year when you can go fishing without a license. The program is rigged so you can't walk away without catching something. You'll be fishing at Shadow Cliffs Regional Recreation Area, located near Pleasanton, in a specially stocked fishing hole. The park will even provide the fishing pole, reel, bait and everything else that's needed. Just bring yourself, your kids and a desire to have a whole lot of fun. Advance registration is required. There's a $3 per person fee.

To reach Shadow Cliffs, take Interstate 580 to Pleasanton and the Santa Rita Road exit. Head south on Santa Rita to Valley, turn left, then left again on Stanley. The park is on the right. There is a day-use parking fee of $4.

For information, contact the East Bay Regional Parks District, 2950 Peralta Oaks Court, Oakland, CA 94605-0381; (510) 636-1684, ext. 2609.

Special Kids Fishing Derby

June 13, 1995 [S] ☎ • 8 a.m. to 1 p.m.

(see #19 on map page 180)

If you're looking for a good neighborhood program to volunteer with, what could be better than helping up to 100 kids with disabilities who come out with a gleam in their eyes and excitement in their voices, all eager to wet a fishing line? While you won't be catchin' whales, you can't help but get caught up in the fun and excitement these kids experience. All volunteers will have to attend an early morning breakfast and orientation session. Following the orientation, you'll spend the remainder of the day helping some really deserving kids have the time of their lives fishing for the big one. The program is held at Lake Temescal in Oakland.

For information, contact Lake Temescal; (510) 652-1155.

Tilden Nature Area Tuesday Twilight

June 13, 1995 [S] ☎ • 7 p.m. to 9 p.m.

(see #16 on map page 180)

This evening program will take a look at some of the critters that wander around near nightfall—those wild things that stay hidden most of the time, at least when people are around. You and a naturalist will be looking for all those wild animal tracks and their homes. The program is open to all ages.

To reach the Tilden Nature Area from Oakland, head east on Highway 24 and pass through the Caldecott Tunnel to the Fish Ranch Road exit. Head west on Fish Ranch to the Grizzly Peak Boulevard intersection, where you'll turn right and enter the park's south entrance. To reach the nature area, turn left once inside.

For information, contact the Tilden Nature Area, Environmental Education Center, Berkeley, CA 94708; (510) 525-2233.

Thursday Morning Bird Walk

June 15, 1995 **S** 🖋 • 7 a.m. to 9 a.m.
(see #46 on map page 181)

This is a wonderful time of year to look at all the young fledglings that are testing their wings. Come out to Ardenwood Regional Preserve in the East Bay and spend the morning looking for and watching the newest additions to the bird world. Bring binoculars and a birding field guide if you have them. Ardenwood Regional Preserve is located near the junction of Highway 84 and Ardenwood Boulevard in Fremont.

For information, contact Ardenwood Regional Preserve; (510) 769-0199 or (510) 796-0663.

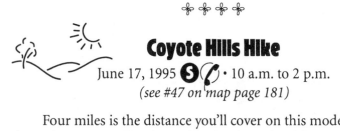

Coyote Hills Hike

June 17, 1995 **S** 🖋 • 10 a.m. to 2 p.m.
(see #47 on map page 181)

Four miles is the distance you'll cover on this moderate hike through Coyote Hills Regional Park. There should be some really good birding opportunities on this hike. It's open to all ages. Bring water, lunch and a friend or two to share the day.

For information, contact the East Bay Regional Parks District, (510) 636-1684; or Coyote Hills Regional Park, 8000 Patterson Ranch Road, Fremont, CA 94555, (510) 795-9385.

Old-Fashioned Campfire Sing-Along

June 18, 1995 **S** 〇 • 5:30 p.m. to 8 p.m.
(see #16 on map page 180)

Bring your longest roasting stick and hot dogs or marshmallows to stick on the end of it and join the naturalist for a roasting, eating, singing good old time at the East Bay's Tilden Nature Area. There will be a roaring campfire to cook your dinner over and a couple of hours for swapping stories, singing songs and having a good time. You should dress appropriately, because summer fog is a frequent evening visitor to the Bay, and while the fire might be warm, it won't last all night. Meet at the Environmental Education Center; the leader will walk you up to the hillside campfire circle as a group. There's no fee and all ages are welcome. To reach the Tilden Nature Area from Oakland, head east on Highway 24 and pass through the Caldecott Tunnel to the Fish Ranch Road exit. Head west on Fish Ranch to the Grizzly Peak Boulevard intersection, where you'll turn right and enter the park's south entrance.

For information, contact the Tilden Nature Area, Environmental Education Center, Berkeley, CA 94708; (510) 525-2233.

❖ ❖ ❖ ❖

Wilderness Fair Nature Rides

June 18, 1995 **S** 〇 • 11 a.m., 1 p.m., 2 p.m. and 3 p.m.
(see #49 on map page 181)

Here's a great chance to try your hand, or actually another portion of your body, at horseback riding. An interpretive aide from Sunol Regional Wilderness will accompany folks on these 30-minute introductory rides into the wilds of the park. The aide will try to answer your questions about the natural and cultural history of the area, point out some of the more fascinating sights and provide encouragement to novice equestrians. There's a fee of about $12 per person for the rides and a $3 parking fee. To reach the Sunol-Ohlone Wilderness from the intersection of interstates 580 and 680, drive south on Interstate 680 for about eight miles to the Highway 84/

Calaveras Road exit. Head south on Calaveras Road approximately four miles to Geary Road. Turn left on to Geary and drive to the park entrance and the visitor center.

For information, contact the East Bay Regional Parks District, 2950 Peralta Oaks Court, Oakland, CA 94605-0381; (510) 636-1684, ext. 2609.

✤ ✤ ✤ ✤

Garin Regional Park Tuesday Twilight

June 20, 1995 **S** ⏱ • 7 p.m. to 9 p.m.
(see #43 on map page 181)

This is an evening look at the cultural and natural history of Garin Regional Park. Join a couple of naturalists to learn a little about the area, the plants that thrive here, the animals that wander about (even if you can't see them), and a few of the park's "secret" places. And all the time, you'll be having some family fun. To reach Garin Regional Park, take Highway 238 south from Hayward about four miles to Garin Road. Turn left and enter the park. There is a $3 parking fee.

For information, contact Garin Regional Park, 1320 Garin Avenue, Hayward, CA 94544; (510) 795-9385.

✤ ✤ ✤ ✤

Senior Safari—Ardenwood Regional Preserve

June 22, 1995 **S** ⏱ • 10 a.m. to 4 p.m.
(see #46 on map page 181)

Join a naturalist for a special bus tour through Niles Canyon, transporting you quickly back to the year 1900 on a 200-acre Fremont farm. You'll have a chance to ride a wagon or horse-drawn carriage to the Patterson Mansion, a 19th-century farmhouse that has been restored. It was built by George Patterson, a '49er who failed at gold mining, but prospered in farming. Today, Patterson's 6,000 acres are still used as a working farm. You'll get to tour the inside of the home and have time to enjoy demonstrations of some of the special skills that were needed to live on a turn-of-the-century farm. The program is designed for older adults and there's a $10 fee. Registration is required.

For information, contact the Pleasanton Senior Center; (510) 636-1684.

❖ ❖ ❖ ❖

Natural History of Lake Fish

June 23, 1995 **$** 🐟 • 9:30 a.m. to 11:30 a.m.
(see #19 on map page 180)

Ask any expert angler and he or she will tell you that you need to know about the life cycles and habits of fish in order to outsmart them. This two-hour class will explore the natural history of some of the fish that live in the East Bay's lakes and rivers. Why and when do fish prefer deeper, colder water? When do they tend to move into the shallows? How big and how fast will fish grow? What will fish eat, when and why? These and more questions that you can think of, as well as a few that you probably never thought to ask, will be answered in the class. This is a must for those folks new to the sport of fishing and for those who seldom catch anything when they do go.

Meet at the Lake Temescal fishing pier. You'll need a fishing license and an East Bay Regional Parks fishing access permit in order to participate. Call to find out what's required and to confirm the dates, times, meeting locations and subjects of each class. Advance registration is required for each of the classes. There is a $3 fee. The program is designed for all ages.

For information, contact Lake Temescal Marina, 6500 Broadway, Oakland, CA 94618, (510) 652-1155; or East Bay Regional Parks District, 2950 Peralta Oaks Court, Oakland, CA 94605-0381, (510) 636-1684.

❖ ❖ ❖ ❖

JUNE

Old Ways Workshop: Weekend in the Stone Age

June 23, 24 & 25, 1995 **S**⌀
Friday noon to Sunday 5 p.m.
(see #49 on map page 181)

If you'd like to spend an entire 54 hours experiencing a close approximation of life back in the Stone Age, then shed all your modern contrivances and conveniences and join this small group of people at remote Camp Ohlone. You'll be starting fires without matches or lighters and cooking without metal pots or pans. No metal tools, no cellular phones, no high-tech tents—it's no joke, but an awful lot of fun. You'll learn bead stringing, tool making, string making and other very basic, but long-forgotten skills practiced by the earliest settlers in this land. You must be at least 12 years old to participate and advance registration is required. Camp Ohlone is located in the Sunol-Ohlone Regional Wilderness, east of Fremont. There will be a fee of approximately $40 for kids and $50 for adults. A higher fee is charged for those who live outside the East Bay Regional Parks District.

For information, contact the East Bay Regional Parks District 2950 Peralta Oaks Court, Oakland, CA 94605-0381; (510) 636-1684.

❖ ❖ ❖ ❖

The Dry Creek Challenge

June 25, 1995 **S**⌀ • Starts at 9 a.m.
(see #43 on map page 181)

If you're a runner and would enjoy running along the scenic trails of Garin and Dry Creek regional parks instead of on stinky city streets, come on up into the Hayward foothills and try this five-mile fun run. The run's route will take you through sections of both parks, over gently rolling hills and through the valley that the creek has carved over eons. Dry Creek, by the way, isn't always dry, in spite of its name. So grab your shorts, your shoes and your wallet and join the fun. Advance registration is required. There will be a fee, probably $12, for each runner.

For information, contact the East Bay Regional Parks District, 2950 Peralta Oaks Court, Oakland, CA 94605-0381; (510) 636-1684, ext. 2609.

Dynamic Delta

June 27, 1995 **$** *• 3:30 p.m. to 4:30 p.m.
(see #31 on map page 181)

This is a tour of the Sacramento River Delta that never leaves the library. Sit back and enjoy a slide program that will show you in one enjoyable hour more about the backwaters of the Delta than you could see by boat in a week. Although it might not be as much fun, it will teach you about the history that surrounds the towns and levees that make up the rich and beautiful water wonderland. Meet in the Pittsburg Library, located at 80 Power Avenue in Pittsburg. All ages are invited to this free program.

For information, contact Black Diamond Mines Regional Preserve, 5175 Somersville Road, Antioch, CA 94509; (510) 757-2620.

JUNE

Black Diamond Mines Tuesday Twilight

June 27, 1995 **$** *• 7 p.m. to 9 p.m.
(see #33 on map page 181)

A naturalist will help you explore the evening world of park wildlife. You may not see a lot of animals, except maybe a few birds, lizards and bats, but you'll find out where they go and why. Do critters vanish during the day because they don't like people, or is there another reason?

To reach Black Diamond Mines Regional Preserve, take Highway 4 east into Antioch and take the Somersville Road exit. Drive south about three miles to the park entrance.

For information, contact Black Diamond Mines Regional Preserve, 5175 Somersville Road, Antioch, CA 94509; (510) 757-2620.

Thursday Morning Bird Walk

June 29, 1995 • 7 a.m. to 9 a.m.

(see #35 on map page 181)

This morning bird stroll will wander through the Diablo foothills along the Pine Creek area. Riparian habitats attract their own special avian visitors and residents. This walk will help you take a closer look at them. Bring binoculars and a bird field guide if you have them.

To reach Black Diamond Mines Regional Preserve, take Highway 4 east into Antioch and take the Somersville Road exit. Drive south about three miles to the park entrance.

For information, contact Black Diamond Mines Regional Preserve, 5175 Somersville Road, Antioch, CA 94509; (510) 757-2620.

✤ ✤ ✤ ✤

Breeding Bird Survey

July 1, 1995 • 6 a.m. to 9 a.m.

(see #46 on map page 181)

Get out early and help survey the Ardenwood farm for nesting birds. With a little direction from a naturalist, you'll spend the morning exploring some of the areas of the park that don't see a great many people. You'll also learn about the habits and whereabouts of such wonderful little feathery creatures as Nuttall's woodpeckers, dark-eyed juncos, rufous-sided towhees, flycatchers, orioles, jays and many more breeding birds. Bring your binoculars and bird field guide if you have them. Ardenwood Regional Preserve is located near the junction of Highway 84 and Ardenwood Boulevard in Fremont.

For information, contact Ardenwood Regional Preserve; (510) 796-0199 or 796-0663.

✤ ✤ ✤ ✤

Sunol Valley Horseback Nature Rides

July 1, 1995 **$** *(• 11 a.m. to 11:30 a.m.*
(see #49 on map page 181)

This 30-minute horseback ride will meander through East Bay's Sunol-Ohlone Regional Wilderness for a quick look at the natural beauty of the area. Besides having an opportunity to see how you like riding a horse, you'll also learn about the area's cultural and natural history. Advance registration is required and there's a $12 fee for the horse rental and ride. To reach the Sunol-Ohlone Regional Wilderness from the intersection of interstates 580 and 680, drive south on Interstate 680 for about eight miles to the Highway 84/ Calaveras Road exit. Head south on Calaveras Road approximately four miles to Geary Road. Turn left on to Geary and drive to the park entrance and the visitor center. There's a $3 parking fee.

For information, contact the East Bay Regional Parks District, 2950 Peralta Oaks Court, Oakland, CA 94605-0381; (510) 636-1684, ext. 2609.

❖ ❖ ❖ ❖

Tilden Nature Area Hike

July 1, 1995 **$** *(• 10 a.m. to 3 p.m.*
(see #16 on map page 180)

The Wildcat Creek watershed in the Tilden Nature Area is the ultimate destination of this six-mile hike. The terrain you'll cover is only moderately rough, so most people should be able to make it, although you've got to be at least five years old to participate. Bring drinking water, lunch, a camera and binoculars, if you have them. It should be a good, warm day.

To reach the Tilden Nature Area from Oakland, head east on Highway 24 and pass through the Caldecott Tunnel to the Fish Ranch Road exit. Head west on Fish Ranch to the Grizzly Peak Boulevard intersection, where you'll turn right and enter the park's south entrance. For the nature area, turn left.

For information, contact the East Bay Regional Parks District, 2950 Peralta Oaks Court, Oakland, CA 94605-0381; (510) 636-1684.

JULY

Nature Detectives

July 1, 1995 • 10:30 a.m. to 11:30 a.m.

(see #23 on map page 180)

Everything in nature is in some way connected to everything else. This program is designed for kids ages three to five and their parents. Since this program is a Fourth of July activity, everyone will get to "sign" the center's special Declaration of Interdependence. Space is limited, so advance reservations are required.

To reach the Hayward Shoreline Interpretive Center, head out of central Hayward on Highway 92 (Jackson Street) and take the Clawiter Road turnoff. From the stop sign, proceed straight for 200 feet, then turn left onto Breakwater Avenue for one mile. Most of the programs are free. Call to make sure it is being offered again this year.

For information, contact the Hayward Recreation and Park District, Hayward Shoreline Interpretive Center, 4901 Breakwater Avenue, Hayward, CA 94545; (415) 881-6751.

Return of the Wind Birds Walk

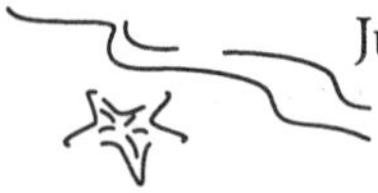

July 2, 1995 • 7:45 a.m. to 9:45 a.m.

(see #23 on map page 180)

You see them every time that you venture near any shoreline, all those strange little birds chasing waves back and forth along the beach and promptly sticking their long, curved beaks into the sand in hopes of finding creatures to eat. The naturalist leader of this walk will help you learn to identify many of those shoreline birds such as plovers, sandpipers, dowithchers and maybe even some of those hordes of gulls that chase after anyone foolish enough to toss food into the air. Bring binoculars and bird field guides, if you have them. You must register in advance for this hike. It will be held at the Hayward Regional Shoreline in the East Bay.

For information, contact the East Bay Regional Parks District, 2950 Peralta Oaks Court, Oakland, CA 94605-0381; (510) 636-1684.

Wilder Ranch Old-Fashioned Fourth of July Picnic

July 4, 1995 • 10 a.m. to 4 p.m.
(see #29 on map page 180)

The Fourth of July hasn't always been celebrated by thousands of fireworks stands selling rather expensive fizzles to the parents of grinning, wild-eyed, excited kids. And there weren't always wild and crazy aerial fireworks displays in nearly every community. Wilder Ranch recreates the old days, when the community came together for a giant picnic and cake walk, square dancing and music. Plus you can enjoy tours around the old ranch house complex.

Wilder Ranch State Park is located right off Highway 1, three miles north of Santa Cruz. There's a $6-per-vehicle entry fee into the park. It should be really nice weather, once the fog has burned off.

For information, contact Wilder Ranch State Park; (408) 688-3141.

❖ ❖ ❖ ❖

Half Moon Bay Ol' Fashion Fourth of July Parade

July 4, 1995 • Starts at noon
(see #25 on map page 180)

JULY

If you've always wanted to be in a parade instead of standing on the sidelines watching, here's your big chance. This is a small town celebration where everyone can participate, especially the youngsters. There are a number of parade categories, including one for horseback riders, people, floats, marching units and animals other than horses and ponies. For kids, the decorated bicycles and trikes and other types of kid transportation are the most fun. Help your youngsters decorate their chosen modes of transportation, then be in the parade line by 11:30 a.m. and you'll be included in the fun.

The parade will travel down Half Moon Bay's Main Street, off US 101, located about 25 miles south of San Francisco. There's a $5 fee for most parade entrants, although entry is free for kids on bikes and trikes. Expect any fog to burn off, bringing sunshine before noon.

For information, contact the Ol' Fashion Fourth of July Committee, P.O. Box 848, Half Moon Bay, CA 94019; (415) 726-4201.

❧ ❧ ❧ ❧

Thursday Morning Bird Walk

July 6, 1995 **$**⟨⟩ • 7 a.m. to 10:30 a.m.
(see #22 on map page 180)

Meet with a naturalist to search for the elusive California least tern, a beautiful and endangered shoreline bird. You'll be wandering around the Crab Cove Visitor Center near the Alameda Naval Air Station and should see terns, along with a great many other shoreline bird species. Bring binoculars and a bird field guide if you have them. To reach the Crab Cove Visitor Center from Oakland, take Interstate 880 to the Broadway exit and turn right. Continue to Webster, turn right and go through the Alameda Tunnel. Turn onto Central, then turn left on McKay. The park entrance is on the left.

For information, contact the Crab Cove Visitor Center, (510) 521-6887.

❧ ❧ ❧ ❧

Catching the Big One

July 7, 1995 **$**⟨⟩ • 9:30 a.m. to 11:30 a.m.
(see #32 on map page 181)

If you've spent much time watching others fish lake waters around the East Bay, you may have seen some really big fish caught. There are some secrets for catching bigger fish, including knowing where they are and what kind of real and fake edibles are best for attracting them to your hook. Learn the inside tips in this program designed for all ages. You'll need a fishing license and an East Bay Regional Parks fishing access permit in order to participate. Call to find out for certain what's required and to confirm the dates, times, meeting locations and subjects of each class. Advance registration is required for each of the classes. There will be a $3 fee per person, plus a $4 vehicle parking fee. Meet at Contra Loma Regional Park, south of Antioch, just off Contra Loma Boulevard.

For information, contact Contra Loma Regional Park, 1200 Frederickson Lane, Antioch, CA 94509, (510) 757-0404; or the East Bay Regional Parks District, 2950 Peralta Oaks Court, Oakland, CA 94605-0381, (510) 636-1684.

Family Camping for Beginners

July 7, 21 & 22, 1995
(see #49 on map page 181)

If you've never been camping and would like to find out what it's all about, and if all you need to get started in this great American pastime is a little guidance, then this class and camping trip are for you. The Friday evening class will cover all the basics of what to expect and what others expect of you when you're out there in any of the thousands of campgrounds in the West. Everything from building campfires to cooking and cleaning will be covered. The book learnin' is followed by an overnight camping trip with the group at the Sunol-Ohlone Regional Wilderness family campground. You and your family will have a great time, the first of a lifetime of wonderful adventures. There is a $20 fee for the entire family.

To reach the Sunol-Ohlone Regional Wilderness from the intersection of interstates 580 and 680, drive south on Interstate 680 for about eight miles to the Highway 84/Calaveras Road exit. Head south on Calaveras Road approximately four miles to Geary Road. Turn left on to Geary and drive to the park entrance and the visitor center. There's a $3 parking fee.

For information, contact the East Bay Regional Parks District, 2950 Peralta Oaks Court, Oakland, CA 94605-0381; (510) 636-1684.

Exploring the Delta by Bus

July 8, 1995 • 9 a.m. to 2:30 p.m.

(see #33 on map page 181)

This is a great trip for exploring the Delta. You'll be boarding a bus at Black Diamond Mines Regional Preserve, then heading off for an adventure you won't soon forget. The first stop is scheduled to be Locke Slough to investigate the plants and animals of the Delta. That will be followed by a tour of the Dai Loy Museum in the old Chinese river town of Locke to look at the art of the Sacramento River Delta. The last part of the day will be lunch at Brannan Island State Recreation Area and a tour of the park's visitor center. You'll need to make reservations for this tour. The fee will be about $20, and you must be at least 10 years old in order to participate.

For information, contact the East Bay Regional Parks District, 2950 Peralta Oaks Court, Oakland, CA 94605-0381; (510) 636-1684.

Junior Farm Ramblers

July 8, 1995 • 9:30 a.m. to noon

(see #47 on map page 181)

Farm life is something most kids, or adults for that matter, never get a chance to experience. But it doesn't have to be that way. The Junior Farm Ramblers lets kids get down and dirty with farm animals and farm chores. They'll be gathering eggs, feeding animals, hoisting hay and doing all the other things that farm kids do everyday. But the day is not all work and no play. There'll be games to divert the crew and food from the country kitchen to snack on. The program is designed for kids ages five to seven and registration is required. There's a fee of $5 per child.

For information, contact Coyote Hills Regional Park, 8000 Patterson Ranch Road, Fremont, CA 94555; (510) 795-9385.

Lake Chabot Challenge Half Marathon

July 9, 1995 **$** *•* Starts at 8 a.m.
(see #38 on map page 181)

For real runners, this 13.1-mile half marathon is a good challenge and the scenery around Lake Chabot is wonderful; in fact, it might even keep your mind off the pain of the run if you're into running hard or not in the greatest shape. The race course travels over dirt fire roads, paved hiking trails and dirt horse trails. This is a very challenging run, so do yourself a favor and don't attempt this if you aren't in shape to complete a run of this distance over less than flat and level ground. Advance registration is required; it's only $15 if you do it in advance, rather than $18 if you wait until race day. The profits collected will be used to pay for trail maintenance around Lake Chabot.

For information, contact Lake Chabot; (510) 484-1339.

Old-Fashioned Campfire Sing-Along

July 9, 1995 **$** *•* 5:30 p.m. to 8 p.m.
(see #16 on map page 180)

For details about this roasting, eating, singing good old time at Tilden Nature Area, see page 239. Meet at the Environmental Education Center; the leader will walk the group up to the hillside campfire circle. There's no fee and all ages are welcome. To reach the Tilden Nature Area from Oakland, head east on Highway 24 and pass through the Caldecott Tunnel to the Fish Ranch Road exit. Head west on Fish Ranch to the Grizzly Peak Boulevard intersection, where you'll turn right and enter the park's south entrance.

For information, contact the Tilden Nature Area, Environmental Education Center, Berkeley, CA 94708; (510) 525-2233.

JULY

Dynamic Delta

July 11, 1995 **S** 🖉 • 1 p.m. to 2 p.m.
(see #32 on map page 181)

This is another tour of the Sacramento River Delta that never leaves the library. Sit back and enjoy a slide program that will show you in one hour more about the backwaters of the Delta than you might see by boat in a week. Although it might not be as much fun, it will teach you about the rich history that surrounds the towns and levees that make up this rich and beautiful water wonderland. Meet in the Antioch Library, located on 18th Street, between G and D streets in the Delta town of Antioch. All ages are invited to attend this free program and no advance registration is required.

For information, contact Black Diamond Mines Regional Preserve, 5175 Somersville Road, Antioch, CA 94509; (510) 757-2620.

❖ ❖ ❖ ❖

Sunol Wilderness Tuesday Twilight

July 11, 1995 **S** 🖉 • 7 p.m. to 9 p.m.
(see #49 on map page 181)

You've probably wandered along a stream in the middle of the day, but have you ever spent time really exploring the same place in late evening? A naturalist will lead this hike through the woodland and stream habitats of Sunol-Ohlone Regional Wilderness during the last couple hours of daylight. You'll get a new look at some of the same old things as they take on a whole new light in the quiet evening hours. To reach the Sunol-Ohlone Regional Wilderness from the intersection of interstates 580 and 680, drive south on Interstate 680 for about eight miles to the Highway 84/Calaveras Road exit. Head south on Calaveras Road approximately four miles to Geary Road. Turn left onto Geary and drive to the park entrance and the visitor center. There's a $3 parking fee.

For information, contact Sunol-Ohlone Regional Wilderness, P.O. Box 82, Sunol, CA 94586; (510) 862-2244.

❖ ❖ ❖ ❖

Thursday Morning Bird Walk

July 13, 1995 **S** • 7 a.m. to 9 a.m.

(see #43 on map page 181)

Garin Regional Park is located in the East Bay just south of Hayward and is a great spot for birding. This particular early morning walk is designed especially for beginning birders. The naturalist will be focusing on the sounds that different bird species make, so you will actually be able to identify these small, feathered creatures not just by sight. Bring your bird field guide, if you have one, and a pair of binoculars, so you can see where the sounds are coming from. To reach Garin Regional Park, take Highway 238 south from Hayward about four miles to Garin Road. Turn left and enter the park. There is a $3 parking fee.

For information, contact Garin Regional Park, 1320 Garin Avenue, Hayward, CA 94544; (510) 795-9385.

❖ ❖ ❖ ❖

Sunol Teen Peak Hike

July 13, 1995 **S** • 9 a.m. to noon

(see #49 on map page 181)

JULY

If you're a teenager looking for something exciting and different to do this summer, try this first in a series of hikes to various peaks in East Bay regional parks. The challenge of this hike to Flag Hill is not too great, with a distance of only 2.5 miles, but it's enough to get your heart pumping and your lungs working. Bring water and a light snack for energy and meet at Sunol-Ohlone Regional Wilderness. You must be somewhere between the ages of 13 and 18 in order to participate. Advance registration is required and there will be a parking fee of $3.

For information, contact the East Bay Regional Parks District, 2950 Peralta Oaks Court, Oakland, CA 94605-0381; (510) 636-1684.

❖ ❖ ❖ ❖

Facts and Fables of Lake Angling

July 14, 1995 Ⓢ☎ • 9:30 a.m. to 11:30 a.m.
(see #38 on map page 181)

There are all kinds of stories about when and how to best catch fish, some of which are true and some of which are figments of someone's vivid imagination. For instance, does it really make a difference if you fish just before or just after a storm? How about when there's a full moon, or in the early morning, instead of the middle of the day? Some of these tricks do seem to make a difference and some don't. Come to this two-hour class and learn the truth about lake angling. Meet at Lake Chabot, which is located near San Leandro, just off Interstate 580 and Lake Chabot Road. You'll need a fishing license and an East Bay Regional Parks fishing access permit in order to participate. Call to confirm the dates, times, meeting locations and the subject of each class. Advance registration is required. There's a $3 fee for the program.

For information, contact the East Bay Regional Parks District, 2950 Peralta Oaks Court, Oakland, CA 94605-0381; (510) 636-1684.

Sunol Valley Horseback Nature Ride

July 15, 1995 Ⓢ☎ • 11 a.m. to 11:30 a.m.
(see #49 on map page 181)

This 30-minute horseback ride meanders through Sunol-Ohlone Regional Wilderness for a quick look at the natural beauty of the area. Besides having an opportunity to see how you like riding a horse, you'll also learn about the area's cultural and natural history. Advance registration is required. There's a $12 fee for the horse rental and ride. To reach the Sunol-Ohlone Regional Wilderness from the intersection of interstates 580 and 680, drive south on Interstate 680 for about eight miles to the Highway 84/Calaveras Road exit. Head south on Calaveras Road approximately four miles to Geary Road. Turn left onto Geary and drive to the park entrance and the visitor center. There's a $3 parking fee.

For information, contact the East Bay Regional Parks District, 2950 Peralta Oaks Court, Oakland, CA 94605-0381; (510) 636-1684.

❖ ❖ ❖ ❖

Ardenwood Farm Ramblers

July 15, 1995 • 9:30 a.m. to noon
(see #47 on map page 181)

This program is the same as the Junior Farm Ramblers, tentatively held the previous weekend, but this one is for older kids. If you've got a few spare 8- to 10-year-olds who might like to spend a Saturday on the farm doing farm chores and eating good old down-home farm cooking, then this is a great place to be. Registration is required and the fee is $5 per child.

For information, contact Coyote Hills Regional Park, 8000 Patterson Ranch Road, Fremont, CA 94555; (510) 795-9385.

❖ ❖ ❖ ❖

Kule Loklo Big Time

July 15, 1995 • 11:30 a.m. to 4:30 p.m.
(see #5 on map page 180)

California's Native Americans lived a relatively rich life along the Pacific Coast. Big Time is a chance to see what life was like in California before Europeans arrived and changed the land and the people who lived here. This annual celebration will be held at Kule Loklo, which means Bear Valley in the dialect of the Coast Mi-wok. Kule Loklo is a reconstructed display of a traditional village where Native American demonstrators will perform tribal dances and demonstrate flint knapping, clamshell bead making and basketry. A large assortment of handmade items, including baskets, jewelry, clothing and artwork, will be available for purchase. These are always fun events, with opportunities to see and experience a bit of California's past. Kids will have a chance to try their hand at traditional Native American skills, such as drilling sea shells with a pump drill, grinding acorns and perhaps making fire without matches or a lighter. There is always plenty of good food and beverages available if you choose not to bring your own picnic lunch, but the lines can get pretty long. Sunscreen and hats can be a welcome relief from the sun. Bring your cameras and video cams because most of the activities can be photographed. (Dancers may request that a few of their dances not be photographed, generally those with religious significance. Please respect their wishes.)

Kule Loklo is located a half-mile walk from the Bear Valley Visitor Center, which is located off Bear Valley Road, about a half mile from the Highway 1 turnoff at the small community of Olema. There's no cost for the program. Summer's early morning fog should give way to heat and sun for most of the day.

For information, contact Bear Valley Visitor Center, Point Reyes National Seashore, Point Reyes, CA 94956; (415) 663-1092.

❖ ❖ ❖ ❖

Lafayette-Moraga Trail Hike

July 16, 1995 • 3:30 p.m. to 9 p.m.
(see #17 on map page 180)

A naturalist will lead this six-mile evening hike, exploring the history of this trail and the nearby communities. Since you won't get back until around dark, you should probably bring a flashlight along. You may get a chance to view some of the more secretive, nocturnal creatures that are fairly abundant in the East Bay parklands. The hike is open to all ages. Call for the planned meeting place and to confirm the time.

For information, contact the East Bay Regional Parks District, 2950 Peralta Oaks Court, Oakland, CA 94605-0381; (510) 636-1684.

❖ ❖ ❖ ❖

Standoff at the Patterson Ranch

July 16, 1995 $ • 6 p.m. to 8:30 p.m.
(see #46 on map page 181)

It's a story that could have been the plot of a Hollywood movie, and in many ways it has been. On the morning of July 16, 1877, facing a hostile group of armed men, a railroad construction crew laid track across the land of a very uncooperative farmer. Since part of the evening's program includes a ride on rails aboard an 1880s handcar, you've already got an idea of how the armed standoff turned out 118 years ago. You can also take an evening train ride, enjoy the surrounding farmland and learn a little bit about the history of the area. There will also be a reenactment of the conflict between the farmer named Patterson and the railroaders. The program is held at Ardenwood Regional Preserve, which is located near the junction of Highway 84 and Ardenwood Boulevard in Fremont.

For information, contact Ardenwood Regional Preserve; (510) 796-0199 or (510) 796-0663.

JULY

✤ ✤ ✤ ✤

Family Camping Series

July 16, 22 & 23, 1995
(see #37 on map page 181)

This is one of several East Bay Regional Parks camping trips designed for novice campers who want to find out what camping in the great outdoors is all about. The initial two-hour meeting will be a discussion of what you'll need and what to expect if you decide to participate in the following weekend's camping trip. The campout will be held at Anthony Chabot Campground in Anthony Chabot Regional Park. There's a $25 fee per family for the program.

For information, contact the East Bay Regional Parks District, 2950 Peralta Oaks Court, Oakland, CA 94605-0381; (510) 636-1684.

✤ ✤ ✤ ✤

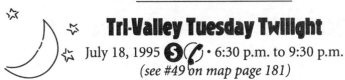

Tri-Valley Tuesday Twilight

July 18, 1995 **S** ⚬ • 6:30 p.m. to 9:30 p.m.
(see #49 on map page 181)

Pleasanton Ridge in Sunol-Ohlone Regional Wilderness is a wonderful place to spend a couple of evening hours enjoying scenic vistas of the area's hilltops. There will be a naturalist along to explain the land forms and the natural history of the area. And you should always be watching for wildlife emerging from hiding places this time of evening. To reach the Sunol-Ohlone Regional Wilderness from the intersection of interstates 580 and 680, drive south on Interstate 680 for about eight miles to the Highway 84/Calaveras Road exit. Head south on Calaveras Road approximately four miles to Geary Road. Turn left onto Geary and drive to the park entrance and the visitor center. There's a $3 parking fee.

For information, contact Sunol-Ohlone Regional Wilderness, P.O. Box 82, Sunol, CA 94586; (510) 862-2244.

❋ ❋ ❋ ❋

Exploring the California Delta by Boat

July 18, 1995 **S** ⚬ • 10 a.m. to 2:30 p.m.
(see #33 on map page 181)

With 57 islands dotting the 1,000 miles of waterways of the Sacramento River Delta, there is no end to the exploration that's possible here, providing you have a boat. If you don't have a boat, but would still like to explore the Delta, join this six-island journey with a naturalist from the East Bay Regional Parks District. You'll meet at Black Diamond Mines Regional Preserve near Antioch, then board a bus to the Ryer Island Ferry, where you'll be jumping onto a boat. The day ends with a picnic lunch at Brannan Island State Recreation Area near Rio Vista and a tour of the visitor center. Advance registration is required and there's a fee of about $15. Participants must be at least 10 years old to join the group.

For information, contact the East Bay Regional Parks District, 2950 Peralta Oaks Court, Oakland, CA 94605-0381; (510) 636-1684.

Parks Express Shoreline Festival

July 20, 1995 **S** 🞉 • 9:30 a.m. to 3 p.m.
(see #9 on map page 180)

If you'd like to volunteer to help a few of the 500 inner-city kids, senior citizens and folks with disabilities who participate in this event, then come on out to Martinez Regional Shoreline and join a group of dedicated individuals who enjoy helping others understand and enjoy the great outdoors. You'll spend the day helping a whole bunch of deserving folks fly kites, study nature and do a little fishing. There will be music, refreshments and lunch provided to all volunteers. You must be at least 16 years old to participate as a volunteer. Registration is required.

For information, contact Martinez Regional Shoreline; (510) 635-0138, ext. 2205.

✤ ✤ ✤ ✤

Fishing San Pablo Bay

July 21, 1995 **S** 🞉 • 10:30 a.m. to 1 p.m.
(see #7 on map page 180)

Historically, San Pablo Bay was a fantastic fishery. While the fishing today isn't what it was 100 or even 25 years ago, there's still some good fishing to be had. All you have to know is how and when to approach these salty waters. You might want to bring your lunch for this one. This naturalist-led class will meet on Friday at Pinole Point fishing pier, just north of the town of San Pablo, off Giant Highway and Atlas Road. You'll need a fishing license in order to participate. Call to confirm the dates, times, meeting locations and the subject of each class. Advance registration is required. The class is open to all ages and there will be a $3 fee.

For information, contact the East Bay Regional Parks District, 2950 Peralta Oaks Court, Oakland, CA 94605-0381; (510) 636-1684.

✤ ✤ ✤ ✤

JULY

Historic Workboat Rendezvous

July 22, 1995 **S** ⋅ Noon to 6 p.m.
(see #6 on map page 180)

China Camp is an historic shrimp fishing village that has kept its connection with the past. Today, with the shrimp industry no longer centered in San Pablo Bay, the park is a quiet refuge for an old way of life. The pier, the old buildings, a remnant boat and nets set out to dry in the warm sun provide a proper backdrop for the historic boats that are the focus of this summer day. It's a wonderful time to see the old ways of a lost industry.

China Camp State Park is located north of San Francisco on US 101. Take the North San Pedro Road exit. Drive east until you enter the park. There will be a $3 fee per vehicle entering the park. It should be warm and sunny, unless the ocean fog rolls in.

For information, contact China Camp State Park; (415) 456-0766.

❖ ❖ ❖ ❖

Old Ways Workshop: Indian Village Workday

July 23, 1995 **S** ⋅ 9:30 a.m. to 4 p.m.
(see #47 on map page 181)

Fremont's Coyote Hills possess a number of Ohlone village sites and one of the oldest is used for various educational programs. A replica of an Ohlone village has been built on the site to further enhance the educational experience. Like any facility, the village is in need of ongoing maintenance and volunteers are the best way to get the work done. If you're at least 10 years old and want to help, then come on by and lend a hand cutting new cattails for the huts, thatching, cleaning and weaving tule mats, and assisting with a few dozen other tasks that need to be completed. To reach Coyote Hills from Fremont, take Interstate 880 (Nimitz Freeway) to the Decoto Road/Highway 84 exit and head west to the Thornton Avenue/Paseo Padre Parkway exit. Turn north and go one mile to Patterson Ranch Road, then turn left and drive into the park. There's a $3 parking fee on weekends and holidays.

For information, contact Coyote Hills Regional Park, 8000 Patterson Ranch Road, Fremont, CA 94555; (510) 795-9385.

❀ ❀ ❀ ❀

Drawing Women Into the Garden

July 23, 1995 **S**🖉 · 2 p.m. to 4 p.m.
(see #46 on map page 181)

If you have even the slightest interest in creating art, then join this look at the botany of 19th-century gardens and the style of drawing and painting practiced by Victorian women. Artists of all skill levels are welcome to join in this different way of viewing Ardenwood Regional Preserve's lush and colorful gardens. Bring your own drawing or painting materials; the naturalist will provide the background information that should inspire you to do your best work. Both men and women are welcome to attend and participate. Ardenwood Regional Preserve is located near the junction of Highway 84 and Ardenwood Boulevard in Fremont.

For information, contact Ardenwood Regional Preserve; (510) 796-0199 or (510) 796-0663.

❀ ❀ ❀ ❀

Briones Tuesday Twilight

July 25, 1995 **S**🖉 · 7 p.m. to 9 p.m.
(see #16 on map page 180)

Here's an evening walk through Briones Regional Park in the Martinez hills. A naturalist will lead this exploration of grassland and woodland habitats. It should be quite a pleasant way to spend an evening. Bring a flashlight with you, one with fresh batteries. Briones Regional Park is located in the hills south of Martinez and north of Lafayette. From Lafayette, take Happy Valley Road north from Highway 24 for about four miles, to the intersection with Bear Creek Road. Turn right onto Bear Creek Road and drive about a half mile to Briones Road, which enters the southwest portion of the park.

For information, contact Briones Regional Park, (510) 229-3020.

✤ ✤ ✤ ✤

Sunol Teen Peak Hike

July 27, 1995 **S** 🕐 • 9 a.m. to 1 p.m.
(see #49 on map page 181)

Teens between the ages of 13 and 18 are invited to break the summer boredom by pitting themselves against the physical challenges of one of the East Bay's parks. This is a 4.7-mile hike to the top of Maguire Peaks in Sunol-Ohlone Regional Wilderness. Bring water and food and $3 to take care of the park's entrance fee. There should be some really great views from the mountains and you'll gain some personal pleasure from having completed the hike. Advance registration is required.

For information, contact the East Bay Regional Parks District, 2950 Peralta Court, Oakland, CA 94605-0381; (510) 636-1684.

✤ ✤ ✤ ✤

Thursday Morning Bird Walk

July 27, 1995 **S** 🕐 • 8 am. to noon
(see #32 on map page 181)

Whether you're a novice birder or have been at it for a few years, you still may have trouble identifying water and shoreline birds. This four-hour walk will focus your binoculars and bird field guides on identifying shore birds that live in the Delta near Antioch Marina and the Ironhouse Sanitary District. Call to confirm the date, time and meeting place.

For information, contact Black Diamond Mines Regional Preserve, 5175 Somersville Road, Antioch, CA 94509; (510) 757-2620.

✤ ✤ ✤ ✤

Concours d'Elegance

Fourth Sunday in July [S] ☎ • 10 a.m. to 4 p.m.

(see #17 on map page 180)

For owners and connoisseurs of old and elegant sports cars, or wannabe owners and connoisseurs of old and elegant sports cars, Lafayette is the place to be in late July. Each year, hundreds of pre-1969 automobiles arrive to compete for best of show in one of California's Sports Car Club of America's premier events. While 1994 saw Italian sports cars highlighted, 1995 will feature Germany Mercedes Benz creations from the early to mid-1900s. While the 300 to 400 cars compete for the judges' notice, many people bring their pride and joy out just to be admired by all. Bring your camera to capture a big part of America's history. The program is held at Acalanes High School, which is located at 1200 Pleasant Hill Road in Lafayette, northeast of Oakland, off Highway 24. There's a $10 entry fee. The weather should be real warm.

For information, contact the Lafayette Chamber of Commerce, 100 Lafayette Circle #103, Lafayette, CA 94549; (510) 284-7404.

Nestling Birders Academy

Fourth week in July [S] ☎ • 9:30 a.m. to 11:30 a.m.

(see #47 on map page 181)

This four-day outdoor educational program is geared toward giving four- and five-year-olds a better understanding of the birds that live in and pass through the Bay Area. This will be a chance for the kids to sing, eat and live like birds, so to speak. The youngsters will earn their wings at graduation from the Nestling Birders Academy. The program is held in Coyote Hills Regional Park and costs just $20 per child. Registration is required. To reach Coyote Hills from Fremont, take Interstate 880 (Nimitz Freeway) to the Decoto Road/Highway 84 exit and head west to the Thornton Avenue/Paseo Padre Parkway exit. Turn north and go one mile to Patterson Ranch Road, then turn left and drive into the park. There's a $3 parking fee on weekends and holidays.

For information, contact Coyote Hills Regional Park, 8000 Patterson Ranch Road, Fremont, CA 94555; (510) 795-9385.

❖ ❖ ❖ ❖

Shoreline Exploration and Sunfish Surprise

July 28, 1995 **S** *∅* • 9:30 a.m. to 11:30 a.m.
(see #39 on map page 181)

The stream and small reservoir at Cull Canyon provide good places for kids and adults to catch sunfish. These smaller fish seem to thrive around the shallower waters near the shoreline, especially if there's a little cover where they can dodge some of the bigger bass, crappie or other small-fish eaters. Grab your pole and join the naturalists to learn the secrets of catching these little fish, which are good to eat if you want to clean them, or you can simply toss them back so they'll grow bigger. Meet at Cull Canyon Regional Recreation Area, which is located just northeast of Castro Valley, off Interstate 580 and Crow Canyon Road. You'll need a fishing license and an East Bay Regional Parks fishing access permit in order to participate. Call to confirm the dates, times, meeting locations and subject of each class. Advance registration is required. There's a $3 fee for the class.

For information, contact the East Bay Regional Parks District, 2950 Peralta Oaks Court, Oakland, CA 94605-0381; (510) 636-1684.

❖ ❖ ❖ ❖

Summer Farm Fair

July 29 & 30, 1995 **S** *∅* • 10 a.m. to 4 p.m.
(see #46 on map page 181)

This is farm life at its best. With the summer wheat ready for harvest, you can get a little exercise and have fun helping with the threshing. There will be many demonstrations of 19th-century farm chores, including mowing, binding, stacking, baling and milling. Should the little ones grow tired of all that work and no play, there will also be craft demonstrations and toy-making sessions. The fair is held at Ardenwood Regional Preserve, which is located near the junction of Highway 84 and Ardenwood Boulevard in Fremont. The fee hasn't yet been determined.

For information, contact Ardenwood Regional Preserve; (510) 796-0199 or (510) 796-0663.

✤ ✤ ✤ ✤

Berry Basket Workshop

July 30, 1995 **S** 🖋 • 10 a.m. to 2 p.m.
(see #47 on map page 181)

California's Native Americans were expert basket makers and this is a great introductory basket-making class for anyone interested in this ancient art. You'll have an opportunity to make a small basket from the native tule plant—the kind of basket used by the Native Americans to gather and carry berries. There's a $25 fee for the class and you must be at least 12 years old to participate. Advance registration is required. It will be held at the Coyote Hills Regional Park Visitor Center in Fremont. To reach Coyote Hills from Fremont, take Interstate 880 (Nimitz Freeway) to the Decoto Road/Highway 84 exit and head west to the Thornton Avenue/Paseo Padre Parkway exit. Turn north and go one mile to Patterson Ranch Road, then turn left and drive into the park. There's a $3 parking fee on weekends and holidays.

For information, contact the East Bay Regional Parks District, 2950 Peralta Oaks Court, Oakland, CA 94605-0381; (510) 636-1684.

JULY

✤ ✤ ✤ ✤

Sunol Valley Horseback Nature Ride

July 30, 1995 **S** 🖋 • 11 a.m. to 11:30 a.m.
(see #49 on map page 181)

This 30-minute horseback ride will meander through Sunol Regional Wilderness for a quick look at the natural beauty of the area. Besides having an opportunity to see how you like riding a horse, you'll also learn about the area's cultural and natural history. Advance registration is required and there's a $12 fee for the horse rental and ride. To reach the Sunol-Ohlone Wilderness from the intersection of interstates 580 and 680, drive south on Interstate 680 for about eight miles to the Highway 84/Calaveras Road exit. Head south on Calaveras Road approximately four miles to Geary Road. Turn left onto Geary and drive to the park entrance and the visitor center. There's a $3 parking fee.

For information, contact the East Bay Regional Parks District, 2950 Peralta Oaks Court, Oakland, CA 94605-0381; (510) 636-1684.

�֎ �֎ �֎ ✖

Shadow Cliffs Tuesday Twilight

August 1, 1995 $ ℓ • 6:30 p.m. to 8:30 p.m.
(see #42 on map page 181)

Arroyos aren't always well understood, at least their importance to the surrounding wildlife. Join a naturalist for this look at the secrets of the park's arroyo during this evening walk and talk. You may get lucky and see some of the nocturnal wildlife emerging from their hiding places to begin another evening of feeding.

For information, contact Del Valle Regional Park, 7000 Del Valle Road, Livermore, CA 94550; (510) 373-0332.

✖ ✖ ✖ ✖

Dynamic Delta

August 1, 1995 $ ℓ • 2 p.m. to 3 p.m.
(see #8 on map page 180)

This is a tour of the Sacramento River Delta that never leaves the library. Sit back and enjoy a slide program that will show you in one hour more about the backwaters of the Delta than you could probably see by boat in a week. Although it might not be as much fun as a boat ride, it will teach you about the rich history that surrounds the towns and levees that make up the rich and beautiful water wonderland. Meet in the Martinez Library located at 740 Court Street. All ages are invited to this free program.

For information, contact Black Diamond Mines Regional Preserve, 5175 Somersville Road, Antioch, CA 94509; (510) 757-2620.

❀ ❀ ❀ ❀

Batting by Boat

August 3, 1995 ❸ ⬭ • 7 p.m. to 9:30 p.m.
(see #38 on map page 181)

Although we're well into the baseball season in August (hopefully), this trip has nothing to do with the national pastime. Instead, this is a look at the fascinating world of those black and brown creatures that fill our night skies, ridding the woods of a lot of flying bugs. You'll be boarding the *Chabot Queen* on Lake Chabot and heading off on the short trip to Raccoon Point. Bring a picnic dinner because you'll be spending the evening here listening to facts and folklore about bats. After the sun sets, you'll sit around waiting for the bats to emerge from their daytime hiding places. You'll be walking the 1.5 miles back to the marina with the group, so wear some comfortable shoes. Advance registration is required and there is a $5 fee for adults and a $3 fee for kids.

For information, contact the East Bay Regional Parks District, 2950 Peralta Oaks Court, Oakland, CA 94605-0381; (510) 636-1684.

AUGUST

❀ ❀ ❀ ❀

Thursday Morning Bird Walk

August 3, 1995 ❸ ⬭ • 7 a.m. to 9 a.m.
(see #43 on map page 181)

This morning hike is in the East Bay's Garin Regional Park, which is south of Hayward. A naturalist will lead the group along the Dry Creek Trail for a look at the diversity of wildlife that makes this area of the hills their home. Bring binoculars and a bird field guide if you have them, and wear some good walking shoes or hiking boots. To reach Garin Regional Park, take Highway 238 south from Hayward about four miles to Garin Road. Turn left and enter the park. There is a $3 parking fee.

For information, contact Garin Regional Park, 1320 Garin Avenue, Hayward, CA 94544; (510) 795-9385.

❈ ❈ ❈ ❈

Natural History of Bay Fish

August 4, 1995 **S**⟋ • 9:30 a.m. to 11:30 a.m.
(see #9 on map page 180)

Here's an opportunity to learn all about the fish that live in the waters between San Pablo Bay and Suisun Bay. One of the things that will become apparent is that the kinds of fish that spend their time in these waters tend to change with the seasons. You'll learn something about anadromous fish, such as salmon and steelhead, which spend most of their lives in the deep waters of the Pacific, coming through the bays and on up into the freshwater rivers to spawn. And you'll learn about the native fish that tend to linger near the piers and along the shoreline—and how you can go about catching them. Meet at Martinez Regional Shoreline's Martinez Pier. You'll need a fishing license in order to participate. Call to confirm the dates, times, meeting locations and the subject of each class. Advance registration is required. There's a $3 fee for the class.

For information, contact the East Bay Regional Parks District, 2950 Peralta Oaks Court, Oakland, CA 94605-0381; (510) 636-1684.

❈ ❈ ❈ ❈

Sunol Valley Horseback Nature Ride

August 5, 1995 **S**⟋ • 11 a.m. to 11:30 a.m.
(see #49 on map page 181)

This 30-minute horseback ride will meander through East Bay's Sunol-Ohlone Regional Wilderness for a quick look at the natural beauty of the area. Besides having an opportunity to see how you like riding a horse, you'll also learn about the area's cultural and natural history. Advance registration is required and there's a $12 fee for the horse rental and ride. To reach the Sunol-Ohlone Regional Wilderness, from the intersection of interstates 580 and 680, drive south on Interstate 680 for about eight miles to the Highway 84/Calaveras Road exit. Head south on Calaveras Road approximately four miles to Geary Road. Turn left onto Geary and drive to the park entrance and the visitor center. There's a $3 parking fee.

For information, contact the East Bay Regional Parks District, 2950 Peralta Oaks Court, Oakland, CA 94605-0381; (510) 636-1684.

❖ ❖ ❖ ❖

Bay Views Hike
August 6, 1995 ⓈⒸ • 12:30 p.m. to 4:30 p.m.
(see #22 on map page 180)

The hike begins at Crab Cove in Alameda and five miles later drops you at Bayfarm Island. This is an easy, level-terrain hike open to all ages. Although the hike is free, there may be a parking fee. Bring water and a snack, and wear some comfortable hiking shoes or boots. To reach the Crab Cove Visitor Center from Oakland, take Interstate 880 to the Broadway exit and turn right. Continue to Webster, turn right and go through the Alameda Tunnel. Turn onto Central, then turn left on McKay. The park entrance is on the left.

For information, contact the East Bay Regional Parks District, 2950 Peralta Oaks Court, Oakland, CA 94605-0381; (510) 636-1684.

AUGUST

❖ ❖ ❖ ❖

Sibley Volcanic Preserve Tuesday Twilight
August 8, 1995 ⓈⒸ • 6:30 p.m. to 8:30 p.m.
(see #18 on map page 180)

Here's your chance to explore an active volcanic area on a special mid-week evening walk and talk. Were there really volcanoes around the Bay? Are they still active? These and many more puzzling questions can be answered by a naturalist during this two-hour program. It is held at the East Bay's Robert Sibley Volcanic Regional Preserve, which is located near Highway 24 along Skyline Boulevard.

For information, contact the Crab Cove Visitor Center; (510) 521-6887.

✤ ✤ ✤ ✤

Exploring the Delta's Water Flow

August 8, 1995 **S** 🖉 • 10 a.m. to 2 p.m.
(see #33 on map page 181)

Join this trip hosted by the California Department of Water Resources for a firsthand look at the water of the Sacramento River Delta—where it comes from, where it goes and the important role it plays in the life and death of an intricate ecosystem. With fish, farmers, recreationists and city water-users all needing adequate supplies of this liquid gold, there is plenty of competition and plenty of argument over who gets what, especially when nature decides to prolong the drought conditions that are so familiar to most Californians. You'll meet at Black Diamond Mines Regional Preserve, then travel by bus to various Delta stops, including Brannan Island State Recreation Area near Rio Vista. Advance registration is required and there's a fee of about $15 per person. Children under age 10 are not allowed on the trip. To reach Black Diamond Mines Regional Preserve, take Highway 4 east into Antioch and take the Somersville Road exit. Drive south about three miles to the park entrance.

For information, contact the East Bay Regional Parks District, 2950 Peralta Oaks Court, Oakland, CA 94605-0381; (510) 636-1684.

✤ ✤ ✤ ✤

Sunol Teen Peak Hike

August 10, 1995 **S** 🖉 • 9 a.m. to 4 p.m.
(see #48 on map page 181)

This is a really challenging 9.2-mile hike that will test some of the most in-shape teens out there. The hike goes to the top of Mission Peak and back. Wear some good hiking boots and take plenty of water, lunch and some energy snacks to keep you going strong. The hike is for anyone between 13 and 18 years old who is willing and able to cover the entire distance. Preregistration is required.

For information, contact the East Bay Regional Parks District, 2950 Peralta Oaks Court, Oakland, CA 94605-0381; (510) 636-1684.

❁ ❁ ❁ ❁

Thursday Morning Bird Walk

August 10, 1995 • 7 a.m. to 9 a.m.

(see #47 on map page 181)

Coyote Hills Regional Park, located near Fremont, is the site of this bird walk. You'll be focusing your binoculars on the swallow's second nesting cycle. These fascinating bug-chasers provide a lot of entertainment for your viewing pleasure. If you have some, bring your binoculars and a bird field guide. To reach Coyote Hills from Fremont, take Interstate 880 (Nimitz Freeway) to the Decoto Road/ Highway 84 exit and head west to the Thornton Avenue/Paseo Padre Parkway exit. Turn north and go one mile to Patterson Ranch Road, then turn left and drive into the park. There's a $3 parking fee on weekends and holidays.

For information, contact Coyote Hills Regional Park, 8000 Patterson Ranch Road, Fremont, CA 94555; (510) 795-9385.

❁ ❁ ❁ ❁

Parks Express Field Day

August 10, 1995 • 9:30 a.m. to 3 p.m.

(see #12 on map page 180)

Miller-Knox Regional Shoreline in Richmond will be the site for fishing fun and nature study for 600 inner-city and disabled kids and senior citizens. Plenty of volunteers are needed to help so many people have a fun day fishing and studying nature. Lunch is provided to all the volunteers. You need to be at least 16 years old and must register in advance.

For information, contact Miller-Knox Regional Shoreline; (510) 635-0138, ext. 2205.

❁ ❁ ❁ ❁

Gummy Worm Bait for Finned Lunkers

August 11, 1995 **S** 🖉 • 9:30 a.m. to 11:30 a.m.
(see #42 on map page 181)

There are secrets and then there are *real* secrets to catching the big lunkers that inhabit the East Bay's reservoirs. People have used lots of things that most people, non-fisherpeople that is, would never think a fish would be dumb enough to put into their mouths. Rubber worms, plastic jigs, shiny pieces of metal, marshmallows, cheese and...Gummy Bears? Well, you'll have to attend the two-hour class to find out how and why someone might be moved to use Gummy Bears as fish bait. Meet at Shadow Cliffs Regional Recreation Area. You'll need a fishing license if you're 16 years old or older, and an East Bay Regional Parks fishing access permit in order to participate. Call to confirm the dates, times, meeting locations and the subject of the class. Advance registration is required. There will be a $3 fee for the class, plus a $3 parking fee. To reach Shadow Cliffs, take Interstate 580 to Pleasanton and the Santa Rita Road exit. Head south on Santa Rita to Valley, turn left, then left again on Stanley. The park entrance is on the right.

For information, contact the East Bay Regional Parks District, 2950 Peralta Oaks Court, Oakland, CA 94605-0381; (510) 636-1684.

❖ ❖ ❖ ❖

Bear Creek Hike

August 12, 1995 **S** 🖉 • 10 a.m. to 3 p.m.
(see #13 on map page 180)

Join the folks and a naturalist at the East Bay's Briones Regional Park for a six-mile exploration of the Bear Creek watershed. The terrain isn't overly difficult, but it's tough enough to restrict the trip to those who have reached age 10 or older. Wear some good walking shoes or boots and bring drinking water and lunch.

For information, contact the East Bay Regional Parks District, 2950 Peralta Oaks Court, Oakland, CA 94605-0381; (510) 636-1684.

❖ ❖ ❖ ❖

Rock Climbing Basics

August 13, 1995 [S] ☎ • 9 a.m. to 5 p.m.
(see #49 on map page 181)

If you're a teenager or older and you're looking for a real summer rush, try a little rock climbing. You'll have to call and register in advance because space is limited in the class, but what a way to get ready for summer fun! You'll join a small group and hike about a mile out to Cave Rocks and then spend the afternoon learning many of the basics that will make your rock climbing endeavors much more fun, safe and successful. The instructors will teach climbing safety, knots that stay tied, belaying, rappelling and other skills. Here's a chance to impress your friends with your "rock star" status. Bring lunch and water to Sunol-Ohlone Regional Wilderness on Geary Road in Sunol. The program is also held in April. There's a $10 fee for the program, although the amount is subject to change.

For information, contact Sunol-Ohlone Regional Wilderness, P.O. Box 82, Sunol, CA 94586; (510) 862-2244.

Morgan Territory Tuesday Twilight

August 15, 1995 [S] ☎ • 6 p.m. to 8 p.m.
(see #33 on map page 181)

Here's an evening exploration of the east side of Mount Diablo. A naturalist will be looking at the history of this beautiful mountain and at the wildlife that call this place home. You might want to bring a snack and binoculars. Call ahead to confirm the date, time and meeting place.

For information, contact Black Diamond Mines Regional Preserve, 5175 Somersville Road, Antioch, CA 94509; (510) 757-2620.

Senior Safari—Del Valle Regional Park
August 16, 1995 **S** 🖉 • 9:30 a.m. to 2 p.m.
(see #45 on map page 181)

Come along on a bus ride for an exploration of the scenic Livermore Valley en route to Del Valle Lake. At the lake, a naturalist will lead an exploration of its natural and cultural wonders and discuss the importance that this body of water plays in the ecosystem. The bus holds only 20 passengers, so you'll have to make your reservations early. There's a $12 fee for residents and $15 for nonresidents.

For information, contact the Pleasanton Senior Center; (510) 636-1684.

❖ ❖ ❖ ❖

Thursday Morning Bird Walk
August 17, 1995 **S** 🖉 • 7 a.m. to 9 a.m.
(see #20 on map page 180)

Redwood forests offer a very unique home environment for birds. The naturalist on this morning walk among the giant redwoods will take a look at the birds that inhabit Redwood Regional Park, located just east of Piedmont and Highway 13. Bring your binoculars and bird field guide if you have them.

For information, contact the East Bay Regional Parks District, 2950 Peralta Oaks Court, Oakland, CA 94605-0381; (510) 636-1684 or (510) 796-0199.

❖ ❖ ❖ ❖

Fishing the Incoming Tide
August 18, 1995 **S** 🖉
(see #30 on map page 181)

There's a reason for fishing the incoming tide, rather than the outgoing tide. It makes sense if you think about it for a few minutes, especially if it's something like salmon that you're hoping to catch. With the natural flow of water heading out to sea, fish aren't as dumb as some people, so rather than fight the current, they wait until the tide rolls in and use that upstream current to help them along on their journeys inland. There are some other reasons, but for those you'll have to come to this class. Meet at Antioch Regional Shoreline's Antioch Pier. You'll need a fishing license in order to participate. Call to confirm the date, time, meeting location and the subject of the class. Advance registration is required. There's a $3 fee for the class.

For information, contact the East Bay Regional Parks District, 2950 Peralta Oaks Court, Oakland, CA 94605-0381; (510) 636-1684.

❖ ❖ ❖ ❖

Old Ways Workshop: Brain-Tanned Buckskin
August 20, 1995 **$** • 9 a.m. to 5 p.m.
(see #47 on map page 181)

If you have an interest in leather tanning, here's an excellent opportunity to learn the ancient techniques that California's Native Americans used. There will be several deer skins available to learn firsthand the steps needed to properly tan hides. You'll be using cooked brains, lots of rubbing and scraping, as well as wood smoke to cure the hides. The naturalist will discuss both wet and dry scraping techniques; at the end of the day, you'll be able to take a piece of your tanned hide home. Advance registration is required and there's a fee of about $20. Kids who wish to participate must be at least 12 years old. The program is held at Coyote Hills Regional Park, near Fremont. To reach Coyote Hills from Fremont, take Interstate 880 (Nimitz Freeway) to the Decoto Road/Highway 84 exit and head west to the Thornton Avenue/Paseo Padre Parkway exit. Turn north and go one mile to Patterson Ranch Road, then turn left and drive into the park. There's a $3 parking fee on weekends and holidays.

For information, contact Coyote Hills Regional Park, 8000 Patterson Ranch Road, Fremont, CA 94555; (510) 795-9385.

❖ ❖ ❖ ❖

Delta Tuesday Twilight

August 22, 1995 **S** 🍃 • 6 p.m. to 8 p.m.
(see #33 on map page 181)

While the idea of exploring the Ironhouse Sanitary District may not sound particularly appealing, you might be amazed at the number of wildlife species that live and breed in the nearby Sacramento River Delta lands and waterways. A naturalist will be leading this look at life on the edge of the Delta. Bring binoculars and your favorite plant and bird field guides. Call ahead to confirm the date, time and meeting place.

For information, contact Black Diamond Mines Regional Preserve, 5175 Somersville Road, Antioch, CA 94509; (510) 757-2620.

✤ ✤ ✤ ✤

Sunol Teen Peak Hike

August 24, 1995 **S** 🍃 • 7 a.m. to 5 p.m.
(see #49 on map page 181)

This is the mother of all the teens-only mountaintop hikes offered this summer in the East Bay's Sunol Regional Wilderness. The hike will go to the top of Rose Peak and will cover 12.2 miles, beginning to end. You must be between 13 and 18 years old to participate. Hopefully, you've done a fair amount of hiking before jumping into this one. Bring water, lunch and snacks. Wear some good hiking boots. Advance registration is required to participate. To reach the Sunol-Ohlone Regional Wilderness, from the intersection of interstates 580 and 680, drive south on Interstate 680 for about eight miles to the Highway 84/Calaveras Road exit. Head south on Calaveras Road approximately four miles to Geary Road. Turn left onto Geary and drive to the park entrance and the visitor center. There's a $3 parking fee.

For information, contact East Bay Regional Parks District, 2950 Peralta Oaks Court, Oakland, CA 94605-0381; (510) 636-1684.

✤ ✤ ✤ ✤

Thursday Morning Bird Walk

August 24, 1995 **S**/ • 7 a.m. to 9 a.m.
(see #33 on map page 181)

Join a naturalist for this two-hour walk in the East Bay's Black Diamond Mines Regional Preserve, just south of Antioch. During the hike, you will be looking at the birds in Shady Canyon, both the year-round residents and the late-summer and early-fall migrants. Bring your binoculars and a bird field guide if you have them. To reach Black Diamond Mines Regional Preserve, take Highway 4 east into Antioch and take the Somersville Road exit. Drive south about three miles to the park entrance.

For information, contact Black Diamond Mines Regional Preserve, 5175 Somersville Road, Antioch, CA 94509; (510) 757-2620.

❀ ❀ ❀ ❀

Dynamic Delta

August 24, 1995 **S**/ • 2 p.m. to 3 p.m.
(see #34 on map page 181)

This is a tour of the Sacramento River Delta that never leaves the library. Sit back and enjoy a slide program that will show you in one hour more about the backwaters of the Delta than you could probably see by boat in a week. Although it might not be as much fun as a boat ride, it'll teach you about the rich history that surrounds the towns and levees that make up the rich and beautiful water wonderland. Meet at the Brentwood Library, which is located at 751 Third Street. All are invited to this free program.

For information, contact Black Diamond Mines Regional Preserve, 5175 Somersville Road, Antioch, CA 94509; (510) 757-2620.

❀ ❀ ❀ ❀

AUGUST

Lake Ecology and Fishing Tricks

August 25, 1995 **S** *Ø* • 9:30 a.m. to 11:30 a.m.
(see #40 on map page 181)

Knowing a lake's ecology and being able to identify a healthy lake versus a sick lake will go a long way toward helping you decide whether or not you should even try fishing some waters. This basic knowledge will also help you know where the big ones are most likely hiding and what kind of creatures they're most likely to be attracted to when feeding time comes around. Meet at Don Castro Regional Recreation Area, located just north of Hayward, off B Street and Interstate 580. You'll need a fishing license and an East Bay Regional Parks fishing access permit in order to participate. Call to confirm the date, time, meeting location and subject of the class. Advance registration is required. There's a $3 fee for the class and a $3 parking fee.

For information, contact the East Bay Regional Parks District, 2950 Peralta Oaks Court, Oakland, CA 94605-0381; (510) 636-1684.

❖ ❖ ❖ ❖

Sunol Valley Horseback Nature Ride

August 26, 1995 **S** *Ø* • 11 a.m. to 11:30 a.m.
(see #49 on map page 181)

This 30-minute horseback ride will meander through Sunol-Ohlone Regional Wilderness for a quick look at the natural beauty of the area. Besides having an opportunity to see how you like riding a horse, you'll also learn about the area's cultural and natural history. Advance registration is required and there's a $12 fee for the horse rental and ride. To reach the Sunol-Ohlone Regional Wilderness from the intersection of interstates 580 and 680, drive south on Interstate 680 for about eight miles to the Highway 84/Calaveras Road exit. Head south on Calaveras Road approximately four miles to Geary Road. Turn left onto Geary and drive to the park entrance and the visitor center. There's a $3 parking fee.

For information, contact the East Bay Regional Parks District, 2950 Peralta Oaks Court, Oakland, CA 94605-0381; (510) 636-1684.

Exploring the California Delta Water Projects

August 26, 1995 **S** 🚻 • 9 a.m. to 2:30 p.m.
(see #33 on map page 181)

This bus ride heads from Black Diamond Mines Regional Preserve to the south Sacramento River Delta. You and the rest of your tour group will look at the water projects that move so much of California's water from where it is naturally to where people have decided it should be. The Department of Water Resources will host this tour of several of their facilities, including the Banks Pumping Plant, the Skinner Fish Facility and the Clifton Court Forebay. Advance registration is required; you must be at least 10 years old to participate. There's a fee of about $20 per person. To reach Black Diamond Mines Regional Preserve, take Highway 4 east into Antioch and take the Somersville Road exit. Drive south about three miles to the park entrance.

For information, contact the East Bay Regional Parks District, 2950 Peralta Oaks Court, Oakland, CA 94605-0381; (510) 636-1684.

❖ ❖ ❖ ❖

Redwood Forest Festival

August 27, 1995 **S** 🚻 • Noon to 4 p.m.
(see #22 on map page 181)

Come celebrate the redwoods that make the tree-lined canyon of Crab Cove in Alameda unique. The day will be filled with hikes, music and other special outdoor programs. Naturalists will lead walks and talks to help you and your kids better understand the importance of our forests, how we use and abuse them and what all of us can do to help protect these valuable resources for both people and wildlife.

To reach the Crab Cove Visitor Center from Oakland, take Interstate 880 to the Broadway exit and turn right. Continue to Webster, turn right and go through the Alameda Tunnel. Turn onto Central, then turn left on McKay. The park entrance is on the left.

For information, contact Crab Cove Visitor Center; (510) 521-6887.

AUGUST

Joaquin Miller Tuesday Twilight

August 29, 1995 **$** *◊* • 6 p.m. to 8 p.m.
(see #19 on map page 180)

There's nothing that's better than a quiet evening stroll through redwoods. Bring the entire family for this casual walk and talk by a naturalist through Joaquin Miller Regional Park's beautiful redwood grove and learn a little about the forest's natural history.

For information, contact the Tilden Nature Area, Environmental Education Center, Berkeley, CA 94708; (510) 525-2233.

Boardwalk Marsh Walk

Early September Saturday **$** *◊* • 2 p.m. to 3 p.m.
(see #24 on map page 180)

Forget the gooey slush of the marsh's mud as you, a naturalist and other visitors stroll the boardwalk in San Francisco Bay National Wildlife Refuge's New Chicago Marsh. Wear comfortable shoes, since they won't be getting too wet, and bring your binoculars for this look at the plants and wildlife of the wetland. To reach the center from Interstate 880 near Milpitas, exit on Highway 237 toward Alviso (Mountain View), then turn north onto Zanker Road. Continue for two miles and make a sharp right turn at Grand Boulevard into the center.

For information, contact the San Francisco Bay Wildlife Society, P.O. Box 524, Newark, CA 94560-0524; (510) 792-4275.

Old-Fashioned Campfire Sing-Along

September 3, 1995 **$** *◊* • 5:30 p.m. to 8 p.m.
(see #16 on map page 180)

For details about this roasting, eating, singing good old time at the Tilden Nature Area, see page 239. Meet at the Environmental

Education Center; the leader will walk the group up to the hillside campfire circle. There's no fee and all ages are welcome. To reach the Tilden Nature Area from Oakland, head east on Highway 24 and pass through the Caldecott Tunnel to the Fish Ranch Road exit. Head west on Fish Ranch to the Grizzly Peak Boulevard intersection, where you'll turn right and enter the park's south entrance.

For information, contact the Tilden Nature Area, Environmental Education Center, Berkeley, CA 94708; (510) 525-2233.

✤ ✤ ✤ ✤

Water Ecology

First Sunday in September Ⓢ ☎ • 2 p.m. to 4 p.m.

(see #16 on map page 180)

With all the people and development in the East Bay, have you ever thought about what the water quality is like? Here's your chance to get out to the Tilden Nature Area and check out the water chemistry of Wildcat Creek. The health of the East Bay's watersheds and marshland, those filters that sift out various things not so good for the Bay, are good indicators of how the health of the surrounding environment is fairing. There should also be a few water-oriented creatures in the area that you might get a good look at. A naturalist will lead this short hike to a good creek access point to begin your exploration. To reach the Tilden Nature Area from Oakland, head east on Highway 24 and pass through the Caldecott Tunnel to the Fish Ranch Road exit. Head west on Fish Ranch to the Grizzly Peak Boulevard intersection, where you'll turn right and enter the park's south entrance. To reach the nature area, turn left once inside.

For information, contact the Tilden Nature Area, Environmental Education Center, Berkeley, CA 94708; (510) 525-2233.

✤ ✤ ✤ ✤

Drakes Beach Sand Castle Contest

Sunday, Labor Day weekend **$**
(see #4 on map page 180)

Building sand castles is a tradition on California's beaches. Who said it was just for kids? Put your architectural designs of fancy and building skills to the ultimate test on the sandy beach of Drakes Bay. And while castles may be the name of this competition, creating your own sand sculptures of seals, whales and other creatures of the deep is certainly welcomed. Call the park for the scheduled judging time and the categories, or simply show up early, stake your claim to a parcel of sand (taking into account the changing tide level), and have at it. Drakes Bay is part of Point Reyes National Seashore, located about 26 miles north of the Highway 1 and US 101 intersection, north of San Francisco Bay. Take the Bear Valley Road turnoff into the park off Highway 1 at Olema and follow the signs for about 16 miles to the beach.

For information, contact Point Reyes National Seashore, Point Reyes, CA 94956; (415) 663-1092.

❖ ❖ ❖ ❖

Shorebirding Safari Workshop

Second weekend in September **$**
3 p.m. to 5 p.m. on Saturday;
8:30 a.m. to 10:30 a.m. and 2 p.m. to 4 p.m. on Sunday
(see #38 on map page 181)

Have you ever walked along the beach and seen all those little birds poking their extra-long bills into the sand time after time? Well, that's their way of fixing breakfast and dinner, depending upon the time of day. These birds depend upon the action of waves and tidal waters to continually bring in new meals for all. Saturday's program will be indoors to view a slide show, handouts and study skins, all of which are designed to help you identify some of the many different shorebirds that you're going to see on Sunday's field trip. You'll be wandering around mud flats, marshes and the brackish waters that are rich in food, thus favorite places for birds to spend most of their time. The program will meet initially at the Nike Classroom at Lake Chabot. Call to confirm the workshop times, which are scheduled according to when the birds are most active.

For information, contact the East Bay Regional Parks District, 2950 Peralta Oaks Court, Oakland, CA 94605-0381; (510) 636-1684.

❀ ❀ ❀ ❀

Lifestyles of the Environmentally Friendly

Mid-September Sunday **$** · 11 a.m. to 4 p.m.
(see #24 on map page 180)

Spend an afternoon learning new ideas for decreasing the human impact on Mother Earth, from saving water and energy to composting, recycling and much more. In 1994, participants got cloth shopping bags and water-saving kits; if they're available, workshop leaders may distribute them again this year. Meet at the San Francisco Bay National Wildlife Refuge's Environmental Education Center. To reach the center from Interstate 880 near Milpitas, exit on Highway 237 toward Alviso (Mountain View), then turn north onto Zanker Road. Continue for two miles and make a sharp right turn at Grand Boulevard into the center.

For information, contact the San Francisco Bay Wildlife Society, P.O. Box 524, Newark, CA 94560-0524; (510) 792-4275.

❀ ❀ ❀ ❀

Natural History of Big Sur

Mid-September Saturday **$** · 2 p.m. to 4 p.m.
(see #24 on map page 180)

Since it's a little difficult to travel to Big Sur and tour the area in just two hours, the folks at the San Francisco Bay National Wildlife Refuge have come up with an alternative. Offered in 1994, and hopefully again in 1995, biologist Paul Henson and environmental consultant Donald Unser will present a slide show on Big Sur, then

SEPTEMBER

stick around to answer questions and sign copies of their book, *The Natural History of Big Sur.* To reach the San Francisco Bay National Wildlife Refuge Visitor Center from Interstate 880 or US 101, take Highway 84 toward the east end of the Dumbarton Bridge. Take the Thornton Avenue exit and drive south for one mile. The refuge is on the right side. Follow the road to the stop sign and turn left into the parking lot.

For information, contact the San Francisco Bay Wildlife Society, P.O. Box 524, Newark, CA 94560-0524; (510) 792-4275.

✢ ✢ ✢ ✢

Star Struck

Mid-September Saturday **S** • 8 p.m. to 10 p.m.
(see #24 on map page 180)

No, this isn't a tour of Hollywood, but an escape from the city lights to the star-filled night skies above the San Francisco Bay National Wildlife Refuge. An astronomer will help you learn to recognize a few of the more easily identified stars and constellations. You'll also hear a few of the legends and myths that have been around since people began looking at the night sky. Bring warm clothing and binoculars. To reach the San Francisco Bay National Wildlife Refuge Visitor Center from Interstate 880 or US 101, take Highway 84 toward the east end of the Dumbarton Bridge. Take the Thornton Avenue exit and drive south for one mile. The refuge is on the right side. Follow the road to the stop sign and turn left into the parking lot.

For information, contact the San Francisco Bay Wildlife Society, P.O. Box 524, Newark, CA 94560-0524; (510) 792-4275.

✢ ✢ ✢ ✢

Ohlone Day at Henry Cowell Redwoods

September 23, 1995 [S] ☎ • 10 a.m. to 4 p.m.

(see #28 on map page 180)

Native Americans lived on this land for many centuries before Europeans arrived on the scene. How did they survive? Where did they find food? These and many other questions about California's first citizens will be answered during the annual Ohlone Day. You'll learn how they prepared food, used plants and made their clothes. Also, there will be a chance to learn some of the games that Native Americans played for fun and to listen to their music. This is not a boring "watch me" demonstration, but a real hands-on experience. While in the park, which has a campground, visitor center, gift shop and picnic area, take advantage of the short trails that pass through some of the redwood groves. There are some really beautiful, short and level trails, so everyone can enjoy these magnificent trees. Henry Cowell Redwoods State Park is located north of Santa Cruz, just off Highway 9 in the town of Felton. There's a $5-per-vehicle fee to enter the park. There may be some fog early in the day, but it should burn off by late morning.

For information, contact Henry Cowell Redwoods State Park; (408) 335-7077.

❀ ❀ ❀ ❀

Angel Island Jubilee

September 23, 1995 [S] ☎ • 11 a.m. to 4 p.m.

(see #14 on map page 180)

They've been celebrating this jubilee for the past 32 years. You can look forward to a living history with all the island's historic sites open. Remember, the island has seen a great deal of history during the past 100 years. It's served as an entry point for Chinese immigrants, a Japanese prisoner-of-war camp, a Nike missile base, a U.S. Army base and now, a state park. Bring your picnic lunch, maybe a bicycle to ride around the island or just bring yourself. The only way to Angel Island is by boat. If you don't own one, you can take a ferry from Tiburon, (415) 435-2131, or one of San Francisco's

Red and White Fleet, (800) 229-2784. Be sure to bring a light jacket, because there's a pretty good chance that there will be fog in the morning. Otherwise, it should be warm.

For information, contact Angel Island State Park; (415) 435-1915.

❖ ❖ ❖ ❖

Geotalk! Geowalk!

Late September Sunday **S**⟡• 2 p.m. to 4 p.m.
(see #26 on map page 180)

Walk to the talk of geologists as you learn everything you ever wanted to know about the geology of California and San Francisco—and a few things you'd probably prefer not to know, if lurking in your subconscious is a fear of earthquakes. This presentation starts with a slide show and ends with a short walk to look at the real stuff. Learn how San Francisco Bay came to be and how bays, lakes and ponds all end their natural life cycles filling with sediment and terrestrial plants. Unfortunately, since the Gold Rush days, humans have done more than their share to speed the transformation of the bay. To reach the San Francisco Bay National Wildlife Refuge Visitor Center, from Interstate 880 or US 101, take Highway 84 toward the east end of the Dumbarton Bridge. Take the Thornton Avenue exit and drive south for one mile. The refuge is on the right side. Follow the road to the stop sign and turn left into the parking lot.

For information, contact the San Francisco Bay Wildlife Society, P.O. Box 524, Newark, CA 94560-0524; (510) 792-4275.

❖ ❖ ❖ ❖

The Ohlone Way

Late September **S**⟡• 1 p.m. to 2 p.m.
(see #24 on map page 180)

For hundreds of years before Europeans arrived and began filling in the bay with their landfills, creating salt ponds and dumping both treated and untreated sewage into the waterways, the Ohlone lived along its shore. Their way of life was as interesting and their culture as rich as anything you'll find today. Learn all about their world in a slide show and talk. Meet at the San Francisco Bay National Wildlife Refuge's Environmental Education Center. To reach the center from Interstate 880 near Milpitas, exit on Highway 237 toward Alviso (Mountain View), then turn north onto Zanker Road. Continue for two miles and make a sharp right turn at Grand Boulevard into the center.

For information, contact the San Francisco Bay Wildlife Society, P.O. Box 524, Newark, CA 94560-0524; (510) 792-4275.

❖ ❖ ❖ ❖

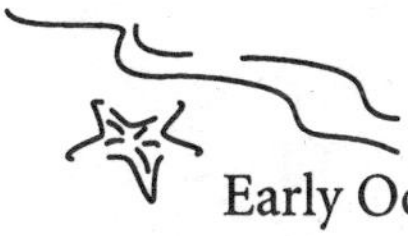

Coast Clean-up

Early October Saturday [S] ☎ • 8:30 a.m. to noon

(see #24 on map page 180)

Annually, thousands of Californians join forces and spend a day cleaning the state's beaches and shorelines. Join the party and provide a great service in helping to protect San Francisco Bay by picking up trash along its shores. This is a time for old clothes, gloves, sturdy shoes or boots, and a lot of enthusiasm for an ugly but immensely rewarding job. Bring friends, family or just yourself. Registration is usually between 8:30 a.m. and 10 a.m.; coordinators will offer clean-up instructions and directions to the coast's most critical areas. Meet at the San Francisco Bay National Wildlife Refuge's Environmental Education Center. To reach the center from Interstate 880 near Milpitas, exit on Highway 237 toward Alviso (Mountain View), then turn north onto Zanker Road. Continue for two miles and make a sharp right turn at Grand Boulevard into the center.

For information, contact the San Francisco Bay Wildlife Society, P.O. Box 524, Newark, CA 94560-0524; (510) 792-4275.

❖ ❖ ❖ ❖

Coast Care Faire

Early October Saturday $5 • 10 a.m. to 2 p.m.
(see #24 on map page 180)

Finished with Coast Clean-up? Then head on over to the San Francisco Bay National Wildlife Refuge Visitor Center to learn about what else you can do to help protect the bay and our other precious waterways. If you've never heard of the Marine Science Institute, the Tri-City Ecology Center or the San Francisco Bay Wildlife Society, here's the perfect opportunity to learn about what they are doing and what you can do to help them save the bay. To reach the Visitor Center from Interstate 880 near Milpitas, exit on Highway 237 toward Alviso (Mountain View), then turn north onto Zanker Road. Continue for two miles and make a sharp right turn at Grand Boulevard into the lot.

For information, contact the San Francisco Bay Wildlife Society, P.O. Box 524, Newark, CA 94560-0524; (510) 792-4275.

❖ ❖ ❖ ❖

Santa Cruz Mission Fiesta

October 7, 1995 $5 • 10 a.m. to 4 p.m.
(see #51 on map page 181)

A special treat awaits you during this fiesta, because there's more to see and do than simply take a walk or short tour through the mission, although even that is well worth your time. On this particular Saturday, there will be tours, of course, but also corn-husk doll making and candle dipping, along with other period games, music, crafts and food. You can expect to be among the roughly 1,000 people who usually attend this event. Santa Cruz Mission State Historic Park is located in downtown Santa Cruz at 144 School Street. The cost of the fiesta is $2 for adults and $1 for seniors and kids under 12. It should be a pretty nice day, but it may be a little cool, so dress accordingly.

For information, contact Santa Cruz Mission State Historic Park; (408) 425-5849.

❖ ❖ ❖ ❖

Welcome Back Monarch Day

October 8, 1995 • Noon to 4 p.m.

(see #51 on map page 181)

The famed monarchs begin arriving in large numbers in October, much to the delight of entomologists (bug scientists), kids and adults with cameras. There will be park staff and volunteers on hand to provide information about the life cycle of these creatures. You can browse the small visitor center and gift shop for T-shirts, books, cups and any number of other monarch-related gift items for friends and family. More importantly, to those more interested in live butterflies than in make-believe images on cloth and paper, there is a boardwalk trail that meanders into a grove of eucalyptus trees. The trees serve as the winter home for the monarchs. When you tire of the butterflies, walk the couple of hundred yards down to Natural Bridges State Beach. If the tide is low, you can walk through the stone arch that gives the beach its name, a prime attraction for visitors here. Natural Bridges State Beach, and the returning monarchs, can be found at the end of West Cliff Drive in Santa Cruz. To get into the park, there's a $6-per-vehicle entrance fee, but if you don't mind a little walk, you can park outside the park for nothing. The weather should be warm and comfortable, unless the fog happens to roll in.

For information, contact the Santa Cruz Visitors Bureau, 701 Front Street, Santa Cruz, CA 95060; (408) 425-1234 or (800) 833-3494.

Fall Color Fest

Mid-October Sunday [S] ☎ • 1 p.m. to 3 p.m.

(see #24 on map page 180)

The colors of fall may not be as striking here in the East Bay as they are in high mountain country or in the eastern United States, but the subtleties of the bay's fall transformations are just as beautiful. So you won't feel like you're missing something, a slide show will probably precede the casual wander through the refuge highlighting the fall colors of other parts of the country. Wear comfortable clothes. To reach the San Francisco Bay National Wildlife Refuge from Interstate 880 near Milpitas, exit on Highway 237 toward Alviso (Mountain View), then turn north onto Zanker Road. Continue for two miles and make a sharp right turn at Grand Boulevard into the lot.

For information, contact the San Francisco Bay Wildlife Society, P.O. Box 524, Newark, CA 94560-0524; (510) 792-4275.

❖ ❖ ❖ ❖

Bike the Bay

Mid-October Saturday [S] ☎ • 10 a.m. to noon

(see #24 on map page 180)

Get out of your car and try a slightly slower mode of transportation—you'll discover a whole new world out there. This is a slow and easy bike tour of the marshes and salt ponds along the dirt levees and trails in the San Francisco Bay National Wildlife Refuge. Learn how plants have adapted to the harsh environment that is created by changing tides, salty water and almost constant winds. Helmets and fat tires are recommended. Reservations are required. To reach the visitor center from Interstate 880 near Milpitas, exit on Highway 237 toward Alviso (Mountain View), then turn north onto Zanker Road. Continue for two miles and make a sharp right turn at Grand Boulevard into the parking lot.

For information, contact the San Francisco Bay Wildlife Society, P.O. Box 524, Newark, CA 94560-0524; (510) 792-4275.

❖ ❖ ❖ ❖

Wild Edibles

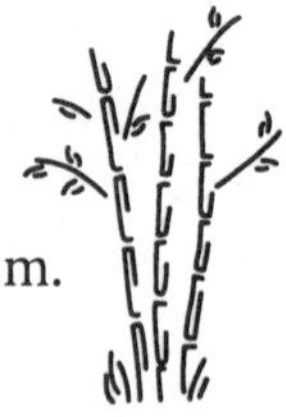

Mid-October Sunday [S] ☎ • 11:30 a.m. to 12:30 p.m.

(see #24 on map page 180)

Browse, if that's the best choice of words, with a naturalist as he searches for wild edible plants in San Francisco Bay National Wildlife Refuge. You might wonder what anyone, except a duck, would find appetizing about things growing in the wetland and dry land of the refuge. Well, you might just be surprised. You'll be able to sample some of the delectably delicious marshy treats while you learn which ones you can feast on and which ones are better left to the slugs, bugs and bigger beasts. Meet at the San Francisco Bay National Wildlife Refuge's Environmental Education Center. To reach it from Interstate 880 near Milpitas, exit on Highway 237 toward Alviso (Mountain View), then turn north onto Zanker Road. Continue for two miles and make a sharp right turn at Grand Boulevard into the lot.

For information, contact the San Francisco Bay Wildlife Society, P.O. Box 524, Newark, CA 94560-0524; (510) 792-4275.

✤ ✤ ✤ ✤

The Life and Times of the California Clapper Rail

Mid-October Saturday 🆂 🖉 · 2 p.m. to 3 p.m.
(see #24 on map page 180)

Join a naturalist, or perhaps photographer Katherine Rambo, in an exploration of San Francisco Bay National Wildlife Refuge's marshland for a look at the life and home of the endangered California clapper rail, a bird which is only found in the salt marshes of San Francisco Bay. While there's a chance you'll see a few clapper rails during this short walk, in a special slide show you'll be able to get a better idea who they are and why the marsh is so important to their survival. To reach the San Francisco Bay National Wildlife Refuge Visitor Center from Interstate 880 or US 101, take Highway 84 toward the east end of the Dumbarton Bridge. Take the Thornton Avenue exit and drive south for one mile. The refuge is on the right side. Follow the road to the stop sign and turn left into the parking lot.

For information, contact the San Francisco Bay Wildlife Society, P.O. Box 524, Newark, CA 94560-0524; (510) 792-4275.

✤ ✤ ✤ ✤

OCTOBER

Botanical Wanderings

Mid-October Sunday [S] ☎ • 2 p.m. to 4 p.m.

(see #24 on map page 180)

Most plants that we are familiar with around our homes or in the valleys and mountains won't be found in the marshes and tidelands of the San Francisco Bay. Join a refuge naturalist and learn the secrets of plants that have developed unique ways of thriving in their salty environment, an environment deadly to most everything else that grows green. You'll have an opportunity to see the transition of plant adaptations from the shallows of the wetlands to the higher, dryer and unsalty lands above. To reach the San Francisco Bay National Wildlife Refuge Visitor Center from Interstate 880 or US 101, take Highway 84 toward the east end of the Dumbarton Bridge. Take the Thornton Avenue exit and drive south for one mile. The refuge is on the right side. Follow the road to the stop sign and turn left into the parking lot.

For information, contact the San Francisco Bay Wildlife Society, P.O. Box 524, Newark, CA 94560-0524; (510) 792-4275.

Pollution Solution

Mid-October Sunday [S] ☎ • 1 p.m. to 2 p.m.

(see #24 on map page 180)

Did you realize that you could be a contributor to the bay's pollution problem and not even know it? Lot's of common household products are deadly when they make their way into the Bay. Learn about safe substitutes and what you can do to help. Meet at the San Francisco Bay National Wildlife Refuge's Environmental Education Center. To reach the center from Interstate 880 near Milpitas, exit on Highway 237 toward Alviso (Mountain View), then turn north onto Zanker Road. Continue for two miles and make a sharp right turn at Grand Boulevard into the center.

For information, contact the San Francisco Bay Wildlife Society, P.O. Box 524, Newark, CA 94560-0524; (510) 792-4275.

Hawk-Watching Workshop

Mid-October weekend **$** *(/)*
(see #38 on map page 181)

The hills overlooking the Golden Gate Bridge are some of the best places to view the annual fall migration of hawks. If you've had little or no experience trying to identify these beautiful hunters on the wing, this workshop is one of the best ways to get into the sport. Friday's two-hour session will be held indoors and will include a slide show, study skins, handouts and special instructions about the secrets for identifying high-flying hawks. You'll also learn about their feeding habits and general behavior, and all about their annual migrations. On Saturday, it's out in the field, exploring the haunts of the East Bay where hawks are generally found. Then, on Sunday, it's onto one of the favorite hawk-watching hills, a place across the bridge in Marin County known appropriately as Hawk Hill. The classroom portion of the program is held in the Nike Classroom at the East Bay's Lake Chabot. There's a fee of about $20 for adults for the three-day program. Reservations are required, because space is limited.

For information, contact the East Bay Regional Parks District, 2950 Peralta Oaks Court, Oakland, CA 94605-0381; (510) 636-1684.

✤ ✤ ✤ ✤

Brine Shrimp Lab

Late October Saturday **$** *(/)* · 10 a.m. to 11:30 a.m.

(see #24 on map page 180)

Sweep your small net through the salt pond and you might be surprised at what you'll find. Here we're looking for brine shrimp and will probably find them. Back at the lab, there's an opportunity to learn some fascinating facts about these curious creatures that serve as tasty treats for more than a few animals in the marsh. If all goes according to plan, and the waters haven't changed significantly, you should be able to see little, bitty boatmen and sea monkeys in the green water samples that you capture. Meet at the San Francisco

OCTOBER

Bay National Wildlife Refuge's Environmental Education Center. To reach the center from Interstate 880 near Milpitas, exit on Highway 237 toward Alviso (Mountain View), then turn north onto Zanker Road. Continue for two miles and make a sharp right turn at Grand Boulevard into the center.

For information, contact the San Francisco Bay Wildlife Society, P.O. Box 524, Newark, CA 94560-0524; (510) 792-4275.

❖ ❖ ❖ ❖

Halloween in Henry Cowell
October 31, 1995 **S**🕭
(see #28 on map page 180)

This is a special day set aside for kids ages 4 to 11 to meet some make-believe redwood forest creatures. Volunteers will be dressed as owls, bats and other creatures of the night for a fun and educational program. While the program is designed for kids, the youngsters must be accompanied by an adult so the program doesn't turn into a babysitting service for the parents' night out. Besides, if you've never been to the park, this is a perfect opportunity to wander a few of the shorter or longer trails that meander through the redwood groves, if you're up to them. Henry Cowell Redwood State Park is located about five miles north of Santa Cruz on Highway 9, near the town of Felton. There's a $5-per-vehicle fee to get into the park. The weather should be a little cool, so dress accordingly.

For information, contact Henry Cowell Redwood State Park; (408) 335-7077.

❖ ❖ ❖ ❖

Exploring the Eastern Town Sites of the Mount Diablo Coal Field
First Sunday in November **S**🕭 · 10 a.m. to 2 p.m.
(see #33 on map page 181)

Take yourself and your family on this relatively easy three-mile hike to explore some of the historic town sites on Mount Diablo.

The hike will begin near the old Judsonville town site, cross over to West Hartley and finally move on to explore around the Stewartville town site. You'll learn the history of the towns and of the coal mining that went on in the area for many years. Bring your lunch, water and a flashlight for exploring Prospect Tunnel. The weather could be a little cool, so dress appropriately. The initial meeting place will be at Black Diamond Mines Regional Preserve. To reach the preserve, take Highway 4 east into Antioch and take the Somersville Road exit. Drive south about three miles to the park entrance.

For information, contact Black Diamond Mines Regional Preserve, 5175 Somersville Road, Antioch, CA 94509; (510) 757-2620.

✣ ✣ ✣ ✣

Avocet Festival '95

November 4 & 5, 1995 $\textbf{S}$ 🖉 • 9 a.m. to 5 p.m.
(see #24 on map page 180)

This festival celebrates the American avocet, a rather large shorebird that may reach a height of 20 inches, most of which appears to be made up of its long legs. Avocets have long, up-curved bills that they sweep through shallow waters of marshes and shallow ponds or shorelines, hoping to catch tiny crustaceans. With Californians draining and filling so many fresh and saltwater marshes, the birds' breeding and feeding territories have been severely impacted or simply eliminated. If you or some natural predator happens to walk or stalk through an area where avocets are nesting and get a little too close to an unoccupied nest, the bird whose territory you've invaded will often send out a screaming cry for assistance. Generally, other avocets will come to the rescue, diving into and mobbing the intruder, driving him or her away. Sounds fun, huh? This annual wildlife arts and crafts fair brings nature artists out to sell their paintings, pottery, jewelry, wood carvings and photographs. There's also an environmental fair where many of the local conservation organizations enlist support in their efforts to protect the Bay. Here's a great chance to get a head start on your Christmas shopping. To reach the San Francisco Bay National Wildlife Refuge Visitor Center

NOVEMBER

from Interstate 880 or US 101, take Highway 84 toward the east end of the Dumbarton Bridge. Take the Thornton Avenue exit and drive south for one mile. The refuge is on the right side. Follow the road to the stop sign and turn left into the parking lot.

For information, contact the San Francisco Bay Wildlife Society, P.O. Box 524, Newark, CA 94560-0524; (510) 792-4275.

✢ ✢ ✢ ✢

Benicia Capitol Christmas Open House

December 1, 1995 **$** 𝒪 • 6 p.m. to 10 p.m.
(see #10 on map page 180)

Few people realize that Benicia served for a short time as the capital city of California. That privilege, or curse, depending on what you think about politicians, didn't last long and the entire operation was moved to Sacramento. But not before the good folks of Benicia had constructed a building to house the politics of the state. As the Christmas season approaches, the old Capitol and the adjacent Fischer Hanlon House are decorated for a traditional Christmas. About 1,500 people will show up during the day to tour the buildings and enjoy the 1800s ambience that the docents and staff have created. Benicia Capitol State Historic Park is located at 115 West G Street, at the corner of 1st Street, in Benicia. Dress for cool weather and expect a possibility of rain.

For information, contact Benicia Capitol State Historic Park; (707) 745-3385.

✢ ✢ ✢ ✢

Bird Walk: On the Wings of Winter

Early December Sunday **$** 𝒪 • 8 a.m. to 10 a.m.
(see #47 on map page 181)

The weather has changed significantly from summer and so have the birds that inhabit the wilds of the East Bay. This special walk will introduce you to all the newcomers who have left colder, snowy lands to the north and east and are feasting among the bushes, trees and grasses in the relatively mild California climate. If you're not really good at identifying the many different birds that inhabit the area, then here's your chance to spend some time with people who can, people who want to share their knowledge of this fun pastime. Plan on seeing thrushes and flickers among the trees and bushes, while out on the waters there should be canvasbacks, pintails and egrets strutting their stuff. If you have binoculars, bring them along, although there will be a few pairs available that you can borrow. Also, if you happen to have a birding field guide, be sure to toss it in your day pack. Dress warmly and hope for no rain. The program is held in Coyote Hills Regional Park. To reach Coyote Hills from Fremont, take Interstate 880 (Nimitz Freeway) to the Decoto Road/Highway 84 exit and head west to the Thornton Avenue/Paseo Padre Parkway exit. Turn north and go one mile to Patterson Ranch Road, then turn left and drive into the park. There's a $3 parking fee on weekends and holidays.

For information, contact the East Bay Regional Parks District, 2950 Peralta Oaks Court, Oakland, CA 94605-0381; (510) 636-1684.

✤ ✤ ✤ ✤

Las Posadas
December 9, 1995 • 5 p.m. to 7 p.m.
(see #51 on map page 181)

Special evening tours through Santa Cruz Mission will be led by staff and volunteers lighting the way with tin-can luminaria. In addition to the tours, there will be an opportunity to make your own tin-can luminaria and paper flowers. There will also be Latin American cookies and hot chocolate to chase away any chill that should invade this pleasant evening. Santa Cruz Mission State Historic Park is located one block from Plaza Park on School Street in Santa Cruz. There's a fee of $2 for adults and $1 for seniors and kids under 12.

For information, contact Santa Cruz Mission State Historic Park; (408) 425-5849.

✤ ✤ ✤ ✤

DECEMBER

Decorating for the Birds

Late December Sunday **S** 🕐 • 10 a.m. to 11:30 a.m.
(see #24 on map page 180)

Spend an hour or two at San Francisco Bay National Wildlife Refuge's Environmental Education Center learning how to make a special outdoor treat for our feathery friends, one that is both attractive and nutritious for the birds in your neighborhood. The birds will thank you with a winter-long display of fanciful flights and chattering songs. Meet at the San Francisco Bay National Wildlife Refuge's Environmental Education Center. To reach the center from Interstate 880 near Milpitas, exit on Highway 237 toward Alviso (Mountain View), then turn north onto Zanker Road. Continue for two miles and make a sharp right turn at Grand Boulevard into the center.

For information, contact the San Francisco Bay Wildlife Society, P.O. Box 524, Newark, CA 94560-0524; (510) 792-4275.

San Francisco Bay Area Seasonal Hikes & Programs

Over the Hills Gang Hikes

Ongoing, year-round, one morning each month **S** 🚶
(various East Bay locations)

How can you be "over the hill" if you're making it over the hills? Each month, Black Diamond Mines Regional Preserve naturalist Carole Richmond will lead a fun-and-exercise hike in a different East Bay regional park for adults age 55 and older. The program started in 1994 and was a big success, with some hikes drawing up to 40 participants. Each morning hike covers between two and four miles of easy terrain in three to four hours; some hikes will be followed with a bring-your-own picnic lunch. The following destinations are scheduled: January—Manhattan Canyon at Black Diamond Mines; February—Briones Regional Park; March—Diablo Foothills Regional Park; April—Morgan Territory; May—Contra Costa Trails; July—Point Pinole; August—Martinez Regional Shoreline; September—Macedo Ranch in Mount Diablo State Park; October—Morgan Territory; November—Sibley Volcanic Regional Preserve; and December—Lake Chabot. Wear good hiking shoes and bring your own water. All hikes are free and Carole will identify birdlife and native plants and wildflowers along the way. Call ahead for exact dates, times and meeting places.

For information, contact Black Diamond Mines Regional Preserve, 5175 Somersville Road, Antioch, CA 94509; (510) 757-2620.

SEASONAL

Snorkel and Scuba Exploration

Ongoing, year-round **S** 🖊
(see #42 on map page 181)

Whether you're a beginner who wants to learn the basics of snorkeling and scuba diving or a certified diver looking for a little refresher training or an early season workout, the place to head to is the East Bay's Shadow Cliffs Regional Recreation Area. Working with some of the local dive shops, staff at the park offer snorkeling and scuba sessions in a freshwater environment. You'll have fun learning and practicing underwater navigation and buoyancy skills. You'll also have an opportunity to try your underwater skills at night. Classes are offered on an ongoing basis; the schedule is set in May, with the times, fees and exact dates to be announced. This is an adults-only program that you must preregister for; it will be held in Shadow Cliffs Regional Recreation Area in Pleasanton. To reach Shadow Cliffs, take Interstate 580 to Pleasanton and the Santa Rita Road exit. Head south on Santa Rita to Valley, turn left, then left again on Stanley. The park is on the right. There is a day-use parking fee of $4.

For information, contact Shadow Cliffs Regional Recreation Area; (510) 846-3000. You can also contact your nearest dive shop located within the boundaries of the East Bay Regional Parks District for the most recent schedule.

Point Reyes Lifeboat Station

Last Sunday of each month **S** 🖊 · 2 p.m. to 4 p.m.
(see #2 on map page 180)

The Point Reyes Lifeboat Station is situated near Chimney Rock, the tiny sliver of land that separates Drakes Bay from the Pacific Ocean. This is a rare opportunity to tour this historic structure and learn about the maritime history of Point Reyes. There is a slide show at 2 p.m., so you may want to get here a little early, not only to get a seat for the show, but to spend time wandering around the area. The cliffs crumble, so don't get too close, either on top or down below along the beach areas. The Point Reyes Lifeboat Station is a good 20-mile drive inside the park. Point Reyes National Seashore is located just off Highway 1, about 26 miles north of its intersection with US 101, north of San Francisco Bay. The weather is really variable, but look for a possibility of fog in the morning with warm sunshine later in the day.

For information, contact Point Reyes National Seashore, Point Reyes, CA 94956; (415) 663-1092.

❀ ❀ ❀ ❀

Wilderness Explorers

Spring through summer, one day each month
(see #44, #49 on map page 181)

If you're looking for a program that will introduce your kids to the wilder side of the East Bay Regional Parks, the naturalists at Sunol-Ohlone Regional Wilderness and Del Valle Regional Park have just the thing. This is an exploration of the parks' land and water resources. The program is designed for younger kids who are willing to spend some time crawling in the grasslands, hiking in the woods and scooping critters from the parks' waterways. And what kid isn't? You are encouraged to participate, as much as you dare, with your kindergarten through second-graders. One part of the program is an overnight camping trip, although there are some prerequisites, which you can find out about by calling the park. Preregistration is required for the program. There's a $3 fee for children for the day programs and a $10 charge for the overnight trip.

To reach Sunol-Ohlone Regional Wilderness from the intersection of interstates 580 and 680, drive south on Interstate 680 for about eight miles to the Highway 84/Calaveras Road exit. Head south on Calaveras Road approximately four miles to Geary Road. Turn left onto Geary and drive to the park entrance and the visitor center. To get to Del Valle Regional Park, take Interstate 580 to Livermore and exit on North Livermore Road. Go south on North Livermore, which turns into South Livermore and then Tesla Road.

SEASONAL

After about two miles, turn left onto Mines Road. Continue about four miles, then turn right onto Del Valle Road, which leads to the park entrance and the Rocky Ridge Visitor Center.

For information, contact Del Valle Regional Park, 7000 Del Valle Road, Livermore, CA 94550, (510) 373-0332; or Sunol-Ohlone Regional Wilderness, (510) 862-2244.

Wilderness Trekkers

Spring through summer, one day each month
(see #44, #49 on map page 181)

While the younger kids get to participate in the Wilderness Explorers program, the older kids will be out on more advanced treks in this program offered at the East Bay's Sunol-Ohlone Regional Wilderness and Del Valle Regional Park. It's designed for third- through fifth-graders and parents are encouraged to participate; in some instances, parental participation is required. You and yours will spend time on foot and on horseback exploring the wilds of the parks. Grasslands, woodlands and the parks' aquatic resources will be the destinations of these afternoon and evening treks. There's also an overnight trip for the kids. There's a $3 charge per child for the day trips and a $10 fee for the overnighter, plus $25 for the horseback trip. Call for meeting places, times and dates.

To reach Sunol-Ohlone Regional Wilderness from the intersection of interstates 580 and 680, drive south on Interstate 680 for about eight miles to the Highway 84/Calaveras Road exit. Head south on Calaveras Road approximately four miles to Geary Road. Turn left onto Geary and drive to the park entrance and the visitor center. To get to Del Valle Regional Park, take Interstate 580 to Livermore and exit on North Livermore Road. Go south on North Livermore, which turns into South Livermore and then Tesla Road. After about two miles, turn left onto Mines Road. Continue about four miles, then turn right onto Del Valle Road, which leads to the park entrance and the Rocky Ridge Visitor Center. Exact directions to the meeting place will be provided when you make the reservation. There is a fee of about $3 per child, and advanced registration is required.

For information, contact Del Valle Regional Park, 7000 Del Valle Road, Livermore, CA 94550, (510) 373-0332; or Sunol-Ohlone Regional Wilderness, (510) 862-2244.

✤ ✤ ✤ ✤

Summer Science Weeks

Week-long sessions, June through August **S** 🖉 · 10 a.m. to 4 p.m.
(see #16 on map page 180)

There's something for everyone here, at least for kids who range in age from 9 to 12 years old. These programs are in-depth looks at everything from animal skulls and owl pellets to flowers, dirt and the bugs that bug them. But other creatures of nature won't be ignored: Snakes, butterflies, pond critters, birds and those creatures that have become so rare that they are now endangered are also part of the fun of learning. This is a thinking kid's program with a variety of take-home projects. Registration is required. There's a $60 fee for the week-long programs. To reach the Tilden Nature Area from Oakland, head east on Highway 24 and pass through the Caldecott Tunnel to the Fish Ranch Road exit. Head west on Fish Ranch to the Grizzly Peak Boulevard intersection, where you'll turn right and enter the park's south entrance.

For information, contact the Tilden Nature Area, Environmental Education Center, Berkeley, CA 94708; (510) 525-2233.

✤ ✤ ✤ ✤

Estuary Explorers

Third Wednesday in June, July and August **S** 🖉 · 3 p.m. to 5 p.m.
(see #22 on map page 180)

The San Francisco Estuary is the center of explorations for 8- to 10-year-olds during each of these two-hour programs. A naturalist will lead the groups in different natural history subjects. Each month's program will focus on a different creature, such as birds in June, fish in July and tide pool critters in August. Registration is required and the fee is just $5 per person. To reach the Crab Cove Visitor Center from Oakland, take Interstate 880 to the Broadway exit and turn right. Continue to Webster, turn right and go through the Alameda Tunnel. Turn onto Central, then turn left on McKay. The park entrance is on the left.

For information, contact the Crab Cove Visitor Center; (510) 521-6887.

✤ ✤ ✤ ✤

Junior Naturalist Academy

Two week-long sessions in June **S**(◌) • 9:30 a.m. to 12:30 p.m.
(see #47 on map page 181)

The Junior Naturalist Academy is meant for kids between the ages of 6 and 10 who are interested in natural history and want to spend time investigating the world around them. This is a flexible program that works around each child's interests and learning styles. Registration is required. The fee is $25 per child. To reach Coyote Hills from Fremont, take Interstate 880 (Nimitz Freeway) to the Decoto Road/Highway 84 exit and head west to the Thornton Avenue/Paseo Padre Parkway exit. Turn north and go one mile to Patterson Ranch Road, then turn left and drive into the park. There's a $3 parking fee on weekends and holidays.

For information, contact Coyote Hills Regional Park, 8000 Patterson Ranch Road, Fremont, CA 94555; (510) 795-9385.

✤ ✤ ✤ ✤

Native American Studies

Fridays in late June and July **S**(◌) • 10 a.m. to 11:30 a.m.
(see #47 on map page 181)

Each week, an expert in California Native American cultures will discuss the life and times of a different central California tribe. You'll learn games and make traditional Native American toys. The program is designed for kids ages 9 to 12 years old. Registration is required and the fee is $20. To reach Coyote Hills from Fremont, take Interstate 880 (Nimitz Freeway) to the Decoto Road/Highway 84 exit and head west to the Thornton Avenue/Paseo Padre Parkway exit. Turn north and go one mile to Patterson Ranch Road, then turn left and drive into the park. There's a $3 parking fee on weekends and holidays.

For information, contact Coyote Hills Regional Park, 8000 Patterson Ranch Road, Fremont, CA 94555; (510) 795-9385.

❖ ❖ ❖ ❖

Volunteer Bicycle Patrol

Ongoing, year-round **S**(̃
(various East Bay locations)

While bicycles are becoming increasingly popular, not everyone is educated in the etiquette of riding on busy trails. Volunteers are always needed to assist the East Bay Regional Parks District's Police Department by observing and reporting less-than-socially-acceptable rider behavior. There is also an emphasis on volunteers educating the public in proper biking etiquette. You are required to be in generally good health and have a bicycle in good working order. Helmets are also required, as is a bell for your bike. This is an ongoing, year-round program, so you can pretty much pick your own hours. You must be at least 18 years old.

For information, contact the East Bay Regional Parks District, 2950 Peralta Oaks Court, Oakland, CA 94605-0381; (510) 636-1684.

❖ ❖ ❖ ❖

Volunteer Flight Medics

Ongoing, year-round **S**(̃
(various East Bay locations)

This is a little more exciting than the bicycle patrol, but it's also a lot harder to get involved in. Volunteers are needed to assist the East Bay Regional Parks District's helicopter unit with rescues and medical assistance. You'll accompany the police pilot and an observer on routine park patrols and work closely with local fire and emergency medical service personnel. The work requires that you have had EMS training at or above the EMT/BLS level prior to applying as a volunteer. The need for volunteer flight medics is year-round.

For information, contact the East Bay Regional Parks District, 2950 Peralta Oaks Court, Oakland, CA 94605-0381; (510) 636-1684.

❖ ❖ ❖ ❖

Regional Parks Reserve Police Officer
Ongoing, year-round
(various East Bay locations)

The need for volunteer reserve officers is growing, so if you're inclined to help protect both the environment and the people who head to the parks for rest and recreation, then get yourself involved in the reserve officer program. Reserve officers supplement full-time officers in patrol activities, provide traffic and crowd control at special events and respond to emergency incidents. A uniform and safety equipment is provided, providing that you have the necessary special training and qualifications.

For information, contact the East Bay Regional Parks District, 2950 Peralta Oaks Court, Oakland, CA 94605-0381; (510) 636-1684.

❖ ❖ ❖ ❖

Volunteer Mounted Patrol
Ongoing, year-round
(various East Bay locations)

This work is very similar to that done by the bike patrol volunteers. The only difference is, rather than being mounted on two wheels, you've got four long legs toting you around the parks. You can enjoy riding the trails, while at the same time helping others learn how to ride safely and with consideration for other riders. The patrol officers don't expect, nor do they want, you to chase down the bad guys like in the movies. You simply use your radio to call in those who are trained and paid to do the chasing. You must have access to your own horse, one that can pass the department's certification course. The need for volunteers is year-round, so if you've got some spare time and like to ride, give this a try.

For information, contact the East Bay Regional Parks District, 2950 Peralta Oaks Court, Oakland, CA 94605-0381; (510) 636-1684 or (510) 881-1833.

✤ ✤ ✤ ✤

Open-Water Lap Swim
Late March to October **S** 🏊
(see #16, 19, 32 & 42 on maps page 180-181)

Swimming laps in a regular, concrete, chlorine-filled pool can be pretty boring. Why not try swimming laps in real water, the way Mother Nature intended? The only concession made to regular swimming pools is the lap lanes that are set up. Otherwise, you've got no walls against which to do fancy little flip turns, no white lines to follow and a bottom of gushy mud. If you have a desire to try your swimming skills on an open-water swim, then this is a good chance to hone your skills and find out what swimming in real water is all about. You can bring your own goggles, cap, kick board, pull buoy or hand paddles if you like. The program is available from the end of March all the way to October, during regular park hours. It's offered at Lake Anza in Tilden Nature Area, Lake Temescal, Shadow Cliffs and Contra Loma regional parks. There's a small fee at to swim at Anza and Temescal and a parking fee at Shadow Cliffs and Contra Loma.

For information, contact the East Bay Regional Parks District, 2950 Peralta Oaks Court, Oakland, CA 94605-0381; (510) 636-1684 or (510) 635-0138.

✤ ✤ ✤ ✤

SEASONAL

Open-Water Swim Training

May 11 to September 21, 1995 [S] ☎ • 5:30 p.m. to 6:30 p.m.
(see #16, 19, 32 & 42 on maps page 180-181)

There's nothing like swimming in open water, with no concrete sides to hold you back. But open-water swimming requires a few different skills than pool swimming, like navigation, special strokes and techniques for breathing air rather than water when things get choppy. To learn these skills, join a group that meets with a training lifeguard at the swim site one day each week for about eight weeks. During that time, you'll get some good workouts and excellent instruction and you'll have some fun. In order to get into this little group, you've got to be able to swim a continuous 200 yards in open water and at the site prior to your first workout. The program will be offered at Lake Anza in Tilden Nature Area, Lake Temescal, Shadow Cliffs and Contra Loma regional parks. The registration fee is $35 for residents and $45 for non-East Bay Regional Parks District folks, in addition to any entry and parking fees, all of which are subject to change. You must register in advance to secure a place in the group.

For information, contact the East Bay Regional Parks District, 2950 Peralta Oaks Court, Oakland, CA 94605-0381; (510) 636-1684.

Naturalist-Led Horse Rides

March through May [S] ☎
(various East Bay locations; phone ahead for meeting places and dates)

On horseback is a great way to explore the wilds of East Bay regional parks and wilderness areas. What makes a good ride even better is to have a naturalist along with you to help identify the flowers, birds and other animals you'll see along the trails. You'll also learn about the cultural history of the Native Americans who called this land home for thousands of years. The trips all vary in length and difficulty in order to accommodate all levels of riders. You can sign up for one or some or all of the rides. The fees listed were for the 1994 trail rides, so they may be different in 1995. You will receive a discount from the listed prices if you bring your own horse. Call the East Bay Regional Parks at the telephone numbers listed below for the most current prices and trip schedules. All rides require advance registration, so call early because they are popular.

Bollinger Canyon to Las Trampas Horseback Ride

This ride is scheduled near the first week in March and will cover about three miles along a creekside habitat. The cost will be about $27 and it's designed for ages seven and older. To reach Las Trampas Regional Park from Interstate 680 in Castro Valley, take Crow Canyon Road north to Bollinger Canyon Road. Follow Bollinger Canyon Road into the park. Directions to the staging area will be sent to you when you make the necessary advance registration by calling the East Bay Regional Parks District at (510) 636-1684.

For information, contact Del Valle Regional Park, 7000 Del Valle Road, Livermore, CA 94550, (510) 373-0332; or Sunol-Ohlone Regional Wilderness, (510) 862-2244.

Pleasanton Ridge Trail Ride

Traveling 15 miles on horseback requires more than beginning riding experience, so be prepared for this mid-March trip. This is for ages 12 and up. The cost will be about $87. To reach Pleasanton Ridge Regional Park from Interstate 880 at the city of Pleasanton, take the Bernal Road exit and drive west about a half mile. Turn left onto Foothill Road and drive another two miles. The park is on your right. Directions to the staging area will be sent to you when you make the necessary advance registration by calling the East Bay Regional Parks District at (510) 636-1684.

For information, contact Sunol-Ohlone Regional Wilderness, P.O. Box 82, Sunol, CA 94586, (510) 862-2244; or Del Valle Regional Park, 7000 Del Valle Road, Livermore, CA 94550, (510) 373-0332.

Sunol Horseback Ride

Usually offered about the first week in May, this relatively easy five-mile ride wanders in search of wildflowers. You must be age 12 or older and the cost will be about $50. To reach Sunol-Ohlone

SEASONAL

Regional Wilderness from the intersection of interstates 580 and 680, drive south on Interstate 680 for about eight miles to the Highway 84/Calaveras Road exit. Head south on Calaveras Road approximately four miles to Geary Road. Turn left onto Geary, which deadends at the park's day-use area. Directions to the staging area will be sent to you when you make the necessary advance registration by calling the East Bay Regional Parks District at (510) 636-1684.

For information, contact the East Bay Regional Parks District, 2950 Peralta Oaks Court, Oakland, CA 94605-0381; (510) 636-1684.

Rocky Ridge to Las Trampas Equestrian Trip

Mid-May, when this ride is usually scheduled, is a great time to see some eagles along this five-mile ridge ride. This is for ages 12 and up. The fee is about $40. Directions to the staging area will be sent to you when you make the necessary advance registration.

For information, contact the East Bay Regional Parks District, 2950 Peralta Oaks Court, Oakland, CA 94605-0381; (510) 636-1684.

Ohlone Wilderness Overnight Horseback Ride

This end-of-May ride covers 21 miles in two days, with an overnight camp stay. Because of the distance and packing needs, this is open only to experienced riders. The fee is about $200. Directions to the staging area will be sent to you when you make the necessary advance registration.

For information, contact the East Bay Regional Parks District, 2950 Peralta Oaks Court, Oakland, CA 94605-0381; (510) 636-1684.

❖ ❖ ❖ ❖

Fishing Tour on the Lake Chabot Queen

Saturdays, March through May • 10 a.m. to noon
(see #38 on map page 181)

There are some monster fish in Lake Chabot, but the secret to catching them is knowing where they lurk and how to approach them. To learn the secrets, join Boss Ross on this boat ride to where the 10-pound bass and 20-pound catfish reside. Bring your own fishing gear and bait if you have it, or you can purchase what you need at the marina. You must preregister for this trip. Anyone under the age of 13 must be accompanied by an adult. If you're 16 years old or older, don't forget your fishing license. The cost is about $5 per angler and the trips last about two hours. Advance registration is required.

For information, contact Lake Chabot, (510) 582-2198.

✤ ✤ ✤ ✤

Prescribed Burn Demonstration
Spring ❺ 🖉
(exact dates and locations to be announced)

For the past 50 years, we've been fighting fires in our wildland areas, attacking them with ground crews, airplanes and bulldozers. In that time, we've significantly reduced nature's effectiveness in spreading uncontrolled wildfires over thousands of acres of grasslands, chaparral and forests every year. Fires started by lightning have been around since the beginning of time. Now, rather than waiting for major fires to occur and then trying to fight them with puny human tools, smaller, cooler and well-controlled fires are being introduced into different areas of California's wild landscapes in an attempt to copy what nature had always done. There is a science to prescribing fires, a science based on fuel amounts, size and moisture, and on weather conditions such as temperature, wind speed, direction and humidity. Only when everything is right does an actual burn proceed. Here's an opportunity for you to see the work and preparation that goes into a prescribed burn. Join the East Bay Regional Parks District's Department of Public Safety, Fire Services, for a day in the hills making fire. The dates and times are really subject to weather conditions, but the programs are most likely to be held in early spring and late fall.

For information, contact the East Bay Regional Parks District, 2950 Peralta Oaks Court, Oakland, CA 94605-0381; (510) 636-1684 or (510) 881-1833.

✤ ✤ ✤ ✤

SEASONAL

Lake Ecology and History Boat Programs

Saturdays in May; Saturday & Sundays, June through August
Saturdays 2 p.m. to 4 p.m.; Sundays 1 p.m. to 2:30 p.m.
(see #45 on map page 181)

Spend a couple of hours in the afternoon with an East Bay Regional Parks District naturalist cruising Lake Del Valle by boat. There's a lot of history, both the natural and cultural kind, and if you've never been out on this beautiful reservoir before, here's the perfect opportunity. You can purchase tickets at the West Side Concession starting at 11 a.m. The cost, which is subject to change, is $4 for those age 13 and over, while the younger, pre-teen set gets on board for just $2.50. All children under the age of 13 and all non-swimming adults will be required to wear personal flotation devices, more commonly called life jackets, which will be provided. Meet at the West Side dock to board. If, by chance, fewer than five people are on hand at departure time, the day's trip is subject to cancellation. The trip lasts two hours. The weather should be pretty warm and comfortable. Bring a camera, sunscreen, a hat and sun glasses.

For information, contact Sunol-Ohlone Regional Wilderness, P.O. Box 82, Sunol, CA 94586; (510) 862-2244.

❖ ❖ ❖ ❖

Del Valle Campfire Programs

Saturdays in May; Friday, Saturday & Sunday of Memorial Day weekend; Fridays & Saturdays, June through August
8 p.m. to 9 p.m.
(see #44 on map page 181)

The Del Valle Campground amphitheater is the place to be on summer weekend nights for an hour of educational fun. A naturalist from Sunol will spend some time answering questions about the local plants, animals and the lake. While the program attendees are primarily folks staying in the campground, you don't have to be a camper to stop in for the evening's entertainment. If you're not staying in the campground, they ask that you park in the overflow parking area behind the campground store. To get to Del Valle Regional Park, take Interstate 580 to Livermore and exit on North Livermore Road. Go south on North Livermore, which turns into South Livermore and then Tesla Road. After about two miles, turn left onto Mines Road. Continue about four miles, then turn right onto Del Valle Road, which leads to the park entrance and the Rocky Ridge Visitor Center. There's a $4 parking fee.

For information, contact Sunol-Ohlone Regional Wilderness, P.O. Box 82, Sunol, CA 94586; (510) 862-2244.

❖ ❖ ❖ ❖

History Cruises on Lake Chabot

Summer weekends and holidays
1 p.m. to 2 p.m. & 2:30 p.m. to 3:30 p.m.
(see #38 on map page 181)

One of California's oldest dams, built more than 120 years ago, was created on East Bay Regional Parks District's Lake Chabot, located just east of San Leandro and Interstate 580. This cruise aboard the *Chabot Queen* tour boat will allow for a different look at the lake. You'll hear all about the dam that Anthony Chabot designed. Its construction saw the use of steam water cannons and wild horses, not your usual building techniques; when it was completed, it was widely considered to be one of California's wonders. There's plenty to see and it's really a fun way to spend a couple of weekend hours. There's a fee of about $2.50 for adults and $1.50 for kids.

For information, contact Lake Chabot; (510) 582-2198.

❖ ❖ ❖ ❖

Shuttle Boat Cruises on Lake Chabot

Summer weekends & holidays • 9 a.m., noon & 4 p.m.
(see #38 on map page 181)

If you're into fishing and don't have a boat to get to some of the more distant parts of the East Bay's Lake Chabot, then for a $1 fee you can get a round-trip ticket on the shuttle boat that crisscrosses

SEASONAL

the reservoir. Even hikers take advantage of this easy way to get to hiking trailheads. There are several landings around the lake that you can be dropped off at or picked up from. And park campers can catch the shuttle boat to the marina concession for forgotten supplies.

For information, contact Lake Chabot; (510) 582-2198.

✤ ✤ ✤ ✤

Anthony Chabot Campfire Programs
Saturdays, June through August ❺⟋ • 8 p.m. to 9 p.m.
(see #37 on map page 181)

A naturalist from the Crab Cove Visitor Center in Alameda will spend an hour each summer Saturday entertaining and educating both campers and non-campers at the park's campfire center. Each week will feature a different program, so you can attend several Saturdays and learn about a variety of subjects. The naturalist will also tour the campground on foot to answer questions and invite folks to the evening program. All ages are encouraged to attend and there's no fee for the programs.

For information, contact the Crab Cove Visitor Center; (510) 521-6887.

✤ ✤ ✤ ✤

Point Reyes National Seashore Hikes & Programs
Ongoing, year-round ❺⟋ • Times vary • See listings that follow
(see #5 on map page 180)

Most of the naturalist programs at Point Reyes begin in early May, then continue through Labor Day, although there's always something going on throughout the year. Scheduling these Saturday and Sunday programs more than a year in advance is nearly impossible, so please be sure to contact the park for their most current list of activities. What follows is a sampling of the types of specific hikes that have occurred in past years and will probably be continued in 1995. Point Reyes National Seashore is located north of San Francisco's Golden Gate Bridge, east of Highway 1, between Drakes Bay and Tomales Bay. The primary access road into Point Reyes is

Bear Valley Road, which cuts off from Highway 1 at the town of Olema. Most of the seminars are free. The weather at Point Reyes can be extremely variable during any day and any season. At different points in the park, it varies from cold, stormy and foggy to hot, dry, windy and calm.

For information, contact Point Reyes National Seashore, Point Reyes, CA 94956-9799; (415) 663-1092 or (415) 669-1250.

Birds of Bear Valley

Join a ranger for a one-hour hike along some of the short loop trails located near the Bear Valley Visitor Center for a look at many of the resident birds of Point Reyes. The diverse habitat supports a large number of bird species throughout the year, ranging from marsh hawks and osprey to thrushes and flycatchers. Actually more than 330 bird species have been spotted in the park, many in Bear Valley. If you're into birdwatching, then take this hike at different times of the year to spot all the migratory species that pass through the area. Bring your binoculars and a bird field guide and meet at the Bear Valley Visitor Center. To reach the Visitor Center from the town of Olema along Highway 1, turn west (toward the ocean) onto Bear Valley Road and drive about one-half mile.

Birds of Five Brooks Pond

This is a one-hour, half-mile search for some of the more secretive water-dwelling birds and the nearby forest songbirds. Bring your binoculars and a bird field guide. Meet at the Five Brooks Trailhead, located just off Highway 1, about 3.5 miles south of Olema. Look for the trailhead sign.

Birds of Limantour Estero

A naturalist will lead you to the nearby wetlands of Limantour Estero for a look at resident and migratory shorebirds and waterfowl. With more than 95 percent of California's historic wetlands now just history, here is an opportunity to see an environment that once supported millions of waterfowl and other birds along much of California's rivers and beaches. Bring your binoculars and a bird field guide. From the town of Olema along Highway 1, turn west (toward the ocean) onto Bear Valley Road and drive north, past the park headquarters, to Limantour Estero at the road's end.

Screech Owl Encounter

Meet at the Bear Valley Visitor Center for a personal introduction to a non-releasable screech owl obtained from the Santa Rosa Bird Rescue Center. If you've never seen an owl up close, then this a great opportunity to see how owls have evolved into silent and deadly night hunters. To reach the Visitor Center from the town of Olema along Highway 1, turn west (toward the ocean) onto Bear Valley Road and drive about one-half mile.

Edges

The meeting of land and sea along California's coast is one of the most beautiful places on earth. Here's a chance to learn more about the human history along the edges of both land and sea. This evening program combines music, stories and poetry, each art form its own celebration of the edge. Bring a flashlight and warm clothes to this one. Call (415) 669-1534 ahead of time for reservations. The meeting place is about a 15-minute walk from the parking lot at Chimney Rock, the land point that stands between Drakes Bay and the Pacific Ocean. To reach Chimney Rock from Inverness, continue on Sir Francis Drake Boulevard for about 14 miles and look for the roadside sign indicating the turnoff, then drive another mile to the parking lot.

Point Reyes Evening Lighthouse Tour

While few people ever get a chance to tour a lighthouse, even fewer get an opportunity to do it at night, seeing a lighthouse just as the keepers who lived and worked on the tiny points of land saw these beacons of safety. For reservations, call (415) 669-1534 on the day you plan to visit; space is limited. Bring a flashlight so you can help light the giant crystal lens—it's also nice for finding your way back to the parking lot if you happen to linger here a bit too long into the evening. From Inverness, drive 16 miles to the end of Sir Francis Drake Boulevard at the lighthouse.

Hike to Abbotts Lagoon

This two-hour hike is a little longer than most of the others offered at Point Reyes. Bring drinking water and dress in layers of clothing so you can shed or add them as needed when the fog lifts and the sun warms. Plan to be out for about two hours seeing firsthand the natural history of this fascinating place. Binoculars and a bird field guide will come in handy. To reach Abbotts Lagoon from Highway 1 at Olema, take the Bear Valley Road to a few miles past Inverness, where the road forks. Bear left onto Pierce Point Road. About two miles past the entrance to Tomales Bay State Park, you'll see the Abbotts Lagoon parking lot.

Hike to Tomales Point

Tomales Point is a long finger of land that separates Tomales Bay from the Pacific Ocean. The point is also part of the Tule Elk Reserve. Tule elk by the thousands once roamed these lands, but, as with many other species, they were brought to the brink of extinction by over-hunting and habitat destruction. They have since been reintroduced to the area, so there's a good chance of seeing these noble animals on the hike. But even if you don't, the abundance of other wildlife, from pelicans to seals, makes the hike worth the four hours it takes to complete. From Highway 1 at Olema, take Bear Valley Road to a few miles past Inverness, where the road forks. Keep right, then head toward the intersection at the Tomales Bay State Park entrance and turn onto Pierce Point Road. Follow Pierce Point Road several miles until it deadends at the Tomales Point trailhead, where the hike meets.

Tide Pools of Chimney Rock

Bring your rubber boots or other footwear you don't mind getting wet and join a ranger for a stroll along the tide pools of Drakes Bay. During this hour-plus walk, you'll be introduced to the amazing abundance of life that thrives in the narrow strip of coast that lies between the high and low tide marks. To reach Chimney Rock from Inverness, drive about 14 miles on Sir Francis Drake Boulevard. Look for the signed turnoff for Chimney Rock, then drive another mile to the parking lot.

SEASONAL

Traces of the Past at Kule Loklo

If you can't make the July 17th Kule Loklo Big Time event, then spend an hour with one of Point Reyes' rangers as he or she explores the cultures of the Coast Mi-wok and other Native Americans who once lived in this beautiful land. Kule Loklo is a recreation of what a Coast Mi-wok village probably looked like before the European explorers and settlers arrived. The Mi-wok village is located about one-half mile from the Bear Valley Visitor Center. To reach the Visitor Center from the town of Olema along Highway 1, turn west (toward the ocean) onto Bear Valley Road and drive about one-half mile.

Just for Kids

Here's a chance for younger kids to spend their own special time with a ranger exploring the natural world of Point Reyes. The programs can differ at each meeting, so you should call the Bear Valley Visitor Center, (415) 663-1092, for details about the meeting time and place and the day's subject.

On Shaky Ground

The infamous San Andreas Fault makes its exit to the sea through Point Reyes National Seashore. If you dare, join the ranger for a walk along the fault line. During San Francisco's great 1906 earthquake, this peace of earth separated and moved some 16 feet. Along the half-mile walk, you'll discover fascinating facts about earthquake and geology, as well as find out what you can do to protect yourself and your family during the next great shaker. The hike will meet at the Bear Valley Visitor Center parking lot. To reach the visitor center from the town of Olema along Highway 1, turn west (toward the ocean) onto Bear Valley Road and drive about one-half mile.

Point Reyes National Seashore Field Seminars

Point Reyes National Seashore sponsors a series of weekend seminars for adults on such subjects as natural history, photography, environmental education and the arts. Costs for the classes vary, ranging from $38 for a one-day pastel painting of nature class and

$32 for a Saturday spent studying bugs and butterflies (including a slide show and field excursion) to $95 for a class in block-printing techniques. All classes require preregistration. Point Reyes National Seashore is located north of San Francisco's Golden Gate, east of Highway 1, between Drakes Bay and Tomales Bay. The primary access road into Point Reyes is Bear Valley Road, which cuts off from Highway 1 at the community of Olema. The weather at Point Reyes can be extremely variable during any day and any season—from cold, stormy and foggy to hot, dry, windy and calm.

For a free brochure and to preregister, contact Point Reyes Field Seminars, Point Reyes National Seashore, Point Reyes, CA 94956; (415) 663-1200.

Early Bird Walk

First Saturday of each month, spring and fall 🅢🅟
8 a.m. to 9:30 a.m.
(see #24 on map page 180)

There's a major rush of wings as migrating birds fly over the Bay Area's waters each year looking for safe refuge to feed and rest before heading out again. There's no better place to see all the action than at the San Francisco Bay National Wildlife Refuge. Wildflowers begin to show their flashy heads and the local birds show their own colorful breeding plumage during the spring walks, while fall will see autumn leaves and waterfowl settling in for their winter respite. Meet at the San Francisco Bay National Wildlife Refuge's Environmental Education Center. To reach the center from Interstate 880 near Milpitas, exit on Highway 237 toward Alviso (Mountain View), then turn north onto Zanker Road. Continue for two miles and make a sharp right turn at Grand Boulevard into the center.

For information, contact the San Francisco Bay Wildlife Society, P.O. Box 524, Newark, CA 94560-0524; (510) 792-4275.

Educator Natural History Workshops

Offered in winter and spring $\mathbf{S}$ $\mathscr{O}$

(various locations; call ahead for meeting places and times)

For grammar school and junior high educators, getting factual and classroom-ready information about the natural ecosystems that surround us is not always easy. A series of workshops presented by the San Francisco Bay Wildlife Society has changed that. The following is a description of programs offered in 1994 that will probably be offered again in 1995, although the exact dates and times had not been set when this book went to press. Give the San Francisco Bay Society a call a month or so in advance of the tentative dates listed to confirm the programs being offered and to sign up. Each of the classes has its own meeting place, which will be provided upon registration. The cost of classes varies from $10 to $50.

For information, contact the San Francisco Bay Wildlife Society, P.O. Box 524, Newark, CA 94560-0524; (510) 792-4275.

Adopt An Endangered Species [Grades K-6]

This January class will focus on student and community action that can be taken to protect threatened and endangered species habitat. There's a $10 fee for the class, which includes an implementation manual. Preregistration is required.

As the Water Flows: Creeks, Wetlands and You [Grades 3-8]

This class will probably be offered in March and will emphasize expanding educators' knowledge about creeks and wetlands, their ecology, wildlife and what it is going to take to continue protecting these vital filters, creators and sustainers of life. The cost of the day-long program includes California Aquatic Science Education Consortium guidebooks: *Creek Watchers*, *Wetland Protectors* and *Freshwater Guardians*. Preregistration is required. The cost is $30, tentatively.

Down, Daring and Dirty: Close-up Encounters with San Francisco Estuary [Grades K-12]

The focus here is a close and intimate look at the problems facing San Francisco Bay and what can be done to mitigate those dangers. Preregistration is required and the cost will be about $50, which includes copies of several resource guides, including *San Francisco Estuary*, *Project Wild* and more. A flexible schedule of dates is generally selected in October, so that as many educators as possible can attend.

Tule Technology of the California Indians (Grades 2-6)

How did the California Native Americans sustain their lifestyles? This day-long class will look at their skills at incorporating natural materials, especially tules, into their daily lives. You'll learn how to replicate some of the tule items the land's earliest inhabitants depended upon for their survival. Preregistration is required. The cost for this November class is set at $40 tentatively.

❖ ❖ ❖ ❖

Astronomy Programs on Mount Tamalpais

Saturdays nearest the new moons, April through October **S**
Starts at 8:30 p.m. April through August, 8 p.m. in September,
7:30 p.m. in October
(see #11 on map page 180)

SEASONAL

Each of the programs offers an opportunity to view the heavens through several quality telescopes that are provided by the San Francisco Amateur Astronomers. The Mount Tamalpais Interpretive Association brings in a speaker at each new moon Saturday program as well. The exact subjects of the 1995 programs hadn't been set at press time. If you've never been up to Mount Tam, as it is referred to by many, the evening drive to the top of the mountain offers an absolutely unrivaled view of the surrounding San Francisco and San Pablo bay areas. To reach the park, from US 101, about five miles south of San Rafael, take the Highway 1/Stinson Beach exit. At the first stoplight, turn left onto Shoreline Highway (Highway 1) and drive about two miles, then turn right on the Panoramic Highway. After three-quarters of a mile, the road splits three ways—you want to take the middle fork for about five more miles. Turn right at the Pantoll Ranger Station and continue about 1.5 miles up the winding mountain road to the Rock Springs Parking Area. The Mountain Theater is within easy walking distance from the parking area. It can get pretty cool at night on top of the mountain, so dress accordingly. The programs are free.

For information, contact the Mount Tamalpais Interpretive Association, 89 Dominican Drive, San Rafael, CA 94901; (415) 388-2070 or (415) 454-4715. For their same-day hotline, phone (415) 355-1483. You can have your name added to the Astronomy Programs mailing list by writing to P.O. Box 3318, San Rafael, CA 94912.

❖ ❖ ❖ ❖

Hayward Shoreline Interpretive Center Naturalist Programs

Ongoing, year-round **$** ⏀ • Times vary • See listings that follow
(see #23 on map page 180)

The Hayward Shoreline Interpretive Center offers naturalist programs each Saturday and Sunday through the summer. Even if you visit the center when there are no formal programs scheduled, there is a lot to see and do. There's an area with interesting hands-on exhibits about the world of nature and lab classrooms for students and visitors. The shoreline also offers eight miles of hiking and bike trails to be explored. There's an outdoor observation platform that overlooks the salt marsh and bay. Below is a list of tentative program offerings for 1995. Most of the programs are free. You can get to the Hayward Shoreline Interpretive Center by heading out of central Hayward on Highway 92 (Jackson Street) and taking the Clawiter Road turnoff. From the stop sign, proceed straight for 200 feet, then turn left onto Breakwater Avenue for one mile.

For information, contact the Hayward Recreation and Park District, Hayward Shoreline Interpretive Center, 4901 Breakwater Avenue, Hayward, CA 94545; (510) 881-6751.

The Early Bird Catches the Run

This early-morning, three-mile slow jog is designed to wake you up while the shoreline wildlife is just getting active. There

Foghorn Press
555 De Haro Street, Suite 220
San Francisco, CA 94107

Get a free copy of Adventure West just for speaking your mind!

Please help us provide you with the best possible books on the outdoors by filling out this card. To thank you for your effort, we'll send you a complimentary issue of **Adventure West Maga-zine**, America's award-winning guide to fun and discovery in the 13 Western states, plus western Canada and western Mexico.

Name: _____

Address: _____ Phone: (___) _____

City: _____ State: _____ Zip: _____

Which book did you purchase/receive? _____

Where did you purchase your book? _____

Where did you hear about this book? _____

What other outdoors subjects would you like to see in a book? _____

Comments welcome: _____

Outdoor and Recreation books from
For more information call 1-800-FOGHORN

Foghorn Press
BOOKS BUILDING COMMUNITY.

should be a large assortment of birds, from the ever-present gulls to pelicans and more. The runs are on Saturdays from 8 a.m. to 9 a.m.

In Search of the Elusive Snowy Plover

Snowy plovers are interesting shorebirds that tend to nest in the open beach sand. This has set them in direct competition with humans who tend to develop and use open sandy beaches for recreation and homes, endangering the snowy plover's continued survival. Because their numbers are small, you may not see one of these little birds, but the search is still a lot of fun. Bring binoculars, and if you don't have any, the center has a few pairs to loan. The bird search is held on spring and summer Sundays from 8 a.m. to 10 a.m.

Touch Tank Day

The center has a 20-foot touch tank where a naturalist will be on hand to answer your questions about the feeding barnacles and other creatures inside. You'll have a chance to see little crabs, mud snails and more, all up close. The program is held during the week; call ahead for dates and times.

On the Edge at Robert's Landing

Join this one-and-a-half- to two-mile walk on the Northern Trail for a chance to discover the marsh-edge wildlife that lives here. You'll learn how the special animals of the area adapt to their unique homes and to the changing seasons. Discover bird families, plant life cycles and learn about the continuing restoration plans for this great place. Call for the meeting place, which will probably be in the East Bay Regional Parks District Office parking lot at the west end of Grant Avenue in San Lorenzo. The walk is held on Saturdays from 11 a.m. to 12:30 p.m.; call ahead for dates.

Summer Birds for Beginners

Trying to identify birds on your own with a guidebook and a pair of binoculars isn't really all that easy, unless you're scoping better-known species. Join this class that shows you how to use the bird's shape, size and basic color patterns to more easily identify them. If you have them, bring a bird book and binoculars. The

SEASONAL

center has a few pairs of binoculars to loan. This is a good beginning program for younger people. The class is held on summer Sundays from 11 a.m. to 1 p.m.; call ahead for dates.

Introduction to the Bay Area's Endangered Animals

There are more than a few endangered species living in and around San Francisco Bay. In fact, you can't count them all on the fingers of your two hands. Spend an afternoon viewing videos and slide programs to help you learn about the animals that can use your help. Since most of the endangered species are both few in number and secretive by nature, videos and slides are the best way to get a close-up view of these fascinating creatures. The program is held on Sundays from noon to 1:30 p.m.; call ahead for dates.

Butterfly Watching

Bring your binoculars and butterfly guidebooks for a walk along the bay to find these fluttering beauties. There's usually a quick meeting at the Winton Avenue parking lot for an introduction to butterfly natural history before everyone heads out on the trail to find these elusive insects. There are some binoculars available on loan. The walk is held on spring and summer Sundays from 10:30 a.m. to 1:30 p.m.; call ahead for dates.

Nature Detectives: Salamanders and Such

Nature Detectives is a special program for kids ages three to five. It explores different aspects of nature with each program. Salamanders and Such explores the secretive lives of these cute little lizard-like animals. While salamanders are seldom seen (because they need a moist environment in which to survive), this program will give everyone an opportunity to see these beautiful and special-ized animals up close. The program is held on Saturdays from 10:30 a.m. to 11:30 a.m.; call ahead for dates.

Endangered or Not?

Have you ever asked yourself why some animals are more likely than other animals to become endangered or extinct? Walk the Marsh Trail and learn the real reasons why so many animals have

become endangered and why more animals will continue to do so.
You'll look at the lifestyles of many species of shoreline creatures and
learn why ending habitat destruction is the key to keeping species
populations strong and viable. You'll visit areas where students have
worked to restore habitat. If you can stay around a little longer,
there's a slide show you can view that will offer even more insight
into the lives of our endangered species. The program is held on
Sundays from 10:30 a.m. to noon; call ahead for dates.

Whales of the World

This new game may surprise you with the knowledge that you
already possess about whales. It will also provide some new and
fascinating information about some of the world's biggest animals
that have ever lived, and will continue to live, if we give them a
helping hand. The program is held on winter and spring Saturdays
from 12:30 p.m. to 1:30 p.m.; call ahead for dates.

Marsh Muckers

Bring your bicycle, lunch, water and some peddling energy for
a two-wheeled tour of the Hayward shoreline. The trek begins on
Grant Avenue in San Lorenzo and heads south to the Hayward
Shoreline Interpretive Center. Since the day usually starts out chilly,
wear layers of clothing so you can strip off the layers as the fog
burns off and the day warms. This is a kids program for experienced
six- to eight-year-olds. Parents don't get to join the trip. Reservations are required for this trip because space is limited, so call ahead.
The program is held on spring and summer Sundays from 10 a.m. to
noon; call ahead for dates.

Early Migrant Search

There are many birds that call the shoreline home for only a
short time as they stop to feed and rest on their way to other parts of
California or the world. There's an opportunity to see some of the
normal migrants, along with an occasional rare find. Bring binoculars, if you have them. The program is held on Saturdays from 9:30
a.m. to 12:30 p.m.; call ahead for dates.

Winged Ones of Winton Avenue

Birds and butterflies will be the focus of this walk through several different habitats of the shoreline along Winton Avenue. Bring your lunch, water, field guides for both birds and butterflies, binoculars and dress in layers. The program is held on spring and summer Sundays from 10 a.m. to 1 p.m.; call ahead for dates.

Salt Marsh Water Creatures

Bring your rubber boots or some old tennies that you don't mind getting wet and join in the fun. Using dip nets and tow nets, you'll get a chance to capture some of the smaller creatures that swim in the salty waters and observe them under microscopes. You might want to bring a change of clothes and shoes, because you will get wet if you want to enjoy the full benefits of this afternoon walk. The program is held on Sundays from 12:30 p.m. to 2:30 p.m.; call ahead for dates.

Chapter 6

❋ ❋ ❋

Great Outdoor Events
of
California's Central Coast

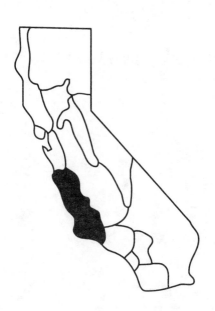

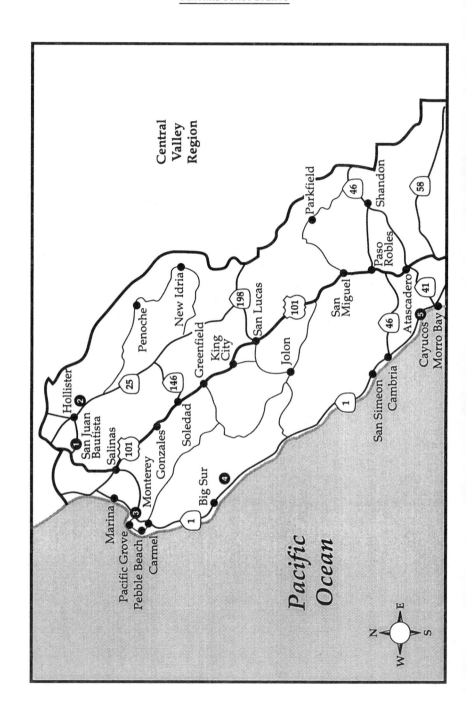

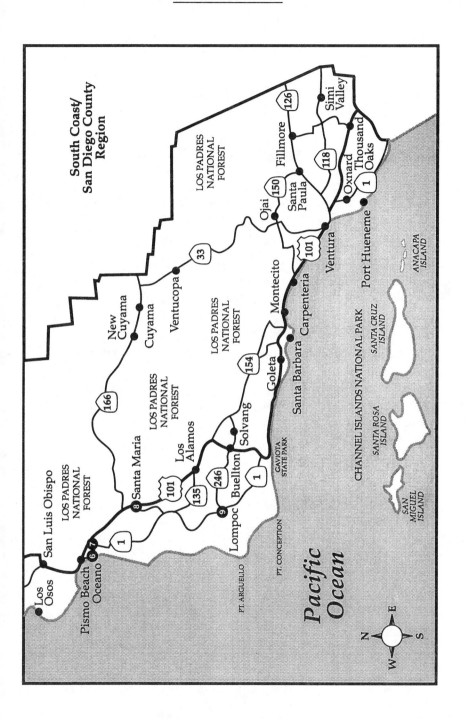

✤ ✤ ✤ ✤

Introduction to the Central Coast

If one were to choose the ideal location anywhere in California to call home, there are more than a few people who, without hesitation, would choose to live somewhere along the rugged coast and inland mountains that stretch from beautiful Monterey down to the vicinity of Ventura. While the exact boundaries of California's central coast can be debated, it's tough to argue that it's anything but a fine place to live, considering the mild climate, the wild landscape and the opportunities for outdoor recreation, which are some of the best in the state.

Drive along Highway 1 and you quickly realize that much of the central coast is isolated, undeveloped and difficult to access. The high cliffs and small number of roads, not to mention a few too many "No Trespassing" signs, limit access to some of the sand beaches that have been carved along the rugged shoreline by the Pacific Ocean. But there remains a significant expanse of mountains and beaches, which can keep even the most ardent explorers busy for a very long time.

If you can bypass the famous golf courses that line Carmel's famed 17-Mile Drive, drive on past Carmel State Beach and stop instead another mile or so south. Point Lobos is one of many public coastal access points, and it is also one of the most beautiful. In the 1800s, Point Lobos served as a whaling port, abalone processing plant and site of a few other less-than-environmentally-acceptable uses. In the ensuing years, it has reformed its practices, but retained its former splendor. You can wander along a gravel beach, watch giant waves crash against jagged cliffs or hike through forest as deer feed peacefully among the pines and wildflowers.

Farther south is Big Sur. Giant redwoods, mile after mile of spectacular coastline, rugged mountains and wilderness areas with few people and fewer towns are what you'll find here. You'll dodge bicyclists puffing their way along the winding highway, stop on top of 200-foot-high cliffs to admire the ocean views, and cross incredible, old concrete bridges that span precipitous creek gorges, escape routes for inland waters flowing relentlessly toward the Pacific.

If you're an off-road-vehicle enthusiast, Pismo Beach has long and wide sandy beaches, wild dunes and easy access that make it a major attraction for anyone who ever dreamed of driving along the edge of crashing waves, spraying water and sand out behind them, seldom mindful of what saltwater does to steel cars.

What you'll find along California's central coast is, well, just about anything you could ever want, with the exception of big cities. The two most heavily populated ones are Monterey and Santa Barbara and even those are relatively small. True, San Francisco and Los Angeles aren't all that far from the north and south ends of the central coast, so if you really need a big-city fix, you're only a short drive away. On the other hand, if you're stuck living in one those big cities, the central coast, with its solitude and beauty, is just as close.

Carlin Soule Memorial Polar Bear Swim
January 1, 1995 **S**
(see #5 on map page 328)

Join a bunch of slightly crazed folks and take one of those New Year's Day swims that always seem to make the local news programs. Since there aren't many chunks of ice floating in the Pacific Ocean off the coast of California, it's not likely this will be spectacle enough to make the national news. Still, the water is cold enough to turn your toes purple and send shivers up and down the spines of most reasonably sane people. Should you ask, Carlin Soule, a local restaurant owner, was the soul who dreamed up this slightly crazy stunt, which now attracts about 300 just as crazy souls each year–or is that soles, as in fish?

Cayucos is located along Highway 1, about six miles north of Morro Bay. There's no fee for the event, except maybe the shivers before, during and after, because the weather could be a little wet and cold on the first day of the new year.

For information, contact Cayucos Chamber of Commerce, 80 North Ocean, Cayucos, CA 93430; (805) 995-1200.

Mountain Transit Authority Mud-N-Yer-Eye
April 9, 1995 **S**
(see #2 on map page 328)

If you own a four-wheel-drive vehicle and want to have some fun, head out to Hollister Hills State Vehicular Recreation Area for a weekend campout and two days of testing your driving skills. You can run your vehicle through obstacle courses of varying degrees of difficulty. The event takes place in the park's Upper Ranch area which is limited to four-wheel-drives, so you don't have to share the hillsides with hordes of buzzing, darting dirt bikes. Hollister Hills State Vehicular Recreation Area is located six miles south of Hollister on Cienega Road. Heading east from Hollister on Highway 156, turn south onto Union Road, then right onto Cienega Road. (Follow the signs, because it's easy to get confused on Cienega.) The cost of the program is $25 per vehicle, but since the weather should be nice, the fun is well worth the money.

For information, contact Hollister Hills State Vehicular Recreation Area; (408) 637-3874.

✤ ✤ ✤ ✤

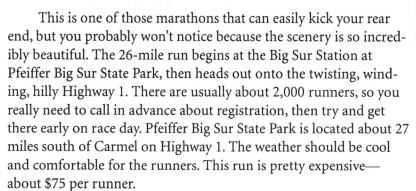

Big Sur International Marathon

April 23, 1995 **S** 🏃
(see #4 on map page 328)

(see #4 on map page 328)

This is one of those marathons that can easily kick your rear end, but you probably won't notice because the scenery is so incredibly beautiful. The 26-mile run begins at the Big Sur Station at Pfeiffer Big Sur State Park, then heads out onto the twisting, winding, hilly Highway 1. There are usually about 2,000 runners, so you really need to call in advance about registration, then try and get there early on race day. Pfeiffer Big Sur State Park is located about 27 miles south of Carmel on Highway 1. The weather should be cool and comfortable for the runners. This run is pretty expensive—about $75 per runner.

For information, contact Pfeiffer Big Sur State Park, c/o Monterey District, 2211 Garden Road, Monterey, CA 93940; (408) 667-2315.

✤ ✤ ✤ ✤

Fremont Peak Day

April 23, 1995 **S** 🏃
(see #1 on map page 328)

(see #1 on map page 328)

If you've never heard of San Benito County, it's time you paid this farm and grape country a visit. You can drive and walk to the top of Fremont Peak to participate in the oldest historic celebration in the county. There's a huge 6-foot by 10-foot U.S. flag that is raised—and whenever you raise a flag, dignitaries invariably have to make speeches and historical pronouncements, right? All that is followed by a picnic lunch and games for kids and adults. Usually, only about 250 people join in the festivities, so it's a good time to enjoy the mountain. To reach Fremont Peak State Park, take Highway 156 to San Juan Bautista, then turn south on the Alameda. From there, take San Juan Canyon Road (G-1) to Fremont Peak. The program is free and the weather should be warm all day.

For information, contact Fremont Peak State Park; (408) 623-4255 or (408) 623-4526.

✤ ✤ ✤ ✤

Beach Party Sand Drags

Last weekend in April **S** 〇 · All day
(see #6 on map page 329)

Pismo Dunes is one of the most popular beaches in California, not just because of its sand and ocean waters, but because you can drive here in your car, truck, motorcycle, motor home or just about anything else you may feel inclined to drive onto the sand. This particular weekend, if all goes as scheduled, there will be a lot more excitement than normal with a four-wheel-drive vehicle competition, a few touring events, a vehicle show, a dance and a great nostalgia beach party. So grab your beach towels, your best sandcastle-building tools, some sunscreen and a camera and head out to the beach for a weekend of great fun. The event is held in Oceano, three miles south of Pismo Beach, off Highway 1. The weather should be great. The fees may change, but they will probably be $4 for each vehicle you take onto the beach, $5 for dune tours, $25 for race registration, $5 for the dance, and $3 for spectators to view the drags.

For information, contact Pismo Dunes State Vehicular Recreation Area, Business Highway 1, Oceano, CA 93445; (805) 473-7230.

✤ ✤ ✤ ✤

Family Day at the Beach

May 6, 1995 **S** • 10 a.m. to 4 p.m.
(see #7 on map page 329)

Ever watched those movies where people drive their cars down wide expanses of ocean beach and splash through the edge of the breaking waves? Well, Pismo Beach is the only spot in California where you can do legally what they do in the movies. On this special family day, there will be demonstrations to show how to use the beach safely, which is especially helpful considering how many people use the beach in so many ways. Off-road-vehicle manufacturers, user groups and other beach-use groups will be present during the day. You can also learn about the ongoing resource management program here, part of which serves to protect the endangered least tern and snowy plover species. Pismo Dunes State Vehicular Recreation Area is located three miles south of the city of Pismo Beach, just off Highway 1. The day is free. Wear a light jacket, because it may be a little foggy in the morning.

For information, contact Pismo Dunes State Vehicular Recreation Area; (805) 473-7230.

✤ ✤ ✤ ✤

Santa Maria Elks Rodeo and Parade

June 1, 2, 3 & 4, 1995 **S**
(see #8 on map page 329)

If you've never been to a real rodeo, here's your chance to see one of the biggest events in the country. Top professional cowboys of the Professional Rodeo Cowboys Association will vie for top honors and dollars in a variety of traditional events, including bronc riding, the always exciting and dangerous bull riding, calf roping and more. There will be a parade to kickoff the events that include, in addition to the rodeo, several concerts and dances. So put on your best cowboy duds and join the 50,000 people who will be here during the event's four days. The rodeo will take place in the Santa Barbara County Fairgrounds' Minetti Arena, located at 937 South Thorn-

MAY

burg Street in Santa Maria, about 20 miles south of San Luis Obispo, on US 101. Entry fees for the rodeo will vary from $6 to $15. The weather should be warm and sunny.

For information, contact Elks Lodge 1538, 1309 North Bradley Road, Santa Maria, CA 93454; (805) 925-4125.

Early Days in San Juan Bautista

June 17 & 18, 1995 [S] ☎

(see #1 on map page 328)

You may have attended living history programs before, but this one adds a special touch. It includes a Victorian Ball to which you're invited. In addition, there are carriage rides and demonstrations of activities that were commonplace in the mid-1800s, such as blacksmithing. The historic and completely restored barroom is sure to see a goodly amount of activity. To reach the park from US 101, take Highway 156 to San Juan Bautista State Historic Park, which is located on the corner of Second and Washington streets. The cost wasn't set at press time, but it probably will be about $15 per person. It should be a pretty warm day, so dress accordingly.

For information, contact San Juan Bautista State Historic Park; (408) 623-4881.

Mountain Man Encampment

August 25, 26 & 27 [S] ☎ • 10 a.m. to 4 p.m.

(see #9 on map page 329)

Mountain men are not real good at paying attention to time, so the date of this encampment reenactment may end up rescheduled. If you've never been to one of these mountain-men weekends, then you've missed a really good time and an opportunity to gain at least a glimpse of what these hardy individuals did to survive in the wilds of the Old West. Look for demonstrations and exhibits, lots of buckskin clothing, hatchets, musket loaders, black powder and animal skins. While historically U.S. mountain men were never really welcome at the Spanish missions, all are welcome on this weekend. By the way, women are also welcome. La Purisima Mission State Historic Park is located at 2295 Purisima Road in Lompoc. The program is free to the public. It should be a warm and pleasant day.

For information, contact La Purisima Mission State Historic Park; (805) 733-3713.

✥ ✥ ✥ ✥

La Purisima Mission Candlelight Tours

October 6 & 7, 1995 **$**🕯

(see #9 on map page 329)

Most tours of California's missions are conducted during the day, of course. While daytime tours are quite enjoyable, why not try a night candlelight tour through one of California's best restored missions? Light from a flickering candle will offer you a completely different perspective on how the missions looked when people lived here in past centuries. Guides will lead tours through the mission by candlelight, while all around docents dressed in period costume will provide a living history, going about the chores that were typically performed in the early 1800s. If you'd like to be transported back to 1822 California on this very special weekend, you must call in advance for reservations. Admission gets you the candlelight tour and a dinner, the menu of which features dishes you might have eaten had you lived here 170 years ago. In the past, this evening has cost about $25 per person, but this year's price hadn't been set at press time. La Purisima Mission State Historic Park is located at 2295 Purisima Road in Lompoc.

For information, contact La Purisima Mission State Historic Park, (805) 733-3713.

OCTOBER

✥ ✥ ✥ ✥

Santa Maria 13th Annual Autumn Arts Festival

October 7, 1995 • 10 a.m. to 4 p.m.

(see #8 on map page 329)

If you're looking for a real family-oriented event, then you've found it. There's a special Kids' World where booths for having fun and testing skills are especially designed for the younger generation. For the older kids in all of us, there's a car show, a fine art show, lots of arts and crafts booths, free prizes, food and a few other things that always seem to spring up at the last minute. The entire event is designed to be affordable for families. Nonprofit organizations from throughout the Santa Maria Valley and central coast sell much of the food to raise funds for their programs. The event will be held at the Veterans' Memorial Cultural Center and Memorial Park at Pine and Tunnell streets in Santa Maria, which is about 20 miles south of San Luis Obispo on US 101. Admission to the festival is free. The weather should be sunny and breezy.

For information, contact the City of Santa Maria Recreation and Parks Department, 313 Tunnell Street, Santa Maria, CA 93454; (805) 925-0951, ext. 206.

La Purisima Mission Founding Day

December 8, 1995 [S] ☎ • evening

(see #9 on map page 329)

This annual event recognizes the founding of the Spanish mission near Lompoc. The event is held in the evening and candles are used to illuminate the trail to the church, creating a strikingly beautiful sight for visitors. A choir is on hand, singing music from the early 1800s, while staff and docents wearing period clothes recreate the atmosphere of bygone days. Expect about 400 people to come here to enjoy the evening festivities. Dress warmly as it can be rather cool, and maybe even wet, during the evening this time of year. La Purisima Mission State Historic Park is located about three miles from Lompoc, along Highway 246 and Purisima Road. There's no cost for the event.

For information, contact La Purisima Mission State Historic Park; (805) 323-0575.

✤ ✤ ✤ ✤

Christmas In Monterey's Adobes

December 8 & 9, 1995 **S** 🖊 • 10 a.m. to 4 p.m.

(see #3 on map page 328)

Monterey is one of California's oldest towns, having been an important part of Spain's holdings in the New World. Some of its homes and other buildings have been around since the early 1800s and many of them have been restored. Unfortunately, many of the restored buildings aren't always open to the public on a daily basis, so this is a great opportunity to visit some of California's history. This being Christmas, the old adobes will be decorated for the season, and there will be refreshments and entertainment available. This is a self-guided tour through old Monterey that will begin in the Pacific House on Custom House Plaza, adjacent to Fisherman's Wharf. There will be docents and staff dressed in period clothing to provide a lot of interesting stories and history about each of the buildings. Tour maps are available in the Pacific House in old Monterey. The cost is just $10 per person. Dress warmly, because this is winter.

For information, contact Monterey State Historic Park; (408) 649-2836.

✤ ✤ ✤ ✤

Central Coast Seasonal Hikes & Programs

Sierra Club Outings

Ongoing, year-round **$** (*) • Times vary
(Various locations; phone ahead for meeting places)

The Los Padres chapter of the Sierra Club offers a significant selection of hikes and outings that are available to both members and non-members. The hikes are specifically designed by trained hike leaders and the scheduling of the hikes is coordinated through the chapter. The listings that follow are from 1994; while most probably will be offered again in 1995, you should contact the Los Padres chapter for their most current outings schedule. For the most part, the hikes occur in the Los Padres National Forest, a few in Angeles National Forest and some in the Santa Monica Mountains, north of Los Angeles. Be sure to wear proper footwear; lugged-sole hiking boots are advised. Bring plenty of water and lunch or something to snack on. Most of the hikes are open to non-members, but you might as well join the Sierra Club (it's only $35 per year). That way, the chapter nearest your home will send you its hike schedule on a regular basis.

For information on Santa Barbara area hikes, write the Los Padres chapter of the Sierra Club at P.O. Box 90924, Santa Barbara, CA 93109-0924; (805) 966-6622.

Wildwood Canyon Geology Walk

Seems there was some kind of song written about a Wildwood Canyon, although maybe not this particular canyon. This is an easy three-mile walk with a 300-foot elevation gain, for a close look at the geologic history of the rugged mountains outside Thousand Oaks. Earthquakes are very much a part of this area, and here's your chance to learn more about the earth's quirks and jerks and how future movement could affect California's mountains and coastline.

Sage Ranch-Simi Mother's Day Adventure

This Mother's Day exploration of the Santa Monica Mountains Conservancy's Sage Ranch will look at the plants that inhabit the rugged countryside and their uses, both in the past and today. This is a three-hour family hike through the Simi Hills, south of the town of Simi Valley, where you'll explore the sandstone outcrops and wonderful oaks. This area is only open to docent-led hikes, making this a rare opportunity to venture into a land that is generally inaccessible to humans.

Big Sur Car Camping

This is one local Sierra Club trip that leaves the Santa Barbara area and heads up the coast to Big Sur. It's generally held in May, but you'll have to call ahead by mid-April to get your reservation in. Besides the beautiful drive up the Coast Highway, you'll have an opportunity to explore the beautiful and rugged Santa Lucia Mountains on trails ranging from easy to strenuous, or just sit back and enjoy the mountains, ocean, redwoods and wildlife. You will need some basic camping equipment, such as a sleeping bag and tent, along with your hiking boots, snacks and water for your daypack.

Matilija Creek—North Fork Ojai

You'll need some good hiking boots for this six- to eight-mile round-trip day hike northwest of Ojai. The group will be looking for those late blooming flowers and edible fruits. You'll even have an opportunity to wade beneath a waterfall. It's a great way to cool yourself off if the day has turned warm. Keep an eye out for black bears, or at least some signs of them, because they're in the neighborhood.

Cambria Pines Memorial Day Weekend

Camp Ocean is in Cambria, nestled in a Monterey pine forest. The views are great and so is the tidepooling and hiking. Besides nature, there's Hearst Castle to tour and the local villages to wander

SEASONAL

through. Saturday is finished off with a campfire and entertainment courtesy of local Sierra Club-members' talent, and most of the meals are included. You'll need to write to the Los Padres chapter in advance to see if this is going to be held again in 1995.

Backpack Sespe Hot Springs

For the more adventurous, this is a 14-mile round-trip backpacking outing northeast of Ojai in the Sespe Wilderness. It has a day layover, so there's plenty of time to enjoy the hot springs. Actually, this isn't a bad trip for beginning backpackers, because the pace is slow and more importantly, since this is just an overnighter, you won't have to bring much more than a sleeping bag and pad, maybe a tent if you're so inclined, as well as a couple of meals and water. Since your load will be light, you might as well toss in a camera, as there should be some great opportunities for pictures. There will probably be a fee of about $10.

Three Pools Beyond Seven Falls

This hike follows a primitive trail north of Santa Barbara, near Gibraltar Reservoir, that winds for about 1.5 miles, part of which includes a short stint of rock scrambling and maybe a little boulder hopping. The whole idea behind this hike is to introduce you to some great swimming holes that the general public will never have an opportunity to see, let alone take a refreshing dip in. Bring your swimsuit and a towel and wear some good hiking boots, because this is a less-than-superhighway type of trail. Remember: You've also got the 1.5 miles back to the trailhead to negotiate.

Rincon Beach Walk

Look out over the waters off the Santa Barbara coast and you'll quickly see why the area is well known for its oil. Giant oil rigs dot the horizon for as far as you can see. This hike is designed to get you even closer to all that black goo so you can understand the geology that fuels the area. This walk along the beach is an easy trek that nearly anyone can participate in. You'll discover some natural oil seeps, explore strange and beautiful rock formations and see lots of driftwood, sea lions and much more. Wear wading shoes for the tide pool explorations and bring a camera and a bag to collect some of the colorful pebbles and stones you'll find along the way. If you're a bit sensitive to the sun, toss a bottle of sunscreen in your daypack, along with some drinking water.

Gibraltar Dam Hike

Here's a seven-mile round-trip hike that uses the road to get to Gibralter Dam and then follows the river trail on the way back, so you won't get bored having to hike the same trail twice. The dam and reservoir are only 10 miles north of Santa Barbara as the crow flies, but, thanks to winding roads, it's about a thirty-mile drive. The hike's leader recommends wearing shorts and wading shoes, because there may be a little high water running across part of the trail. That is assuming California ever again sees anything reminiscent of normal rainfall, whatever that is, or was. This is a reasonably slow-paced hike; bring your swimming suit, or make use of your shorts, because there'll be an opportunity for the group to do a little swimming along the way.

Montecito Peak Annual Sunset Hike

Summer Solstice—June 20, give or take a day—is that day of the year when it stays light the longest. It's also the day for this hike up a rather steep trail that ends at the top of Montecito Peak for a fantastic, panoramic view of the coast. It's a pretty strenuous 7.5-mile hike, so make sure you're in shape to handle the full trek. But even if you're not, all the huffing and puffing is well worth the sunset view. Since the idea here is to sit on the mountaintop watching the sun set, don't forget to bring along a flashlight to make finding your way back to your car just a little bit easier. Montecito Peak is just inland from the town of Montecito.

SEASONAL

CALIFORNIA'S GREAT OUTDOOR EVENTS

Chapter 7

✤ ✤ ✤ ✤

Great Outdoor Events
of
California's Central Valley

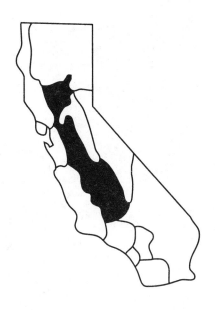

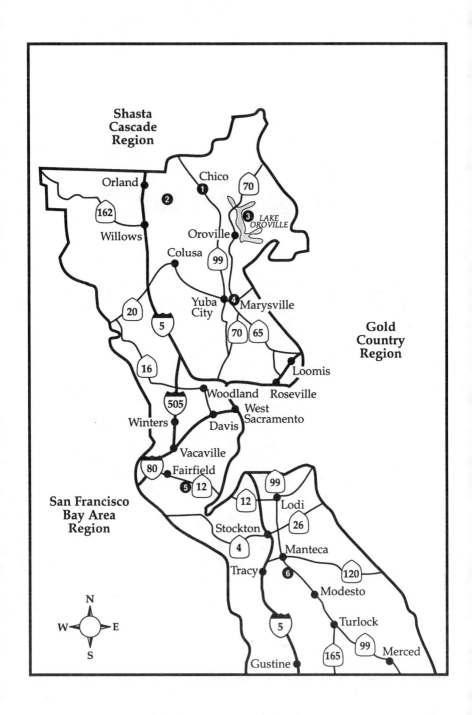

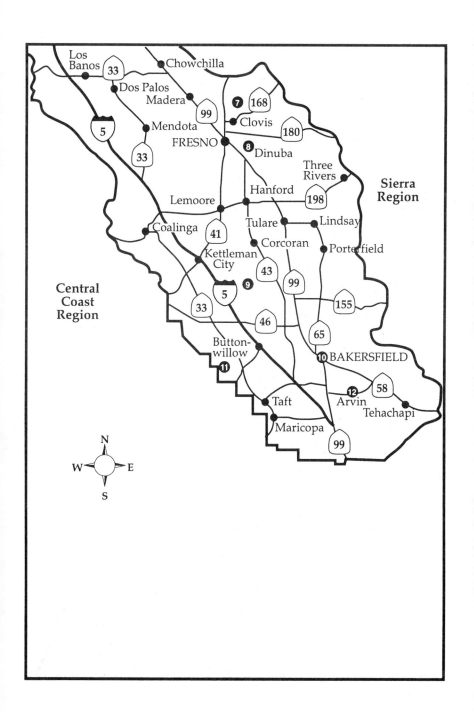

Introduction to the Central Valley

Stretching from near Chico in the north to the Tehachapi Mountains south of Bakersfield, the expansive Central Valley is best known for its agricultural richness, providing fruits and vegetables for the entire country. You may have mixed feelings about the valley if you've ever driven Interstate 5, feelings that are a combination of boredom and irritation. Except for Sacramento, which hasn't been included in this Central Valley chapter because of its close association with Gold Country history, there are very few towns along the route. Every 20 or 30 miles, you run across a fast food and gas oasis off the freeway, in between endless acres of cotton, orchards, overgrazed grasslands and meandering concrete rivers transporting Northern California water to the dry mouths, empty swimming pools and beckoning reservoirs of the parched southland.

Many of the events that occur in the Central Valley tend to focus on the Native Americans who once lived there, on the wildlife that thrives in the few wetlands and wildlands that haven't been converted to farmland, or on the infamous San Andreas Fault, which most of us would not mind about if it took its creaking, groaning and quaking elsewhere, quietly. But since it won't go away, we may as well enjoy the natural world that it has created.

The coming of the Europeans to this rich land transformed it from a marshy wetland filled with ducks and elk to a dry land in need of irrigation to support a lot of nonnative edibles. Lately, we have figured out that such a drastic transformation of an entire ecosystem is not particularly good for either people or wildlife. We have reintroduced endangered tule elk into restored and protected habitat and more agricultural fields are now being flooded to provide winter havens for migrating waterfowl. Today, irrigation strategies that spelled doom for some turn-of-the-century agricultural communities such as Allensworth, along with more recently developed farmlands, are now being revamped.

So the next time you're stuck driving the length of the Central Valley, take time, as they say, to smell the roses. Well, at least once you get far enough away from some of those cattle concentrations and their unique odors. Especially during spring, take a few minutes from your 65-miles-per-hour-plus freeway speeds and explore more than a fast food restaurant's water closet. Drive some of the side roads that meander back into the bordering hill country. You might be surprised at the beauty that awaits you. If you can take a little more time, join some of the organized outdoor hikes and drives through the area listed in this chapter and discover a whole new world.

San Andreas Fault: Gorman to Wallace Creek Tour

January 7, 1995 **S** 🖉
(see #10 on map page 347)

California and earthquakes are synonymous, aren't they? Nowhere in California are earthquakes more prevalent than along the San Andreas Fault. Here is an opportunity to travel with an earthquake expert and discover the problems that this meandering fault line continues to pose for us in California. This trip will take you to the Big Bend segment of the fault line to examine the exposures left by the 1857 Fort Tejon fault scarp, several pressure ridges and sag ponds. If you haven't a clue as to what fault scarps, pressure ridges and sag ponds are, then this is a wonderful opportunity to learn how to identify these prominent geologic indicators of earthquake faults found throughout much of California. The timing of earthquake activity along this stretch of the San Andreas is discussed in relation to the offset drainage at nearby Wallace Creek. There will also be an opportunity to learn about the ongoing efforts to increase the acreage of the Carrizo Plain Natural Area and Wildlife Reserve. This geology tour will probably begin in Bakersfield, but contact the trip leader for specific information. The trip costs $20 per person, which includes transportation. A field guide is also needed; if you don't have one, ask the trip leader for a recommendation.

For information, contact the Bureau of Land Management, 3801 Pegasus Drive, Bakersfield, CA 93308-6837; (805) 391-6081.

❀ ❀ ❀ ❀

Carrizo Birdwatching Tour

Mid-January **S** 🖉
(see #11 on map page 347)

Carrizo Plain Natural Area is home to many wintering birds, but this car tour will focus on the sandhill cranes that visit Soda Lake each year. Yearly water conditions dictate how many hundreds of sandhills winter here, but there is much more to see. The car caravan also will travel to Painted Rock, one of the most significant examples of Native American rock art found in California. There is a three-quarters-of-a-mile walk to the rock from the parking area. Besides a camera and lots of film, bring hiking boots or walking shoes, a jacket, sunscreen, water, food and anything else you may need, because there are no visitor services in the immediate area. Tours are limited to 25 people, so reservations are required. They will begin accepting them after January 12, 1995, at the Goodwin Education and Visitor Center; phone (805) 475-2131.

The Carrizo Plain Natural Area is about 40 miles west of Buttonwillow. Take Highway 58 west to Soda Lake Road, then turn south and continue to the visitor center. There's no cost for the hike. The weather should be sunny and cool, but rain or fog are always possible.

For information, contact the Bureau of Land Management, 3801 Pegasus Drive, Bakersfield, CA 93308-6837; (805) 391-6092.

❊ ❊ ❊ ❊

San Andreas Fault: Coalinga to Pinnacles Tour

February 4, 1995 **S**🖉

(see #10 on map page 347)

California is a land of incredible geologic diversity, much of it created by earthquakes and volcanic activity. Here is an opportunity to travel with a geology expert and discover which natural forces continue to shape the state. This trip will take you to Coalinga Sulfur Spring and also along the San Andreas Fault and into Pinnacles National Monument. The focus will be on the history of earthquake activity including the Coalinga and 1992 Parkfield shakers. This geology tour will probably begin in Bakersfield, but contact the trip leader for specific information. There's a fee of $20 per person, which includes transportation. You should also bring along a field guide to get the most out of the trip.

For information, contact the Bureau of Land Management, 3801 Pegasus Drive, Bakersfield, CA 93308-6837; (805) 391-6081.

❊ ❊ ❊ ❊

Great Valley Tule Fog Fête

Last Sunday in February **S** 🖉 • 10 a.m. to 4 p.m.
(see #6 on map page 346)

If you've ever had the misfortune of having to drive Interstate 5 or Highway 99 through California's Central Valley during winter, when the fog is so thick that flying ducks tend to rear-end each other, then you can maybe appreciate the humor in celebrating tule fog. Caswell Memorial State Park sits smack in the middle of some of the thickest valley fog, so the event's pea soup cook-off is apropos to the theme. There are also lots of activities designed for kids and a series of natural resource interpretive stations set up along the park's nature trails. Call in advance for reservations and to confirm the date and time.

Caswell Memorial State Park is located on Ripon Road, about six miles from Ripon and Highway 99. To get in, you'll have to pay a day-use fee of $5 per vehicle, but call to confirm the fee if money is a concern. You can expect winter sun, hopefully, but count on cold, damp, tule fog—otherwise the fête wouldn't be living up to its name.

For information, contact Caswell State Park, 28000 South Austin Road, Ripon, CA 95366; (209) 599-3810 or (209) 874-2056.

❖ ❖ ❖ ❖

Arvin Wildflower Festival

April 22 & 23, 1995 • 10 a.m. to 6 p.m.
(see #12 on map page 347)

In 1979, a severe windstorm struck the Bear Mountain foothills near the small community of Arvin, destroying most of the wildflowers that covered the hillsides. The community decided to help Mother Nature in her work of reseeding the once plentiful wildflowers. In commemoration of the successful reseeding of the foothills along Bear Mountain Boulevard (Highway 223), a festival is held every year. Today, the festival draws 10,000 people to the arts and crafts displays, food booths, live entertainment, 5K and 10K fun runs, co-ed softball tournament, horseshoe tournament, carnival rides, helicopter flights and parade. Since this is the wildflower season, you should take a drive out into the surrounding hills and enjoy the fruits of the labor completed nearly 20 years ago.

The festival is held at Di Giorgio Park in the town of Arvin, off Highway 223, about 12 miles east of Highway 99 and 12 miles south of Bakersfield. Most of the festival is free, except for foodstuffs and such. The weather should be clear and warm, but there's always a chance that a spring rainstorm might sneak through.

For information, contact the Arvin Chamber of Commerce, P.O. Box 645, Arvin, CA 93203; (805) 854-2265.

✤ ✤ ✤ ✤

Wildflower Century Bicycle Race
April 23, 1995 ❺ ⟁
(see #1 on map page 346)

One of the biggest and best century bicycle tours in Northern California begins in Chico and meanders across the flat Central Valley and into the hills to the east. Actually, several rides are available including the traditional Wildflower 100-miler, the Mildflower 65-miler, the 20-mile Childflower and the 125-mile La Fleur Sauvage. For anyone who wants to participate in either a 30-, 60- or 90-mile ride, a special Flatflower Century avoids the 4,300-foot elevation gains of the Wildflower rides and the 6,500-foot elevation gain of La Fleur Sauvage. Advance check-in is available the night before the Sunday race—and it's a good idea to take advantage of the opportunity because 3,000 riders are expected to join in the fun. With so many participants of varying ages and abilities, there will be no mass start. And with this many people rolling into the relatively small town of Chico, hotel space is at a premium. (Even so, a few of the local hotels offer special rates for cyclists. You can contact the Chico Visitors Bureau for hotel and race information.) The entry fee includes all of the food and drink stops along the courses, dinner and a massage, which should be quite welcomed after 125 miles of cycling. The race will begin in Chico. Contact the Visitors Bureau for pre-race registration locations and the race's starting point. The cost should be about $10 for one of the kids' short races and $25 per cyclist for any of the remaining events. The weather should be warm with a light breeze, but rain is never out of the picture this time of year.

For information, contact the Chico Visitors Bureau, 500 Main Street, Chico, CA 95928; (916) 891-5556 or (800) 852-8570.

✤ ✤ ✤ ✤

Wildflower Caravan
Mid-April **$** 🖊
(see #11 on map page 347)

Carrizo Plain Natural Area protects one of the largest remaining examples of historic San Joaquin Valley grasslands. It's home to nine endangered species, including the giant kangaroo rat, blunt-nosed leopard lizard and the San Joaquin kit fox. Each spring, the San Joaquin Valley explodes into a brilliant palate of wildflower colors. This car tour will lead you to the heart of it. You will be greeted by vast fields of wildflowers, including California poppies, blue bonnets, purple owls, clover and yellow alkali daisies. The car caravan will also visit Soda Lake and Painted Rock, a significant example of Native American rock art. Besides a camera and lots of film, bring good hiking boots or shoes, a jacket, sunscreen, water, food and anything else you may need, because there are no visitor services in the immediate area. Tours are limited to 25 people, so reservations are required. They usually begin accepting them the last week in March at the Goodwin Education and Visitor Center; phone (805) 475-2131. The Carrizo Plain Natural Area is about 40 miles west of Buttonwillow. Take Highway 58 west to Soda Lake Road, then turn south and continue to the visitor center. There's no cost for the hike. The weather should be sunny and mild, but spring storms can bring rain and wind.

For information, contact the Bureau of Land Management, 3801 Pegasus Drive, Bakersfield, CA 93308-6837; (805) 391-6092.

✤ ✤ ✤ ✤

Painted Rock Tour

Mid-April [S]☎

(see #11 on map page 347)

Historically, the Chumash, Yokut and other Native Americans hunted and traded on the Carrizo Plain, an area which today is part of the Carrizo Plain Natural Area. This car tour leads to Painted Rock, one of the most significant examples of Native American rock art in California, a place sacred to many Native Americans. During spring and summer, Painted Rock is also a nesting site for prairie falcons and, except for these special tours, is closed to the public during the nesting period. Carrizo Plain Natural Area protects one of the largest remaining examples of historic San Joaquin Valley grasslands and is home to nine endangered species, including the giant kangaroo rat, blunt-nosed leopard lizard and the San Joaquin kit fox. Besides a camera and lots of film, bring good hiking boots or shoes, a jacket, sunscreen, water, food and anything else you may need because there are no visitor services in the immediate area. Tours are limited to 25 people, so reservations are required and can usually be made beginning the last week in March at the Goodwin Education and Visitor Center; phone (805) 475-2131. The Carrizo Plain Natural Area is about 40 miles west of Buttonwillow. Take Highway 58 west to Soda Lake Road, then turn south and continue to the visitor center. There's no cost for the hike. The weather should be sunny and mild, but spring storms can bring rain and wind.

For information, contact the Bureau of Land Management, 3801 Pegasus Drive, Bakersfield, CA 93308-6837; (805) 391-6092.

Bidwell Bar Day

May 6, 1995 [S]☎ • Noon to 4 p.m.

(see #3 on map page 346)

No, Bidwell Bar Day doesn't honor some famous drinking establishment. The bar refers to a river sandbar and Bidwell was the person who owned all the land in the area of Chico and out toward Oroville back in the last century following the Gold Rush. The celebration is based loosely on the early days of the town named Bidwell Bar that occupied the area for a few years. This is really a family affair with a lot of fun activities, most tied to the history of the area. There's gold panning, various games, a reenactment of a pioneer wedding and loads of other entertainment. Food will be available for sale and there will be a crafts show and sale.

Bidwell Bar is located at Lake Oroville, which fills several canyons with its waters, about seven miles east of Oroville. Just follow the signs once you get to Oroville. There's no cost for the event. It should be warm, hot or very hot; after all, it's almost summer in California.

For information, contact Lake Oroville State Recreation Area; (916) 538-2200.

Jet Ski Regatta

May 13 & 14, 1995 **$**🖊
(see #3 on map page 346)

The scheduled date of this event is tentative, but when you get right down to it, you've really got to be a dedicated jet ski enthusiast to join the other 1,000 people who attend. Temperatures can get well into the 90-degree range, perhaps even into triple digits. There's no shade, no seating and it can get pretty windy out there on the South Forebay at Lake Oroville, which is where the event is generally held. If you like jet skis and want to see some real experts doing their things or participate yourself in this weekend of cool fun, then come on out. If you get bored with the forebay, there's always adjacent Lake Oroville with its many miles of shoreline and coves to explore.

To reach Lake Oroville's South Forebay from Highway 70 in Oroville, take the Grand Avenue exit and drive west for about five miles. There's a park entry fee of $5 per vehicle. Since this is nearly summer, dress appropriately and don't forget the sunscreen.

For information, contact Lake Oroville State Recreation Area; (916) 538-2200.

Allensworth Jubilee Celebration

May 13, 1995 **$** ⚲ · 10 a.m. to 5 p.m.
(see #9 on map page 347)

The annual spring jubilee is a jump back in time to the beginning of this century when Allensworth was the first all-black community in California. Ultimately, bad well water caused the farming community to disband, but the celebration of life in Allensworth never has ended. There are games for the kids, lots of really great food and gospel singing, as well as apple-bobbing and watermelon-eating contests. Several of the old buildings, including Colonel Allensworth's home and the old school house, have been restored and are open to the public. Up to 5,000 people usually take part in the festivities. Colonel Allensworth State Historic Park is located north of Bakersfield, seven miles west of Earlimart and Highway 99, on County Road J22. There's a fee of $3 per person to get into the park for the event. It should be pretty warm, and since you're in the middle of farm country, it can get a bit dusty.

For information, contact Colonel Allensworth State Historic Park; (805) 849-3433.

❖ ❖ ❖ ❖

Magical Moonshine Theatre Performance

May 13, 1995 · 4 p.m. in Spanish & 6 p.m. in English
(see #8 on map page 347)

Before the advent of writing, tribal elders passed their folklore down through the generations through storytelling. Many of the tales spoke of how different native peoples came to inhabit a land, where their food originally came from and how the animals that made up their worlds came to be as powerful or fast or secretive as they were. In this program, the Magical Moonshine Theatre group brings you "Animal Folktales of the Americas," a dramatic presentation for the entire family that is based on many of these ancient folktales. Each performance boasts an ever-changing selection of tales. You might hear how the condor brought food to earth, why the fox and caribou decided to exchange legs, the exploits of Br'er

Rabbit and his buddies, or Native American tales about coyotes, mountain rams and grizzly bears. The wonderful stories are retold using a combination of puppet and mask theater, accompanied by live music played on instruments ranging from modern electronic keyboards to the traditional charango and banjo.

This is a bilingual theater, with the 4 p.m. program in Spanish and the 6 p.m. performance in English. Much of the funding for this program comes from a California Arts Council grant. The event is held at an outdoor stage in Rose Ann Vuich Park at 855 El Monte in the town of Dinuba, about 20 miles south east of Fresno. From Highway 99, take the Mountain View exit and drive about 12 miles east. The program is free and the weather should be wonderful, so expect warm and sunny skies.

For information, contact the City of Dinuba Community Services, 1390 East Elizabeth Way, Dinuba, CA 93618; (209) 591-5940.

Gold Mining Dredge Tour

Third Saturday in May [S] ☎ • 10 a.m. to 3 p.m.

(see #4 on map page 346)

This event really begins in Gold Country, but travels to the Central Valley, where Gold Dredge No. 21 is still in operation today on the Yuba River near Marysville. This is an extremely rare opportunity to visit the old dredge, which is operated by Cal Sierra Development, Inc., located on the Yuba Gold Field. You'll learn about its history and meet some of the people who operate it. A shuttle boat will ferry you out to view the dredge; hard hats and life jackets must be worn during the tour and they will be provided. This tour is for adults only and it's limited to 20 participants. While people may meet up in Nevada City, the tour proper will begin in Marysville, about 45 minutes away via Highway 20. You can get more specific directions when you call for reservations. The tour will cost $18 per person. It should be a pretty nice, warm day for the trip.

For information, contact the Nevada County Land Trust, P.O. Box 2088, Nevada City, CA 95959; (916) 265-0430.

Silver Dollar Fair

May 24 to 29, 1995 **$** *(see #1 on map page 346)*

Some people think that a fair is a fair is a fair...and they're probably right. But fairs are still a lot of fun for families and young lovers. Commercial displays, agriculture, farm animals, wild rides, food, drink and much more can keep you hopping all day and well into the night. Stop in if you're in the Chico neighborhood.

The Silver Dollar Fairgrounds are in Chico, off Highway 99's Park Avenue exit. There's a $4 general admission fee charged. It should be a hot day and a comfortable evening.

For more information, contact the Silver Dollar Fairgrounds, P.O. Box 1158, Chico, CA 95927; (916) 895-4666.

❋ ❋ ❋ ❋

MAY

Allensworth Juneteenth

June 17, 1995 **$** · 10 a.m. to 4 p.m.
(see #9 on map page 347)

The small all-black community of Allensworth, which thrived in California's San Joaquin Valley around the turn of the century, is back in the spotlight for a Juneteenth celebration. Come visit the historic town and enjoy entertainment on three stages, featuring gospel, rhythm and blues and popular music—pretty much something for everyone. There will be guided tours though the historic buildings, including an old schoolhouse, lots of really tasty food and an arts and crafts show, much of which focuses on African art. Up to 3,500 people make the drive out to the park, many coming out the day before and spending the night in the park's campground.

Colonel Allensworth State Historic Park is located north of Bakersfield, seven miles west of Earlimart and Highway 99, on County Road J22. Entry is $3 per person when you drive into the park. During this time of year, the weather can be downright hot and the nearest swimming hole is too far away to think about.

For information, contact Colonel Allensworth State Historic Park; (805) 849-3433.

Brannan Island Kids' Fishing Derby

Mid-June [S] ☎ • 9 a.m. to 2 p.m.

(see #5 on map page 346)

The Sacramento Delta offers unlimited recreation opportunities, and with so many miles of waterways, fishing is one of the most popular pastimes. If your kids have a goodly amount of fishing experience, they can jump right in, so to speak. If they don't, there will be some local fishing experts on hand to offer pointers on the best way to win the fishing derby. Awards will be made for first place overall and in different age groups. There's usually free hot dogs and soft drinks for kids under age 13. Bring your fishing poles, tackle and an ice chest, that is if you want to clean your fish and take them home. Brannan Island State Recreation Area is located near Antioch, on Highway 160, about 3.5 miles south of Highway 12. The park entry fee is $5 per vehicle. It should be hot, with the possibility of cooling afternoon winds.

For information, contact Brannan Island State Recreation Area; (916) 777-6671 or (916) 777-7701.

Millerton Lake Sand Castle Contest

Early August [S] ☎ • 10 a.m. to 4 p.m.

(see #7 on map page 347)

Millerton Lake isn't the ocean. Still, this inland reservoir, like its better-known ocean beach cousins, has the two prime ingredients needed by sand castle builders: sand and water. But what really makes this contest unique is that its contestants are teams from architectural firms who compete head-to-head and bucket-to-bucket in the planning and construction of the most elaborate sand mansions possible. It should be fun to watch the pros try to make their creations rise from sand to prominence, without being made to look like amateurs by nearby kids' sand castles. And the lake does have at least one advantage over an ocean beach—builders won't have to complete their creations before the tide rolls in and washes them away.

Millerton Lake is located about 20 miles northeast of Fresno at the intersection of highways 41 and 145. Take Highway 41 north of Fresno. After nine miles, turn right on Friant Road. Take it 10 miles into the park. There's a $5 entry fee per vehicle. It should be good and hot, so bring sunscreen.

For information, contact Millerton Lake State Recreation Area; (209) 822-2225 or (209) 822-2332.

✤ ✤ ✤ ✤

Bidwell Mansion Almond Festival

September 16, 1995 • 10 a.m. to 5 p.m.
(see #1 on map page 346)

John Bidwell built a mansion to lure his young lover from the East. Over the years, he also introduced a great many innovations into the farming industry during the mid- to late-19th century. His orchards, vineyards and farmland were the beginnings of today's California agricultural industry. This almond celebration highlights just one aspect of the Chico area's agricultural diversity with a crafts and antique show, musical entertainment and refreshments. Bidwell Mansion will also be open for tours and, actually, that alone is worth the trip to Chico. On the tour, you'll learn little historical tidbits, like the fact that John Bidwell's wife, Annie, forbade dancing in the mansion, although it was built with a lavish third-floor ballroom. Annie also banned the making or consumption of alcoholic beverages on the premises. Even John Bidwell's foreman had to keep the grapes that were grown on the estate a secret; Bidwell's grape-growing experiments would turn out to be the beginning of much of California's table grape and wine industry.

The festival has an added bonus for those pack rats who are still saving those cute little statues, dishes and paintings from great-grandmother's attic. Experts will be on hand to offer appraisals of antiques and collectibles, so bring your very best. Event planners anticipate 1,000 or so people to show up at the mansion; arrive early, because parking can be a little bit of a problem. Think about bringing along a picnic lunch and enjoy the open, tree-shaded lawn surrounding the mansion.

SEPTEMBER

Bidwell State Historic Park is located at 525 The Esplanade in Chico. The festival is free, but appraisals will cost you $5, which is a pretty good deal if you've ever gone out looking at what appraisals normally cost. Tours of the mansion will cost $2 for adults and $1 for children, ages 6 to 17. It should be a warm day.

For information, contact Bidwell State Historic Park, 525 The Esplanade, Chico, CA 95926; (916) 895-6144.

❧ ❧ ❧ ❧

California Clean-Up Day

September 16, 1995 [S] ☎ • 10 a.m. to 2 p.m.

(see #5 on map page 346)

Brannan Island is one of the public park areas of California that will probably be participating in this annual clean-up day, as it has in many previous years. If you'd like to volunteer to help clean the junk from a park, grab your work gloves, old clothes and an appetite for having fun while working, if that's possible, and join the 200 or more park lovers. All the volunteers are usually treated to a barbecue at the end of the reasonably short workday. The park will even waive the entrance fee if you're coming to help out. Brannan Island State Recreation Area is located 3.5 miles south of Highway 12 on Highway 160, not far from Antioch. It should be a nice, hot day, but hopefully with cool Delta breezes arriving in the afternoon to cool things down. Sunscreen might be advisable.

For information, contact Brannan Island State Recreation Area; (916) 777-7701.

❧ ❧ ❧ ❧

Chico Expo and National Yo-Yo Championships

Last weekend in September [S] ☎ • 10 a.m. to 6 p.m.

(see #1 on map page 346)

Here's where walking your dog takes on a whole new meaning. Walking the dog, around-the-world and other equally silly-named tricks are accomplished by yo-yo enthusiasts of all ages in this annual competition that is part of the Chico Exposition. Begun as a local event about two years ago in this Central Valley college town, the thrill of victory, or at least the fun of it all, is what everyone stands to gain in what is now dubbed as the National Championship.

The yo-yo competition is held on Saturday only, at Chico's Silver Dollar Fairgrounds. Chico is located about 45 miles north of Marysville on Highway 99. Take the Park Avenue exit off Highway 99. There's a $2.50 general admission fee. There is no fee to compete. It should be a warm and sunny day.

For information, contact the Chico Chamber of Commerce, 500 Main Street, Chico, CA 95828; (916) 891-5556 or (800) 852-8570.

Allensworth Annual Rededication

October 6, 7 & 8, 1995 [S] ☎ • 10 a.m. to 5 p.m.

(see #9 on map page 347)

This is probably the only park that rededicates itself every year, but that's just fine, because any excuse for the fun that is had here is justified. In addition to the interpretive tours through the park's historic buildings, there is lots of entertainment, mostly musical in nature, and some excellent, home-cooked food. The park protects the remnants of California's first and only all-black community which thrived here for quite a few years earlier this century. While the park is located out in the middle of San Joaquin Valley farmland, kind of a long way from major towns and cities, over 5,000 people usually show up for this annual event.

Colonel Allensworth State Historic Park is located north of Bakersfield, seven miles west of Earlimart and Highway 99, on County Road J22. There's a fee of $3 per person to get into the park. The weather should be reasonably warm and nice, but you never know for sure.

For information, contact Colonel Allensworth State Historic Park; (805) 849-3433.

Holiday Fair

October 20, 21 & 22, 1995 **S**✐
(see #1 on map page 346)

After Labor Day, most fairs are nothing more than fond summer memories. Before the holiday season officially arrives, the people of Chico get together for just one more fling. The Holiday Fair bids farewell to summer and welcomes the upcoming winter holiday season. So if you haven't had enough of all the spring and summer fairs, stop by and enjoy good food, great exhibits and all the excitement that accompanies any good-time fair.

Take the Park Avenue exit off Highway 99 in Chico to the Silver Dollar Fairgrounds. There will be an entry fee, but it's not yet been set. It should be a warm and sunny day.

For information, contact the Silver Dollar Fairgrounds, P.O. Box 1158, Chico, CA 95927; (916) 895-4666.

Frontier Christmas

December 2, 1995 **S**✐ • 10 a.m. to 4 p.m.
(see #3 on map page 346)

When the pioneers came rolling or sailing into California, they didn't ignore the Christmas season. Although they may not have had all the comforts of the homes they left in the East, they made do with whatever they could find, however far they were from anything that resembled civilization. This modern-day celebration of the old ways will feature an 1850s theme with old-time entertainment, crafts and games. And if you're needing a little extra money for your Christmas shopping, there will be gold panning opportunities so, who knows, you may strike the big one and be set for life. More than likely, you'll just have a lot of fun and learn a little more about the way California's Gold Rush pioneers celebrated the holidays that were important to them.

Lake Oroville is located about seven miles east of Oroville. Follow the signs from town out to the lake. It's best to call for directions to the event site. There's a $5 fee per vehicle. The weather will probably be cold and damp.

For information, contact Lake Oroville State Recreation Area; (916) 538-2200.

Bidwell Mansion Christmas Open House

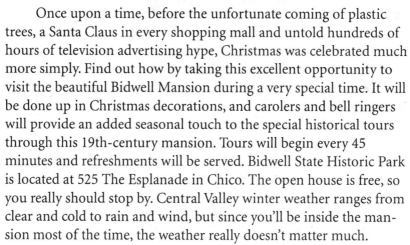

December 3, 1995 • 1 p.m. to 5 p.m.
(see #1 on map page 346)

Once upon a time, before the unfortunate coming of plastic trees, a Santa Claus in every shopping mall and untold hundreds of hours of television advertising hype, Christmas was celebrated much more simply. Find out how by taking this excellent opportunity to visit the beautiful Bidwell Mansion during a very special time. It will be done up in Christmas decorations, and carolers and bell ringers will provide an added seasonal touch to the special historical tours through this 19th-century mansion. Tours will begin every 45 minutes and refreshments will be served. Bidwell State Historic Park is located at 525 The Esplanade in Chico. The open house is free, so you really should stop by. Central Valley winter weather ranges from clear and cold to rain and wind, but since you'll be inside the mansion most of the time, the weather really doesn't matter much.

For information, contact Bidwell State Historic Park, 525 The Esplanade, Chico, CA 95926; (916) 895-6144.

DECEMBER

Central Valley Seasonal Hikes & Programs

Bureau of Land Management Geology, Archaeology & Ecology Tours

Monthly, either first or second Saturdays **$** ✆

(see #10 on map page 346)

Dr. Gregg Wilkerson of the Bureau of Land Management leads a different day-long hiking tour each month that focuses on some aspect or combination of geology, archaeology and ecology. The subjects and destinations of the tours tentatively include the following, although a specific schedule for April through December of 1995 had not been set at press time: Owens Valley to Mono Basin (two days); Ecology of the San Joaquin Valley; Bakersfield to Carpenteria; Bakersfield to Point Sal; Bakersfield to Ojai and Santa Paula; Jamestown to Copperopolis; Placerville to Georgetown; and Breckenridge Mountain to Havilla. Most geology tours begin in Bakersfield, but contact the trip leader for specific information. The cost is usually $20 per person, which includes transportation from the meeting place. It is recommended that you bring along a field guide. Advance registration is suggested.

For information, contact the Bureau of Land Management, 3801 Pegasus Drive, Bakersfield, CA 93308-6837; (805) 391-6081.

Bidwell–Sacramento River State Park Summer Speaker Series

Saturdays in July and August **$** $\wp$ • 10 a.m. to 11 a.m.
(see #2 on map page 346)

This is a great opportunity to learn about Sacramento River ecology from various experts in their fields. Each Saturday, experts from California State University, Chico and from other governmental agencies and organizations will lead easy one-hour walks and talks along the river. Here's a chance to ask questions and get answers about the Central Valley's lifeblood, not only with respect to the irrigation provided to thousands of acres of agricultural lands, but for the habitat that this riparian artery provides in the way of waterfowl refuges, fisheries and homes for numerous other species of wildlife.

Bidwell-Sacramento River State Park can be tough to find. Start at the river crossing for Highway 32 between Chico and Interstate 5, head east for about one mile, then turn south on River Road to the park. There's no fee for the programs.

For information, contact Bidwell-Sacramento River State Park, 12105 River Road, Chico, CA 95926; (916) 342-5185.

Genetic Resource Center Nature Trail Walk

Ongoing, year-round **$** $\wp$ • 7 a.m. to 4:30 p.m.
(see #1 on map page 346)

In 1934, the first kiwis planted here were destined to become the mother and father of all future generations of that exotically sweet and fuzzy fruit grown in North America. Today, a three-quarter-mile, self-guided, wheelchair-accessible nature trail passes alongside those original kiwi, a stand of timber bamboo planted in 1904, the rootstock of the original pistachio introduced in 1929 and many other experimentally introduced species. The nature trail meanders along part of Comanche Creek with its native vines and blackberries. There are picnic tables and benches where you can sit for a snack while enjoying the wildlife. Each season has something special to offer: spring flowers, summer shade, fall color and winter quiet. The Genetic Resource Center is located at 2741 Cramer Lane, off Highway 99, in Chico. There's no cost to hike the nature trail. Dress for the season in which you visit.

For information, contact the U.S. Department of Agriculture, Forest Service, Genetic Resource Center, 2741 Cramer Lane, Chico, CA 95928; (916) 895-1176.

Chapter 8

✢ ✢ ✢ ✢

Great Outdoor Events of California's South Coast & San Diego County

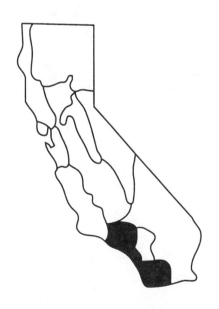

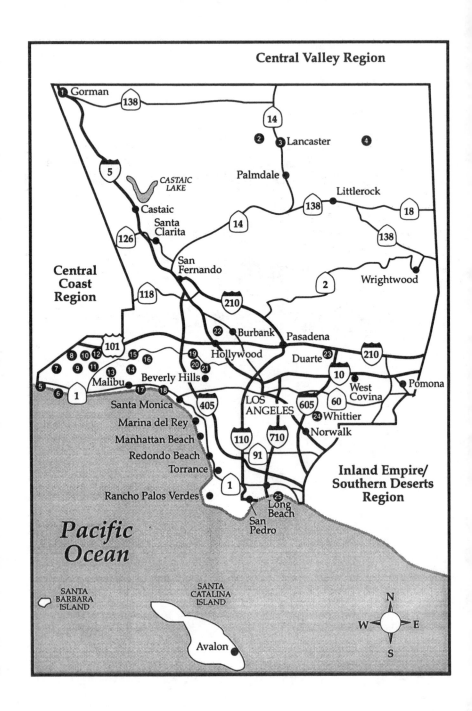

Central Valley Region

Gorman
138
14
Lancaster
Palmdale
Littlerock
18
CASTAIC LAKE
Castaic
Santa Clarita
138
138
Wrightwood
2
San Fernando
Central Coast Region
118
210
Burbank
Pasadena
Hollywood
Duarte
210
Beverly Hills
West Covina
Pomona
Malibu
Santa Monica
LOS ANGELES
Whittier
Marina del Rey
Norwalk
Manhattan Beach
Redondo Beach
Inland Empire/
Torrance
Southern Deserts
Region
Rancho Palos Verdes
Long Beach
San Pedro

Pacific Ocean

SANTA BARBARA ISLAND

SANTA CATALINA ISLAND

Avalon

N
W   E
S

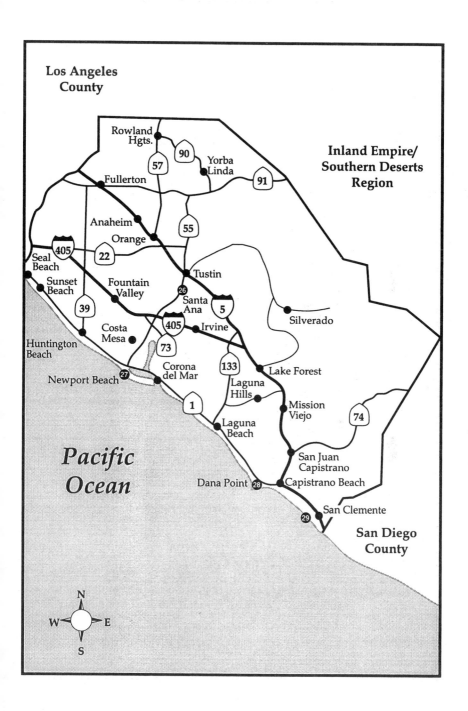

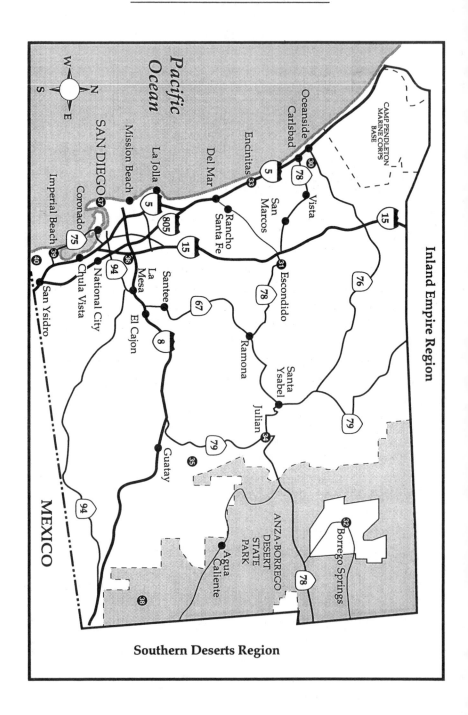

✤ ✤ ✤ ✤

Introduction to the South Coast & San Diego County

Ask many non-Californians to describe Southern California and they tend to mention earthquakes and Los Angeles in the same breath. Once they get past the fear-of-catastrophe stage, their minds focus on the people, millions of them, and the sunny, warm beaches, San Diego, Disneyland and Hollywood. While all of that is certainly Southern California, there's a bunch more. Within a few minutes drive of downtown Los Angeles, *sans* freeway traffic jams anyway, there are rugged mountains, streams, lakes, eagles, bobcats, coyotes, deer and not a lot of people. And each year, just like clockwork, whales on their migrations north and south pass within eyeshot of those people-strewn beaches.

As you look through the listings of hikes and events in this chapter, you're likely to notice that all of San Diego County has been included along with California's South Coast. While San Diego proper is appropriately placed, the county as a whole includes a big hunk of land that stretches well past the coastal hills, over the inland mountains and well into the desert lands to the east.

There are many reasons for including all of San Diego County with the South Coast, but I'll mention only two of them here. First, the California Office of Tourism includes all of San Diego Country in its state maps for tourists, albeit as a separate section from the South Coast. Including all of San Diego County with the South Coast made drawing the boundary lines easier on the map that accompanies this book. Secondly, there isn't much going on out in those deserts much of the year because it's too hot to breathe, let alone do anything. But circumstances do change. During spring, camera-lugging people are crawling all over the deserts, chasing the sometimes elusive wildflower blooms.

Getting back to the South Coast proper, the Santa Monica Mountains offer a handy urban wilderness area that provides several million city people with an escape from their daily grind. Many conservation-oriented nonprofit and government entities offer hikes and other programs through the mountains that once served as home to generations of Native Americans and provide a kaleido-scopic backdrop for the movie industry, from the Korea of TV's "MASH" to the simian-dominated futuristic landscape in *Planet of the Apes*.

So whether you want to hike the wilderness mountains or bang a volleyball on the beach, there is little in the way of recreation that can't be found along California's South Coast or in San Diego County.

Point Loma Whale Watch Weekend

January 21 & 22, 1995 • 9 a.m. to 5 p.m.
(see #37 on map page 372)

Whale watching has become a California tradition and San Diego's Point Loma is a perfect place to see gray whales as they travel from the cold, northern seas to the warm, protected bays of Mexico. What makes this particular whale-watching weekend different is that scientists, educators and photographers will be on hand as guest speakers, each sharing his or her special insights into, and experiences with, California's gray whales. National Park Service rangers will assist visitors in spotting these sometimes elusive creatures as they swim the relatively warm waters off Point Loma, while a musical group will perform historic whaling music. The program is held at Cabrillo National Monument in San Diego, which is located near the southern tip of Point Loma in San Diego. Take Rosecrans Street to Canon Street and turn right. Follow Canon to Catalina Boulevard, then turn left and proceed through the Naval Ocean System Center gates. The cost is $4 per vehicle. Be prepared for clear, cool weather, although rain is not impossible in January.

For information, contact Cabrillo National Monument, P.O. Box 6670, San Diego, CA 92166; (619) 557-5450.

Two Can Day

February 4, 1995 • 10 a.m. to 4 p.m.
(see #26 on map page 371)

Zoos are great places to learn about wildlife from around the world and Two Can Day is the perfect day to save a few bucks while taking a whole bunch of kids to the zoo with you. Kids under age 12 are admitted free when they bring in two empty aluminum cans. There are a couple of prizes, including a free family membership for the kid who brings in the most aluminum cans, and a free zoo T-shirt for second place. The cans will be sold by the zoo and the proceeds used to help pay for the new mixed species rainforest exhibit presently under construction. Co-sponsored by Great Western Reclamation, you'll have the opportunity to see the day's namesake, Toco Toucan, along with all the other animals currently calling the Santa Ana Zoo home. Great Western Reclamation's recycled robot, named Cycler, will be on hand to educate zoo visitors about the importance of recycling.

The Santa Ana Zoo is located at 1801 East Chestnut Avenue in Santa Ana. It's near First and Fourth streets, off Interstate 5. The cost will be about $3 for adults, $1 for seniors and for kids ages 3 to 12, and free to people with disabilities and members of the zoo. The event is free to kids under 12 who donate two empty aluminum cans. It should be a pretty nice day, although maybe a little cool.

For information, contact the Santa Ana Zoo, 1801 East Chestnut, Santa Ana, CA 92701; (714) 953-8555.

✤ ✤ ✤ ✤

Third Annual Native American Days
First weekend in February • 9 a.m. to 5 p.m.
(see #32 on map page 372)

The differences among Native American cultures, even within California, are both remarkable and fascinating. While many of California's Native American cultural events take place in the northern half of the state, here's the perfect opportunity for a look at the desert lifestyles that sustained these rich cultures for hundreds and even thousands of years. Actually, many different cultures are represented during the event, which will include a look at rock art, as well as the Native American philosophy and way of life. This is a really popular event with up to 4,000 people making their way here for the two days. Anza-Borrego Desert State Park is located east of San Diego via Highways 78 and 70 from the east, or via Interstate 8 from the south. The event takes place at the park's beautiful, half-buried visitor center, which is at the west end of Palm Canyon Road out of Borrego Springs. There is no cost for the program. The weather is really quite tolerable at this time of year, although the nights can be cool.

For information, contact Anza-Borrego Desert State Park, 200 Palm Canyon Drive, Borrego Springs, CA 92004; (619) 767-4205.

Juan de Anza Pageant
Late February 💲✎
(see #13 on map page 370)

This day is set aside to commemorate Spanish explorer Juan de Anza and his expedition to this area in 1775, who came with the intention of settling this new land. His ragtag group of 73 adults and 120 children was a melting pot of Europeans, many of whom were also part African (*mulatto*) or part Native American (*mestizo*), as well as people from the Iberian Peninsula (*criollo*). While de Anza's colonization effort was not particularly successful, one of his original immigrants, Jose Bartoleme Tapia, returned to the area in 1802. Tapia was granted permission by the Commandant of the Garrison of Santa Barbara to graze livestock on a rancho in Malibu Canyon. The rancho became known as the Topanga Malibu Simi Sequit Rancho. Today, it is known simply as Malibu Creek State Park and it hosts the annual de Anza Pageant. To reach Malibu Creek State Park, take the Las Virgenes exit off the Ventura Freeway (US 101) in Calabasas heading west. Take Las Virgenes two miles past Mulholland Drive and continue another two miles to the park entrance on the right. While the pageant is free, there's a $5 day-use fee for each vehicle entering the park. The weather in February can range from cold and rainy to warm and beautiful.

For information, contact California State Parks, 39996 Pacific Coast Highway, Malibu, CA 90265; (818) 880-0372.

Duarte Family Wilderness Day

March 18, 1995 • 9 a.m. to 2 p.m.
(see #23 on map page 370)

For a family event that incorporates fitness, wilderness skills and an appreciation for nature, this is one of the best. It's been going on now for about five years and gets more popular each year, which creates a bit of a problem because the program is limited to just 300 people. Part of the day is spent learning orienteering skills (using a map and compass to find your way), followed by a barbecue lunch that begins at 11:30 a.m. Once the basic skills have been covered, there's a hike that begins at the top of Mel Canyon Road and heads through the scenic lower reaches of Mel Canyon to the Van Tassel Trail. The hike continues with some excellent views of the city of Duarte and some of the other canyons. If you want to continue, you can climb to Sawpit Dam and Reservoir, which was built in the 1920s as a flood control project. After another three miles, you'll find yourself on top of 3,700-foot Mount Bliss. All in all, it's a great day for some great fun. The fee for the program is $12 for adults and $9 for kids. There is a discount for early entry. Duarte is located about 11 miles east of Pasadena, just off interstates 210 and 605.

For information, contact the City of Duarte Parks and Recreation Department, 1600 Huntington Drive, Duarte, CA 91010; (818) 357-7931.

Wildflower Show

First weekend in April **S** 🜄 • 10 a.m. to 5 p.m.
(see #9 on map page 370)

Join the fine folks of the California Native Plant Society in the Santa Monica Mountain's Charmlee Nature Preserve for a grand display of native plants and wildflowers. Not only can you see and admire these wonderful plants, but you have an opportunity to purchase many of them for your home gardens. There will also be an art show, strolling musicians and more. The show will probably be held at the Michael Landon Center at Malibu Bluffs Park.

For information, contact the California Native Plant Society, (818) 348-5910; or the Charmlee County Natural Area, (310) 457-7247.

Franklin Canyon Ranch Site Hike

Early April Saturday • 9 a.m. to 11 a.m.
(see #21 on map page 370)

This hike is entitled "Taking Care of Ourselves and Our World," and will cover less than two miles with an accompanying discussion about human wellness and the role ecology plays in it. This is a moderate hike through a beautiful part of the Santa Monica Mountains. Bring water and a snack. It should be a fairly warm day, but there's always a chance of a spring rainstorm. To reach the old ranch site from the Ventura Freeway (US 101), drive south on Coldwater Canyon Drive to Beverly Drive (Beverly Hills Fire Station #2). Turn right onto Beverly Drive and go one mile to Franklin Canyon Drive. Turn right and drive 1.5 miles to Lake Drive. Turn left and go a very short distance, then take a right turn into the Upper Lake area. Drive around the east side of the lake and park in the Sooky Goldman Nature Center lot.

For information, contact the Mountains Education Program, 2600 Franklin Canyon Drive, Beverly Hills, CA 90210, (310) 858-3090; or Mountain Parks Information, (800) 533-7275.

Geology of Southern California

Early April Saturday • 10 a.m. to noon
(see #13 on map page 370)

Southern California's geologic forces have a history of changing the landscape, at times sometimes suddenly and violently. For thousands of years, those changes had little effect, except on the relatively few Native Americans who lived there. Today, with several million people living in and around the mountains, most will sooner or later feel earthquakes, while others are unlucky enough to have their homes subjected to rivers of mud and water, as well as the earth's burps. This program is a chance to take a look at the geologic forces that created these mountains and continue to reshape them. You'll have an opportunity to examine evidence of how those deep-earth, rumbling forces continue to change the face of the Santa Monicas and why the freeways, highrises and homes will likely continue to shake and sometimes tumble into rubble. The hike in Malibu Creek State Park will look at the fascinating rock formations near the creek that meanders through the park. To reach Malibu Creek State Park, take the Ventura Freeway (US 101) to Las Virgenes Road, then head three miles to the intersection with Mulholland Highway. Continue to about one-quarter of a mile south of Malibu Canyon Road. The park entrance is on the right. The weather should be warm. There's a $5 park day-use entry fee.

For information, contact Malibu Creek State Park; (818) 880-0367.

Tots on the Trail

Early April Saturday [S] ☎ • 10 a.m. to noon

(see #21 on map page 370)

Introduce your little ones, ages two to four, to the joys of the great outdoors in the Santa Monica Mountains. Obviously, the kids must be accompanied by their parents or grandparents on this short walk of discovery. Your kids will get to experience the sights, sounds and feel of nature, and you'll get to see them excited about more than their next meal. The program is lots of fun for all. You need advance reservations for the program which will be held at the Sooky Goldman Nature Center. To get to the Sooky Goldman Nature Center from the Ventura Freeway (US 101), drive south on Coldwater Canyon Drive to Beverly Drive (Beverly Hills Fire Station #2). Turn right onto Beverly Drive and go one mile to Franklin Canyon Drive. Turn right and drive 1.5 miles to Lake Drive. Turn left and go a very short distance, then take a right turn into the Upper Lake area. Drive around the east side of the lake and park in the Sooky Goldman Nature Center lot.

For information, contact the Mountains Education Program, 2600 Franklin Canyon Drive, Beverly Hills, CA 90210, (310) 858-3090; or Mountain Parks Information, (800) 533-7275.

❖ ❖ ❖ ❖

Topanga Bird Walk

Early April Sunday **S**🖊 • 8 a.m. to 11 a.m.
(see #14 on map page 370)

APRIL

Topanga State Park began its modern life as part of a huge Spanish rancho, and now offers folks of the greater Los Angeles area a great and easily accessible place where they can wander through some wonderful birding habitat. Early spring morning is a great time to stroll through the valleys and woodlands of this Santa Monica Mountains park. Bring water and a snack, your binoculars and bird identification book, if you happen to have one. The hike will be led by a knowledgeable member of the Sierra Club. There's no fee for the walk. To reach the park, take the Topanga Canyon Boulevard exit south from the Ventura Freeway (US 101). Drive about eight miles to Entrada Road and turn east to the Topanga State Park entrance. There's a $5 day-use entry fee per vehicle. The weather should be warm and mild.

For information, contact the Sierra Club; (213) 387-4287.

❖ ❖ ❖ ❖

Springtime Splendor

Early April Sunday **S**🖊 • 1 p.m. to 3 p.m.
(see #14 on map page 370)

When winter rains finally finish their stay over the southland, warm temperatures combine with the moisture to produce an abundance of wildflowers. And you can often find different flowers in various canyons and varying elevations throughout the Santa Monica Mountains. Join a member of the Temescal Canyon Association for an easy hike in Topanga Canyon looking for and learning about native plants and animals. Bring a camera so you can take home some of the beauty of the spring wildflowers. There's a mammal and bird collection in the park's nature center, so you can see on display some of the wildlife only rarely seen by people in the park. The weather should be pretty nice. Bring water and a snack to keep your energy level up so you can enjoy the park to its fullest. To reach Topanga Canyon State Park, take the Topanga Canyon Boulevard exit south from the Ventura Freeway (US 101). Drive about eight miles to Entrada Road and turn east to the Topanga State Park entrance. There's a $5 day-use fee for each vehicle.

For information, contact the Temescal Canyon Association; (310) 454-4188.

Fire-Followers Wildflower Walk
Early April Sunday **$**⌀ • 10 a.m. to 1 p.m.
(see #16 on map page 370)

Fire has been an integral part of the ecology of the Santa Monica Mountains for thousands of years. Unfortunately, recent wildfires have devastated hundreds of people's homes and tens of thousands of acres of wildlands. Learn about the vital role that fire plays in creating a reproductive hotspot for pioneering wildflowers. Bring a camera for some great photo opportunities; with a naturalist along for the hike, you'll be able to find out the names of the flowers that you photograph. This hike will meander up Cold Creek Canyon Preserve. Advance reservations are required, and bring water and lunch with you. If you happen to own a wildflower field guide, you may want to bring it.

To reach the preserve from the Ventura Freeway (US 101), take Topanga Canyon Boulevard south to Mulholland Drive and turn west (right). Drive one-quarter of a mile and turn left on Mulholland Highway and drive approximately five miles to Stunt Road. Turn left and drive to the preserve entrance on the left. Ask about where to park when you call and make your reservations.

For information, contact the Mountain Restoration Trust; (310) 456-8432.

❈❈❈❈

Malibu Creek Birding Tour

Early April Saturday [S] ☎ • 8 a.m. to 11 a.m.

(see #13 on map page 370)

From thick woodlands and riparian waterways to hillside chaparral and open meadows, Malibu Creek State Park's many habitats support over 160 species of birds. On any one hike through the park, you can see hummingbirds and golden eagles, flycatchers and quail. You'll have to return many times to see all 160 species, since many of them are migratory and may only spend a few hours, days or weeks in the park before moving on. Others can be found here any time of the year. Bring your binoculars and a bird identification book, if you have them, and some water. There will be a knowledgeable birder from the Malibu Docent Association to help you spot and identify birds that you may not be familiar with.

To reach Malibu Creek State Park, take the Ventura Freeway (US 101) to Las Virgenes Road, then head three miles to the intersection with Mulholland Highway. Continue to about one-quarter of a mile south of Malibu Canyon Road. The park entrance is on the right. The weather should be warm. There's a $5 park day-use entry fee.

For information, contact Malibu Creek State Park; (818) 880-0367.

❈❈❈❈

Santa Ana Zoo Spring Fling

April 8, 1995 • 11 a.m. to 2 p.m.

(see #26 on map page 371)

This isn't your normal, run-of-the-mill Easter egg hunt, but an Easter "searchin' safari" egg-citing day of fun and egg-ucation. After all, chickens aren't the only creatures that lay eggs. Kids receive their own passport to adventure as they travel the zoo learning about all those other egg-laying animals. Chicken, snake, rhea and turtle eggs will be on display along with the animals that laid them. And you'll have a chance to learn about those other creepy, sometimes slimy egg-layers, like frogs, spiders and fish. Bring your camera for some great shots of your kids having a really good time, or to photograph the animals and eggs if that's more appealing to you. The Santa Ana Zoo is located at 1801 East Chestnut Avenue in Santa Ana. It's near First and Fourth streets, off Interstate 5. Admission is $3 for adults and $1 for seniors and kids ages 3 to 12; people with disabilities and members of the zoo get in free. This should be a great weather day.

For information, contact the Santa Ana Zoo, 1801 East Chestnut, Santa Ana, CA 92701; (714) 953-8555.

✤ ✤ ✤ ✤

March for Parks

Mid-April weekend 🌑📷

(see #8 on map page 370)

Here is an opportunity to visit Paramount Ranch, most recently the location used to film "Dr. Quinn, Medicine Woman," for a fundraising day of fun. The festival will bring together environmental groups and various park agency representatives to offer information on their parklands and programs. Craftspersons and retailers specializing in outdoor recreation will also be on hand, providing a wide variety of booths and activities related to the day's environmental theme. You'll have an opportunity to participate in nature walks, ride ponies and listen to some great music. The proceeds from the event will help support naturalist-led park learning adventures for inner-city kids.

To reach Paramount Ranch, exit the Ventura Freeway (US 101) at Kanan Road, just west of Agoura Hills, then continue south on Kanan about three-quarters of a mile, turning left on Cornell Road. Veer right, continuing about 2.5 miles to the entrance, which is on the right. The cost of the weekend event is $4 for adults and $2 for kids. You should expect pleasant, sunny spring weather.

For information, contact California State Parks, 39996 Pacific Coast Highway, Malibu, CA 90265; (310) 457-8142.

Where Your Folks Used to Frolic

Mid-April Saturday **S**🚶 · 10 a.m. to noon
(see #11 on map page 370)

Join this tour through the oak woodland of the Peter Strauss Ranch. It's an easy walk for people who enjoy nature and want to learn a little more about the world of the Santa Monica Mountains. With a little imagination, you can envision this land where people once came and played, until the highway was punched through and changed the nature of the area. Bring water and lunch. Meet in the parking lot. To reach the Peter Strauss Ranch from the Ventura Freeway (US 101), take the Kanan Road exit west of Agoura Hills and head south for 2.8 miles to Troutdale Road. Turn left on Troutdale, then turn left again on Mullholland Highway. Drive right under the arch into the parking lot. Walk back across the bridge on Mulholland Highway and enter the main gate into the ranch.

For information, contact the Topanga Canyon Docents; (818) 881-9063.

✿ ✿ ✿ ✿

Let's Walk Around the Lake

Mid-April Saturday **S**🚶 · 10 a.m. to 11:30 a.m.
(see #21 on map page 370)

Take an easy stroll around Upper Franklin Canyon Reservoir. A naturalist will be along to answer questions and provide information about the area's plants and animals. There will also be a talk about the Native Americans who once inhabited the Santa Monica Mountains and Franklin Canyon, long before someone thought to build a reservoir here. The program will be held at the Sooky Goldman Nature Center. To get there from the Ventura Freeway (US 101), drive south on Coldwater Canyon Drive to Beverly Drive (Beverly Hills Fire Station #2). Turn right onto Beverly Drive and go one mile to Franklin Canyon Drive. Turn right and drive 1.5 miles to Lake Drive. Turn left and go a very short distance, then take a right turn into the Upper Lake area. Drive around the east side of the lake and park in the Sooky Goldman Nature Center lot.

For information, contact the Mountains Education Program, 2600 Franklin Canyon Drive, Beverly Hills, CA 90210, (310) 858-3090; or Mountain Parks Information, (800) 533-7275.

❧ ❧ ❧ ❧

Discovering Nature

Mid-April Saturday • 1:30 p.m. to 3 p.m.
(see #21 on map page 370)

If you have children and would like to introduce them to the world of nature, then join a naturalist for a short walk to look at what kinds of homes animals make, a special meeting with a special tree and a chance to watch the fascinating world of bugs. If you're a little squeamish when it comes to bugs, you can just turn your head when your youngster picks one up and tries to eat it—well, hopefully that won't happen. Space is limited, so call ahead for reservations. The program is held at the Sooky Goldman Nature Center. To get there from the Ventura Freeway (US 101), drive south on Coldwater Canyon Drive to Beverly Drive (Beverly Hills Fire Station #2). Turn right onto Beverly Drive and go one mile to Franklin Canyon Drive. Turn right and drive 1.5 miles to Lake Drive. Turn left and go a very short distance, then take a right turn into the Upper Lake area. Drive around the east side of the lake and park in the Sooky Goldman Nature Center lot.

For information, contact the Mountains Education Program, 2600 Franklin Canyon Drive, Beverly Hills, CA 90210, (310) 858-3090; or Mountain Parks Information, (800) 533-7275.

❧ ❧ ❧ ❧

Twilight Hike Plus Marshmallows

Mid-April Saturday **S** ⬙ • 4:30 p.m. to 7 p.m.
(see #9 on map page 370)

Come along on this easy hike and your reward will be a great view of a beautiful sunset over the Pacific Ocean. As the sun sets, a campfire will chase away any evening chill that happens to invade, while providing a perfect opportunity to roast a few marshmallows, tell some stories and just have a fun Saturday night. Bring a flashlight, water and skewers of some sort to hold your marshmallows over the coals, because they really don't want you chopping off tree and bush branches just to roast a marshmallow or two. The hike is held at Charmlee County Natural Area. To reach the park, take the Pacific Coast Highway about three miles south of the Ventura County line and turn inland on Encinal Canyon Road. Drive about four miles to the park entrance, which is on the left side of the road.

For information, contact the National Park Service; (818) 597-9192.

❖ ❖ ❖ ❖

Birding for Beginners

Mid-April Sunday **S** ⬙ • 8 a.m. to 10 a.m.
(see #21 on map page 370)

Sometimes it's not always that easy to spot small birds hiding in thick brush. Join this hike and learn a few tricks for using binoculars to spot the little critters and field guides to identify them. There will be discussions about the natural history of many bird species and how they have adapted to different environmental demands in order to survive in the Santa Monica Mountains. Bring water and a pair of binoculars, if you have them. If you don't, there will be a few pairs to share. The weather should be nice for birding. This hike will be held at the Sooky Goldman Nature Center. To get there from the Ventura Freeway (US 101), drive south on Coldwater Canyon Drive to Beverly Drive (Beverly Hills Fire Station #2). Turn right onto Beverly Drive and go one mile to Franklin Canyon Drive. Turn right and drive 1.5 miles to Lake Drive. Turn left and go a very short distance, then take a right turn into the Upper Lake area. Drive around the east side of the lake and park in the Sooky Goldman Nature Center lot.

For information, contact the Mountains Education Program, 2600 Franklin Canyon Drive, Beverly Hills, CA 90210, (310) 858-3090; or Mountain Parks Information, (800) 533-7275.

❖ ❖ ❖ ❖

T'ai Chi Walk

Mid-April Sunday **S** 🖉 • 9 a.m. to 11 a.m.
(see #21 on map page 370)

For centuries, the Chinese have had a special way of communing with nature while improving their minds and bodies. Whether you are a total beginner or have had a little experience with t'ai chi, you're welcome to join this morning program. The leader will discuss the environment and demonstrate a very special exercise program geared toward bringing your mind and body in tune with nature. The walk will be held at the Sooky Goldman Nature Center in the Santa Monica Mountains. To get there from the Ventura Freeway (US 101), drive south on Coldwater Canyon Drive to Beverly Drive (Beverly Hills Fire Station #2). Turn right onto Beverly Drive and go one mile to Franklin Canyon Drive. Turn right and drive 1.5 miles to Lake Drive. Turn left and go a very short distance, then take a right turn into the Upper Lake area. Drive around the east side of the lake and park in the Sooky Goldman Nature Center lot.

For information, contact the Mountains Education Program, 2600 Franklin Canyon Drive, Beverly Hills, CA 90210, (310) 858-3090; or Mountain Parks Information, (800) 533-7275.

❖ ❖ ❖ ❖

Backpacking Survival Fun

Mid-April Sunday **S** 🗭 • 11 a.m. to 12:30 p.m.
(see #21 on map page 370)

If you already backpack or if you'd like to backpack for the first time, one of the most important things for you to know is how to survive emergency situations in the wilds of the Santa Monica Mountains, or anywhere else for that matter. Come along with a backpacking expert and learn those tricks for dealing with emergency situations that most of us never want to experience. Remember, Mother Nature can provide great pleasures, but she can be unforgiving when you go unprepared, either mentally or physically. The program will be held at the Sooky Goldman Nature Center. From the Ventura Freeway (US 101), drive south on Coldwater Canyon Drive to Beverly Drive (Beverly Hills Fire Station #2). Turn right onto Beverly Drive and go one mile to Franklin Canyon Drive. Turn right and drive 1.5 miles to Lake Drive. Turn left and go a very short distance, then take a right turn into the Upper Lake area. Drive around the east side of the lake and park in the Sooky Goldman Nature Center lot.

For information, contact the Mountains Education Program, 2600 Franklin Canyon Drive, Beverly Hills, CA 90210, (310) 858-3090; or Mountain Parks Information, (800) 533-7275.

✤ ✤ ✤ ✤

Nature & Awareness

Mid-April Sunday **S** 🗭 • 12:30 p.m. to 2 p.m.
(see #21 on map page 370)

The 1960s and '70s are still with us, at least the parts that were physically and mentally beneficial. Join a nature guru on this guided meditation followed by an easy, slow-paced walk on some of the trails around the Sooky Goldman Nature Center. Meditation helps to center you, allowing the serenity and power of nature to penetrate your being to its full extent. You'll seek the state of mind that people like Muir and Leopold captured, living in complete harmony with nature. The program will be held at the Sooky Goldman Nature Center. To reach the center from the Ventura Freeway (US 101), drive south on Coldwater Canyon Drive to Beverly Drive (Beverly Hills Fire Station #2). Turn right onto Beverly Drive and go one mile to Franklin Canyon Drive. Turn right and drive 1.5 miles to Lake Drive. Turn left and go a very short distance, then take a right turn into the Upper Lake area. Drive around the east side of the lake and park in the Sooky Goldman Nature Center lot.

For information, contact the Mountains Education Program, 2600 Franklin Canyon Drive, Beverly Hills, CA 90210, (310) 858-3090; or Mountain Parks Information, (800) 533-7275.

❖ ❖ ❖ ❖

Photo Fun In Franklin Canyon

Mid-April Sunday **S**🕿 • 3 p.m. to 4:30 p.m.
(see #21 on map page 370)

If you have a camera, a tripod and lots of film, bring them. If you don't, then just come along on this very slow-paced photo shoot at the Sooky Goldman Nature Center to enjoy nature and to learn from someone who has quite a few years behind a camera. You can get some pointers on how to look at nature from a different perspective, perhaps expanding your vision beyond the everyday. And once you're seeing the world around you a little differently, you'll be on your way to matching the photography of the masters. To get to the Sooky Goldman Nature Center from the Ventura Freeway (US 101), drive south on Coldwater Canyon Drive to Beverly Drive (Beverly Hills Fire Station #2). Turn right onto Beverly Drive and go one mile to Franklin Canyon Drive. Turn right and drive 1.5 miles to Lake Drive. Turn left and go a very short distance, then take a right turn into the Upper Lake area. Drive around the east side of the lake and park in the Sooky Goldman Nature Center lot.

For information, contact the Mountains Education Program, 2600 Franklin Canyon Drive, Beverly Hills, CA 90210, (310) 858-3090; or Mountain Parks Information, (800) 533-7275.

❖ ❖ ❖ ❖

The Walk of Life, Sound & Light

Mid-April Sunday **S** *⌀* • 5 p.m. to 6:30 p.m.
(see #21 on map page 370)

This is another class focusing on meditation as a vehicle for becoming one with nature. In this evening program, you will be guided through the interplay of nature's often subtle, always powerful sound and light. Join the group at the Sooky Goldman Nature Center for this unique look at our own special place in the cycle of life on planet Earth. To get to the Sooky Goldman Nature Center from the Ventura Freeway (US 101), drive south on Coldwater Canyon Drive to Beverly Drive (Beverly Hills Fire Station #2). Turn right onto Beverly Drive and go one mile to Franklin Canyon Drive. Turn right and drive 1.5 miles to Lake Drive. Turn left and go a very short distance, then take a right turn into the Upper Lake area. Drive around the east side of the lake and park in the Sooky Goldman Nature Center lot.

For information, contact the Mountains Education Program, 2600 Franklin Canyon Drive, Beverly Hills, CA 90210, (310) 858-3090; or Mountain Parks Information, (800) 533-7275.

❖ ❖ ❖ ❖

Babes In the Woods

Mid-April weekday **S** *⌀* • 10 a.m. to noon
(see #21 on map page 370)

If you have a stroller-aged infant and would like to spend time in a pleasant, natural setting, then come along with other mothers and fathers for an easy walk around the National Park Service's Upper Franklin Canyon Reservoir. Take this opportunity to get your child out of the noise and confusion of city life and relax with the joys that only nature can provide. Advance reservations are required in order to limit the number of participants, since the idea here is to enjoy nature's serenity and not have 50 parents screaming at their kids to quiet down and behave. The program will be held at the Sooky Goldman Nature Center. To reach the center from the

Ventura Freeway (US 101), drive south on Coldwater Canyon Drive to Beverly Drive (Beverly Hills Fire Station #2). Turn right onto Beverly Drive and go one mile to Franklin Canyon Drive. Turn right and drive 1.5 miles to Lake Drive. Turn left and go a very short distance, then take a right turn into the Upper Lake area. Drive around the east side of the lake and park in the Sooky Goldman Nature Center lot.

For information, contact the Mountains Education Program, 2600 Franklin Canyon Drive, Beverly Hills, CA 90210, (310) 858-3090; or Mountain Parks Information, (800) 533-7275.

Nursery Nature Walk

Mid-April weekday [S] ☎ • 10 a.m. to noon

(see #12 on map page 370)

In the continuing tradition of Nursery Nature Walks in the Santa Monica Mountains, this is a naturalist-led walk through the oak woodlands of Rocky Oaks, with you and your infant-to-kindergarten-age child. One of the walk's stops will be at a pond to watch the birds flutter and listen to the frogs croak. If you're lucky, you may even see a fish jump. There are also some amazing rock formations that some of the older youngsters who have graduated from crawling to walking might enjoy exploring. The Rocky Oaks Site is operated by the National Park Service. To get there from the Ventura Freeway (US 101), take the Kanan Road exit and head south. Turn west (right) on Mulholland Highway and right again into the parking lot. From the Pacific Coast Highway, turn inland on Kanan-Dume Road and go north until you reach Mulholland Highway. Turn west (left) and then right into the parking lot.

For information, contact Nursery Nature Walks; (310) 364-3591.

Runyon Canyon Trail Hike

Mid-April Saturday **S** 🚶 • 9 a.m. to 11 a.m.
(see #22 on map page 370)

Right in the middle of the Hollywood Hills, there exists a wilderness. It doesn't require hours to drive to and then many more miles of hiking before you step foot in nature's backyard. But as close to the great Los Angeles urban scene as Runyon Canyon is, there's some amazingly strenuous hiking available. This hike will explore some of the steeper passages through the canyon. Make sure that your leg muscles and lungs are up to par for this quick little two-hour hike. There should be plenty of wildflowers, birds and other wildlife to see. Bring some water along and wear good, sturdy shoes or hiking boots. To reach Runyon Canyon Park, take the Hollywood Freeway (US 101) and turn south onto Highland Avenue. Take Highland to Franklin Avenue and turn west, then turn north on Fuller. Park where the street ends.

For information, contact Friends of Runyon Canyon; (213) 666-5004.

❀ ❀ ❀ ❀

Mountaintop Views

Mid-April Saturday **S** 🚶 • 9:30 a.m. to 2:30 p.m.
(see #7 on map page 370)

There are many rugged and beautiful canyons in the Santa Monica Mountains and this six-mile, fairly strenuous hike will take you to the top of the highest point for a spectacular view. Along the way, a National Park Service ranger will help you identify the trail-side plants and wildflowers and better understand their relationships to the individual ecosystems and the larger bio-region. The hike will follow the Mishe Mokwa Loop Trail. Come prepared with good hiking boots; bring lunch and water. You might want to toss some binoculars and a field guide or two into your day pack. The trail is part of the Santa Monica Mountains' more extensive Backbone Trail. Meet at the Backbone Trail parking lot at the Circle X Ranch Site. Following the Pacific Coast Highway through Malibu, take the

APRIL

Coldwater Canyon exit and drive south to its intersection with Mulholland Drive. The entrance is on the east (left) side of the intersection.

For information, contact the National Park Service; (818) 597-9192.

Wildflowers Go Wild

Mid-April Saturday **S** 🏃 • 10 a.m. to 1 p.m.
(see #13 on map page 370)

Malibu Creek meanders through Malibu canyon, creating a riparian habitat that supports a wide range of plants and animals. Some of the prettiest of those plants are out in all their glory during spring, their red, orange, blue and yellow flowers attracting pollinating bees and other insects, setting the stage for next year's flowery show. Join a volunteer from the Malibu Creek Docent Association who will lead you to some of the secret wildflower spots off the beaten path. You'll have fun learning about the different plant families, which in turn will help you to more easily identify wildflowers on your own using some of the many field books that are available at your local bookstore. Actually, some of these guides are available in the park's small ranch house visitor center near the bridge, which you should visit.

Meet at the lower parking lot near the entrance to the park. To reach Malibu Creek State Park, take the Ventura Freeway (US 101) to Las Virgenes Road, then head three miles to the intersection with Mulholland Highway. Continue to about one-quarter of a mile south of Malibu Canyon Road. The park entrance is on the right. The weather should be warm. There's a $5 park day-use entry fee.

For information, contact Malibu Creek State Park; (818) 880-0367.

Evening Birds

Mid-April Saturday **S**⬤ • 6 p.m. to 7:30 p.m.
(see #21 on map page 370)

This is a wonderful walk for both beginning birders and those who have well-worn pages in their field guides. Birds, like most people (with the exception of Southern California sun worshipers), tend to look for cool places to hide during the heat of the day. Then they emerge from their daytime haunts to feed and play and look for mates during the evening hours, also much as most people do. The leader of this hike will offer insights into the habits of the seasonal avian creatures that pass through the Franklin Canyon area, while helping you learn where to look and listen for each of them. Bring binoculars, if you have them, and a flashlight. To reach the Sooky Goldman Nature Center from the Ventura Freeway (US 101), drive south on Coldwater Canyon Drive to Beverly Drive (Beverly Hills Fire Station #2). Turn right onto Beverly Drive and go one mile to Franklin Canyon Drive. Turn right and drive 1.5 miles to Lake Drive. Turn left and go a very short distance, then take a right turn into the Upper Lake area. Drive around the east side of the lake and park in the Sooky Goldman Nature Center lot.

For information, contact the Mountains Education Program, 2600 Franklin Canyon Drive, Beverly Hills, CA 90210, (310) 858-3090; or Mountain Parks Information, (800) 533-7275.

✤ ✤ ✤ ✤

Malibu Creek Bird Walk

Mid-April Sunday **S**⬤ • 8 a.m. to 11 a.m.
(see #13 on map page 370)

Grab your favorite bird field guide, if you have one, a pair of binoculars, and join this group of birders for a stroll through part of Malibu Creek State Park, looking at the more common birds that live here, and also at those that are merely passing through this time of year. You'll learn what birds find to eat to survive in a place where we would starve—and how what they eat, like millions of crawling bugs and flying insects, help maintain nature's delicate balance, in spite of human efforts to unbalance the entire thing. Bring some water and food for the walk, and maybe even your camera, since there should be a good number of wildflowers blooming this time of year. To reach Malibu Creek State Park, take the Ventura Freeway (US 101) to Las Virgenes Road, then head three miles to the intersection with Mulholland Highway. Continue to about one-quarter of a mile south of Malibu Canyon Road. The park entrance is on the right. The weather should be warm. There's a $5 park day-use entry fee.

For information, contact the Sierra Club; (213) 387-4287.

✤ ✤ ✤ ✤

Sunday Morning Circle X Ranch Hike
Mid-April Sunday 🅢 📞 • 8:30 a.m. to 4:30 p.m.

(see #7 on map page 370)

How does an entire day communing with nature, accompanied by others wanting to do the same, sound to you? This is a long and fairly strenuous hike, so you need to be ready to hike for eight hours, with a few rest stops and a lunch break tossed in just to keep everyone alive. The hike begins at the Circle X Ranch and finally ends in Sycamore Canyon, with your route taking you through Serrano Canyon. Plan on it being hot, dry, cool, sunny and shady—all of the above—along the way, with a few creeks to wander past and over, or perhaps through, if you please. Since this is a one-way hike, everyone planning to go should meet at Temescal Canyon parking lot to arrange participant carpools back to Circle X Ranch where the hike will begin. You really don't want to hike all the way back in the dark, so please, help arrange the carpools. To get to the Circle X Ranch parking area from the Pacific Coast Highway, turn inland on Yerba Buena Road and drive about 6.5 miles to the Circle X entrance. There's a large parking lot near the east gate of the ranch.

For information, contact the Temescal Canyon Association, (310) 454-4188.

✤ ✤ ✤ ✤

March for Parks

April 16, 1995 **$** 🖊 • 10 a.m. to 3 p.m.
(see #8 on map page 370)

Head for the hills in this celebration of spring in the Santa
Monica Mountains. Spring represents renewal and new growth; this
hike, which will begin at the Paramount Ranch, represents our
efforts to renew our commitment to our kids. March for Parks is
sponsored by the National Park Service as a fundraiser designed to
provide an ongoing opportunity to send children to naturalist-led
outdoors education programs. The day is designed to get the entire
family to enjoy the great outdoors with their kids; of course, you can
also come alone. To reach Paramount Ranch, exit the Ventura
Freeway (US 101) at Kanan Road, just west of Agoura Hills, then
continue south on Kanan about three-quarters of a mile, turning left
on Cornell Road. Veer right, continuing about 2.5 miles to the
entrance, which is on the right. There may be a small fee for the
event.

For information, contact the National Park Service Visitor
Center, (818) 597-9192; or Mountain Parks Information, (800)
533-7275.

❋ ❋ ❋ ❋

Senior Saunter

Mid-April Sunday **$** 🖊 • 10 a.m. to noon
(see #21 on map page 370)

This slow-paced hike will begin at the Sooky Goldman Nature
Center and is designed for those whose numerical age happens to be
in the upper third or so of the general population, but whose spirit
is as young as ever. You'll meet a docent from the nature center who
will lead you through portions of Upper Franklin Canyon. Learn
about nature, or if you already are a much-learned citizen, share
your knowledge with others, while spending a pleasant morning
with other nature-loving folks. Bring water and maybe a snack, a
wildflower field guide and binoculars, if you have them. To get to the
Sooky Goldman Nature Center from the Ventura Freeway (US 101),

drive south on Coldwater Canyon Drive to Beverly Drive (Beverly Hills Fire Station #2). Turn right onto Beverly Drive and go one mile to Franklin Canyon Drive. Turn right and drive 1.5 miles to Lake Drive. Turn left and go a very short distance, then take a right turn into the Upper Lake area. Drive around the east side of the lake and park in the Sooky Goldman Nature Center lot.

For information, contact the Mountains Education Program, 2600 Franklin Canyon Drive, Beverly Hills, CA 90210, (310) 858-3090; or Mountain Parks Information, (800) 533-7275.

❖ ❖ ❖ ❖

Great Rendezvous & John Muir Birthday Party

Mid-April Sunday • 10 a.m. to 1:30 p.m.
(see #14 on map page 370)

John Muir is probably the hippie ancestor of the environmental movement in the West, a bearded man dedicated to doing some rather strange things during his lifetime of exploring the West's wilderness areas, especially the Sierra. While Muir, with his long hair and shaggy beard, is gone, you might glimpse his spirit, and you're sure to learn more about his incredible life on this annual hike. The hike's final destination is the Trippet Ranch for a birthday celebration. The hike will leave from Topanga State Park and follow Dead Horse Trail. You'll need to bring water and lunch; you may want to include a camera, because there's bound to be a lot of wildflowers and some exceptionally beautiful views. The entrance to Topanga State Park is located on Entrada Road, east of Topanga Canyon Boulevard, eight miles south of US 101, six miles north of Santa Monica.

For information, contact the Sierra Club; (213) 387-4287.

❖ ❖ ❖ ❖

Cultural History Walk

Mid-April Sunday **S** ⏀ • 1 p.m. to 2 p.m.
(see #22 on map page 370)

More than a few of the people who have lived in such places as Malibu and Beverly Hills have been well-known personalities. And some of them have definitely left their marks on this land. Come to Runyon Canyon Park and spend an hour with a local historian to learn about the canyon's part in Los Angeles history, from the Frank Lloyd Wright project site to the proposed Metro Rail tunnel route. To reach Runyon Canyon Park, take the Hollywood Freeway (US 101) and turn south onto Highland Avenue. Take Highland to Franklin Avenue and turn west, then turn north on Fuller. Park where the street ends.

For information, contact the Friends of Runyon Canyon; (213) 665-5004.

�֍ �֍ ✖ ✖

Point Mugu 14th Annual Trail Days

April 21, 22 & 23, 1995 **S** ⏀ • 8:30 a.m. to 4 p.m.
(see #5 on map page 370)

Grab your favorite work gloves and persuade some willing (or not-so-willing) family members and friends to join in the fun and hard work. You'll be helping a popular coastal park by building new trails, repairing some well-used older trails or assisting in much-needed habitat restoration projects. There is something for just about everyone to do. So if you want to do a little community service in the wide open spaces of the Santa Monica Mountains, bring water, lunch and a healthy appetite for helping the environment. Call in advance for specific information and reservations. Your helping hand will be much appreciated. Point Mugu State Park is located along the Pacific Coast Highway, four miles west of the Ventura County line. Enter the park at the Sycamore Canyon Campground.

For information, contact the Santa Monica Mountains Trails Council; (818) 222-4530 or (818) 222-4531.

John Muir Birthday Party

April 21, 1995 • Starts at 8 p.m.

(see #29 on map page 371)

Back in the mid- to late-19th century, John Muir did much to help light the way for the environmental movement that was in its infancy in the nation at that time. Bring along a folding chair and join ranger Jim Long for this special evening celebrating Mr. Muir. Long will show his nationally-renowned slide program about Muir, entitled "A Range of Light." He'll also offer his own special insights into Muir's life and the environmentalist's lifelong contributions that helped to create not only Yosemite National Park, but California's state park system. Come and enjoy a beautiful spring evening on San Clemente State Beach. In keeping with the birthday tradition, cake and refreshments will be served. San Clemente State Beach is off Interstate 5 at Calafia Street, just south of San Clemente. Expect the weather to be a little cool, so bring a jacket or sweater.

For information, contact California State Parks, 3030 Avenue del Presidente, San Clemente, CA 92672; (714) 492-0802.

Earth Day in the Desert

April 22, 1995 [S] ☎ • 9 a.m. to 5 p.m.

(see #32 on map page 372)

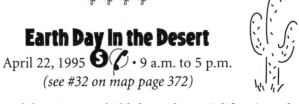

Earth Day celebrations are held throughout California and there's no place more wide open and primitively earthy than the southern deserts of the state. At this event, there will be a series of speakers who can reacquaint you with the ongoing needs of Mother Earth. Displays and other conservation-related activities will entertain and enlighten you and your kids. The events are held at the Anza-Borrego Desert State Park Visitor Center, a unique building integrated with the surrounding environment. The center is semi-buried in a desert hillside, nearly indistinguishable from surrounding sand, rock and vegetation. Paths and interpretive panels surround it. Anza-Borrego Desert State Park is located east of San

Diego via highways 78 and 70 from the east, or from Interstate 8 from the south. The event takes place at the park's visitor center which is at the west end of Palm Canyon Road out of Borrego Springs. The program is free. The weather should be comfortable during the day and a little cold at night.

For information, contact Anza-Borrego Desert State Park, 200 Palm Canyon Drive, Borrego Springs, CA 92004; (619) 767-4205.

California Poppy Festival

April 22 & 23, 1995
9 a.m. to 5 p.m. on Saturday; 10 a.m. to 5 p.m. on Sunday
(see #3 on map page 370)

APRIL

This annual event celebrates the city's most popular spring visitor, the California poppy. Surrounding Lancaster are thousands of open acres of semidesert lands that explode in waves of gold, purple and yellow each year, although some years are better than others. The poppies are what attract most people out here, and while the festival is held in town and Lancaster City Park, there's an opportunity to take a helicopter fly-over of the California Poppy Reserve for $25 per person. The festival itself includes crafts booths, kids entertainment and information about wildflowers. There will also be a 27-mile bike race and 5K and 10K poppy runs. Admission is $1 for adults and seniors; kids under age 12 are admitted free. Lancaster is located on Highway 14, about eight miles north of Palmdale.

For information, contact the City of Lancaster, 44933 North Fern Avenue, Lancaster, CA 93534; (805) 723-6089.

Point Mugu State Park Trail Days

Late April weekend **S**𝒪
(see #5 on map page 370)

Here is the perfect opportunity to get out and help restore portions of the many trails that meander through the hills of this coastal park. There should be lots of wildflowers and perhaps some great views of the Pacific (depending on which trails are receiving maintenance attention), as well as an opportunity to spend quality time with friends and family. It's also a good time to meet a few new people. The day is capped off with an evening campfire program; for those participants who wish to camp, complimentary sites will be available. Point Mugu is located just off US 101, about 31 miles northwest of Santa Monica. There's no cost to participate. Expect the weather to be clear and warm, so there's little chance that you'll be able to get out of work because of rain.

For information, contact California State Parks, 39996 Pacific Coast Highway, Malibu, CA 90265; (310) 457-8142.

⚜ ⚜ ⚜ ⚜

Birdwatching for Beginners

Late April Saturday **S**𝒪 • 8 a.m. to 11 a.m.
(see #13 on map page 370)

This walk in Malibu Creek State Park is really meant for beginners. If you've ever wondered what kinds of birds are fluttering around your home garden each spring and summer, here's your chance to learn how to identify them. If you don't already own one, purchase a good bird field guide to use on this hike. If you're unsure what guide might work best, come along on the hike anyway and see what most folks are using. Bring binoculars, if you have them—all serious or even semi-serious birders own a pair. After all, most wild birds don't let you get close enough so you can carefully study all their colors, beaks and body shapes and sizes. There are hundreds of species of birds in Southern California, and after three hours of basic instruction, you'll be well on your way to understanding how to tell the difference between a flycatcher and a horned lark. To reach Malibu Creek State Park, take the Ventura Freeway (US 101) to Las Virgenes Road, then head three miles to the intersection with Mulholland Highway. Continue to about one-quarter of a mile south of Malibu Canyon Road. The park entrance is on the right. The weather should be warm. There's a $5 park day-use entry fee.

For information, contact Malibu Creek State Park; (818) 880-0367.

✤ ✤ ✤ ✤

Conditioning Hike

Late April Saturday **S** ⏱ • 9 a.m. to 11 a.m.
(see #21 on map page 370)

If you're looking to get into shape, and have at least begun the process (so you're not simply rolling off a couch and into a pair of never-before-used hiking boots), then why not give this rather brisk, five-mile hike a try? If you're out of shape, this one hike won't leave you 100-percent ready to tackle the entire 64 miles of the Santa Monica Mountains' Backbone Trail, but it's a way to start. Wear good hiking shoes or boots, bring water and maybe a snack to replenish your energy reserves and come join the other adults and teens who will be giving this little jaunt a try. The hike starts at the Sooky Goldman Nature Center. To reach the center from the Ventura Freeway (US 101), drive south on Coldwater Canyon Drive to Beverly Drive (Beverly Hills Fire Station #2). Turn right onto Beverly Drive and go one mile to Franklin Canyon Drive. Turn right and drive 1.5 miles to Lake Drive. Turn left and go a very short distance, then take a right turn into the Upper Lake area. Drive around the east side of the lake and park in the Sooky Goldman Nature Center lot.

For information, contact the Mountains Education Program, 2600 Franklin Canyon Drive, Beverly Hills, CA 90210, (310) 858-3090; or Mountain Parks Information, (800) 533-7275.

Full Moon Hike

Late April Saturday **S** 🖊 • 6:30 p.m. to 9 p.m.
(see #21 on map page 370)

Exploring Franklin Canyon during the day is a wonderful way to spend some time, but for a whole different world, try coming back at night under the light of a full, or nearly full, moon. There's a whole world of creatures out there—owls, foxes, coyotes, all those animals that tend to hide during the day and emerge to feed in the late evenings. And even if you don't *see* any of the nocturnal wildlife, the sounds they make can thrill you to the marrow—or is that frighten you to the bone? Anyway, seeing all those city lights in the valley below is well worth the energy it takes to walk up the canyon from the hike's start at the Franklin Canyon Ranch Site. To get there from the Ventura Freeway (US 101), drive south on Coldwater Canyon Drive to Beverly Drive (Beverly Hills Fire Station #2). Turn right onto Beverly Drive and go one mile to Franklin Canyon Drive. Turn right and drive 1.5 miles to Lake Drive. Turn left and go a very short distance, then take a right turn into the Upper Lake area. Drive around the east side of the lake and park in the Sooky Goldman Nature Center lot.

For information, contact the Mountains Education Program, 2600 Franklin Canyon Drive, Beverly Hills, CA 90210, (310) 858-3090; or Mountain Parks Information, (800) 533-7275.

Lagoon Birdwatching Walk

Late April Sunday **S** 🖊 • 8:30 a.m. to 11:30 a.m.
(see #17 on map page 370)

Most folks who aren't entirely familiar with birds probably assume that the only thing you'll see flying around the ocean beaches are plain old seagulls. Even if that were true, which it isn't, an experienced birder would tell you that there are actually many species of gulls attacking the beaches and bombing folks from above. Many of the same species of gulls have completely different colorations, depending upon how old they happen to be. Come along on this hike and, as you move ever so slightly inland along the creek and lagoon at Malibu Lagoon State Beach, you'll discover a vast assortment of birds, each segregated into its own special environmental niche, constantly searching for food. This is an easy walk for both beginners and experts who would like to spend anywhere from one to three hours observing birds. Bring binoculars and a bird field guide, if you have one.

Malibu Lagoon State Beach is located just off the Pacific Coast Highway, a quarter mile west of the Malibu Pier and 1.5 miles east of Malibu Canyon Road. Parking lots are located on both sides of the Pacific Coast Highway.

For information, contact the Santa Monica Bay Audubon Society; (310) 454-9962.

APRIL

❖ ❖ ❖ ❖

Kids' Scavenger Hunt

Late April Sunday **S** 🏃 • 10 a.m. to noon
(see #21 on map page 370)

Help your kids build an awareness of the importance of nature and a respect for the natural world around them. With an introduction to nature like this one, they'll quickly begin to develop a sense of how the human species fits into the scheme of the natural world and what we can do to either help or hurt Mother Nature. This scavenger hunt for things natural is designed for kids, ages 8 to 12. Advance reservations are required.

To get to Franklin Canyon and the Sooky Goldman Nature Center from the Ventura Freeway (US 101), drive south on Coldwater Canyon Drive to Beverly Drive (Beverly Hills Fire Station #2). Turn right onto Beverly Drive and go one mile to Franklin Canyon Drive. Turn right and drive 1.5 miles to Lake Drive. Turn left and go a very short distance, then take a right turn into the Upper Lake area. Drive around the east side of the lake and park in the nature center lot.

For information, contact the Mountains Education Program, 2600 Franklin Canyon Drive, Beverly Hills, CA 90210, (310) 858-3090; or Mountain Parks Information, (800) 533-7275.

❖ ❖ ❖ ❖

Welcome to Los Angeles

Late April Sunday 🟢 🖉 • 1 p.m. to 3:30 p.m.
(see #21 on map page 370)

If you're new to the City of Angels, or if you've lived here for a lifetime but never ventured far from the freeways and shopping centers, here's your invitation to meet your other neighbors, the trees of Franklin Canyon. This is a leisurely-paced walk, ideal for anyone who isn't in a hurry. A naturalist will lead you through the woods of the canyon and identify the numerous plant and animal species that call this place home. You might want to bring water to drink and a camera. To get to Franklin Canyon from the Ventura Freeway (US 101), drive south on Coldwater Canyon Drive to Beverly Drive (Beverly Hills Fire Station #2). Turn right onto Beverly Drive and go one mile to Franklin Canyon Drive. Turn right and drive 1.5 miles to Lake Drive. Turn left and go a very short distance, then take a right turn into the Upper Lake area. Drive around the east side of the lake and park in the Sooky Goldman Nature Center lot.

For information, contact the Mountains Education Program, 2600 Franklin Canyon Drive, Beverly Hills, CA 90210, (310) 858-3090; or Mountain Parks Information, (800) 533-7275.

✤ ✤ ✤ ✤

Rancho Sierra Vista Moonlight Adventure

Late April Sunday 🟢 🖉 • 7 p.m. to 8:30 p.m.
(see #10 on map page 370)

If you've never sat quietly and watched a big, yellow moon rise slowly above a woodland meadow, you're in for a real treat on this easy walk. The only thing that might be different than planned is if the smog happens to be hanging heavy over the basin—that tends to color the moon more of an anguished orange, but it's still pretty. Bring yourself, a flashlight and a special friend, if you have one. The exact date of this event will be determined by the closest full moon to a late April weekend. The Rancho Sierra Vista/Satwiwa Site is operated by the National Park Service. From the Ventura Freeway (US 101), take the Wendy Drive exit at Newbury Park and head south to Potrero Road. Turn west (right) on Potrero Road and drive until you reach its intersection with Pinehill Road, where the park entrance is located.

For information, contact the Sierra Club; (213) 387-4287.

✤ ✤ ✤ ✤

Full Moon Over Runyon

Late April (under a full moon) Ⓢ ⬮ • 7:30 p.m. to 9:30 p.m.
(see #22 on map page 370)

APRIL

This hike is generally scheduled for the evening of the full moon, even if it falls on a weekday. It's a moderately strenuous hike, so come prepared to do some walking. Bring water and a flashlight and come enjoy a whole new experience, if you've never hiked under the light of the moon. The hike will last a couple of hours and the leader will take you through sections of Runyon Canyon. To reach Runyon Canyon Park, take the Hollywood Freeway (US 101) and turn south onto Highland Avenue. Take Highland to Franklin Avenue and turn west, then turn north on Fuller. Park where the street ends.

For information, contact the Friends of Runyon Canyon; (213) 666-5004.

✤ ✤ ✤ ✤

Post-Fire Chaparral Chatter

Late April weekday Ⓢ ⬮ • 8 a.m. to noon
(see #16 on map page 370)

For untold thousands of years, fire was actually a friend to the hills and canyons of the Santa Monica Mountains. It removed thickets of chaparral, allowing new plants to come in and providing renewed food supplies for wildlife. Now that humans have moved in permanently, fire is no longer the welcome neighbor it was in past centuries. Still, we haven't been entirely successful, and probably never will be, in keeping it from returning to reignite its ancient ties with the hillsides of its old home. This hike will take you through some recently fire-ravaged areas to look at the damage fire does, as well as the benefits it bestows on the land. You'll walk away from this morning hike with a better understanding of why fire, under very controlled circumstances, should be allowed to return periodically to the hills. Bring water and a snack, if you like. Be sure to call and verify the date of the walk.

The meeting place is at Cold Creek Canyon Preserve. To get there from the Ventura Freeway (US 101), take the Topanga Canyon Boulevard exit. Follow Topanga Canyon Boulevard to Mulholland Drive. Turn west (right) and drive one-quarter mile, then turn right on Mulholland Highway. Drive five more miles to Stunt Road. Turn left and drive to the preserve entrance.

For information, contact the California Native Plant Society, (818) 348-5910; or the Mountain Restoration Trust, (310) 456-5625.

❖ ❖ ❖ ❖

Late Spring Migrants
Last Saturday in April **S** 🕊 • 7:30 a.m. to 10 a.m.
(see #21 on map page 370)

The migratory bird population can change weekly in the hills of the Santa Monica Mountains. With summer only about three weeks away, it's time to take another hike through the Franklin Canyon area to check out the new arrivals. The leader will take you on a walk along the lakeside and through some chaparral areas in search of new birds. You'll need good hiking shoes or boots and binoculars. If, by some strange weather quirk, a late spring rainstorm hits, the hike will be canceled. Be sure to call ahead to verify the date and time of this hike. To get to Franklin Canyon/Sooky Goldman Nature Center from the Ventura Freeway (US 101), drive south on Coldwater Canyon Drive to Beverly Drive (Beverly Hills Fire Station #2). Turn right onto Beverly Drive and go one mile to Franklin Canyon Drive. Turn right and drive 1.5 miles to Lake Drive. Turn left and go a very short distance, then take a right turn into the Upper Lake area. Drive around the east side of the lake and park in the Sooky Goldman Nature Center lot.

For information, contact the Mountains Education Program, 2600 Franklin Canyon Drive, Beverly Hills, CA 90210, (310) 858-3090; or Mountain Parks Information, (800) 533-7275.

Evening Campfire Hike

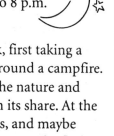

Last Saturday in April **S** *⌀* • 5 p.m. to 8 p.m.
(see #13 on map page 370)

Spend an evening in Malibu Creek State Park, first taking a short, slow-paced hike, then sitting and relaxing around a campfire. On the hike, you'll learn a little something about the nature and history of the park, both of which it has more than its share. At the campfire, you'll enjoy listening to stories and songs, and maybe participate in a skit or watch a slide show. Bring water and a flashlight. To reach Malibu Creek State Park, take the Ventura Freeway (US 101) to Las Virgenes Road, then head three miles to the intersection with Mulholland Highway. Continue to about one-quarter of a mile south of Malibu Canyon Road. The park entrance is on the right. The weather should be warm. There's a $5 park day-use entry fee.

For information, contact Malibu Creek State Park; (818) 880-0367.

Butterflies & Bees at Work

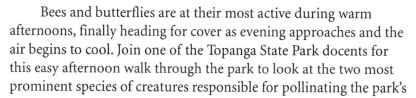

First Sunday in May **S** *⌀* • 1 p.m. to 3 p.m.
(see #14 on map page 370)

Bees and butterflies are at their most active during warm afternoons, finally heading for cover as evening approaches and the air begins to cool. Join one of the Topanga State Park docents for this easy afternoon walk through the park to look at the two most prominent species of creatures responsible for pollinating the park's wildflowers and more than a few people's gardens. Bring your butterfly field guide if you have one, a camera if you're a quick shooter and water for your thirst, as the afternoon is sure to be warm. Arrive a little early, or a lot early, and wander through the park's nature center to view the mammal and bird collection. The entrance to Topanga State Park is located on Entrada Road, east of Topanga Canyon Boulevard, eight miles south of US 101, six miles north of Santa Monica.

For information, contact the Topanga Canyon Docents; (818) 881-9063.

❖ ❖ ❖ ❖

Canyon Loop Hike

Early May Saturday **$** 〇 • 8:30 a.m. to 2:30 p.m.
(see #19 on map page 370)

This is a perfect time of year for a nice long hike through several canyons. You should be able to see plenty of hawks and possibly even an eagle or two flying high overhead or cruising low over a meadow, looking for mice or squirrels. There ought to be plenty to view over the hike's 10 miles. The hike will meander in and out of valleys, over ridges and along some of the Santa Monica Mountains' oak savannah. A National Park Service ranger will lead you through Cheeseboro and Palo Comado canyons. Bring your lunch, lots of water and sunscreen; wear some comfortable hiking boots. A camera wouldn't be a bad idea. To reach the Cheeseboro Canyon parking lot, take the Ventura Freeway (US 101) to the Coldwater Canyon exit. Head south to the intersection with Mulholland Drive. The park entrance is on the east (left) side of the intersection. Expect some fairly warm temperatures.

For information, contact the National Park Service; (818) 597-9192.

❖ ❖ ❖ ❖

Starlight Hike

Early May weekday **S** 🖋 · 7 p.m. to 9 p.m.
(see #21 on map page 370)

Join this group of nocturnal sky watchers and hike up the hills of Franklin Canyon to view the stars. There will be a star navigator along to point out planets, constellations and single, major stars twinkling in the heavens. Bring binoculars, if you have them, and a flashlight, because the hike is generally scheduled for a night with no moonlight to wash out the glow of stars. If it's cloudy, the hike will be canceled. To get to the Franklin Canyon/Sooky Goldman Nature Center from the Ventura Freeway (US 101), drive south on Coldwater Canyon Drive to Beverly Drive (Beverly Hills Fire Station #2). Turn right onto Beverly Drive and go one mile to Franklin Canyon Drive. Turn right and drive 1.5 miles to Lake Drive. Turn left and go a very short distance, then take a right turn into the Upper Lake area. Drive around the east side of the lake and park in the Sooky Goldman Nature Center lot.

For information, contact the Mountains Education Program, 2600 Franklin Canyon Drive, Beverly Hills, CA 90210, (310) 858-3090; or Mountain Parks Information, (800) 533-7275.

❖ ❖ ❖ ❖

Wheels to the Sea

May 4, 1995 **S** 🖋
(see #5 on map page 370)

Here is an excellent opportunity for the physically challenged to enjoy an exciting four-mile descent from a mountaintop in Point Mugu State Park, along appropriate dirt roads, with a final race to the edge of the Pacific Ocean. There are some spectacular views from the top, and some not-too-shabby views on the way down the hillside. Volunteers are needed, and welcome, to serve as assistants for the participants. There's no cost for the program. The entrance to Point Mugu is about 31 miles northwest of Santa Monica, just off the Pacific Coast Highway (Highway 1). You can pretty much count on warm and clear weather, but there is potential for light fog this time of year.

For information, contact California State Parks, 39996 Pacific Coast Highway, Malibu, CA 90265; (818) 880-0350.

❖ ❖ ❖ ❖

Cinco de Mayo Celebration

May 5, 6 & 7, 1995 • 10 a.m. to 4 p.m.
(see #37 on map page 372)

Old Town San Diego is a colorful and fun place to visit any time of the year, but it gets even better during the annual weekend Cinco de Mayo celebration. This year, the event will begin with a celebration of the 194th anniversary of Pio Pico's birthday. Pico was the last Mexican governor of California, before the United States took over. Grab your camera and capture all the wild and colorful costumes of the dancers, the special flowers and other finery. There will be plenty of good food, lively music and good times in the plaza and along the streets of Old Town. This is a really popular event, with over 100,000 people participating over the course of the weekend. Old Town San Diego State Historic Park is located off Interstate 5, between San Diego Avenue and Twiggs Street. Entry into the park is free. Expect warm and comfortable weather.

For information, contact Old Town San Diego State Historic Park, (619) 237-6770 or 237-6766.

❖ ❖ ❖ ❖

Coming Home to Pio Pico

May 5, 1995 • 10 a.m. to 4 p.m.
(see #24 on map page 370)

Few people realize that the last Mexican governor to rule California had his home in what is now Whittier. Governor Pio Pico, born on May 5, 1801, loved a good fiesta and this annual event recreates that same ambience in the state historic park bearing his name. Last year, 1994, marked the first year of the festival and it was an extremely successful and popular day for residents from throughout the area. Plans were set to continue the event annually. There will be lots of music, food, old-time demonstrations, displays of historic significance and official government proclamations and commendations. Pio Pico State Historic Park is located in Whittier at 6003 Pioneer Boulevard. There is no cost for the event; the weather should be warm and sunny.

For information, contact Pio Pico State Historic Park; (714) 780-6222.

✢ ✢ ✢ ✢

Mother's Day Special Stroll

May 7, 1995 • 10 a.m. to noon
(see #11 on map page 370)

(see #11 on map page 370)

After a wonderful breakfast, treat your Mom to a very special Mother's Day with a pleasant stroll beneath the shady oaks of the Peter Strauss Ranch Site. If she's an outdoors lover at all, then she'll be delighted by the ferns and wildflowers of this lovely mountain park. Bring something to drink and meet the docent hike leader in the parking lot. It'll be one of Mom's most memorable Mother's Days. To get to the ranch from the Ventura Freeway (US 101), take the Kanan Road exit, west of Agoura Hills, then head south for 2.8 miles to Troutdale Road. Turn left on Troutdale, then turn left again on Mullholland Highway. Head right under the arch into the parking lot. Walk back across the bridge on Mulholland Highway and enter the main gate into the ranch.

For information, contact the Topanga Canyon Docents; (818) 881-9063.

Malibu Tile and Floral Festival

May 11, 12 & 13, 1995 **S** 🎧 • Call for the start time
(see #17 on map page 370)

The title of this event makes it sound like a bathroom decorators' convention, but such is not the case. The historic Adamson House, which is perched on the beach overlooking the Pacific Ocean and Malibu Lagoon, is decorated with some incredibly beautiful handmade tiles. The festival will give you an opportunity to tour the house and see how the original owners designed so much handmade tile into their home. There also will be demonstrations of tile making, an art form that has deep historical roots. Docents and staff will show slide programs and provide tours of the gardens. Art pieces will be available for sale and, for an additional fee, a gala dinner and buffet luncheon will be provided; call ahead to make reservations. Malibu Lagoon State Beach is located just off the Pacific Coast Highway, a quarter mile west of the Malibu Pier and 1.5 miles east of Malibu Canyon Road. Parking lots are located on both sides of the Pacific Coast Highway.

For information, contact Malibu Lagoon State Beach; (310) 456-8432 or (310) 456-1684.

Ultra Distance Trail Run

May 13, 1995 **S** 🎧 • 9 a.m. to 5 p.m.
(see #38 on map page 372)

This run is not meant for beginning joggers, nor for the faint of heart. It's a trail footrace that begins in Anza-Borrego Desert State Park and heads upward and westward, finally ending 50 miles later in Cuyamaca Rancho State Park. The stated purpose of the run is to acquaint runners with the parklands, but after 20 or 30 miles of running on what will probably be a downright hot day, enjoying the desert and high-mountain scenery probably won't be a high priority. About 100 people generally participate. The starting point for the Ultra Distance Trail Run will be at Pinyon Wash, which can be reached via Highway 78E from Julian. Call for more specific directions and to verify that it's still going to cost you $50 to participate. It's going to be pretty warm in the desert and possibly a little cooler in the higher mountains of Cuyamaca.

For information, contact Anza-Borrego Desert State Park; (619) 767-4205.

❖ ❖ ❖ ❖

Riffles & Rills

Mid-May Saturday **S** 🔦 • 9 a.m. to 1 p.m.
(see #16 on map page 370)

The effects of fire on oak woodlands and grasslands of the mountains are readily apparent, but what about the streams in an area laid to waste by wildfires? With hillsides denuded of vegetative cover, erosion becomes a major factor in the lives of frogs, fish and other creek-dwelling creatures. They, unfortunately, are unable to escape their watery world, even when it fills with silt and the blackened charcoal ooze of burned plant life. What do the animals do? How have they adapted to starkly different living conditions? Or have they? Join a knowledgeable member from the Mountain Restoration Trust at Cold Creek Canyon for a look at what's happening in the burned lands of the Santa Monica Mountains. Advance reservations are required. To get to the Cold Creek Canyon meeting place, from the Ventura Freeway (US 101), take Topanga Canyon Boulevard south to Mulholland Drive and turn west (right). Drive one-quarter of a mile, turn left on Mulholland Highway and drive approximately five miles to Stunt Road. Turn left and drive to the preserve entrance on the left. Ask for parking information when you call to make your reservations.

For information, contact the Mountain Restoration Trust, (310) 456-8432.

❖ ❖ ❖ ❖

Life After Fire

Mid-May Saturday [S] ☎ • 9:30 a.m. to noon
(see #10 on map page 370)

Here's an opportunity to accompany a National Park Service ranger as he or she documents the return of wildlife to the Satwiwa Site following the Santa Monica Mountains wildfire. The ranger will talk about fire ecology, the periodic use of small, controlled fires to significantly reduce the ravages of major wildfires. You may be able to assist as the ranger gathers evidence of the presence of wildlife and documents it both in writing and with photography. To get to the Rancho Sierra Vista/Satwiwa Site, take the Ventura Freeway (US 101) to the Wendy Drive exit in Newbury Park. Head south on Wendy Drive to Potrero Road and turn west (right). The park entrance is at the intersection of Potrero Road and Pinehill Road. Park at the Pinehill Road parking lot.

For information, contact the National Park Service; (818) 597-9192.

Sunday Morning Hike

Mid-May Sunday [S] ☎ • 10 a.m. to 5 p.m.
(see #14 on map page 370)

This hike will take you along the Bay Tree Trail, on up to Rogers Road, with the return route running through Temescal Canyon. This is a pretty tough hike that will take about seven hours, with a few breaks for rest and lunch. Come prepared to cover a lot of ground and see some beautiful sights while enjoying a day of hiking in the Santa Monica Mountains. Bring lunch and plenty of water; wear good hiking boots that your feet will thank you for. The meeting place is scheduled tentatively for Topanga State Park, which is located on Entrada Road, east of Topanga Canyon Boulevard, eight miles south of US 101 and six miles north of Santa Monica. Call to confirm.

For information, contact the Temescal Canyon Association; (310) 454-4188.

Julian Wildflower Show

May 13 to 21, 1995
10 a.m. to 4 p.m. weekdays; 10 a.m. to 5 p.m. on weekends
(see #34 on map page 372)

Now in its 69th year, this annual show features wildflowers from a 15-mile radius around Julian. The flowers, ranging from desert cacti to mountain dogwood, are gathered from private property, with the land owners' permission, of course. Each of the wildflower specimens is clearly identified for those who want to know what they're seeing each spring along the highways. The yearly displays depend entirely on what the winter and early spring weather has been like. More rain tends to bring more wildflowers, so during drought years things aren't quite as good, but still well worth the drive to Julian. Alongside the wildflower show, you'll find an art show. If you have a group of 35 to 50 people who would like to travel to the wildflower show and would also like a special luncheon arranged for them, the Julian United Methodist Church Women's Group can put one together. The wildflower show is held in the Julian Town Hall in Julian, which is near the intersection of highways 78 and 79, about 41 miles east of Escondido and Interstate 15. There's no cost, but donations are accepted. The weather should be warm and dry.

For information, contact the Julian United Methodist Church Women's Club, P.O. Box 393, Julian, CA 92036; (619) 765-0436.

Doheny Grunion Night

Mid-May Ⓢ ☎ • 10 p.m. to after midnight
(see #28 on map page 371)

Grunion are those bizarre and elusive little fish that beach themselves during spring high tides in order to spawn in the moist sand. Their eggs then hatch during the next high tide and are swept back out to sea. While the grunion fishing season is not yet open during this event, a ranger will be here to talk about these seven-inch fish and their strange spawning rituals. Then you'll know where to look and how to catch the wily little creatures (with your hands only) when the season does open later in the year. The Doheny Interpretive Center will be open late during this special night so you can enjoy the tide pool and aquarium exhibits. Bring a flashlight, warm clothes and a beach chair, if you'd rather sit while waiting for the grunion to start their show. There will be a campfire, so bring a coat hanger or other roasting stick for the free marshmallows. The Doheny State Beach entrance is located on Del Obispo Street, off the Pacific Coast Highway at Dana Point. It generally costs $6 to get into the park, but it'll be free if you remember to mention to the person in the entry kiosk that you are coming in for Grunion Night. While the days may be warming up by this time of year, it can get pretty cool after the sun goes down, especially around midnight when the grunion finally start doing their thing.

For information, contact California State Parks, 3030 Avenue del Presidente, San Clemente, CA 92672; (714) 496-6172.

❖ ❖ ❖ ❖

Topanga 10K Run

May 27, 1995 • Starts at 8 a.m.
(see #14 on map page 370)

This annual event is tied to Topanga Days County Fair and is designed to offer a little fun and fitness to local community participants. The best part, beyond the fun and fitness, is that this course meanders through some of the 9,000 acres of Topanga State Park in the Santa Monica Mountains. It's always difficult to believe that several million people live within a 30-minute drive of these rugged mountains. Preregistration for this event is important, because they sometimes limit the number of runners. The entrance to Topanga State Park is located on Entrada Road, east of Topanga Canyon Boulevard, eight miles south of US 101, six miles north of Santa Monica. There's a $15 entry fee for race participants and a $5 day-use parking fee for each vehicle. The day should be warm and sunny, unless, of course, there happens to be a little morning fog.

For information, contact California State Parks, 20825 Entrada Road, Topanga, CA 90290; (310) 454-8212 or (310) 455-2465.

❖ ❖ ❖ ❖

Early Summer Residents

Late May Saturday **S** 📞 • 7:30 a.m. to 10 a.m.
(see #21 on map page 370)

This hike is generally held in Franklin Canyon toward the end of May. If you happened to have attended the earlier spring resident bird hikes offered in Franklin Canyon, many of the species you saw then will be nowhere in sight on this day. There will be new arrivals to spy through your binoculars and try to identify in your field guide. It should be a pleasant morning for a walk and the birds you see will be an added enjoyment. Beginning and expert birders alike are invited to participate. To get to the Franklin Canyon/Sooky Goldman Nature Center from the Ventura Freeway (US 101), drive south on Coldwater Canyon Drive to Beverly Drive (Beverly Hills Fire Station #2). Turn right onto Beverly Drive and go one mile to Franklin Canyon Drive. Turn right and drive 1.5 miles to Lake Drive. Turn left and go a very short distance, then take a right turn into the Upper Lake area. Drive around the east side of the lake and park in the Sooky Goldman Nature Center lot.

For information, contact the Mountains Education Program, 2600 Franklin Canyon Drive, Beverly Hills, CA 90210, (310) 858-3090; or Mountain Parks Information, (800) 533-7275.

❖ ❖ ❖ ❖

History & Arts

Late May Saturday **S** 📞 • 10 a.m. to 11 a.m.
(see #11 on map page 370)

Meet a National Park Service ranger for an informative walk along the creek as she or he describes the history of the Peter Strauss Ranch estate. There will be discussions of the lives and culture of the

Chumash, the first people to live here. You'll learn about the Spanish missions and Mexican ranchos that ultimately drove the Indians from the Santa Monica Mountains. Then the talk will focus on the entertainment industry, which arrived here soon after the invention of motion pictures. There will also be an arts and crafts show that will exhibit the creative creations of staff and docents. You can view some really neat stuff and have an opportunity to create some equally neat stuff yourself. To reach the ranch from the Ventura Freeway (US 101), take the Kanan Road exit, west of Agoura Hills, and head south for 2.8 miles to Troutdale Road. Turn left on Troutdale, then turn left again on Mullholland Highway. Drive right under the arch into the parking lot. Walk back across the bridge on Mulholland Highway and enter the main gate into the ranch.

For information, contact the National Park Service; (818) 597-9192.

❖ ❖ ❖ ❖

Will Rogers State Historic Park
Nursery Nature Walk

Late May weekday **S** 🕐 · 10 a.m. to noon
(see #18 on map page 370)

There's a lot more to Will Rogers State Historic Park than rope twirling, polo ponies and old movies and newsreels of Will's cracker-barrel wisecracks. The nursery nature walk program is offered in various parks throughout the Santa Monica Mountains during spring and summer and is designed for families with kids from infants to six years of age. At Will Rogers Park, there are horses and a picnic area to augment the singing and learning about the natural world that lies so close to the big city. A donation is requested. Will Rogers State Historic Park is located at 14253 Sunset Boulevard in Pacific Palisades, about eight miles inland from the Pacific Coast Highway. Watch for the entrance sign on the left side of the road, because it's easy to miss on the first pass.

For information, contact Nursery Nature Walks; (310) 998-1151.

❖ ❖ ❖ ❖

Leo Carrillo Underwater Treasure Dive

June 10, 1995 **S** 🤿
(see #6 on map page 370)

While the chance of discovering a 17th-century treasure chest filled with gold doubloons may dance through the participating divers' heads, seashells will be the most prominent windfall to come anyone's way during this underwater expedition. But all is not lost, because the seashells can be exchanged for prizes. Kids under 12 years old can participate in their own treasure hunt on the beach, and while their dreams may not be as wild as the adult divers, their excitement certainly will be. There will be a raffle for additional prizes. Lunch is available for a small cost to non-participants, and it is included in the registration fee for beach and ocean-bottom treasure hunters. Proceeds from the event will go toward building a park visitor center. Leo Carrillo State Beach is about 25 miles west of Santa Monica along the Pacific Coast Highway. Adult registration for the program is $30 and kids are $7.50. If you're only interested in the lunch and raffle, the cost is $15. There is a $6 per vehicle day-use fee. The weather should be warm and sunny for the beach treasure hunters and very wet for the divers.

For information, contact California State Parks, 39996 Pacific Coast Highway, Malibu, CA 90265; (310) 457-8142 or (310) 454-8212.

❖ ❖ ❖ ❖

San Pasqual Battlefield Living History

June 25, 1995 **S** 🤿 · 10 a.m. to 4 p.m.
(see #40 on map page 372)

Before California was officially part of the United States, there was a battle between the U.S. Cavalry and what they thought was a ragtag Mexican Army. Well, that ragtag army won the battle, although Mexico lost the war not long afterward and all now is history. Reenactments of the battle, displays and other living history demonstrations of how people lived in the last century are all part of the day. Bring a picnic lunch and plan to join about 500 other people for a fun day out in the country. To reach San Pasqual Battlefield State Historic Park, take Highway 15 south to Valley Parkway and exit to the left. Then turn right onto San Pasqual Road and follow the signs to the park. If you can find the San Diego Wild Animal Park, then the battlefield park is just one mile east. There's no cost for the program. The weather should be very warm, but pleasant.

For information, contact San Pasqual Battlefield State Historic Park, (619) 238-3380.

✤ ✤ ✤ ✤

Estuary Family Nature Walk

Late June weekday Ⓢ ☎ • 3:15 p.m. to 4:45 p.m.
(see #39 on map page 372)

If you head south from San Diego, down to the border that separates the United States and Mexico, you'll discover a wetland area that historically has been a prime home for wildlife, especially waterfowl. Today, much of this wetlands is protected by both national and state preserves. The folks at the Tijuana Estuary are anxious to introduce you to the wild part of this marvelously rich meeting of land and water. On this particular hike, a ranger or naturalist will lead you to the uplands of the estuary, where the birds and plants differ from those that thrive on the salty waters of the wetlands. Wear sturdy shoes and bring water to drink. The hike is free.

For information, contact the Tijuana Estuary Visitor Center, 301 Caspian Way, Imperial Beach, CA 91932; (619) 575-3613.

✤ ✤ ✤ ✤

Tijuana Estuary Visitor Center Garden Tour

Late June Saturday Ⓢ ☎ • 9 a.m. to 10 a.m.
(see #39 on map page 372)

For those who are unable or unwilling to hike any great distance, here's a perfect chance to see and enjoy the color of the wetlands without any strenuous hiking. This walk through the

Tijuana Estuary Visitor Center's garden will expose you to the world of wildflowers. Learn which flowers thrive in these special wetlands and how they fit into the world of the estuary. You'll also discover how other plants, insects and animals depend upon one another to survive and prosper. Reservations are required for this walk.

For information, contact the Tijuana Estuary Visitor Center, 301 Caspian Way, Imperial Beach, CA 91932; (619) 575-3613.

❊ ❊ ❊ ❊

Beach & Dune Walk

Late June Saturday **S** 🞔 • 9 a.m. to 11:30 a.m.
(see #18 on map page 370)

This is a family hike along the sandy beach and dunes where the Tijuana River empties into the Pacific Ocean. You'll have an opportunity to search for insects and nests occupied by a couple of endangered species, such as least terns and snowy plovers, birds that settle along the sandy beach. Learn why these birds have come to the brink of extinction and what management programs are being implemented to protect them along parts of California's coast, including some in areas normally covered by human sun worshipers. Bring binoculars and a bird field guide, if you have them. A camera will also get you some beautiful photographs. While everyone is welcome to join the hike, kids under the age of 10 must be accompanied by an adult. The hike leaves from the south end of Seacoast Drive in Imperial Beach. Reservations are required for the hike, so call the Tijuana Estuary Visitor Center ahead of time.

For information, contact the Tijuana Estuary Visitor Center, 301 Caspian Way, Imperial Beach, CA 91932; (619) 575-3613.

❊ ❊ ❊ ❊

Will Rogers State Historic Park 5K & 10K Race

July 4, 1995 • 6 a.m. to 9:30 a.m.

(see #18 on map page 370)

Join the 3,000 to 4,000 other runners in this annual fundraiser that directly benefits Will Rogers State Historic Park. The park was the ranch home of the late political satirist and homespun philosopher. After the race, take time to tour the ranch house or see a short film about the man and his extraordinary life. The footrace begins near the parking lot next to the polo field and heads out the entrance road toward Sunset Boulevard, passing some breathtaking views of the mountains and ocean. The race will cost you $15 if you preregister and $20 if you register on the day of the race. It should be a warm, sunny day for a run. Will Rogers State Historic Park is located at 14253 Sunset Boulevard in Pacific Palisades, about eight miles inland from the Pacific Coast Highway. Watch for the entrance sign on the left side of the road, because it's easy to miss on the first pass.

For information, contact Will Rogers State Park Historic Park, 1501 Will Rogers Road, Pacific Palisades, CA 90272; (310) 454-8212.

Sunday Park Tour

Mid-July Saturday • 11 a.m. to 12:30 p.m.

(see #20 on map page 370)

If you've never had an opportunity to spend any time in the Santa Monica Mountains' Coldwater Canyon, here's a good chance for you to meet with a small group of other people for a short tour of the highlights of the park. In addition to the park, the hike leader will also take you through the TreePeople's environmental headquarters. TreePeople is a nonprofit group whose members help to combat the greenhouse effect by planting millions of trees throughout California. They also encourage proper stewardship of our fragile environment by providing educational programs and community action training. You'll get a firsthand look at recycling and composting and learn some more of the history of the park. You need a reservation for the tour. To get to Coldwater Canyon Park, take the Ventura Freeway (US 101) to the Coldwater Canyon exit. Drive south to the intersection with Mulholland Drive. The entrance is on the east (left) side of the intersection.

For information, contact TreePeople; (818) 753-4600.

❖ ❖ ❖ ❖

Horse Poker Ride

July 15 to 16, 1995 **$**
(see #35 on map page 372)

You have to have a horse and at least a little ability to ride in order to participate in this event. Riders follow a prearranged course, obtaining a poker playing card at each checkpoint. At the end of the ride, poker hands are compared and a winner is proclaimed. Overnight camping is available in the horse camp. The ride is held at Cuyamaca Rancho State Park and riders will travel through portions of the park's 24,000 acres of rambling hills and mountains, through oak woodlands and pine forests. Usually about 80 riders participate in the ride. Even if you don't have an interest in horse poker, if you have a horse and love to ride in the wide open spaces, Cuyamaca Rancho is a perfect place to camp and spend several days exploring. To reach Cuyamaca Rancho State Park, drive east from San Diego on Interstate 8, then head north on Highway 79 into the park. Once inside the park, follow signs to Vaqueros Horse Camp. There's a fee of $75 per rider, with a $6 per vehicle park entrance fee. Expect some very warm, but not uncomfortable, weather.

For information, contact Cuyamaca Rancho State Park; (619) 765-0755.

❖ ❖ ❖ ❖

Cold Creek Canyon Photo Walk

Early July Saturday [S]☎ • 9 a.m. to 1 p.m.
(see #16 on map page 370)

Have you spent a lot of money on film, hoping to get some really great shots, imagining how the view in front of you will look transformed into a giant photograph on your wall, only to be disappointed with the results? Join this photo walk and learn how to make the best use of filters, fill flash and different lenses. Pack along your camera, lenses and any other photo equipment that you may have—and be sure to bring your questions. Besides calling to check on the date for this, you'll need reservations to participate. To reach the preserve from the Ventura Freeway (US 101), take Topanga Canyon Boulevard south to Mulholland Drive and turn west (right). Drive one-quarter of a mile, turn left on Mulholland Highway and drive approximately five miles to Stunt Road. Turn left and drive to the preserve entrance on the left. Parking information will be given when you call and make your reservations.

For information, contact the Mountain Restoration Trust; (310) 456-8432.

Canyon Reverie

Mid-July Sunday [S]☎ • 10 a.m. to 12:30 p.m.
(see #16 on map page 370)

In 1993, a devastating fire swept through portions of the Santa Monica Mountains and this hike will take you through fire-ravaged Cold Creek Canyon for an exploration of nature's regenerative powers. The canyon was transformed by fire, as it has been many times before throughout its history. You'll begin to understand the sequence in which plants grow and provide nutrients, shade and competition for the plants that follow. Learn how fire, when properly controlled, can be a great management tool for preventing potentially destructive wildfires. Meet at the Cold Creek Canyon Preserve lower gate. To get there from the Ventura Freeway (US 101), take the Topanga Canyon Boulevard exit. Follow Topanga

Canyon Boulevard to Mulholland Drive. Turn west (right) and drive one quarter of a mile, then turn right on Mulholland Highway. Drive five more miles to Stunt Road. Turn left and drive to the preserve entrance.

For information, contact the Cold Creek Docents; (818) 591-9363.

❖ ❖ ❖ ❖

Cultural History Hike

Mid-July Sunday **S** 𝒪 • 1 p.m. to 2 p.m.
(see #22 on map page 370)

More has happened in and around the Santa Monica Mountains during the past 100 years than has occurred here in the past 1,000 years. Some of it has been good, some not so good, but all of it has been interesting. Spend an hour with a local historian and learn about this playground of the rich and famous, from the Frank Lloyd Wright project site to the proposed Metro Rail tunnel route. You'll travel through 100 years of Santa Monica Mountains history, all in just one short hour. The hike will be held in Runyon Canyon Park. To reach Runyon Canyon Park, take the Hollywood Freeway (US 101) and turn south onto Highland Avenue. Take Highland to Franklin Avenue and turn west, then turn north on Fuller. Park where the street ends.

For information, contact Friends of Runyon Canyon; (213) 666-5004.

❖ ❖ ❖ ❖

Calcium Carbonate & Cultural History Walk and Talk

Mid-August Saturday **S** 𝒪 • 9 a.m. to 1 p.m.
(see #16 on map page 370)

Author and naturalist Milt McAuley will be the guest leader of this get-together in the Santa Monica Mountains' Cold Creek Canyon Preserve. Spend some time exploring the preserve's waterfalls and learn about the geologic history of the surrounding mountains and valleys, a geology that continues to evolve, however imperceptibly, with each passing year. But geology isn't the entire story here. Between the Native Americans who inhabited this land for thousands of years and the present composite of rich and famous (and poor and wanna-be-famous), there's 200 years of people-history that isn't always studied. While it's a short history, it has done more to change these mountains than any other force in the past 1,000 years. To reach the preserve from the Ventura Freeway (US 101), take Topanga Canyon Boulevard south to Mulholland Drive and turn west (right). Drive one-quarter of a mile, turn left on Mulholland Highway and drive approximately five miles to Stunt Road. Turn left and drive to the preserve entrance on the left. Ask about where to park when you call and make your reservations.

For information, contact the Mountain Restoration Trust; (310) 456-8432.

✤ ✤ ✤ ✤

Estuary Bird Walk
Late August Saturday **S** ⬤ • 8 a.m. to 9:30 a.m.
(see #39 on map page 372)

So where do all the birds go when they head south for the winter? Even before the first hints of winter in the far north begin to show, many birds start their long flight to the warm, rich waters of the Tijuana Estuary, south of San Diego. Each time you visit the estuary, you're likely to encounter new arrivals, because the birds that depend upon the estuary change in both numbers and species throughout the year. Winter brings travelers from the far north, while summers see different visitors who come and join the full-time residents. This walk is specially designed to find and identify the earliest arrivals from the north, those still wearing their summer plumage. Bring water, binoculars and a bird field guide; wear some good hiking boots. The number of people allowed on this hike is limited, so call in advance for reservations. There is no fee.

For information, contact the Tijuana Estuary Visitor Center, 301 Caspian Way, Imperial Beach, CA 91932; (619) 575-3613.

August Allure

Late August Saturday S ⦿ • 9 a.m. to 11:30 a.m.
(see #16 on map page 370)

This is a special, late-summer exploration of Cold Creek Canyon that will take you into some secret places known only to those who are intimately knowledgeable of the preserve. While fire has done its destructive work in parts of the canyon, nature's ability to recover is an amazingly powerful force and you can see her work in action. Toss a bottle of water in your day pack and join the group for this little adventure. Meet at the Cold Creek Canyon Preserve lower gate. To get there from the Ventura Freeway (US 101), take Topanga Canyon Boulevard south to Mulholland Drive and turn west (right). Drive one-quarter of a mile, turn left on Mulholland Highway and drive approximately five miles to Stunt Road. Turn left and drive to the preserve entrance on the left.

For information, contact the Cold Creek Docents; (818) 591-9363.

✤ ✤ ✤ ✤

Tijuana Estuary Workshop

Late August Saturday S ⦿
(see #39 on map page 372)

This workshop is designed primarily for kids, but anyone who wants to participate will have an opportunity to look at the nests and nesting habits of two endangered species, the light-footed clapper rail and the least tern. The Tijuana Estuary is situated on the United States' side of the line that tells Mexico where its land stops. The wetland area is a primary resting and wintering ground for tens of thousands of migrating birds. During this workshop, which will introduce you and your kids to this wonderful escape from city life, you'll get a chance to view some of nature's wonders to be found here. Oh, and you and your kids can also create art projects that will serve as remembrances of your trip to the estuary for a long time to come. There's a $2 fee per child for the workshop.

For information, contact the Tijuana Estuary Visitor Center, 301 Caspian Way, Imperial Beach, CA 91932; (619) 575-3613.

AUGUST

Tijuana Estuary Workshop for Teachers

Late August Saturday Ⓢ ☎

(see #39 on map page 372)

If you are a teacher planning to bring your class out to the estuary for a field trip, then you must attend this two-day workshop. You'll learn about the ecology of the coastal wetland and how to present the subject to your elementary grade students. There will be everything from flashcards and posters to videos and lots of direct field experience. Workshop materials are available in both English and Spanish. Lunch, described as "yummy," is included in the $50 workshop fee ($20 extra for second-language materials). Reservations are required to assure a place in the workshop, because space is limited.

For information, contact the Tijuana Estuary Visitor Center, 301 Caspian Way, Imperial Beach, CA 91932; (619) 575-3613.

Annual Antelope Valley Indian Museum Celebration

September 16, 1995 Ⓢ ☎ • 10 a.m. to 5 p.m.

(see #3 on map page 370)

A fair distance inland, yet not that far of a drive from Los Angeles, the Antelope Valley Indian Museum throws an annual party celebrating the simple fact that it exists, which is as good a reason as any to have a celebration. This annual celebration marks the seasonal opening of the museum with Native American dancers, displays, crafts and storytelling. Volunteers and rangers will lead nature hikes around the area and through the museum. So if you've got nothing better to do, and maybe even if you do, you ought to drive out of the city and enjoy the desert lands to the east. Following the celebration, the museum will be open each weekend until the following June, from 11 a.m. to 4 p.m.

To reach the Antelope Valley Indian Museum, take Highway 14 to Lancaster, then head east on Avenue K to 150th Street. Turn right (south) on 150th Street and drive to Avenue M, then turn left and continue one mile to the museum. There's a $2 entry fee for adults and $1 for kids ages 6 to 12. It'll probably be hot, so dress appropriately.

For information, contact the Antelope Valley Indian Museum; (805) 942-0662.

✤ ✤ ✤ ✤

Encinitas Family Day

September 23, 1995 • 10 a.m. to 5 p.m.
(see #33 on map page 372)

Annually for the past 10 years, the coast city of Encinitas has celebrated the family with a day designed for the whole crew. The start time for most of the day's events is 10 a.m., but for those interested in getting an early jump on the fun, there's a 5K run or walk that begins at 7:30 a.m. and meanders along the coastline. You can join others as they help clean up the beach starting at 8 a.m., then get some free refreshments and possibly a special pass into Sea World for just $2. Following the run and the clean-up, it's time to eat a pancake breakfast and enjoy the information booths and the Firemen and Sheriffs Tug-of-War competition. There is a special Kids' Zone for the younger ones and live entertainment at the center stage. The events are held at Moonlight Beach, 400 B Street in Encinitas, which is just off Highway 101, about 31 miles north of San Diego. There's no cost for the program and the weather should cooperate with sunny skies.

For information, contact Encinitas Community Services, 505 South Vulcan Avenue, Encinitas, CA 92024; (619) 633-2740.

SEPTEMBER

Malibu Coast Clean-Up

Late September or early October weekend **$** 🖋
(various locations)

Each year, thousands of people gather along parts of California's coast and spend the day cleaning beaches or nearby lands of trash and debris that has collected over the year. Usually, there are good-natured contests for collecting the biggest, strangest, most and other categories of garbage. So come on out and join your neighbors in cleaning up a small part of California's coast. The location of the planned clean-up changes each year, depending upon which part of the Malibu Coast is most in need of attention, so call to find out where to meet. There's no cost to participate, unless you count a few sore muscles that you're likely to discover the following day. The weather should be quite pleasant for a day of work.

For information, contact California State Parks, 39996 Pacific Coast Highway, Malibu, CA 90265; (310) 457-8142.

Cabrillo Festival

September 24 through October 1, 1995 • 10 a.m. to 4:30 p.m.
(see #37 on map page 372)

For 30 years, this annual festival has commemorated Juan Rodriguez Cabrillo's exploration of California's coast. In 1542, Cabrillo sailed along the southern coast, claiming for Spain the lands he discovered. The highlight of this year's celebration will be a reenactment of Cabrillo, his priest and soldiers coming ashore from a historic replica of his ship at Point Ballast, the explorer's original landing site. While Cabrillo's expedition went on to explore more than 800 miles of coastline, the festival will remain here, with entertainment provided by dancers and singers representing the United States, Spain, Portugal and Mexico. Dignitaries will oversee a special ceremony commemorating the explorer's voyage of discovery and you can enjoy traditional foods from the represented countries. If that's not enough, you can also explore the area's beautiful tidepools, Old Point Loma Lighthouse (built in 1855), and remnants of World War I and II coastal fortifications. The festival will be held at Cabrillo National Monument, which is located near the southern tip of Point Loma in San Diego. Take Rosecrans Street and turn right on Canon Street, then turn left onto Catalina Boulevard. Proceed through the Naval Ocean System Center gates to the park. The festival is free to the public. You can probably expect San Diego's usual warm and sunny weather.

For information, contact Cabrillo National Monument, P.O. Box 6670, San Diego, CA 92166; (619) 557-5450.

❖ ❖ ❖ ❖

Annual Birding Event
October 6 & 7, 1995
7 p.m. to 10 p.m. Friday; 7 a.m. to 1 p.m. Saturday
(see #39 on map page 372)

This annual birders' event begins on Friday evening with a reception at the Tijuana Estuary, which will feature a guest speaker, artist or author well known in the world of birding. The real fun begins on Saturday morning as birders gather in the Tijuana River Valley for a morning of great birding. The area is nationally recognized for its rare birds and the overall numbers of species found here. You may see red-throated pipits, longspurs, flocks of horned larks, northern waterthrushes, yellow-billed cuckoos, herons and many, many other species. If you're new to birding, this is a good opportunity to learn a few identification tricks and also to discover where to look for some of those rare sightings. To cap off the day, lunch will be served at Border Field State Park, which overlooks the entire valley.

The main field event will be held at Tijuana River Valley Regional Park, which is located near the Mexican border. Head 12 miles south of San Diego on Interstate 5, then take the Coronado Avenue exit. At the traffic light, turn south on Hollister Boulevard and continue 1.5 miles. Turn west on Sunset Boulevard and continue to Saturn Boulevard, then turn left and drive into the parking

OCTOBER

lot for Meyers Ranch (currently Effie May Farms). Call the San Diego County Parks and Recreation Department for the exact meeting place, because it can get a little tricky on these back roads. The event will cost about $20 per person. The weather should be very pleasant this time of year.

For information, contact San Diego County Parks and Recreation Department, 5201 Ruffin Road, Suite P, San Diego, CA 92123; (619) 694-3049.

❧ ❧ ❧ ❧

Mountain Bicycle Poker Ride
October 8, 1995 $ 🚲
(see #35 on map page 372)

This is a take-off on the horseback poker rides that have been held for years. Mountain bikers are finally catching onto the fun, at least those who have a love for gambling. Just about anyone who can ride a mountain bike and has the vaguest idea of how poker is played can participate. Riders travel on a pre-planned trail with several stops established where each participant must check in. The check-in involves receiving a card from a poker deck and continuing on to the next stop to repeat the process. At the end of the trail, each rider has a complete poker hand, and if she or he is lucky, it will be the winning hand. Prizes, fun and exercise are all part of this day spent riding through portions of Cuyamaca Rancho State Park's 18,000 acres. About 50 riders are expected to participate. To reach Cuyamaca Rancho State Park, drive east from San Diego on Interstate 8, then head north on Highway 79 into the park. Once inside the park, follow signs to Vaqueros Horse Camp. There's a fee of $75 per rider, with a $6 per vehicle park entrance fee. Expect some very warm, but not uncomfortable, weather.

For information, contact Cuyamaca Rancho State Park; (619) 765-0755.

❧ ❧ ❧ ❧

Cara's Oak Day

October 21, 1995 • 10 a.m. to 3 p.m.
(see #31 on map page 372)

California's Native Americans depended upon the fall acorn harvest for much of their yearly food supply. Gather with a couple hundred other people to celebrate the autumn acorn harvest with a day of storytelling, games, nature hikes and tree plantings. The event is held on the 53 acres of hills and oaks in Felicita Park and is sponsored by the Cara Knott Foundation and the California Oak Foundation. There will be information available about the plight of California's remaining and threatened oak woodlands, along with suggestions about what you can do to help restore and protect California's great oaks. Felicita Park is located at 742 Clarence Lane in Escondido. There's a $1 entry fee into the park. Plan on some cool and pleasant weather.

For information, contact San Diego County Parks and Recreation Department, 5201 Ruffin Road, Suite P, San Diego, CA 92123; (619) 694-3049.

Annual Antique Gas & Steam Engine Show & Dutch Oven Cookoff

October 21 & 22, 1995 • 9 a.m. to 4:30 p.m.
(see #30 on map page 372)

These two events may not seem to have much in common, and they don't, except for the fact that both require heat to work. This is the San Diego County Parks Department's annual Dutch oven cookoff and it's open to folks of all ages, with various categories of cooking events. The Antique Gas & Steam Engine Show features everything from blacksmith and wheelwright shops, demonstrations of last century's farming equipment, gristmill and sawmill operations, draft horses, a farrier and vintage fashions to music, square dancing and demonstrations of turn-of-the-century farming skills. There's an antique tractor parade every afternoon about 1 p.m. To get to Guajome County Park, drive about six miles east of Oceanside

OCTOBER

on Highway 76, then turn onto Highway S14 (North Santa Fe Avenue). Drive about two miles to the park entrance. The event will cost $5 for adults; those under age 15 are free. There is also a registration fee for the cookoff, but call for more information. The weather can range from warm to cool.

For information, contact San Diego County Parks and Recreation Department, 5201 Ruffin Road, Suite P, San Diego, CA 92123; (619) 694-3049.

Annual Halloween at Los Penasquitos Adobe

October 27, 1995 • 6:30 p.m. to 10 p.m.
(see #36 on map page 372)

Halloween is always a special night no matter where you are, but spending this spookiest of all spooky nights in a 150-year-old adobe can only add to the scariness. This will be a little different than most Halloween programs, with the emphasis on ranger-led nightlife programs, a campfire and storytelling. There's also a hayride and crafts for everyone to enjoy. It's designed for kids from kindergarten through eighth grade—and their parents, of course. The program is held at the Los Penasquitos Preserve and Adobe. The park is located about 20 miles north of San Diego, off Interstate 15. Take the Mercy Road exit and drive west to Black Mountain Road, then turn north and drive to Park Village Road. Make a U-turn and return south, then turn right at the entrance to Canyonside Park. Follow the road west to the adobe. It will cost $10 per person. It may get a little cool as the evening progresses, so dress accordingly.

For information, contact San Diego County Parks and Recreation Department, 5201 Ruffin Road, Suite P, San Diego, CA 92123; (619) 694-3049.

Cuyamaca Ride & Tie
October 26 to 29, 1995 **S**
(see #35 on map page 372)

If you ever thought that a horse race wasn't good exercise for people, better think again. A ride and tie isn't like any horse race you've ever seen. This is a two-person team effort, with the twist being that there is only one horse per team. The idea here is for one person to ride the team's horse a set distance along the race course, stop, tie the horse and then continue down the trail on foot as fast as possible. At the same time, the team's second member runs on foot to get to where the horse has been tied, jumps on and gallops down the trail, passing the teammate, then riding to the next stop, where he or she ties the horse and heads out on foot. This alternating run-ride-tie-run process continues through the 30-mile course to the finish line. The first complete team (horse, rider and runner) to cross the finish line is declared the exhausted winner. Prizes are awarded. To reach Cuyamaca Rancho State Park, drive east from San Diego on Interstate 8, then head north on Highway 79 into the park. Once inside the park, follow signs to the event's starting location. The cost is $135 per team, with a $6 park entrance fee per vehicle. The weather should be cool and pleasant, hopefully.

For information, contact Cuyamaca Rancho State Park; (619) 765-0755.

✤ ✤ ✤ ✤

Point Mugu Poker Run Bicycle Ride
Mid-October weekend **S**
(see #5 on map page 370)

Here is an opportunity to combine gambling and exercise in a public service fundraising event. Participants compete in a variety of bicycle rides in which playing cards are collected at designated stops. In the end, the rider with the best poker hand wins the event's prize. There will be many prizes awarded, with a raffle held for even more opportunities to win. Food will be available for those not wishing to bring their own. The event is designed to help raise money for a much-needed visitor center. Point Mugu State Park is located on the Pacific Coast Highway, about 31 miles northwest of Santa Monica. The cost of the program hasn't been set yet, but probably will be about $20 per person. The weather should be cool, but comfortable.

For information, contact California State Parks, 39996 Pacific Coast Highway, Malibu, CA 90265; (805) 986-8483.

❖ ❖ ❖ ❖

Wheels to the Sea
Mid-November weekend **$** 📞
(see #5 on map page 370)

Here is an excellent opportunity for the physically challenged to enjoy an exciting four-mile descent from a mountaintop in Point Mugu State Park, along dirt roads, finally reaching the sea. There are some spectacular views from the top. Volunteers are needed to serve as assistants for the participants in wheelchairs. The entrance to Point Mugu State Park is located about 31 miles northwest of Santa Monica along the Pacific Coast Highway. Preregistration is required; exact directions to the starting point will be sent with the registration confirmation. The program is free to participants. The weather is usually clear, unless an early winter rainstorm rolls in from the Pacific.

For information, contact California State Parks, 39996 Pacific Coast Highway, Malibu, CA 90265; (805) 986-8484.

❖ ❖ ❖ ❖

Old Point Loma Lighthouse Anniversary
November 15, 1995 • 10 a.m. to 4 p.m.
(see #37 on map page 372)

This almost-annual celebration offers a rare opportunity to climb the stairway that leads to the Old Point Loma Lighthouse tower for a spectacular view of San Diego and the harbor. After three years of construction and another year waiting for the special

Fresnel lens to arrive from France, the oil lamp was lit for the first time on November 15, 1855. For the next 36 years, the lighthouse, perched 422 feet above sea level, provided a guiding light for ships passing Point Loma and entering San Diego Bay. One of eight original West Coast lighthouses still open to the public, the Old Point Loma Lighthouse has been restored as closely as possible to its 1880s appearance.

Old Point Loma Lighthouse is located within Cabrillo National Monument, near the southern tip of Point Loma in San Diego. Take Rosecrans Street to Canon Street and turn right, then left onto Catalina Boulevard. Proceed through the Naval Ocean System Center gates into the park. There's a park entry fee of $4 per vehicle. Hopefully, the weather will cooperate and not be too wet.

For information, contact Cabrillo National Monument, P.O. Box 6670, San Diego, CA 92166; (619) 557-5450.

❖ ❖ ❖ ❖

Backbone Trail Month

Mid-November ❺ 🦶
(various locations in the Santa Monica Mountains)

The wilds of the Santa Monica Mountains are administered by a mind-boggling assortment of government, quasi-government and nonprofit organizations, all determined to acquire and protect as much of these beautiful and rugged lands as possible. Throughout the month of November, many of these organizations sponsor numerous hikes and a couple of ceremonies to highlight their year's efforts to acquire new lands and complete the remaining few miles of trail still under construction. The 64-mile Backbone Trail, which runs along ridges through the length of the Santa Monica Mountains, is about 90 percent complete, so a major celebration is fast approaching. Generally, the hikes and year-end trail work parties are scheduled only a couple of months in advance. Give a call for a schedule of events and programs, then take a day to join in on the fun and see one of Southern California's best-kept secrets, at least kept best from the rest of the world that sees Los Angeles as nothing

NOVEMBER

more than skyscrapers and beaches. There really is a whole world of nature just freeway minutes away from the jumble of downtown Los Angeles.

There are numerous access points into the Santa Monica Mountains including Malibu Creek State Park, Topanga Canyon, Point Mugu and more. Check a local map, or call the number below for information on specific event dates and meeting places. There is generally no cost, although some of the parks may require you to pay an entry fee of $5 or less. Expect typical South Coast fall weather. Hopefully, it will be mild and balmy, but there could be rain this late in the year.

For information, call Mountain Parks Information; (800) 533-7275.

✤ ✤ ✤ ✤

San Pasqual Battlefield Reenactment
December 3, 1995 • 10 a.m. to 4 p.m.
(see #40 on map page 372)

We hear very little about the Battle of San Pasqual, especially in our history books, since it saw the Mexican Army defeating a detachment of U.S. Cavalry. Still, even though Mexican forces were victorious, the Battle at San Pasqual marked the beginning of the end of Mexico's control of California. In this historic reenactment, there will be lots of muzzle loaders exploding, fancy uniforms, galloping horses, general excitement and no bloodshed. The historic battlefield is located about one mile east of the San Diego Wild Animal Park, east of Escondido on Highway 78.

For information, contact California State Parks; (619) 238-3380.

✤ ✤ ✤ ✤

Holiday In Old Town San Diego

December 8 & 9, 1995
(see #37 on map page 372)

After the sun sets over California's South Coast, the ambience of Old Town San Diego State Historic Park changes. Gone are most of the tourists and their kids running, yelling and having fun. Many of the shops and historic buildings have closed their doors. But this weekend, when the sun sets, Old Town stays awake, with its historic buildings remaining open well into the night for you to take candle-light tours through them. The Christmas season fills the air and Old Town comes alive with holiday cheer. Old Town San Diego State Historic Park is located off Interstate 15 in San Diego, between San Diego Avenue and Twiggs Street. The cost is $5 for adults and $3 for kids ages 6 to 16. The weather should be cool, but comfortable, unless it rains.

For information, contact Old Town San Diego State Historic Park; (619) 237-6770.

Old Town Merchant's Open House & Luminaries

December 9, 1995
(see #37 on map page 372)

San Diego has been around for a couple of centuries, and from its Spanish beginnings to its multi-cultural present day, Christmas has always been a special time here. On this particular day, you can wander through historic Old Town San Diego and enjoy the season with songs and entertainment. Many of the shops will offer samples of food, and there will be a luminaries lighting program that will add a special ambience to the historic setting. When you finish wandering and eating, there should still be some time left to get a little holiday shopping done in some of the many shops. Old Town San Diego State Historic Park is located off Interstate 15 in San Diego, between San Diego Avenue and Twiggs Street. The program is free to the public. Hopefully, the weather will be cool with no rain.

For information, contact Old Town San Diego State Historic Park; (619) 237-6770.

DECEMBER

Las Posadas & Luminaries

December 14, 1995 **$** ⟨⟩
(see #37 on map page 372)

In the early 1800s, the residents of San Diego began a Christmas season tradition. The townsfolk would gather to portray the journey of Mary and Joseph as they sought shelter for the Christ child. On this evening, docents and staff wearing 19th-century costumes will keep the tradition alive with an historical reenactment along a route lined with luminaries. Old Town San Diego State Historic Park is located off Interstate 15 in San Diego, between San Diego Avenue and Twiggs Street. The program is free to the public. The weather might be a little cool and possibly even wet.

For information, contact Old Town San Diego State Historic Park; (619) 237-6770

South Coast & San Diego Seasonal Hikes & Programs

Antelope Valley California Poppy Display

Every day, mid-March through April **S** ⏱ · 9 a.m. to 4 p.m.
(see #2 on map page 370)

Winter rains, followed by spring sunshine, bring a colorful renewal of life to the dry hills and valleys of Antelope Valley. Entire hillsides are splashed with the brilliant orange hue of our state's flower, the California poppy. Bring your camera and spend an hour or two walking through the vividly colorful fields. There's a visitor center featuring displays of wildflower paintings and also a gift shop. Since weather plays a key role in determining the quality and the peak period of each season's wildflower display, it's a good idea to call the park ahead of time for information on how the bloom is looking. On spring weekends, the parking lot can fill, so you might want to get here early. To reach the Antelope Valley Poppy Reserve, drive out Highway 14 and take the Avenue I exit in Lancaster. Head west for 15 miles to the reserve entrance. There's a $5 per vehicle entrance fee. It may be warm, or a little cool and breezy.

For information, contact the Antelope Valley California Poppy Reserve, 1051 West Avenue M, Suite 201, Lancaster, CA 93534; (805) 943-5183.

SEASONAL

Hungry Valley Wildflower Tours

Weekends, April through June [S] ☎ • 1 p.m. to 3 p.m.

(see #1 on map page 370)

Many areas of California boast beautiful spring wildflower shows. One of the lesser known areas, but also one of the most spectacular, is Hungry Valley State Vehicular Recreation Area located near Tejon Pass. Park rangers lead weekend tours throughout the wildflower season, and the best part is that you don't have to walk unless you would like to get out on your own. The 15-mile vehicle tour route is over dirt roads, all of which can be traversed by passenger cars, although your car may need a good dusting-off by the time you're done. A special wildflower guide is available for visitors who wish to canvas the area on their own. Bring a camera and plenty of film because the poppies, coreopsis, lupine, baby blue eyes, owl's clover and dozens of other colorful wildflowers make for some beautiful photographs. Hungry Valley State Vehicular Recreation Area is off Interstate 5 in Gorman, about 68 miles north of Los Angeles. There's a $4 per vehicle entry fee into the park, but the actual wildflower tour is free. It will probably be pretty warm, especially the closer to June that you go.

For information, contact the Hungry Valley District Office, P.O. Box 1360, Lebec, CA 93243; (805) 248-7007.

Saddleback Butte State Park Hikes

Saturdays: March 4 to June 24 & September 2 to November 25

[S] ☎ 9 a.m. to 11 a.m.

(see #4 on map page 370)

Spring and fall are the best times to hike the desert country of Saddleback Butte and there's a ranger-led hike that can introduce you to the wonders of this land. The hikes usually vary in distance and destinations, but none are too difficult. There are wildflowers during spring and giant colonies of antelope ground squirrels to see any time of year, although they may be hiding from the heat during much of the day. Rabbits, roadrunners, quail, and various flying birds and other creatures of the desert are also likely to be seen. Well, as far as roadrunners go, at least their tracks in the sand are visible.

To reach Saddleback Butte State Park from Highway 14 in Lancaster, drive east on East Avenue J (N5) for 17.5 miles to its intersection with 170th Street East. The park is on the corner.

For information, contact Saddleback Butte State Park; (805) 942-0662.

✤ ✤ ✤ ✤

Tijuana Estuary Nature Hike

First three Saturdays of each month **$** *• 9 a.m. to 11 a.m.*
(see #39 on map page 372)

Where there's water, there's life, and when you combine the flow of freshwater with the nutrients of saltwater, a special environment is created, richer in wildlife than one might imagine. With something on the order of 90 percent of all wetlands in California having been filled, drained or destroyed in some other imaginative manner, the estuary that fills the void between Mexico and California is a special and rare place. Join a ranger or naturalist who will take you on a guided walk where you'll see the ways that plants and animals have adapted in order to survive in a rich, yet not always hospitable home (at least not always hospitable when the impacts of the human species are introduced into the equation). The hike will go rain or shine, although rain is not something that regularly falls on this particular part of California. Meet at the corner of 5th and Iris streets in Imperial Beach. The weather will vary, depending upon the time of year. There's no cost for the nature hikes.

For information, contact the Tijuana Estuary National Wildlife Reserve; (619) 587-3613.

✤ ✤ ✤ ✤

SEASONAL

Tijuana Estuary Bird Walk

Fourth Saturday of each month **S**⊘ • 8:30 a.m. to 11 a.m.
(see #39 on map page 372)

The wetlands that flow between Mexico and California provide a home for many species of birds, but serve as a stopover for tens of thousands more birds heading either north or south each year. The diverse array of creatures inhabiting the estuary's waters provides a ready, abundant and nutrient-rich food supply for birds. Bring your binoculars and bird field guides, if you have them. Reservations are required for the bird walk and kids must be accompanied by an adult. Meet at the Estuary Visitor Center, which is located at 301 Caspian Way in Imperial Beach. There's no cost to participate in the walks.

For information, contact the Tijuana Estuary National Wildlife Reserve; (619) 587-3613.

❖ ❖ ❖ ❖

Los Penasquitos Adobe Tours

First and third Saturdays each month **S**⊘ • 11 a.m. and noon
(see #36 on map page 372)

Several days each month, tours and interpretive programs focus on the earliest days of the Los Penasquitos Preserve and Adobe and the life that was centered around the historic rancho. The history of the rancho began in 1823, when California's first Mexican governor awarded over 4,000 acres of land to Captain Francisco Maria Ruiz, the veteran commandant of the Presidio, as reward for his service. The following year, Ruiz completed construction of his adobe *casa.* In 1862, George Alonzo Johnson, upon marrying the daughter of Ruiz's grandnephew, incorporated the old adobe into a larger residence. The adobe stayed in the family until the 1880s, when financial setbacks (which were not uncommon for many of the early ranchos) caused the property to pass through the hands of several owners.

The ranch has significant history attached to it. It was the first stopping place of Brigadier General Stephen Watts Kearny and his half-starved remnant Army of the West after their defeat at the Battle of San Pasqual in 1846. Later, the U.S. Army ran supply trains through the rancho to provision its Fort Yuma outpost on the Southern Emigrant Trail. Finally, in 1962, San Diego County purchased the land around the adobe and worked toward restoration of the rancho's early character. The Los Penasquitos Preserve and Adobe is located about 20 miles north of San Diego, off Interstate 15. Take the Mercy Road exit and drive west to Black Mountain Road, then turn north and drive to Park Village Road. Make a U-turn and return south, then turn right at the entrance to Canyonside Park. Follow the road west to the adobe. The program is free, unless you wish to make a donation.

For information, contact San Diego County Parks Society, 5201 Ruffin Road, Suite P, San Diego, CA 92123; (619) 694-3049.

❈ ❈ ❈ ❈

Quail Botanical Gardens Tours

Saturdays & first Tuesday of each month for children's tours
tours start at 10 a.m.; children's tours start at 10:30 a.m.
(see #37 on map page 372)

This is an absolutely beautiful botanical garden featuring over 3,000 plant species, including rare and unusual plants. There's a waterfall and an overlook offering a special view of the 30-acre garden. The tours are led by trained docents who can answer your questions about the many trees, flowers and other plants. Quail Botanical Gardens is located at 230 Quail Gardens Drive in San Diego. There's a $2 entry fee per person.

For information, contact the Quail Botanical Gardens Foundation, (619) 436-8301.

❈ ❈ ❈ ❈

Volcan Mountain Nature Hikes

Second Saturday of each month • 9:30 a.m. to 11:30 a.m.
(see #34 on map page 372)

Enter through the stone gateway to this 228-acre preserve and you'll know immediately that this is a special place. The preserve is in the mountains east of San Diego near the town of Julian. The docent-led Saturday hikes generally focus on a different subject each month, such as the geology of Volcan Mountain, Native American uses of plants (allowing you to sample some of the wild foods found in the woodlands), oak trees in the mountains, endangered habitats and birds of prey. Then again, you might just hike to the top of the mountain. Hikes aren't held in August and September generally, but the trails are open to the public. Remember to bring plenty of water and stay on the trails. The preserve meeting place is outside Julian. Take Highway 78/79 west into Julian to Farmer Road. Turn left onto Farmer Road and continue 2.2 miles, turning right on Wynola Road for about 100 yards, then turning left, back onto Farmer Road. Go another 100 yards and park on the shoulder of the paved road by the preserve's signed entrance. The hikes are free. As far as weather goes, you'll see all four seasons here, from hot in the summer to freezing in the winter.

For information, contact the Volcan Docents, San Diego County Parks, 5201 Ruffin Road, Suite P, San Diego, CA 92123; (619) 694-3049.

Whale Watching at Newport Beach

January 1 to March 31, 1995 • All day
(see #27 on map page 371)

Whale watching is always popular in winter, and if you can spot 'em from their shores, most coastal cities and towns promote the activity. Actually, about the only thing you'll see from the shore are the spouts erupting skyward from whales that are several hundred yards or more off the coast. The best way to see these huge, beautiful beasts is to join one of the many whale-watching tours that leave several times each day. While the boats aren't allowed to directly chase the whales, they can shut down their engines as they see whales approaching and allow the creatures to swim as near to your boat as they may be willing to go.

Newport Beach is located about 16 miles south of Long Beach

on Highway 1. It won't cost you anything to watch the whales from the shore; boat trips out to where the whales are swimming can cost from $20 and up. The weather is generally pretty nice, unless a winter storm happens to be blowing through.

For information, contact the Newport Beach Conference and Visitors Bureau, 366 San Miguel #200, Newport Beach, CA 92660; (800) 94-COAST.

✤ ✤ ✤ ✤

Whale Watching at Long Beach

January 1 to March 31, 1995 • All day
(see #25 on map page 370)

While you won't see many whales from Long Beach Harbor, it's a great place to catch a boat out to where the whales are plentiful and playful. You can also hitch a ride out to Avalon on Santa Catalina Island for a day of fun and whale watching along the way.

Long Beach is located about 24 miles from Los Angeles. You can call the Long Beach Area Convention and Visitors Bureau for the current boat tour costs and contact telephone numbers. The weather should be good, unless a winter storm wanders through.

For information, contact the Long Beach Area Convention and Visitors Bureau, One World Trade Center #300, Long Beach, CA 90831-0300; (800) 4LB-STAY.

✤ ✤ ✤ ✤

Singles Walk

Sundays, April through September **S** 🚶 • 10 a.m. to noon
(see #21 on map page 370)

If you're single, enjoy nature and want to meet other people in the same situation, why not spend a couple of hours with other single folks on a quiet walk in Upper Franklin Canyon? This part of the Santa Monica Mountains offers a lot to see, so enjoy the canyon on a warm spring afternoon with some newfound friends. And you've still got Saturday night for other pursuits, if that's in the wind. The weather should be pretty nice. The walk begins at the Sooky Goldman Nature Center. To get there from the Ventura Freeway (US 101), drive south on Coldwater Canyon Drive to Beverly Drive (Beverly Hills Fire Station #2). Turn right onto Beverly Drive and go one mile to Franklin Canyon Drive. Turn right and drive 1.5 miles to Lake Drive. Turn left and go a very short distance, then take a right turn into the Upper Lake area. Drive around the east side of the lake and park in the Sooky Goldman Nature Center lot.

For information, contact the Mountains Education Program, 2600 Franklin Canyon Drive, Beverly Hills, CA 90210, (310) 858-3090; or Mountain Parks Information, (800) 533-7275.

❀ ❀ ❀ ❀

Caballero Canyon Twilight Hike

Fridays, April through September ⓢ ⎰ • 7 p.m. to 10 p.m.
(see #15 on map page 370)

This leisurely evening hike will cover three miles from Caballero Canyon to Mulholland Drive in the Santa Monica Mountains. As the sun sets, you could get an opportunity to see wildlife that generally stays well hidden during daylight hours. Bring water, wear hiking boots and carry a good flashlight. This is an easy hike that even beginners can enjoy. To get to the hike's meeting place, take the Ventura Freeway (US 101) to the Reseda Boulevard exit. Turn south and drive 1.9 miles to just past the fountain on the left side of Reseda Boulevard. Park on the street. The hikes are free.

For information, contact the Sierra Club; (213) 387-4287.

❀ ❀ ❀ ❀

Incredible Edibles

Sundays, April through August ⓢ ⎰ • 10 a.m to 1 p.m.
(see #21 on map page 370)

Before the advent of restaurants, delis and supermarkets, what did the folks who lived in this land do when they where hungry?

Hard to imagine such a time or that the mountains around the Los Angeles area provided a well-balanced diet for Native Americans, isn't it? Well, hook up with a naturalist at the Franklin Canyon Ranch Site and head off on this expedition to find and identify plants that are edible, along with those that will make you either dead, or wish you were, if you eat them. There will also be a special presentation on fruits and vegetables, the ones that are a little more familiar to us than leached acorns and cattail roots. The size of this group must be limited, so advance reservations are required. To get to the Sooky Goldman Nature Center from the Ventura Freeway (US 101), drive south on Coldwater Canyon Drive to Beverly Drive (Beverly Hills Fire Station #2). Turn right onto Beverly Drive and go one mile to Franklin Canyon Drive. Turn right and drive 1.5 miles to Lake Drive. Turn left and go a very short distance, then take a right turn into the Upper Lake area. Drive around the east side of the lake and park in the Sooky Goldman Nature Center lot.

For information, contact the Mountains Education Program, 2600 Franklin Canyon Drive, Beverly Hills, CA 90210, (310) 858-3090, ext. 115 or Mountain Parks Information, (800) 533-7275.

Magic Lantern Walk: The Movies

Saturdays, April through September [S] ☎ • 9 a.m. to 11 a.m.

(see #21 on map page 370)

Hollywood's movie industry has always needed wild places to film wild movies and they wanted those places nearby. Take a couple of hours to walk with a guide who will show you around Franklin Canyon Ranch, one of many areas in the Santa Monica Mountains where Hollywood has been turning the hills, trees and streams of Southern California into nearly everywhere else on the planet, and in some cases turning them into other planets, for the past 60 years. You'll also see how far the movie industry is going these days to protect the environment that it so dearly loves to film.

To get to Franklin Ranch from the Ventura Freeway (US 101), drive south on Coldwater Canyon Drive to Beverly Drive (Beverly Hills Fire Station #2). Turn right onto Beverly Drive and go one mile to Franklin Canyon Drive. Turn right and drive 1.5 miles to Lake Drive. Turn left and go a very short distance, then take a right turn into the Upper Lake area. Drive around the east side of the lake and park in the Sooky Goldman Nature Center lot.

For information, contact the Mountains Education Program, 2600 Franklin Canyon Drive, Beverly Hills, CA 90210, (310) 858-3090; or Mountain Parks Information, (800) 533-7275.

From Set to Screen

Saturdays, April through September [S] ☎ • 10 a.m. to 11 a.m.
(see #8 on map page 370)

Moviemaking has been a nearly everyday occurrence in the mountains near Malibu, and one of the favorite places to film is at the Paramount Ranch. Western towns and science fiction sets have been created here for years. Most recently, "Dr. Quinn, Medicine Woman" has been shot here. So to see some of the magical places created by some of the most famous moviemakers and movie stars, join a National Park Service ranger for an easy stroll back through some of Hollywood's fascinating history. To reach the Paramount Ranch, take the Ventura Freeway (US 101) to the Kanan Road exit near Agoura Hills and go south for about three-quarters of a mile. Turn left at the Cornell Road sign and veer to the right. Drive south another 2.5 miles. The entrance is on the right side of the road.

For information, contact the National Park Service; (818) 597-9192.

L.A.: Valley of Smokes, Land of Tongva

Saturdays, April through September [S] ☎ • 2 p.m. to 4 p.m.
(see #21 on map page 370)

Take a walk on the wild side and see how this land that is used by hikers and bikers today served the peoples who lived here 225 years ago. A naturalist will show you some of the foods they ate, the plants they turned into baskets and the stones they transformed into tools. This is a relatively easy walk through the old Franklin Canyon Ranch site, located near Beverly Hills. To get to Franklin Canyon Ranch/Sooky Goldman Nature Center from the Ventura Freeway (US 101), drive south on Coldwater Canyon Drive to Beverly Drive (Beverly Hills Fire Station #2). Turn right onto Beverly Drive and go one mile to Franklin Canyon Drive. Turn right and drive 1.5 miles to Lake Drive. Turn left and go a very short distance, then take a right turn into the Upper Lake area. Drive around the east side of the lake and park in the Sooky Goldman Nature Center lot.

For information, contact the Mountains Education Program, 2600 Franklin Canyon Drive, Beverly Hills, CA 90210, (310) 858-3090; or Mountain Parks Information, (800) 533-7275.

Satwiwa Sundays

Sundays, April through September **$** 🖊 · 10 a.m. to 5 p.m.
(see #10 on map page 370)

Here's an opportunity to visit the Santa Monica Mountains' Satwiwa Native American Indian Culture Center and have your questions about the earliest inhabitants of this land answered by a Native American guest speaker. If, by chance, a Native American speaker is unable to attend, a knowledgeable National Park Service ranger will be on hand to offer informational assistance. To get to the Rancho Sierra Vista/Satwiwa Site, take the Ventura Freeway (US 101) to the Wendy Drive exit in Newbury Park. Head south on Wendy Drive to Potrero Road and turn west (right). The park entrance is at the intersection of Potrero Road and Pinehill Road.

For information, call Friends of Satwiwa, (805) 499-2837; or the National Park Service, (818) 597-9192.

SEASONAL

Trail Building

Saturdays, April through September **S**🖊 • 8 a.m. to 2 p.m.
(various locations in the Santa Monica Mountains)

If you're looking for a way to pay nature back for some of the pleasures you get to experience in the Santa Monica Mountains, why not help with the ongoing trail building programs? There's almost always work to do repairing old trails, building new ones and revegetating trails that were originally ill-planned or came into existence as short cuts that served only to speed the erosion process. The meeting and work sites change weekly, so call to find out where you can go to help.

For information, contact the Sierra Club; (213) 387-4287.

❖ ❖ ❖ ❖

Trim and Tread

First Sunday of each month **S**🖊 • 11 a.m. to 3 p.m.
(various locations in the Santa Monica Mountains)

With all the organizations associated with the Santa Monica Mountains, you'd think that every trail had been fixed and additional trail work was no longer needed. Wrong. And if you join the Mountain Restoration Trust's monthly trail crew, you'll see for yourself how much work it takes to keep the trail system in working condition. Spend part of a day cutting weeds and trimming back brush in a spectacular setting. Bring water, lunch and some good leather work gloves. Tools and crew size are limited, so you must call in advance to reserve a place. Work locations change, so call in advance.

For information, contact the Mountain Restoration Trust; (310) 456-5625.

❖ ❖ ❖ ❖

Nursery Nature Walk

April weekdays **S**⌀ · 10 a.m. to noon
(see #20 on map page 370)

If you're stuck at home with a really young child, somewhere between three months and six years old, bring him or her—or both or all—and yourself, for a quiet stroll through the natural beauty of Coldwater Canyon Preserve. This is a guided walk that will introduce you and your youngsters to the fascinating world of nature. There's also a visit to TreePeople, a nonprofit group whose members help to combat the greenhouse effect by planting millions of trees throughout California. There you'll have a chance to see chickens and the recycling center. Reservations are required for this one, so call ahead. Donations are accepted. To get to Coldwater Preserve from the Ventura Freeway (US 101), take the Coldwater Canyon exit and head south to the intersection of Mulholland Drive. The preserve's entrance is on the left (east) side of the intersection.

For information, contact Nursery Nature Walks; (310) 998-1151.

❖ ❖ ❖ ❖

Canyon Tykes Hike

Ongoing during summer **S**⌀ · 1:30 p.m. to 4:30 p.m.
(see #21 on map page 370)

For the slightly older-than-toddler crowd, this hike is designed to introduce kids ages four to seven to the fascinating world of nature in the Santa Monica Mountains. All kids must be accompanied by an adult for this exploration of trails, a look at animal homes and the area's fascinating ecosystem. The walk will begin at the Sooky Goldman Nature Center. Advance reservations are required. To get to the Sooky Goldman Nature Center from the Ventura Freeway (US 101), drive south on Coldwater Canyon Drive to Beverly Drive (Beverly Hills Fire Station #2). Turn right onto Beverly Drive and go one mile to Franklin Canyon Drive. Turn right and drive 1.5 miles to Lake Drive. Turn left and go a very short distance, then take a right turn into the Upper Lake area. Drive

SEASONAL

around the east side of the lake and park in the Sooky Goldman Nature Center lot.

For information, contact the Mountains Education Program, 2600 Franklin Canyon Drive, Beverly Hills, CA 90210, (310) 858-3090; or Mountain Parks Information, (800) 533-7275.

✤ ✤ ✤ ✤

Weed War

Sundays, April through September **S** 🕐 • 9 a.m. to 1 p.m.
(various locations)

When the Spanish, and later the pioneers, came to California, they brought with them animals such as sheep and cattle that trampled and munched the native grasses into near extinction. Both purposely and accidentally, alien plant species were introduced from the old world. Far too many of those transplanted weeds are still with us, choking out the reproductive abilities of oaks and other native plants and wildflowers. Join in the continuing efforts to eradicate non-native weeds so the native ones can return to their old stomping grounds. The locations vary monthly, so you'll need to call for the meeting place on the Sunday you decide to participate.

For information, contact the California Native Plant Society, (808) 348-5910.

✤ ✤ ✤ ✤

Learning Adventures for Children

Thursdays, June through August **S** 🕐 • 3:15 p.m. to 4:45 p.m.
(see #39 on map page 372)

This environmental education program is designed for younger kids. If your kids are older than pre-school age, you aren't required to attend the program, unless you want to learn a few things yourself. The program is usually a storytelling that may answer questions such as why a raven never tangos with an octopus. Other programs will explore the worlds of bugs, birds or animals, or they may look at ancient Native American folklore.

For information, contact the Tijuana Estuary Visitor Center, 301 Caspian Way, Imperial Beach, CA 91932; (619) 575-3613.

❊ ❊ ❊ ❊

Fitness Hikes

Weekends, June through September 🆂⊘ • 10 a.m. to noon
(see #21 on map page 370)

Most of these hikes are meant for intermediate or advanced hikers because of the terrain, distance and pace that is set. A hike leader will take you on some of the trails around the Sooky Goldman Nature Center, where in addition to getting a lot of good exercise, you'll have an opportunity to learn a little something about this special part of the Santa Monica Mountains. You might want to bring some water with you, because the hills and valleys can get a little warm by noon, the hike's scheduled ending time. To get to the Sooky Goldman Nature Center from the Ventura Freeway (US 101), drive south on Coldwater Canyon Drive to Beverly Drive (Beverly Hills Fire Station #2). Turn right onto Beverly Drive and go one mile to Franklin Canyon Drive. Turn right and drive 1.5 miles to Lake Drive. Turn left and go a very short distance, then take a right turn into the Upper Lake area. Drive around the east side of the lake and park in the Sooky Goldman Nature Center lot.

For information, contact the Mountains Education Program, 2600 Franklin Canyon Drive, Beverly Hills, CA 90210, (310) 858-3090; or Mountain Parks Information, (800) 533-7275.

SEASONAL

❊ ❊ ❊ ❊

Weekend Estuary Nature Walks

Saturdays, June & July 🆂⊘ • 9 a.m. to 11:30 a.m.
(see #39 on map page 372)

This is an easy stroll though the upland areas of the estuary to view the birds, flowers and other plants found in this rich and wonderful world. All ages are welcome to attend. Bring water and binoculars, if you have them. The hike leaves from Fifth and Iris streets in Imperial Beach. There is no fee.

For information, contact the Tijuana Estuary Visitor Center, 301 Caspian Way, Imperial Beach, CA 91932; (619) 575-3613.

✤ ✤ ✤ ✤

First Saturday at Cold Creek Valley Preserve

First Saturday of the month, June through August 🅢✆
5:30 p.m. to 7:30 p.m.
(see #16 on map page 370)

Leave the coastal beaches and the inland valleys and discover the rugged sandstone peaks of Cold Creek. Hiking here in the early evening is a special treat. The light is soft, the colors warm and the company you'll have on the hike is wonderful. Meet the hike leader at the Stunt High Trailhead. To reach the preserve from the Ventura Freeway (US 101), take Topanga Canyon Boulevard south to Mulholland Drive and turn west (right). Drive one-quarter of a mile and turn left on Mulholland Highway and drive approximately five miles to Stunt Road. Park on the wide dirt area on the right side of the road.

For information, contact the Cold Creek Docents; (818) 591-9363.

✤ ✤ ✤ ✤

Chronicles of the Canyon

First Sunday of the month, June through September
10 a.m. to 12:30 p.m.
(see #21 on map page 370)

Want a list of the folks who've called the Santa Monica Mountains' Franklin Canyon their home? First, there were the Native Americans, who lived here for thousands of years. Then, the Spanish pushed the Native Americans aside, only to be pushed back to Europe by the American settlers. Today, modern filmmakers come here to bring Hollywood's magical transformations of reality into make-believe to the silver screen. Come and explore the canyon with a naturalist/historian who will fill you in on all the good stuff, and the ugly stuff that has occurred here. Bring water and a snack for this relatively easy hike. To reach Franklin Canyon from the Ventura Freeway (US 101), drive south on Coldwater Canyon Drive to Beverly Drive (Beverly Hills Fire Station #2). Turn right onto Beverly Drive and go one mile to Franklin Canyon Drive. Turn right and drive 1.5 miles to Lake Drive. Turn left and go a very short distance, then take a right turn into the Upper Lake area. Drive around the east side of the lake and park in the Sooky Goldman Nature Center lot.

For information, contact the Mountains Education Program, 2600 Franklin Canyon Drive, Beverly Hills, CA 90210, (310) 858-3090; or Mountain Parks Information, (800) 533-7275.

✤ ✤ ✤ ✤

Plant Adventures In Franklin Canyon

Second Saturday of the month, July and August 🅂 ✆
9 a.m. to noon
(see #21 on map page 370)

This hike is especially designed for adults who want to learn more about the plants of the Santa Monica Mountains. From cactus to chaparral, oaks to sycamores, the plants of these beautiful mountains are well adapted to the warm and dry climate that most people who live here find quite agreeable. If you have a camera, bring it with you. If you happen to have one or more plant or wildflower field guides, you should bring them as well. Also toss some water into your day pack, along with lunch or a snack. To reach Franklin Canyon from the Ventura Freeway (US 101), drive south on Coldwater Canyon Drive to Beverly Drive (Beverly Hills Fire Station #2). Turn right onto Beverly Drive and go one mile to Franklin Canyon Drive. Turn right and drive 1.5 miles to Lake Drive. Turn left and go a very short distance, then take a right turn into the Upper Lake area. Drive around the east side of the lake and park in the Sooky Goldman Nature Center lot.

For information, contact the Mountains Education Program, 2600 Franklin Canyon Drive, Beverly Hills, CA 90210, (310) 858-3090; or Mountain Parks Information, (800) 533-7275.

SEASONAL

Chapter 9

✤ ✤ ✤ ✤

Great Outdoor Events of California's Inland Empire & Southern Deserts

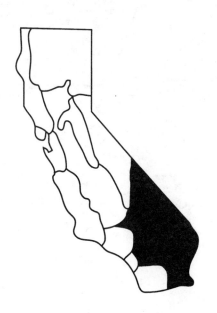

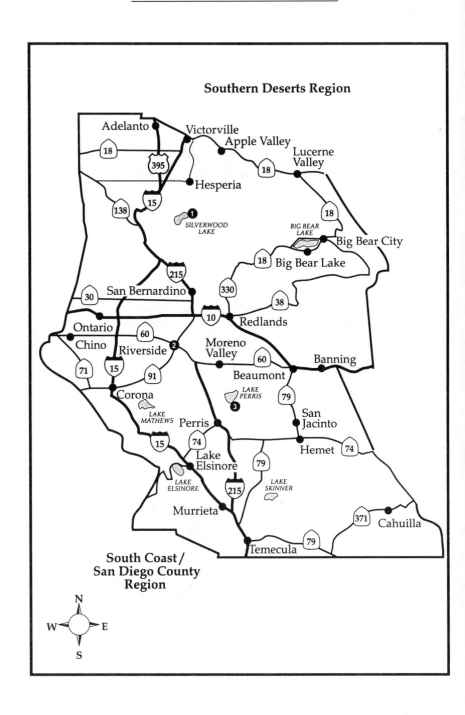

Southern Deserts Region

Adelanto

Victorville

Apple Valley

Lucerne Valley

18

395

18

Hesperia

138

15

18

1 *SILVERWOOD LAKE*

BIG BEAR LAKE

Big Bear City

18 Big Bear Lake

215

30 San Bernardino

330

38

10 Redlands

Ontario

60

2

Moreno Valley

Chino

Riverside

60

Banning

71

15

91

Beaumont

Corona

LAKE PERRIS

79

LAKE MATHEWS

Perris

3

San Jacinto

15

74

Hemet

74

Lake Elsinore

79

LAKE ELSINORE

215

LAKE SKINNER

Murrieta

371 Cahuilla

South Coast / San Diego County Region

79

Temecula

N
W   E
S

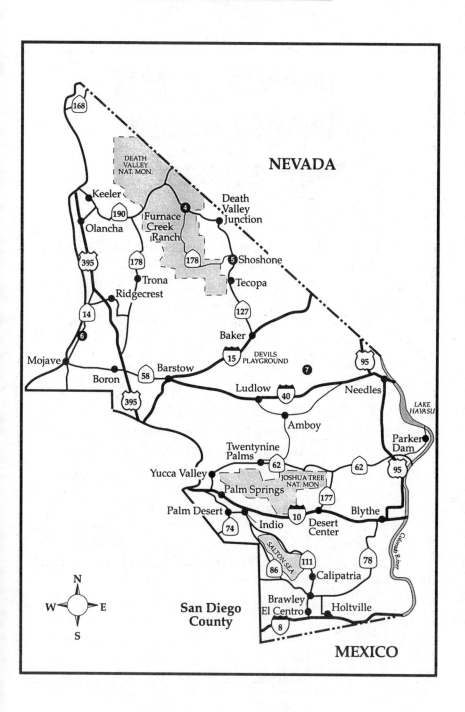

✤ ✤ ✤ ✤

Introduction to the Inland Empire & Southern Deserts

Drive across what has become known as the Inland Empire and what you find is contrast. Climb twisting, narrow roads up to high mountain lakes and you find conifer forests and ski resorts. Drop off the back side of the mountains and continue eastward, and you find desert lands, broad and dry, where more rugged mountains and cactus-like Joshua trees provide a strange yet picturesque backdrop for each spring's wildflower show.

First appearances can be deceiving. Look beyond the dry desolation of the eastern lands, with names like Death Valley, Mojave Desert and Eureka Dunes, and you find a wonderland covered with plants and thriving with wildlife. You say you don't see the wildlife? How about those lizards and snakes? These creatures are all the wilder for having adapted to life in these arid lands, surviving in areas that seldom see more than a few inches of rain each winter. But there is much more. Cool springs, shady oases and fuzzy creatures like kangaroo mice and mountain goats survive and actually thrive in these lands, at least if people leave them alone.

While cruising many of the dunes, canyons and badlands in four-wheel-drives and dirt bikes is a popular form of recreation during winter and spring, so is hiking, backpacking or simply driving the family sedan over the paved and reasonably well-maintained dirt roads that meander across the great deserts. But come summer, with temperatures that cruise well into suffocating triple digits, animals that can't leave the area are forced to hide during the heat of day, venturing out only during the cooler evenings to look for food and water. People, on the other hand, are able to leave, or simply avoid the deserts during summer, instead heading to the higher mountains of the Inland Empire. Summer recreational pursuits are much more appealing in the tall pines of Angeles, San Bernardino and Cleveland national forests, where cool mountain breezes and the refreshing waters of Big Bear, Arrowhead and Silverwood lakes beckon.

With the exception of a week or two at some of the prime spring wildflower viewing sites, the deserts are almost never crowded with people. That contrasts sharply with our national forests, where during summer or winter you can seldom escape the presence of other humans. Of course, there are exceptions, if you're into backpacking in the more remote wilderness areas. But there is nothing more strikingly beautiful than the desert at sunrise as the first rays of a new day dance across the rocks and cliffs with warm, soft light. Unless, of course, it's a desert sunset, as the last rays of light paint the sky with brilliant shades of pink, orange and blue.

Bald Eagle Celebration Day

Mid-February [S] ☎

(see #1 on map page 462)

Just because recently bald eagles have been recommended for removal from the endangered species list doesn't mean that everybody is going to have a chance to see these majestic birds. However, there are several places in California where the big birds winter, always around large water sources that can support their fish-feeding habits and where isolation is at least marginally attainable. For Southern Californians, one of the best places to see bald eagles is around Silverwood Lake, one of those fake lakes created by the California Aqueduct. While the date of this event is not set far in advance, you can bet that up to 1,000 people will find out about it and drive to this reservoir, which literally straddles the high desert and high mountains. Here's your chance to see an eagle, but even if you don't, the booths and displays here should give you plenty to do. The emphasis at the event is on educating school kids, but everyone can benefit from the program.

Silverwood Lake is located in the San Bernardino Mountains, 11 miles east of Interstate 15 on Highway 138, or about 20 miles north of San Bernardino on highways 18 and 138. The event is free, but you may be subject to a $6 per vehicle day-use fee. The weather can be almost anything from cold and stormy to warm and sunny.

For information, contact Silverwood Lake State Recreation Area, 14651 Cedar Circle, Hesperia, CA 92345-9799; (619) 389-2303.

Lake Perris Earth Day Trail Celebration

April 21, 1995 [S] ☎ • 8 a.m. to 4 p.m.

(see #3 on map page 462)

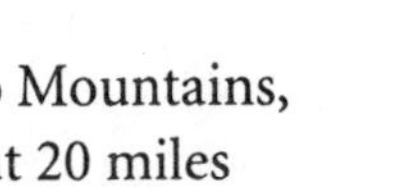

Celebrating Earth Day in conjunction with Trail Day is popular in many California state, national and local parks, and Lake Perris is no different. While most activities at the park are usually focused on or around the lake, the waterslide or the grassy picnic areas, there are many miles of trails that meander through the hills around the perimeter of the park. Rugged mountains, ancient Native American petroglyphs and spectacular wildflower displays in spring make a day of trail work a real adventure. After a good rain, you can count on dozens of beautiful waterfalls cascading over the rock formations in the surrounding mountains. At the Earth Day Trail Celebration, there are special presentations held at the Indian Museum, which sits on the bluff overlooking the lake. The programs will provide an opportunity to learn more about the natural environment and what we can do to stem our destructive impact on it. If the day gets a little too warm and you need to take a quick dip, or if you would like to come early and try a little fishing, then Lake Perris is waiting for you and your family. Lake Perris State Recreation Area is located about 11 miles south of Riverside, via Highway 60 or Interstate 215. There's a $6 fee per vehicle for day-use entry into the park.

For information, contact Lake Perris State Recreation Area, 17801 Lake Perris Drive, Perris, CA 92370; (909) 657-0676 or (909) 657-6150.

APRIL

❖ ❖ ❖ ❖

Orange Blossom Festival

April 22 & 23, 1995 • 10 a.m. to 5 p.m.
(see #2 on map page 462)

There is nothing sweeter than the fragrance of orange blossoms that fill the air here each year. Even with the neverending encroachment of civilization on the 100-year-old orange groves, there are still plenty of trees left. In recognition of the historical significance of the citrus industry in Southern California, a new state park was opened in Riverside in 1993, which was only somewhat coincidentally the 100th anniversary of Sunkist, the famous orange company. This event features lots of orange-related booths, food and activities for kids. The park is easy enough to spot among the orange groves and swaying palm trees. You'll be greeted by one of those giant oranges that once dotted California's highways, from which vendors sold fresh orange juice and other delectable citrus squeezings. To get to California Citrus State Historic Park, first head to Riverside. From the Interstate 215 and Highway 91 interchange in Riverside, take the Highway 91 freeway west about eight miles to the Van Buren Boulevard exit. Drive south on Van Buren Boulevard for one mile, then turn left on Victoria Avenue and continue for one-half mile. Turn right on Jackson Street, then right again on Dufferin Avenue to the park entrance. The park is located at the corner of Dufferin Avenue and Jackson Street. The program is free and the weather should be very nice.

For information, contact California Citrus State Historic Park, 1879 Jackson Street, Riverside, CA 92504; (909) 657-0676.

❀ ❀ ❀ ❀

Tommy Thomas Fishing Derby
April 23, 1995 **Ⓢ** ✎ • 7 a.m. to 2 p.m.
(see #3 on map page 462)

This is a special program designed for kids ages 7 to 15. The day begins with a quick class that teaches the secrets of catching sunfish at Lake Perris. Then everybody grabs their poles and heads down to the lake to try their luck with such secret fishing baits as cheese and marshmallows, or some of the more traditional attractants like worms, salmon eggs or lures. The morning catch is tallied and the winners in several fish-catching categories (biggest, smallest, most and others) are announced later in the day. Even if your kids don't win in any of the categories, they'll win smiles on their faces after a great day in the outdoors. Usually, about 500 kids compete, so don't be late, although there's plenty of shoreline to fish from. Lake Perris State Recreation Area is located about 11 miles south of Riverside, via Highway 60 or Interstate 215. It should be warm and sunny, so bring the sunscreen and something cool to drink. There's a $6 per vehicle day-use entry fee.

For information, contact Lake Perris State Recreation Area, 17801 Lake Perris Drive, Perris, CA 92370; (909) 657-0676 or (909) 657-6150.

❀ ❀ ❀ ❀

Handicapped Fishing Derby

April 29, 1995 **$** 𝒪 · Call for time
(see #1 on map page 462)

This program is designed for kids and adults with physical disabilities who would love to spend a day fishing in a real derby. Silverwood Lake is a reservoir located near the end of the California Aqueduct. This is actually kind of a strange place, because one side of the reservoir sits at the upper edge of the high desert with all those scrubby little desert plants, while another part of the reservoir is surrounded by tall pine trees. As odd as that may seem, it's also very beautiful. The handicapped fishing derby is sponsored by several organizations, including the staff at Silverwood Lake State Recreation Area, the Department of Fish and Game's Mojave Fish Hatchery and some of the local bass clubs. The event will be held along Cleghorn Beach. Bring your fishing pole, if you have one, and maybe an extra one to share with someone who doesn't. Usually, about 100 very happy people participate in the program—and they take quite a few fish from the waters of Silverwood. The lake can be reached via Highway 138, about 11 miles east of Interstate 15, or from San Bernardino by traveling about 20 miles via highways 18 and 138. There's a $6 park day-use entry fee per vehicle. It should be a warm day.

For information, contact Silverwood Lake State Recreation Area; (619) 389-2281 or (619) 389-2303.

❀ ❀ ❀ ❀

Waterski Competition

May 19 & 20, 1995 **$** 𝒪 · 10 a.m. to 4 p.m.
(see #1 on map page 462)

Waterskiing has never really caught on like snow skiing and it probably never will. Still, competition on the water is just as fierce as it is on the slopes. If you have the competitive spirit and even a little ability, here's your chance to test your skills. If you prefer, you can join the other 1,000 people or so who come just to watch the fun.

The event is held on Silverwood Lake, a Southern California reservoir filled with Northern California water that has been transported and pumped southward and upward via the California Aqueduct. This is a fun day for the entire family. Plan for a warm day on the beach with a few dips in the cool waters of the lake. Silverwood Lake can be reached via Highway 138, about 11 miles east of Interstate 15, or from San Bernardino by traveling about 20 miles via highways 18 and 138. There's a $6 day-use fee per vehicle.

For information, contact Silverwood Lake State Recreation Area; (619) 389-2281 or (619) 389-2303.

❖ ❖ ❖ ❖

Hispanic Cultural Heritage Day
September 24, 1995 • 10 a.m. to 4 p.m.
(see #3 on map page 462)

Lake Perris sits in what was once a shallow valley where potatoes were grown. Today, that same valley has been pumped full of water that traveled several hundred miles through the California Aqueduct. The day's activities, celebrating the culture of the large Hispanic population living in the area, will include mariachi and Latin music, folk dancers and, for the kids, piñatas to swing at and prizes to scramble for. Bring your own picnic lunch, a fishing pole and a bathing suit for a full day of fun. Lake Perris State Recreation Area is located 11 miles south of Riverside via Highway 60 or Interstate 215. There is a $6 day-use entry fee per vehicle. Count on it being hot, so bring the sunscreen.

For information, contact Lake Perris State Recreation Area, 17801 Lake Perris Drive, Perris, CA 92370; (909) 657-6150.

❖ ❖ ❖ ❖

Underwater Pumpkin-Carving Contest

October 29, 1995 [S] ☎ • 10 a.m. to 2 p.m.

(see #3 on map page 462)

This rather unique approach to carving Halloween pumpkins is designed for scuba divers, unless of course you're able to hold your breath for extremely long periods of time. The contest is held in the waters of Lake Perris, which are not always of the utmost clarity. For the youngsters too young and the oldsters to old to dive, there also will be a landlubbers' pumpkin-carving contest. The finished pumpkins will be judged for a variety of artistic and other categories, with prizes awarded to the winners and probably more than a few of the losers. Bring your diving gear and your favorite pumpkin-carving knife, if you have one. Lake Perris State Recreation Area is located 11 miles south of Riverside via Highway 60 or Interstate 215. There's a $6 day-use fee per vehicle. It should still be pretty warm during the day, but if you're wearing a wetsuit it probably won't matter too much.

For information, contact Lake Perris State Recreation Area, 17801 Lake Perris Drive, Perris, CA 92370; (909) 657-0676.

Death Valley Fall Festival

November 4, 1995 [S] ☎ • All day

(see #5 on map page 463)

Fall is a great time to see Death Valley, and with all that's planned for the day, there's something for everyone to do. If you've never been to Death Valley, here's your chance to learn a lot about this amazing land's history and the people who have called it home, as well as those who didn't find a way to adapt to the rocky, sandy, mountainous terrain. There's a gem and mineral show, a Shoshone craft show and an open air market. There are several guided tour events including a trail rider, if you have your own horse, and an off-road caravan, if you have a four-wheel-drive vehicle in reasonably good condition. Entertainment includes old-time fiddlers, a mesquite deep-pit barbecue, an off-road bike event, a Volksmarch (non-competitive walk) and special games for kids. For those with a good arm and an equally good eye, there also will be a horseshoe tournament. Most of the events will take place in the small town of Shoshone, located on Highway 127, north of Baker and Interstate 15.

For information, contact Death Valley Chamber of Commerce at P.O. Box 157, Shoshone, CA 92384; (619) 852-4524.

✤ ✤ ✤ ✤

Death Valley 49ers Encampment
First week in November **$**🌙
(see #4 on map page 463)

This is the biggest gathering you'll find in Death Valley. About 40,000 people, most in RVs of some sort, show up for all the activities. There are special walks to some of the nearby attractions and historic areas, guided four-wheel-drive caravans, a fiddling contest, gold panning for those who want to strike it rich, square dancing, golf (yes, there is a golf course in the middle of this desert of deserts), and a fine art show. There's lots more to keep you from being bored, including a costume contest, a photography show, a liar's contest, wagon rides and evening campfire song fests. Call ahead for reservations, because the place does fill up early in the week. Most of the events will start from Death Valley's Furnace Creek, which is located on Highway 190, east of Olancha and US 395.

For information, contact Death Valley 49ers, P.O. Box 157, Shoshone, CA 92384; (619) 852-4524.

✤ ✤ ✤ ✤

Underwater Clean-Up

November 11, 1995 **$** 🖊 • 8 a.m. to 4 p.m.
(see #3 on map page 462)

If you're a scuba diver and want to join what has become an annual clean-up event, bring your dive gear to Lake Perris and be prepared to have fun working. With thousands of people using Lake Perris each weekend during a very long boating, swimming and fishing season, a large selection of junk, trash and garbage is tossed or dropped from boats and from shore. Divers generally bring up about two tons of trash each year. The event begins on the boat launch ramps, so bring your tanks, your boat if you have one, and a lot of energy. Lake Perris State Recreation Area is located 11 miles south of Riverside via Highway 60 or Interstate 215. The cost is $6 per vehicle to enter the park, and another $5 to launch your boat. The weather might even be a little cool by November.

For information, contact Lake Perris State Recreation Area, 17801 Lake Perris Drive, Perris, CA 92370; (909) 657-0676.

NOVEMBER

Inland Empire & Southern Desert Seasonal Hikes & Programs

Red Rock Canyon State Park Hikes

Sundays from March 5 to June 25 & September 3 to November 26
S ✆ • 9 a.m. to 11 a.m.
(see #6 on map page 463)

A series of hikes is offered in the wilds of Red Rock Canyon each Sunday. While the destination of each hike is determined by the leading ranger, any destination here is worth the effort, because there's more than first meets the eye in this vast and beautiful landscape. The great cliffs have attracted the Hollywood movie crowd since the birth of moving pictures and they still do. Probably the best known recent movie to be filmed here, at least in part, was *Jurassic Park*. And scenery that attracts Hollywood will more than fill your own camera's viewfinder with spectacular images. In parts of the park, you'll encounter Joshua trees, spring wildflowers and more than a few hawks, eagles and other birds. If you want to get a jump on the ranger's hike, there's a self-guided nature trail that begins near the park's campground. Being so far from city lights, the night skies are great for stargazing, so bring your star maps, telescopes and imaginations. Red Rock Canyon State Park is located about 25 miles northeast of Mojave on Highway 14.

For information, contact Red Rock Canyon State Park; (805) 942-0662.

Mitchell Caverns Natural Preserve Tours

Mid-September to mid-June **S** Ⓒ
10 a.m., 1:30 p.m. & 3 p.m. weekends & holidays;
1:30 p.m. weekdays
(see #7 on map page 463)

You have to drive seemingly forever across the desert in order to get to these limestone caves, which are part of Providence Mountains State Recreation Area. Now, you definitely don't want to come here in the middle of summer, but fall and spring can't be beat in this magical land. The tours through the caves are led by a ranger, and going on one of the 90-minute tours is the only way to get in. Only 25 people are allowed on each tour, and on holiday weekends the tours can fill up pretty quickly, so you might want to get your tickets early in the day. If you've got a group of 10 or more folks, please call the park in advance so arrangements can be made. Tour fees are $4 for adults and $2 for kids, ages 6 to 17. Mitchell Caverns is located 100 miles east of Barstow and 17 miles from Interstate 40 on Essex Road.

For information, contact Mojave District Office; (805) 942-0662.

SEASONAL

�֍ ✤ ✤ ✤

Appendices

California's Five Best Fourth of July Fireworks Shows

Undoubtedly, I'll create my own share of fireworks by trying to decide where you'll find the top five fireworks displays in California, especially considering that most communities have some kind of fireworks exhibitions exploding above them. I'll attempt to reduce the large load of complaint mail from those community fathers and mothers who feel that they have the best pyrotechnic display going.

Let's face it, fireworks are fireworks are fireworks. About the only thing that separates one display from another is the length of the show, that grand finale of exploding aerial bombs and the magic of where it's all happening. And these are the things that I've used to decide which shows should be the best in 1995. Oh, one final criterion: Because our forefathers signed the Declaration of Independence on a Thursday, not waiting until Friday or Monday in order to give themselves a three-day weekend, the modern celebration must occur on the Fourth of July in order to be considered here. After all, we've already recast most of our dead presidents' birthdays for our own three-day-weekend convenience. Let's keep the Fourth of July on July 4th.

Except perhaps for the first listing, the remainder aren't in any particular order, mostly because it didn't occur to me 20 or 30 years ago to start traveling to every city, town and block party in California to view and pick the five best Fourth of July fireworks displays for this book. As a consequence, I've been forced to evaluate the occasionally exaggerated claims of some very helpful city chambers of commerce. Based on the above four loosely defined points, what follows is my list of the best five places to view fireworks this coming Fourth of July:

Tahoe City

Take one part high Sierra mountains, add the splash of a cobalt blue lake, toss in at least three parts Fourth of July fireworks and you've got the best place in California to enjoy an incredible evening of celebration. Usually, there are at least three fireworks displays here on the Fourth, but that's due to a little cheating, because two of them are actually held on the Nevada side of the big lake. There's one at South Shore, another at Incline Village, but the biggest is usually held in Tahoe City on the California side. You have a couple of options here for viewing the fireworks. Probably the best view, and certainly the most romantic, is from a boat bobbing gently off shore a couple hundred yards. No boat? There are several piers for viewing the fireworks at Tahoe City, one of the most popular being the public pier at Tahoe State Recreation Area. And all you have to do is to look over either shoulder to catch the shows at Incline Village and South Shore.

Now, there is one drawback to the Tahoe City fireworks and that is the massive traffic jam along the narrow two-lane highways 89 and 28 in town after the show ends. The best thing to do is to hit one of the restaurants or other places that serve liquid libations of various sorts—give the traffic an hour or so to clear.

For information, contact the Tahoe North Visitors & Convention Bureau, P.O. Box 5578, Tahoe City, CA 96145; (916) 583-3494.

San Francisco

Star of stage, screen, musical scores and more, the city, the bay, the Golden Gate...San Francisco is one of those special places that makes you feel alive just being there. And the energy that permeates your soul moves into the night skies on the Fourth of July. There probably isn't a bad place to be for viewing the aerial skyrockets exploding over the bay, but if you want to be really close, try heading out near Pier 39, along Fisherman's Wharf. You should probably get there well before dark if you want the best viewing spot. Another interesting approach might be to stroll out to the middle of the Golden Gate Bridge, although it can get a little cool suspended out there, especially if the summer fog decides to blow in off the Pacific and pay an evening visit to the bay, which could impact your appreciation of the star bursts. If you happen to have a boat, there would probably be nothing finer than to anchor your big schooner in the bay and celebrate the Fourth while sipping a little champagne, kicking back and watching the fun explode above. Come over early to miss the traffic and stay late to enjoy the ambience of Northern California's greatest city.

For information, contact the San Francisco Convention &

Visitors Bureau, P.O. Box 429097, San Francisco, CA 94142-9097; (415) 974-6900.

Santa Barbara

The beautiful Spanish architecture, quiet streets, a broad sandy beach, wonderful weather and a great boardwalk combine to create one of California's most beautiful cities. Add a special fireworks display on the Fourth of July and you've got one especially spectacular sight. Last year was the first time in five years that fireworks had even been exploded over the city's waterfront, but the people here are already planning the 1995 fireworks show and it should be bigger, louder and better than 1994's.

And there's something here that you probably won't see in most fireworks displays. The entire show is synchronized to music. All you have to do is to tune your radio to 99.9 KTYD on the FM dial or 990 KQSB on the AM dial, crank up the volume and enjoy the fireworks in a whole new light.

Where's the best place to watch the show? There's not really a bad place. The wide open beach will be one of the most popular viewing sites and certainly the boardwalk will fill with people early in the evening. Probably, the window tables in the many restaurants that line the boardwalk or Cliff Drive, across from the beach, will be prime viewing locations. What might be interesting is to drive up Highway 154 which rises rapidly from the beach-level city. From not too far up, there are some spectacular views of Santa Barbara and the channel waters.

Wherever you decide to set up for an evening of exploding fire and light, you ought to get here early. Better yet, spend the day in one of California's oldest towns. Museums, the boardwalk and city shops, the courthouse, mission and presidio are all open to public and well worth the time to visit.

Before the show you can enjoy a few other activities including an eclectic car show and a parade.

For information, contact SPARKLE (Santa Barbara Patriotic Association for the Return of Kabooms and Light for Everyone), (805) 962-9926; or call the Santa Barbara Chamber of Commerce, (805) 965-3021.

Cal Expo, Sacramento

This might seem like a strange place to see fireworks, the California Exposition and State Fair site, but it has consistently had one of the biggest and best programs I've ever seen. It generally had more massive aerials bombs, shot off over a longer period of time, than you can imagine. In most fireworks displays, there's always a finale where dozens of aerial rockets are exploded in the last few seconds. At Cal Expo, about the time you think you've seen the finale, it gets even wilder as dozens more of the things streak skyward and explode, spreading their giant sprays of red and gold and green light in 360-degree arcs.

The overall view is great, since the entire show is held near the lake that covers much of the center of the horse racetrack. You can choose to sit either in the grandstand or stand down near the track, although since they are tending to do a lot more of the ground display shows, you may want to try for a seat in the stands.

There are some downsides to the Cal Expo Fourth of July extravaganza. First, you have to pay a few bucks to get inside the racetrack. And each year the promoters try to add more ground-level displays that can't be seen by anyone outside the track bleachers, which is great if you're inside, not so great if you're trying to sneak a view from the huge shopping center a few blocks away or from near Cal Expo's parking lot. A second problem is trying to get out of the parking lot after the show. Suffice to say, simply don't be in a hurry, cause you ain't goin' nowhere for quite some time. But, you ask, is it worth the admission fee to get in and the parking tangle afterward? You bet!

For information, contact California Exposition and State Fair, 1600 Exposition Boulevard, Sacramento, CA 95815; (916) 263-3000.

Long Beach

Long Beach Harbor and the *Queen Mary* have become synonymous since the big luxury ocean liner was made a permanent resident and tourist attraction. If you get to the harbor early in the evening of the Fourth, take the time to enjoy a tour of the ship. There are various displays on board that recall the glory days of Atlantic crossings by the big ship, and there's plenty more to do, like eat and shop, either aboard the ship or in the adjacent Queen Mary Marketplace. If you decide to watch the fireworks display from the ship, better find a vacant spot along the railing fairly early, or else you may have a little problem. Now, fireworks are exploded over the harbor every Saturday evening during summer (at least that's what the city is tentatively planning), but there's a special Fourth of July spectacular that is the best of their pyrotechnics shows of the summer season. Like many of the other best places to watch fireworks, there's a harbor where, if you happen to own your own boat, you can float the evening show away bobbing quietly directly below the not-so-quiet exploding rockets. It'll cost you about $7 for adults to get aboard the *Queen Mary* and there's another $5 fee for a special behind-the-scenes tour of the big boat. Or you can pay $4 for a special audio tour. Maybe the best thing to do is to book one of the 365 staterooms for the night. The *Queen Mary* is located in the Queen Mary Seaport, which is located at 1126 Queen's Highway, near the south end of the Long Beach Freeway (Interstate 710).

For information, contact the Long Beach Area Visitor and Convention Bureau, One World Trade Center, Suite 300, Long Beach, CA 90831-0300; (310) 436-3645. For *Queen Mary* information, contact (310) 435-3511.

California's Ten Best Food FEASTivals

If you had to think of the one thing that truly represents California, it's unlikely you could. Well, it's unlikely that your choice would gain the consensus of any group of people, at least any group larger than yourself and your own alter ego. Cars, beaches, mountains, weird hair, weird clothes, San Francisco, Los Angeles, Hollywood...the list could fill this book, but I'll refrain. But consider a scientific survey of Japanese tourists visiting California which was conducted a couple of years back. One of the questions asked was what they remembered most about California. Did they answer the Golden Gate Bridge? Half Dome in Yosemite? Disneyland? Nope! Their overwhelming response was—oranges. Big, fat, orange oranges.

So, based on the fact that most people love to eat, as evidenced by the large numbers of pleasantly plump folks wiggling in and out of restaurants, and the only slightly smaller number of folks who exercise like crazy so that they can continue eating whatever they please, I have chosen food as the number-one, *ichi ban,* symbol of California's heart, soul and stomach.

Instead of attempting to choose one food, like all those Japanese tourists did, I'll choose the top 10 foods, based entirely on the fact that if a community is crazy enough to create a festival to honor their favorite, locally produced food, then it's probably a pretty significant and memorable representative of California. (Or maybe not, depending upon your tastes.) Of course, there are literally dozens of other food feastivals that are held out there, most of which I didn't mention on the list. Here's a short list of the agricultural also-rans: Cantaloupes, beans, onions, mushrooms, grapefruit, corn, cherries and strawberries—they all have their champions, some more than one champion. If your favorite didn't make it in the list of 10 this year, there's always hope that you'll see it in the next edition. In the meantime, here's the 1995 selection of California's 10 best food feastivals:

Yuba City Prune Festival

Second weekend in September **S** *• 10 a.m. to 7 p.m.*

This is not a sit-in by old folks with irregularity hoping for the miracle cure. Prunes are good. Just ask any of the 25,000 or more people who show up here for this weekend of free-flowing food, fun and musical notes. While the focus is supposed to be on prunes, and indeed there is much ado about prunes (ranging from an educational prune pavilion to a gourmet prune station), there's lots more going on. While not everything had been set when these words were written, some of what was offered at the 1994 Prune Festival is a good example of what will be seen again in 1995. Dixieland jazz was in abundance, featuring such luminaries as Igor's Jazz Cowboys, the Natural Gas Jazz Band, Hot Frogs and the Blue Street Jazz Band. But, since a dark brown, shriveled little fruit is the focus, you can also enjoy celebrity chefs, a farmers market, exotic foods and beverages, wine tasting and something they call Tastes of the Valley, which is lots of ethnic food and dancing. The cost is $6 for adults, $5 for seniors and $4 for kids ages 6 to 12.

The Prune Festival is held at the Yuba-Sutter Fairgrounds, 442 Franklin Avenue in Yuba City.

For information, contact the California Prune Festival, P.O. Box 3006, Yuba City, CA 95992; (916) 673-3436.

Stockton Asparagus Festival

Fourth weekend in April **S** *) • Friday 1 p.m. to 7 p.m.; Saturday and Sunday 10 a.m. to 7 p.m.*

California's great green God smiled upon Stockton and proclaimed it the Asparagus Capital of the World. Most kids seem to scrunch up their faces at vegetables in general and at icky little green spears of asparagus in particular. But for those of us who love this spring vegetable, there is more than enough to make anyone green with envy, especially if the anyone happens to be stuck living in a place like Montana, where it's probably still snowing this time of year. Join the 100,000 or so other people who show up here each year and wrap your lips around such mouth-watering favorites as asparagus pasta, a beef-n-asparagus sandwich, deep fried asparagus, asparagus stir fry and just plain asparagus.

When you finally can't eat anymore, then you can work it all off wandering through the art and crafts fair, admiring the beautiful automobiles in the Asparagus Festival Concours d'Elegance, or enjoying a fun run, a children's entertainment pavilion and strolling entertainment. After all that, it's time to head back for a little asparagus ice cream.

Get here early, because although there is plenty of parking on the flattened farm field across the road from the park where the festival is held, it gets pretty dusty at the far reaches of the makeshift, dirt parking lot. The cost is $6 for adults and $3 for kids and seniors.

The festival is held in Stockton's Oak Grove Regional Park, north of Stockton. Take the Eight Mile Road exit off Interstate 5.

For information, contact the Stockton-San Joaquin Convention and Visitors Bureau, 46 West Fremont Street, Stockton, CA 95202; (209) 943-1987.

Apple Hill Apple Festival

August through October 🅢 📞 · *10 a.m. to 5 p.m. daily*

This is one of those festivals that seems to go on and on and on. Actually, it's not so much a festival as a two- or three-month ripening of different varieties of apples. There are a couple dozen apple ranches covering the few thousand acres that have become collectively known as Apple Hill. Each year, all of these apple ranches keep trying to outdo one another with more happenings, especially when it comes to the subject of apple-related foods, crafts booths and apple-picking opportunities.

Picking your own apples is more than half the fun of going, but if you're not into manual labor, you can certainly choose to grab a bagful, a couple of bushel boxes or an entire truckload, if you like. But if you just walk in and buy a box of them, you miss out on the pure pleasure of plucking a big, bright red apple from the tree and taking a giant bite from some of the juiciest, sweetest fruit in California's foothills. And don't be surprised if you go home feeling a little ill after consuming apple pie, apple turnovers, apple cookies, caramel apples, apple cider and plain old apples.

If you get ambitious and decide to purchase lots of apples, because you plan on peeling and canning or freezing them as apple slices, apple sauce or apple butter, better get yourself one of those automatic apple peelers, slicers and core removers. They cost less than $20, work really slick and are sold all over Apple Hill.

The festival, as it is, is most active on weekends until fall, usually October, when the last of the apples are harvested and shipped away. You'll find different varieties of apples, from red and golden delicious and Arkansas blacks to Gravenstein and pippins, peaking in availability during the season as they ripen.

For information, contact the Apple Hill Growers, P.O. Box 494, Camino, CA 95709; (916) 644-7692.

Patterson Apricot Fiesta

June 3 & 4, 1995 **S** (/) • *Saturday 6 a.m. to dusk; Sunday 6 a.m. to 5 p.m.*

Either you love 'em or you hate 'em. These slimy little orangish-colored nuggets have never really gained the popular worldwide support of California oranges. In time, who knows? Obviously, the people of Patterson have learned to love apricots, because 1995 will mark the 25th year the San Joaquin Valley community has celebrated the sweet fruit.

You'll have fun getting your fill of fresh and dried apricots, apricot jam, apricot pies, apricot ice cream and apricot yogurt. And just in case you want to be reminded of the little fruits during winter when they aren't available fresh, you can take home apricot coffee mugs, apricot wine glasses, apricot beer mugs, apricot T-shirts, apricot magnets, apricot tote bags, and if you still haven't had enough, grab yourself an apricot cookbook so you can create your own apricot delectable.

If there is someone in your group who isn't particularly predisposed to slurping down nice, ripe apricots, there's a lot of other actvities going on. There are hot-air balloons and a horseshoe-tossing tournament on Saturday morning, as well as a petting zoo and dunking booth for kids in the afternoon and fireworks at night. What else might you expect? Well, over the two days, there will probably also be bingo, food booths (including foods other than apricots), a parade, barbecue, firemen's muster and a skydiving exhibition.

The town of 9,000 people create a great atmosphere for the 20,000 people who come to the Apricot Festival each year. The Apricot Capital of the World closes off their downtown "circle" to traffic so you can walk to everything without having to dodge cars. Hay bales are scattered about for seating, so there's plenty of resting places. Best of all, there's no admission fee to the fiesta. Patterson is located south of Tracy, just off Interstate 5. Take the Patterson exit, which is Sperry Avenue, then drive east three miles to town.

For information, contact the Patterson Apricot Fiesta, P.O. Box 442, Patterson, CA 95363; (209) 892-3118.

Holtville Carrot Festival
February 4 through 12, 1995 **S** *(C)* • *daily*

Bugs Bunny made carrots famous, but who would have thought that someone would create a festival for a lowly orange root with a frilly green top knot? Thousands of dieters have learned to despise the many pounds of carrots they eat yearly, in spite of the fact that they really taste good and are good for you. Many of us eat carrots only because Mom said they'd make us see better at night, or something like that.

The best way to describe most people's approaches to cooking carrots is, well, boring. For too many people, it creates brain pain to imagine more than one or two ways to cook a carrot. Most people boil them to mush, while others simply toss them in a stew. A few folks may get fancy and steam them, or cut them into fancy little shapes to brighten a green salad.

One of the best things about food feastivals like this one is that folks tend to get real creative and discover more incredibly wild and delicious gastronomical presentations of that silly wabbit's favorite food than you can possibly imagine. But, should you be able to imagine another recipe, there's a special carrot cooking contest that could be right up your alley.

For those with taste buds wanting a little more sustenance than a bulky vegetable, there's also a rib cook-off. Sounds like a reasonably balanced meal headin' your way.

The whole festival happens in Holtville, which is located just off Interstate 8, 117 miles east of San Diego, and off Highway 115, nine miles east of El Centro.

For information, contact the Holtville Chamber of Commerce, P.O. Box 185, Holtville, CA 92250; (619) 356-2923.

Garlic Festival

Last weekend in July 🟢 ⌓ • *Friday 10 a.m. to 7 p.m.; Saturday and Sunday 9 a.m. to 5 p.m.*

If you like garlic, then Gilroy is the place to be. The self-proclaimed Garlic Capital of the World, this little town of a few thousand grows to over 135,000 over the course of the three-day festival. And while there are the typical quality crafts vendors, music and dancing at the Garlic Squeeze Barn Dance, the star of the show is the highly esteemed, lowly garlic. During the three days of the festival, over four tons of garlic will be ground, squeezed, cooked and eaten.

If the wind happens to be blowing from the right direction as you approach town, you can smell the garlic long before you reach the first sumptuous bites of garlic delicacies. When you wander through Gourmet Alley, you'll have an opportunity to gorge yourself on an endless mountain of garlic bread and huge slabs of beef with rosemary mops dunked in garlic marinade. And of course, there's always the weird stuff like garlic ice cream and the Tour de Garlique bicycle tour.

For the kids, Herbie's Garlic Kids Club is a special place where the youngsters can enjoy music, games and food, even some special non-garlic food for those who have yet to acquire a taste for the pungent bulb.

If you happen to feel that you've developed, or stolen, the best darn garlic recipe anyone has ever tasted, then you have an obligation to enter the garlic recipe cook-off. Original and unpublished recipes are submitted and the top eight finalists are chosen to participate in a cook-off. First prize, in addition to overnight accommodations, is $1,000, with second place receiving $500 and third place netting $300. If you feel the need to enter the recipe contest, call the festival office well in advance at (408) 842-1625 for submission rules and deadlines. Gilroy is located 30 miles south of San Jose on US 101. Once you're in Gilroy, just follow the signs to the southwest edge of town for the festival. The admission may change, but it will probably set you back about $7 for Friday and $8 on Saturday and Sunday. Admission is $2 for kids and seniors on any of the three days.

For more information, contact the Gilroy Garlic Festival Association, P.O. Box 2311, Gilroy, CA 95021; (408) 842-1625.

Orange Blossom Festival

April 22 & 23, 1995 Ⓢ✆ • *Saturday 10 a.m. to 8:30 p.m.; Sunday 10 a.m. to 5 p.m.*

The very first Orange Day Parade was held in downtown Riverside 100 years ago. Why Riverside? It kind of depends on who you talk to. Obviously, the area's fertile soil, perfect weather and the fact that irrigated land was available were some of the biggest reasons for the growth of the orange and citrus industry in Riverside. Another reason was the convincing promotion of the area orchestrated by land speculators. Whatever the reasons, with land for miles around Riverside covered with the sweet-smelling scent of orange blossoms, the clean air, beautiful views of the surrounding snowcapped mountains and the opportunity to become rich growing oranges, who wouldn't have wanted to live here 100 years ago? And people did get rich. For a time, Riverside was the wealthiest city per capita in the nation.

A few things have changed during the past 100 years. The air is not always as clear as it once was, although it still has its picture-postcard days, and a lot of the orange groves have succumbed to the steady creep of urban sprawl. But the folks in Riverside are still celebrating the navel orange and the impact it had on Southern California's agricultural empire in general and on Riverside's growth specifically.

The Orange Blossom Festival weekend kicks off with a citrus parade downtown, then moves on to a country fair, children's programs, steam train rides, art exhibits and fireworks. While much of the weekend activity is focused around Riverside's historic Mission Inn, you must take the antique trolley out to California Citrus State Historic Park for additional festivities, including a special citrus breakfast on Sunday morning. And, unlike downtown Riverside, there are still plenty of orange trees growing at the state park. So come on over to Riverside and have a great time immersed in the sweetness of California oranges.

Riverside is located about 60 miles east of Los Angeles, off highways 60 and 91.

For information, contact the Riverside Visitor and Convention Bureau, 3443 Orange Street, Riverside, CA 92501; (909) 787-7950.

16th Annual Selma Raisin Festival

May 11 to 14, 1995 🝓 🝓 • *daily*

You can buy raisins by the box in grocery stores or find them in your breakfast cereal, but the best place to go for raisins is the Central Valley town of Selma. Every time I've driven past the off ramp that leads to Selma, I've thought of Selma, Alabama and the history that surrounds that town, not shriveled grapes. But it's those shriveled seedless grapes that Selma, California is probably best known for. And the folks of Selma really know how to celebrate their little, dried brown fruit.

If you like raisins, then you really don't want to miss one of the kickoff events, which is Thursday evening's Gourmet Row. If you think that raisins only come in certain breakfast cereals, then you're in for a real surprise and some great taste-tempting delights. It'll cost you about $5 to get into Gourmet Row, but once inside, you'll get to sample the best raisin-filled dishes that all the participating restaurants can devise. Judges will be on hand to determine winners of such categories as "most innovative use of raisins" and "most outstanding raisin dish." You can even cast your own ballot for your favorite raisin dish, which will be given the "people's choice" award. Some past winners have been a raisin flan and a raisin betty crisp.

If you've got your own favorite raisin recipe, there's also a contest for your own cookies, cakes, pies and breads. Most of the categories must contain at least one-half cup of raisins. The first evening is capped off with the crowning of the festival's queen, the Raisin Royalty. The festival also features a parade, walk-a-thons, runs, arts and crafts, lots of food, a carnival, dance exhibitions, art and photography contests, and much, much more.

The many events are held in various locations in Selma, which is located about 14 miles south of Fresno and 20 miles north of Visalia, just off Highway 99.

For information, contact the Selma District Chamber of Commerce, 1802 Tucker Street, Selma, CA 93662; (209) 896-3315.

Half Moon Bay Pumpkin Festival

October 14 & 15, 1995 **S** *(*) • 10 a.m. to 5 p.m.*

Unless you're a gardener or farmer who pulls out the pumpkin seeds for planting in early summer, there are really only two other times of the year when you think about pumpkins. If we skip the Christmas pumpkin pies, then October is the most popular time of year for chasing after these big orange squashes. A week or so before Halloween, we haul the kids out to the local citified version of a pumpkin patch where someone has laid out a couple hundred of the orange balls on some vacant city street corner. The slightly more adventurous drive out to the country where the big orange squashes are actually grown. But people who want the most fun pack up the kids and car and head over to Half Moon Bay's October festival.

Ghosts, goblins and jack-o-lanterns are just part of Half Moon Bay's festival of the pumpkin. The real stars here are such gastronomical delights as pumpkin everything: pie, ice cream, strudel, crêpes, bread, muffins, plus a few new concoctions created annually just to test the fortitude of the human digestive tract. If the kids are into pumpkins, but you hate the big squashes, there's plenty of other food available, including non-pumpkin linguica, tacos, artichokes and a wide selection of beverages designed to help with the smooth transition of food from hand to mouth to gullet. There's plenty of entertainment and lots of artisan vendors.

Beyond the food, there's the Great Pumpkin Parade, a masquerade ball on Saturday night, a 10K fun run and, if you just can't get enough pumpkin, several pumpkin pie-eating contests. There are also pumpkin carving demonstrations and a haunted house filled with spooky witches, goblins, ghosts and ghouls.

For backyard pumpkin growers, you can bring your prized pumpkins, just the really big ones, into town a week early for the great pumpkin weigh-off held on October 9. Now, before you go to all the trouble to load that special, steroid-pumped 300-pound monster you've created in your backyard into the backseat of your Honda in hopes of cashing in on some of the $5,000 in prize money that's offered, think again. The winner of the 1993 weigh-off was an import monster from Puyallup, Washington that nearly broke the scales with its 740-pound heft. If you want to impress your neighbors, you can get your picture taken with the 1995 winning pumpkin.

The festival is not held in a farmer's field, but on a half-mile stretch of Main Street between Miramontes and Spruce streets in the historic downtown section of Half Moon Bay, which is located about 20 miles south of San Francisco on Highway 1. The festival is free and the weather should be cool.

For information, contact the Half Moon Bay Art & Pumpkin Festival, P.O. Box 274, Half Moon Bay, CA 94019; (415) 726-9652 or (415) 726-3491.

Castroville Artichoke Festival

September 16 & 17, 1995 🅂🄲 • *10 a.m. to 4 p.m.*

If you've ever driven through the Castroville area on your way to or from Monterey, you'll understand why the little coastal town refers to itself as the Artichoke Capital of the World. Mile after mile of artichoke bushes fill the fields and there's plenty of places to stop and buy fresh artichokes, deep-fried artichoke hearts, pickled artichokes and probably a few more artichoke delicacies that you've never heard of.

The two-day festival attracts over 40,000 people, most of whom love eating the prickly little green vegetables that are more tough, stringy leaves than edible parts. But that fact doesn't stop people from participating in the artichoke-eating contest. Since most of the thing isn't edible, what you have to do in five minutes is to eat as much of the carefully weighed pile of artichokes set out in front of you as you can. Your refuse is then weighed and the person who has eaten the most is declared the winner.

For those who like to use their imaginations while cooking, there's an artichoke recipe cook-off with cash prizes for the winners. Should you decide to enter the competition, you'll be competing against the likes of the 1992 winner, which was Middle East Lamb Balls in Artichoke Cups with Yogurt Sauce. So go ahead and give it your best shot.

You'll also find all the other things that make a food festival a food festival. An artichoke queen is crowned and there's an arts and crafts show, music and a pancake breakfast. On Sunday, two fun runs, a 5K and a 10K, are scheduled to begin at 7:30 a.m. for those ambitious early risers. The Sunday parade will begin at about 9:30 a.m., with the remainder of the programs and stage events concluding at 4 p.m.

For information, contact the Castroville Artichoke Festival, P.O. Box 1041, Castroville, CA 95012; (408) 633-2465.

California's Five Weirdest Events

Doo Dah Parade

Sunday following Thanksgiving Day **S** *⌀* • *Starts at noon*

This wacky event began in Pasadena as a spoof on the city's annual New Year's Day Rose Parade, although some surmise that it began when a few smog-crazed wackos escaped from the local sanitarium and decided to do something anti-establishment to keep themselves busy. A few words of caution about this one: While most of the parade is just plain fun, you may want to cover your eyes, or your kids' eyes, when a float that is a replica of a throat-slashing execution, complete with squirting blood, passes by. You also might encounter the woman "boob tube," a television set mounted over her chest tuning in a pair of bodacious, bogus bare boobs, or a flock of stuffed seagulls passing overhead, spewing out what appears to be, and hopefully isn't, white seagull exhaust.

On the more wholesome side, you can also hope to catch the Briefcase Precision Drill Team as they march down the street in their black suits and ties, stopping to perform precision military rifle-like drills with their black briefcases. In fact, most of these attaché twirlers are real-life, high-level bank executives. It just goes to show you that the weirdness in Southern California isn't restricted to just the younger generation.

Get here early in order to get a good seat, although you don't have to show up a full two days early like you would for the Rose Parade. An hour or two is usually adequate. Bring your camera and hope that the film isn't confiscated by your local one-hour lab owner and given to the District Attorney as evidence that a very deranged person is running around town doing some really bizarre things. Expect to have a really good time.

You really need to call in September to check on the date for 1995, because it may be moved back to October and it could always begin at 10 a.m. instead of noon.

For information, contact Pasadena Doo Dah, P.O. Box 2392, Pasadena, CA 91102; (818) 796-2591.

APPENDICES

Banana Slug Derby

August 19, 1995 **S** *⚲* • *Noon to 3 p.m.*

In the far northwestern reaches of California, what do folks do with all that spare time on their hands? Well, they race banana slugs. If you've never heard of a banana slug, you're not alone. You must have spent time wandering the trails in those dripping, damp redwood forests to have run across these giant yellowish slugs creepy-crawling their way up a tree or across a rotting stump or trying to play squish between your hiking boot and the forest duff trail.

Why would people purposely go out and capture these six-inch-long slimy banana-looking things just to race them? There's no profit in it. There's no exciting sprint to the finish line. You can't claim racing-breed pedigree and rent your winning entry out to procreate. You can't eat them, or at least you wouldn't want to. About the only reason to race banana slugs that's left is for the sheer glory of it. Winners in different age categories walk away with hand-made trophies and little else, except for their pride. And I imagine that these trophies decorate the mantels of many a good home.

They've been holding these races for 27 years at Prairie Creek Redwoods State Park and about 350 competitors show up annually. You get to wander through an ancient redwood forest, capture one or two banana slugs for the big race day, then cheer your entry on as it slimes its way out of the circle faster than its competitors. All in all, it makes for a major once-in-a-lifetime adventure.

After the race, it's only right that you return your entry to the forest. And remember to wash the slime off your hands before you eat dinner—believe me, banana slug slime is some really tough slime to scrub off.

Prairie Creek Redwoods State Park is located about 50 miles north of Eureka or six miles north of Orick, just off US 101. In late summer, the weather should be foggy in the morning, clearing in the afternoon, unless it rains, which isn't too likely in August. If you aren't already camping in the park, you'll have to pay the park vehicle day-use entry fee of $5. The races are free. Make camping reservations by calling MISTIX at (800) 444-7275, up to eight weeks in advance.

For information, contact Prairie Creek Redwoods State Park, (707) 488-2171.

Angels Camp Jumping Frog Jubilee & Calaveras County Fair

May 18, 19, 20 & 21, 1995 **S** 🖊 *• Starts at 8 a.m.*

Now why would I include as one of the weirdest events taking place in California each year something that has become a venerable Gold Country tradition? Think about this for a moment. First, the entire event is based on what was a tall tale (read fabrication) written by Mark Twain, whose own name was a clever fabrication, all for the purpose of making a buck or two off a bunch of gullible Easterners willing to pay good money for anything written about the weird things that gold-hungry prospectors did for entertainment. And it worked.

And it's still working. You, being of unsound mind, go out to some slimy pond to chase and capture an even slimier frog. Then, if you're doing this according to what the expert frog jumpers recommend, you keep your little frog locked up in a dark box so it doesn't start becoming overly fond of people (fat chance). Then you pay a parking fee, an entry fee to get into the Calaveras County Fairgrounds and yet another fee for the privilege of dumping your freaked-out, slimy green prisoner onto a carpet of fake green grass. To inspire the greatest possible leap, you are forced to jump up and down like some crazed maniacal frog-hater, trying to scare the bumps off this little, defenseless froggy. You scream, you yell, you threaten the little froggy with great bodily harm. All the while, a large audience of well-wishers cheers and jeers you and your frog on. After you've convinced your frog to take three of his most powerful leaps, you grab Kermit and go home, in victory or ignomious defeat. Life is good...and weird. And to think that thousands of people do this for four, fun-filled days each year.

If you want to participate, but just can't bring yourself to do it in person, you can send your entry fee and the fair will bring in a substitute frog jockey to race either your personal frog that you've overnighted to the event, or one they've selected from the communal frog farm.

Now, if your frog happens to win, you can pocket a quick $750, or stuff your pockets really full with $5,000 if you frighten your frog enough so that it beats the current world-record triple jump of 21.5 feet. All in all, this is actually a fun, entertaining, adventurous and potentially profitable event for the entire family. Oh, and there's lots more than just a bunch of crazy frog jumpers. This is also the Calaveras County Fair, featuring all the things that make county fairs so much fun.

Frog Town is located at the Calaveras County Fairgrounds at the south end of Angels Camp, just off Highway 49. Fair entry fees range from $7 to $9 (in 1994) for adults, $2 less for kids under 12. Parking is $2 and it costs $3 for each frog entered into competition, be it your own or one of the borrowed slimers. The weather's almost always warm and dry for frog days.

For information, contact the Calaveras County Fair & Jumping Frog Jubilee, P.O. Box 96, Angels Camp, CA 95222; (209) 736-2561.

World Championship Great Arcata-to-Ferndale Cross-Country Kinetic Sculpture Race

May 27, 28 & 29, 1995 🅢🖉 · *Saturday noon till Monday evening*

The Kinetic Sculpture Race is probably not as weird as it is bizarre, although if you ask Webster the lexicographer, not Webster the spider web swabber, there's really not much difference between the two words. If you feel the urge to expend your creative and physical energies in designing, building and racing a contraption that, while not necessarily street legal or safe, is capable of being propelled by your feet or arms or both, by a single person or multiple bodies, over land and sea at dangerously breakneck speeds, then maybe you have what it takes to enter this ultimate test of zaniness.

While speed is needed to win this race, it is the artistry of the weird and creative mind that makes it so much fun to watch. Pedal power is used to propel creations that would pass as great, bad B-movie monsters over sand, streets, dirt roads, mud and even water. You'll see everything from giant worms and snakes to monster crabs with legs big enough to keep you in crab Louie for years. The race is spread out over three days, starting in Arcata, traveling south through Eureka, across Humboldt Bay, over the Eel River and finally finishing in the restored Victorian town of Ferndale.

If there were a large monetary prize for winning this race, then one might understand why so many people are driven to spend hundreds, and in some cases even thousands, of dollars to design and construct a major, weird, creature-like contraption and spend three days racing it against others of the same ilk. But that's not the case. There is no major cash prize for the winner. It's all for the glory, just for the glory. And local glory at that. Unless, of course, the winner happens to be from out of town and has enough clout to convince the editor of his or her hometown newspaper to run a news story on such a remarkably weird exploit.

Actually, there are a few entry category prizes for such things as art, engineering, speed, costumes and sound effects emitted by these creatures. And to prove that this is no ordinary competition, there's the coveted Medeocar Award for the sculpture that finishes dead middle.

Arcata/Eureka is located about 240 miles north of San Francisco on US 101. The competition will cost about $15 per pilot and is free to spectators, but call to confirm.

For information contact the Ferndale Chamber of Commerce, P.O. Box 325, Ferndale, CA 95536, (707) 786-4477; or Kinetic Sculpture Race, Inc., (707) 725-3851.

Bay to Breakers Footrace

May 21, 1995 🅢 🉐 • *8 a.m. to 1 p.m.*

San Francisco, like many large cities, has it's collection of fun-loving, flamboyant, sometimes eccentric people who help to make it the great and fun city it is. These are the ones who are generally viewed as being a little too "different" by those folks living in places far from the cutting edge or in places without an overabundance of on-ramps to the Information Super Highway.

The 12-kilometer (7.5-mile) Bay to Breakers Footrace starts in downtown San Francisco and winds through town, out to Ocean Beach. You don't have to be a city dweller to participate. Many eccentric, let-it-all-hang-out types show up, some traveling great distances to compete. In an athletic sense, this is not a competitive, push-it-til-you-drop footrace. People dress up in outrageous costumes—you might spot a pair of cows out of Gary Larson's Far Side cartoon or a chiropractic office running as a spinal column—and, in some instances, dress down. (Don't be shocked if you flash on a streaker or two.)

Considering some of the costumes and the sense of fun that permeates the thousands-strong crowd of runners, walkers, crawlers and paraders, being the first to cross the finish line is not first on most people's minds. It's more to see and be seen and to take in the communal wackiness. As everyone straggles into the finish line, there's food and drink and musical entertainment to enjoy.

You don't have to be different, whatever that is, or wear something other than normal jogging clothes to run the Bay to Breakers, but then why wouldn't you want to?

For information about the start time and location, contact the *San Francisco Examiner* Bay to Breakers Footrace, (415) 777-7770.

Leftovers

Many things—soups, beans, stews—are better the second time around. The kinds of events listed as leftovers here aren't necessarily food events. Because they are not necessarily outdoor events, which are the primary focus of this book, they haven't been given complete listings. Still, I thought you should be made aware of a few hundred other things to do during the year, just in case you and yours happen to be looking for something different to do. For the most part, they're just fun things for individuals and families to enjoy on weekends. While most of these events have been offered in the past, a few of the sponsoring parties were slow or noncommittal in confirming the continuation of their specialties for 1995, so, always, always, *always* call and confirm the date, the time and the fact that they exist. The blurbs below include only the briefest of mini-previews, mostly for the benefit of the programs and events that have titles that say nothing about what to expect. While something called "Jonesville Hang Gliding Festival" might be self-explanatory, with a "Jonesville Septemberfest" you don't know what to expect.

North Coast Leftovers

Clam Beach Fun Run
When: January 4, 1995, tentatively
What to expect: Run from Trinidad to Clam Beach with awards and T-shirts
Who to contact: Eureka/Humboldt County Convention & Visitors Bureau, (800) 338-7352

Old-Time Fiddle Contest
When: January 21, 1995
What to expect: Lots of fiddlin' around by some of the best
Who to contact: Cloverdale Historical Society, (707) 894-2067

Victorian Village Mysteries

When: February 3, 4 & 5, 1995
What to expect: Be the sleuth who solves the mystery crime in the
Victorian town of Ferndale
Who to contact: Ferndale Chamber of Commerce, (707) 786-4477

Cloverdale Citrus Fair

When: February 10 to 13, 1995
What to expect: Oranges and other citrus delights to savor
Who to contact: Cloverdale Citrus Fair, (707) 894-3992

Guerneville Fiesta Italiana Crab Feed

When: February 11, 1995
What to expect: Lots of food, but crab is the featured star
Who to contact: Guerneville Rotary Club, (707) 869-0623

Celebration of Black History Month

When: February, date not set
What to expect: Food and exhibits of African American contributions
in California and the U.S.
Who to contact: Yountville, Domaine Chandon Winery, (707) 944-8844

A Taste of Main Street

When: March 23, 1995, tentatively
What to expect: A dozen restaurants in Eureka to tour and sample food
Who to contact: Eureka/Humboldt County Convention & Visitors
Bureau, (800) 338-7352

Redwood Coast Dixieland Jazz Festival

When: March 24, 25 & 26, 1995, tentatively
What to expect: Big bands, jam sessions and Dixieland jazz groups
Who to contact: Eureka/Humboldt County Convention & Visitors
Bureau, (800) 338-7352

Sonoma County Folk Festival

When: Second and third weekends in March
What to expect: Wine tasting, plenty of food and musical and dancing
entertainment
Who to contact: Santa Rosa Chamber of Commerce, (707) 545-1414

Fort Bragg Whaler Beer Fest
When: Fourth Saturday in March
What to expect: Microbrewers and their followers offering good beer and great seafood
Who to contact: Fort Bragg Chamber of Commerce, (800) 726-2780

Crescent City Fiddle Contest
When: First Weekend in April
What to expect: The best fiddle players from the West competing, followed with a barbecue and dance
Who to contact: Crescent City Chamber of Commerce, (800) 343-8300

Apple Blossom Festival
When: First weekend in April
What to expect: Blossoms galore, a parade, a fun run and entertainment
Who to contact: Sebastopol Chamber of Commerce, (707) 823-3032

Bodega Bay Fishermen's Festival
When: Third Sunday in April
What to expect: Decorated boats in a water parade, the blessing of the fleet and kite flying
Who to contact: Bodega Bay Chamber of Commerce, (707) 875-3422

Petaluma Butter & Egg Days Parade
When: Last Saturday in April
What to expect: All kinds of rich food to sample and butter churning
Who to contact: Petaluma Chamber of Commerce, (707) 762-2785

Bicycle Tour of the Unknown Coast
When: May 7,1995, tentatively
What to expect: California's toughest century race, with events for all ages, leaving from Humboldt County Fairgrounds
Who to contact: Eureka/Humboldt County Convention & Visitors Bureau, (800) 338-7352

Windsor Day Festival
When: Second Saturday in May
What to expect: Entertainment and food, featuring a catsup cook-off contest
Who to contact: Windsor Chamber of Commerce, (707) 838-7285

Arcata BeBop & Brew
When: May, Mother's Day
What to expect: Combines jazz bands and 25 microbrewery beers from Western states
Who to contact: Arcata Chamber of Commerce, (707) 822-3619

Willits Community Festival & Collector's Car Show
When: Third Saturday in May
What to expect: Fine old cars, wine and good food
Who to contact: Willits Chamber of Commerce, (707) 459-4113

Russian River Wine Festival
When: Sunday following Mother's Day in May
What to expect: Jazz for the ear and wine for the palate
Who to contact: Healdsburg Chamber of Commerce, (800) 648-9922

Clearlake 1950s Car Show
When: First weekend in June
What to expect: A period-dress dance, wine tasting, crafts booths and old cars
Who to contact: Lakeport Chamber of Commerce, (707) 263-5092

Pony Express Days
When: First weekend in June
What to expect: Food, crafts and celebration of this one-time stop for the Pony Express
Who to contact: McKinleyville Chamber of Commerce, (707) 839-2449

Fish Feed and Art Festival
When: June 11, 1995, tentatively
What to expect: Salmon and whitefish, arts, crafts and more in Trinidad's Town Hall
Who to contact: Eureka/Humboldt County Convention & Visitors Bureau, (800) 338-7352

Crescent City Teddy Bear Picnic
When: A weekend in June
What to expect: Lots of teddy bears, the cuddly kind, for display and sale
Who to contact: Crescent City Chamber of Commerce, (800) 343-8300

Humboldt Folklife Festival
When: Second Saturday in June
What to expect: Music of all sorts celebrating cultures of all sorts
Who to contact: Arcata Chamber of Commerce, (800) 553-6569

Great Grape Stampede
When: Second Saturday in June
What to expect: Grape stompin', grape eatin' and imbibing of fermented
    grape brew
Who to contact: Windsor Chamber of Commerce, (707) 838-7285

48th Annual Rodeo in the Redwoods
When: June 16, 17 & 18, 1995, tentatively
What to expect: Pancake breakfast, rodeo events and more
Who to contact: Eureka/Humboldt County Convention & Visitors
    Bureau, (800) 338-7352

Fifth Annual Arcata Bay Oyster Festival
When: June 17, 1995, tentatively
What to expect: Oyster delicacies presented by 30 local Arcata
    restaurants, with games and music
Who to contact: Eureka/Humboldt County Convention & Visitors
    Bureau, (800) 338-7352

45th Annual Mid-Summer Scandinavian Festival
When: Third weekend in June
What to expect: Summer solstice celebration with a parade, dances,
    food and costumes
Who to contact: Ferndale Chamber of Commerce, (707) 786-4477

Redwood Acres Fair and Rodeo
When: June 21 to 25, 1995, tentatively
What to expect: Fair, rodeo, exhibits, livestock and a carnival in Eureka
Who to contact: Eureka/Humboldt County Convention & Visitors
    Bureau, (800) 338-7352

Art & Jazz on the Lake
When: Fourth weekend in June
What to expect: Crafts, food and entertainment on Benbow Lake
Who to contact: Garberville Chamber of Commerce, (707) 923-2613

Hot Air Balloon Classic
When: Last weekend in June
What to expect: Colorful balloons above, crafts and music on the ground below
Who to contact: Windsor Chamber of Commerce, (707) 838-7285

Mad River Festival
When: July 1 to 31, 1995
What to expect: Music, comedy, puppetry, vaudeville and more at Blue Lake
Who to contact: Eureka/Humboldt County Convention & Visitors Bureau, (800) 338-7352

Arcata Jubilee
When: Fourth of July
What to expect: Crafts, lots of strange and not so strange food, plus fire truck rides and night fireworks
Who to contact: Arcata Chamber of Commerce, (800) 553-6569

Crescent City Fourth of July Celebration
When: Fourth of July
What to expect: Logging show, crafts booths, food and lots of fireworks
Who to contact: Crescent City Chamber of Commerce, (800) 343-8300

World's Largest Salmon BBQ
When: First Saturday in July
What to expect: Lots of music, wine and salmon to munch on down at Noyo Harbor
Who to contact: Fort Bragg Chamber of Commerce, (800) 726-2780

Lake County Rodeo
When: First Saturday in July
What to expect: Rodeo events, along with a dance, barbecue and crafts show
Who to contact: Lakeport Chamber of Commerce, (707) 263-5092

Mendocino Music Festival
When: July 10 through 20, 1995
What to expect: Great music, featuring hippie-ish sounds, in a
beautiful town
Who to contact: Mendocino Chamber of Commerce, (800) 726-2780

Lake County Wine & Food Renaissance
When: Second Saturday in July
What to expect: Great food and wines from some great local wineries
Who to contact: Lakeport Chamber of Commerce, (707) 263-5092

Shakespeare Festival
When: Last weekend in July
What to expect: Works of the great Englander performed beside
Benbow Lake
Who to contact: Garberville Chamber of Commerce, (707) 923-2613

Wildwood Days
When: First weekend in August
What to expect: Lumber mill tour, along with food and a crafts faire
Who to contact: Rio Dell & Scotia Chamber of Commerce,
(707) 764-3436

Klamath Salmon Festival
When: First weekend in August
What to expect: Salmon and other tasty food, boat races, a logging
show and crafts
Who to contact: Klamath Chamber of Commerce, (707) 482-5591

Reggae on the River
When: August 5 & 6, 1995, tentatively
What to expect: The largest outdoor reggae concert in the West,
featuring international bands in Piercy
Who to contact: Eureka/Humboldt County Convention & Visitors
Bureau, (800) 338-7352

Annie & Mary Day
When: August 6, 1995, tentatively
What to expect: Annual celebration with parade, barbecue, a fiddle
contest and crafts at Blue Lake

Who to contact: Eureka/Humboldt County Convention & Visitors Bureau, (800) 338-7352

Santa Rosa Gravenstein Apple Fair
When: Second weekend in August
What to expect: Farm displays, music and apples galore
Who to contact: Sonoma County Farm Trails, (707) 996-2154

Solar Energy Expo & Rally
When: Second weekend in August
What to expect: Solar-powered vehicles, along with food, crafts and music
Who to contact: Willits Chamber of Commerce, (707) 459-4133

Cypress Lane Jazz Festival
When: Third Saturday in August
What to expect: Wine country jazz with wine country refreshments
Who to contact: Windsor Chamber of Commerce, (707) 838-7285

17th Annual Humboldt Folklife Festival
When: August 26, 1995, tentatively
What to expect: Folk music celebration with outdoor stages and ongoing concerts in Arcata
Who to contact: Eureka/Humboldt County Convention & Visitors Bureau, (800) 338-7352

Seafood Festival
When: Labor Day weekend in September
What to expect: Seafood, beer and wine, along with fishing-related exhibits
Who to contact: Crescent City Chamber of Commerce, (800) 343-8300

Sixth Redwood Country Cowboy Classic
When: September 9 & 10, 1995, tentatively
What to expect: Wine, cheese, Senior Pro Rodeo, cowboy poets, barbecue, western dance and art in Eureka
Who to contact: Eureka/Humboldt County Convention & Visitors Bureau, (800) 338-7352

Lakeport Oktoberfest
When: First weekend in October
What to expect: A Wine Country beer event (is that stuff legal here?) with plenty of German food
Who to contact: Lakeport Chamber of Commerce, (707) 263-4936

Shasta Cascade Leftovers

Shasta Dixieland Jazz Festival
When: First weekend in April
What to expect: Lots of jazz bands and other musical treats
Who to contact: Redding Chamber of Commerce, (916) 225-4433

Paul Bunyan Mountain Festival
When: Last weekend in June
What to expect: Country music, country barbecue and country crafts
Who to contact: Westwood Chamber of Commerce, (916) 256-2456

Dunsmuir Railroad Days
When: Third weekend in June
What to expect: Carnival, steam engine demonstrations, music, crafts and more
Who to contact: Dunsmuir Chamber of Commerce, (916) 235-2177

Modoc County Fair
When: Fourth weekend in August
What to expect: Something for just about everybody in this classic small county fair
Who to contact: Cedarville Chamber of Commerce, (916) 233-2819

Red Bluff Arts in the Park
When: First full weekend in September
What to expect: Music, food and, of course, arts and crafts
Who to contact: Red Bluff Chamber of Commerce, (800) 665-6225

Tehama County Museum Jubilee
When: Weekend after Labor Day in September
What to expect: A rare museum jubilee, with fun, food, crafts and tours
Who to contact: Tehama Chamber of Commerce, (916) 384-2251

Sierra Leftovers

Yosemite Chef's Holiday
When: Three weeks in January
What to expect: Great food made by great chefs in a great place
Who to contact: Ahwahnee Hotel, Yosemite National Park, (209) 454-2020

Rainbow Days & Fish Derby
When: April 29, 1995
What to expect: Fish displays plus prizes for kids who catch the largest
    fish, among other categories
Who to contact: Bishop Chamber of Commerce, (619) 873-8405

Bishop Mule Days
When: Memorial Days weekend
What to expect: Mule racing of all sorts, food, crafts and kids' activities
Who to contact: Bishop Chamber of Commerce, (619) 873-8405

Fourth of July Celebration
When: Fourth of July
What to expect: Traditional fun, with mud volleyball and other sports,
    food, crafts and fireworks
Who to contact: Bridgeport Chamber of Commerce, (619) 932-7500

Bishop Fireworks
When: Fourth of July
What to expect: Family activities and nighttime fireworks
Who to contact: Bishop Chamber of Commerce, (619) 873-8405

Loyalton Fourth of July Coming and Going Parade
When: Fourth of July
What to expect: July 4th fun for everyone
Who to contact: Sierra County Chamber of Commerce, (800) 200-4949

Bishop Homecoming and Wild West Junior Rodeo
When: July 8 & 9, 1995, tentatively
What to expect: Rodeo for kids under age 18 only, with barrel racing, dummy roping, goat tying and more
Who to contact: Bishop Homecoming & Junior Rodeo, (619) 873-4404

Eastern Sierra Tri-County Fair
When: Third weekend in July
What to expect: Country music, country cookin' and country crafts
Who to contact: Bishop Chamber of Commerce, (619) 873-8405

Sierraville Western Dance and Rodeo
When: First weekend in August
What to expect: Cowboy stuff and dance for those who can still walk
Who to contact: Sierra County Chamber of Commerce, (800) 200-4949

Rodeo & Tri-County Fair
When: August 30 to September 4, 1995
What to expect: Good times at a real country county fair
Who to contact: Bishop Chamber of Commerce, (619) 873-8405

Wild West Rodeo
When: Labor Day weekend
What to expect: Rodeo, western food, crafts and music
Who to contact: Bishop Chamber of Commerce, (619) 873-8405

Bishop's Fourth Annual Fly-In
When: September 23 & 24, 1995, tentatively
What to expect: Airplane and glider rides, barbecue, vintage military aircraft and entertainment
Who to contact: Bishop Chamber of Commerce, (619) 873-8405

Kernville Stampede Rodeo
When: October 14 & 15, 1995, tentatively

What to expect: Bull riding, bronc busting and all the stuff that goes along with cowboys
Who to contact: Mrs. R. Sanchez, (619) 378-3157

Downieville Holiday on Main Street
When: First Saturday in December
What to expect: Christmas crafts, displays, food and fun
Who to contact: Sierra County Chamber of Commerce, (800) 200-4949

Christmas Parade
When: December 2, 1995, tentatively
What to expect: Angels on horseback, country wagons and Christmas music filling Bishop
Who to contact: Bishop Chamber of Commerce, (619) 873-8405

Gold Country Leftovers

Mariposa Storytelling Festival
When: Last Saturday in January
What to expect: The nation's best storytellers entertain kids and adults
Who to contact: Mariposa Chamber of Commerce, (800) 208-2434

Dandelion Days
When: Third weekend in March
What to expect: Food and fun in the Gold Rush town of Jackson
Who to contact: Calaveras County Visitors Bureau, (209) 736-0049

Rough & Ready Chili Cook-Off
When: First Sunday in April
What to expect: Lots of hot food, hot spices and a hot time
Who to contact: Rough & Ready Chamber of Commerce, (916) 272-4320

Hangtown National Motocross
When: Last weekend in April
What to expect: Extremely popular and wild motorcycle dirt track races
Who to contact: Prairie City Off-Highway-Vehicular Area, (916) 985-7378

Coyote Howl
When: Second weekend in May
What to expect: Howling contest with crafts, games and music
Who to contact: Coulterville Chamber of Commerce, (209) 878-3074

Rough & Ready Secession Days Celebration
When: Fourth Saturday in June
What to expect: Activities, food and fun celebrating the three months that this little town seceded from the government's taxes
Who to contact: Rough & Ready Chamber of Commerce, (916) 272-4320

Folsom Rodeo and Fireworks
When: Fourth of July
What to expect: Rodeo, food, country music and fireworks
Who to contact: Folsom Chamber of Commerce, (916) 985-2698

Downieville Fourth of July
When: Fourth of July
What to expect: Daytime crafts fair, nighttime fireworks and a dance
Who to contact: Sierra County Chamber of Commerce, (916) 289-3619

Fourth of July Parade & Celebration
When: Fourth of July
What to expect: Parade, food, crafts and a fireworks display
Who to contact: Nevada City Chamber of Commerce, (800) 655-6569

Miners Day
When: First Saturday in August
What to expect: Old mining equipment displays, food and fun
Who to contact: Downieville Chamber of Commerce, (916) 289-3619

Apple Hill Festival
When: Labor Day to Christmas
What to expect: Lots of bake shops, apples galore, crafts, food and antiques
Who to contact: Camino Apple Hill Growers Association, (916) 644-7692

Downieville Septemberfest
When: Labor Day weekend in September
What to expect: Donkey rides, donkey racing and arts and crafts
Who to contact: Downieville Chamber of Commerce, (916) 289-3619

Nevada City's Constitution Day Parade & Celebration
When: Second Sunday in September
What to expect: Big parade recognizing famous women and men in history
Who to contact: Nevada City Chamber of Commerce, (800) 655-6569

Downieville Mother Lode Antique Bottle Show and Sale
When: September 9, 1995
What to expect: Lots of old stuff for sale, or just to look at, along with food and drink
Who to contact: Sierra County Chamber of Commerce, (800) 200-4949

Carmichael Founder's Day Celebration
When: Third Saturday in September
What to expect: Food, crafts and music
Who to contact: Carmichael Chamber of Commerce, (916) 481-1002

Downieville Quilt Show
When: First weekend in October
What to expect: Fall colors for a fall show of old quilts, new quilts and quilt-making supplies and demos
Who to contact: Sierra County Chamber of Commerce, (800) 200-4949

San Francisco Bay Area Leftovers

Prune Festival
When: Third weekend in May
What to expect: Music and prune foods of all sorts
Who to contact: Campbell Chamber of Commerce, (408) 378-6252

Los Altos Mayfest
When: Third weekend in May
What to expect: Pet parade, arts, crafts and a flea market
Who to contact: Los Altos Chamber of Commerce, (408) 354-9300

Mill Valley Mountain Plays
When: Last two Saturdays in May and Sundays in June
What to expect: Broadway plays on top of Mount Tamalpais
Who to contact: Mill Valley Chamber of Commerce, (415) 388-9700

Art in the Vineyard
When: Memorial Day
What to expect: Artists and their art at a local winery
Who to contact: Livermore Chamber of Commerce, (415) 447-1606

Strawberry Festival
When: First weekend in June
What to expect: Strawberry deserts galore and more
Who to contact: Los Gatos Chamber of Commerce, (408) 354-9300

Los Gatos Summerfest
When: June weekend
What to expect: Lots of food and crafts booths
Who to contact: Los Gatos Chamber of Commerce, (408) 354-9300

Art & Wine Festival
When: First full weekend in June
What to expect: Lots of premier artists and wines
Who to contact: Sunnyvale Chamber of Commerce, (408) 736-4971

Art & Wine Festival
When: First weekend in June
What to expect: Food, wine, arts and crafts
Who to contact: Walnut Creek Chamber of Commerce, (510) 934-2007

World's Fastest Rodeo
When: First weekend in June
What to expect: Western music, Western art and a Western rodeo
Who to contact: Livermore Chamber of Commerce, (415) 447-1606

Art Under the Oaks
When: Father's Day, June
What to expect: Food, music and an arts and crafts fair
Who to contact: Livermore Chamber of Commerce, (415) 447-1606

Sonoma Marin Fair
When: Third week in June
What to expect: All the things you expect from a fair: food, music, games and fun
Who to contact: Petaluma Chamber of Commerce, (707) 762-2785

Bay Hill Champagne Festival
When: Fourth weekend in June
What to expect: Arts, crafts, food and champagne
Who to contact: San Bruno Chamber of Commerce, (415) 588-0180

Country Vintner's Festival
When: Fourth weekend in June
What to expect: Wine, food, crafts and ocean air
Who to contact: Santa Cruz Convention and Visitors Bureau, (408) 425-1234

Art, Wine & Music Festival
When: Fourth weekend in June
What to expect: Food, music, art and wine
Who to contact: Novato Chamber of Commerce, (415) 897-1164

Saratoga Blossom Festival
When: Last Saturday in June
What to expect: California poppy blossoms, wine, food, arts and crafts
Who to contact: Saratoga Chamber of Commerce, (408) 867-0753

Stars & Stripes Day
When: Fourth of July
What to expect: Wine, food, arts and crafts, games and fireworks
Who to contact: Antioch Chamber of Commerce, (415) 757-1800

Livermore Old Fashioned Fourth
When: Fourth of July
What to expect: Music, games and food
Who to contact: Livermore Chamber of Commerce, (415) 447-1606

Tapestry in Talent
When: Weekend nearest the Fourth of July
What to expect: Art festival with food, music and drink
Who to contact: San Jose Visitor Information Center, (408) 283-8833

Cabrillo Music Festival
When: Third Thursday through fourth Sunday in July
What to expect: Modern and classical music
Who to contact: Aptos Chamber of Commerce, (408) 688-1467

Connoisseur's Market Place
When: Third weekend in July
What to expect: Lots of international foods, crafts and music
Who to contact: Menlo Park Chamber of Commerce, (415) 325-2818

Gilroy Garlic Festival
When: Last full weekend in July
What to expect: Garlic everything, music, crafts and more garlic
Who to contact: Gilroy Visitors Bureau, (408) 842-6437

Art & Wine Festival
When: Last weekend in July
What to expect: Art, wine, food and crafts
Who to contact: Fremont Chamber of Commerce, (510) 795-2244

Country Festival
When: Second weekend in August
What to expect: Country food, local wines, lots of food, music and crafts
Who to contact: Cupertino Chamber of Commerce, (408) 252-7054

Los Gatos Art & Wine Festival
When: Third weekend in August
What to expect: Local wines, food and crafts
Who to contact: Los Gatos Chamber of Commerce, (408) 354-9300

Milpitas Art & Wine Festival
When: Third weekend in August
What to expect: Wine, food, arts, crafts and fun
Who to contact: Milpitas Chamber of Commerce, (408) 262-2613

Hispanic Cultural Festival
When: Last full weekend in August
What to expect: Rides, kids' shows and games, piñata breaking and lots
of south of the border foods
Who to contact: Gilroy Visitors Bureau, (408) 842-6438

Concord Fall Fest
When: Labor Day weekend
What to expect: International foods, wine, crafts and music
Who to contact: Concord Convention and Visitors Bureau,
(415) 685-1184

Livermore Harvest Festival
When: Labor Day weekend
What to expect: Grape harvest, food, crafts and music
Who to contact: Livermore Chamber of Commerce, (415) 447-1606

Millbrae Art & Wine Festival
When: Labor Day weekend
What to expect: Wine, art, food and games
Who to contact: Millbrae Chamber of Commerce, (415) 697-7324

Sausalito Art Festival
When: Labor Day weekend
What to expect: Wine, fine art, fine crafts, games and food
Who to contact: Sausalito Chamber of Commerce, (415) 332-0505

Castro Valley Fall Festival
When: Weekend after Labor Day
What to expect: Wine, food, crafts and music
Who to contact: Castro Valley Chamber of Commerce, (415) 537-5300

Mountain View Art & Wine Festival
When: Weekend after Labor Day
What to expect: Wine, food, games, music and crafts
Who to contact: Mountain View Chamber of Commerce, (415) 968-8378

Capitola Begonia Festival
When: Second Sunday in September
What to expect: Parade of flowers, food, music and crafts
Who to contact: Capitola Chamber of Commerce, (408) 475-6522

Martinez Art in the Park
When: Third Sunday in September
What to expect: Local artists and crafts, food and wine
Who to contact: Martinez Area Chamber of Commerce, (415) 228-2345

Capitola Art & Wine Festival
When: Second weekend in September
What to expect: Art, wine, food and music
Who to contact: Capitola Chamber of Commerce, (408) 475-6522

Benicia Handicraft Fair
When: Second Saturday in September after Labor Day
What to expect: Arts, crafts, food and fun
Who to contact: Benicia Chamber of Commerce, (800) 559-7377

Pittsburg Seafood Festival
When: Second weekend in September
What to expect: Seafood galore, including chowders, clams and
calamari, wine and music
Who to contact: Pittsburg Chamber of Commerce, (415) 432-7301

Coast Fog Fest
When: Third weekend in September
What to expect: Seafood of all sorts, with crafts, music and wine
Who to contact: Pacifica Chamber of Commerce, (415) 355-4122

River Town Jamboree
When: Last weekend in September
What to expect: Food, music, games and crafts
Who to contact: Antioch Chamber of Commerce, (415) 757-1800

San Bruno Street Festival
When: First weekend in October
What to expect: Crafts, food, wine and music
Who to contact: San Bruno Chamber of Commerce, (415) 588-0180

Vallejo Wine & Cheese Exposition
When: First weekend in October
What to expect: Lots of wine, cheese and international foods to enjoy
Who to contact: Vallejo Convention and Visitors Bureau, (707) 642-3653

Bass Derby
When: Second weekend in October
What to expect: Arts, crafts, food, wine, music, plus a little bass fishing
Who to contact: Rio Vista Chamber of Commerce, (707) 374-2700

Brussel Sprouts Festival
When: Second weekend in October
What to expect: Brussel sprouts in just about every kind of food imaginable and unimaginable
Who to contact: Santa Cruz Visitors Bureau, (408) 425-1234

Half Moon Bay Art & Pumpkin Festival
When: Third weekend in October
What to expect: Crafts, music, pumpkin food and pumpkin carving for Halloween
Who to contact: Half Moon Bay Art & Pumpkin Festival, (415) 726-9652 or (415) 726-3491

Los Gatos Children's Christmas & Holiday Parade
When: First Saturday in December
What to expect: Children in costumes, food, crafts and fun
Who to contact: Los Gatos Chamber of Commerce, (408) 354-9300

Central Coast Leftovers

San Luis Obispo Mardi Gras Street Fair
When: February 11, 1995
What to expect: A New Orleans-style street party
Who to contact: San Luis Obispo Visitor & Convention Bureau, (800) 634-1414

Santa Cruz Clam Chowder Cook-Off
When: Fourth Saturday in February
What to expect: The famous boardwalk covered with pots of steamin' chowder
Who to contact: Santa Cruz County Convention and Visitor's Bureau, (800) 833-3494

Santa Barbara International Film Festival
When: Second Friday through third Sunday in March
What to expect: Films, workshops and critics critiquing
Who to contact: Santa Barbara Visitor and Convention Bureau, (800) 927-4688

Paso Robles Wine Festival
When: Third weekend in May
What to expect: Wine sales, wine sampling and music
Who to contact: Paso Robles Chamber of Commerce, (805) 238-0506

Mushroom Festival
When: Memorial Day weekend
What to expect: Lots of mushroom dishes, wine and music
Who to contact: Morgan Hill Chamber of Commerce, (408) 779-9444

Flag & Water Festival
When: Second Saturday in June
What to expect: Music, food, wine and crafts booths
Who to contact: Walnut Creek Chamber of Commerce, (510) 934-2007

Pacific Fine Arts
When: Second weekend in June
What to expect: Ceramics, stained glass and other fine arts
Who to contact: San Carlos Chamber of Commerce, (415) 593-1068

Junefest
When: Second Sunday in June
What to expect: Lots of food, music and fun
Who to contact: Los Osos and Baywood Chamber of Commerce, (805) 528-4884

Burrito Bash and Crafts Faire
When: Third weekend in June
What to expect: Arts and crafts, music and burritos
Who to contact: Watsonville Area Chamber of Commerce, (408) 724-3849

Lompoc Flower Festival
When: Fourth weekend in June
What to expect: Lots of flowers, food and entertainment
Who to contact: Lompoc Valley Festival Association, (805) 736-4567

Mozart Festival
When: Last weekend in July through first weekend in August
What to expect: Festival of chamber music and symphonies
Who to contact: San Luis Obispo Visitor and Convention Bureau,
    (800) 634-1414

Danish Days
When: Second weekend in September
What to expect: Danish dancing, food, beer and music
Who to contact: Solvang Visitor Bureau, (800) 468-6765

Artichoke Festival
When: Third weekend in September
What to expect: Artichokes galore and an arts and crafts fair
Who to contact: Castroville Artichoke Festival, (408) 633-2465

Harbor Festival
When: First weekend in October
What to expect: Wine, seafood, arts and crafts and music
Who to contact: Morro Bay Chamber of Commerce, (800) 231-0592

Pioneer Day
When: Saturday before Columbus Day in October
What to expect: Car show, street dance and inexpensive fun
Who to contact: Paso Robles Chamber of Commerce, (800) 322-3471

Atascadero Colony Days

When: Third Saturday in October
What to expect: Parade, music, arts and crafts booths and firemen's brigade
Who to contact: Atascadero Chamber of Commerce, (805) 466-2044

Octoberfest

When: Last Sunday in October
What to expect: Food, music and arts and crafts booths
Who to contact: Los Osos Chamber of Commerce, (805) 528-4884

❖ ❖ ❖ ❖

Central Valley Leftovers

19th Annual Stockton Ag Expo

When: Third week in January
What to expect: Food, agricultural displays and more food
Who to contact: Greater Stockton Chamber of Commerce, (209) 547-2960

Clovis Big Hat Festival

When: First Saturday in April
What to expect: Wear any old hat and enjoy food, music and a crafts sale
Who to contact: Clovis Chamber of Commerce, (209) 299-7273

Camellia Cup Regatta

When: April 15 & 16, 1995
What to expect: A race for many classes of boats on Folsom Lake
Who to contact: Folsom Lake Yacht Club, (916) 985-3704

Arvin Wildflower Festival

When: Third Saturday in April
What to expect: Food, crafts, kids' games and parade
Who to contact: Arvin Chamber of Commerce, (805) 854-2265

Heritage Days

When: Third weekend in April

What to expect: Wagon rides, staged cowboy gunfights, crafts, food and drink
Who to contact: Bakersfield Convention and Visitors Bureau, (800) 325-6001

Teamsters' Jackass Mail Run
When: Third Saturday in April
What to expect: Races, food and fun
Who to contact: Springville Chamber of Commerce, (209) 539-2312

Big Hat Days & Rodeo
When: Fourth weekend in April
What to expect: Rodeo events, food and fun
Who to contact: Springville Chamber of Commerce, (209) 539-2312

Winton Spring Festival
When: Fourth weekend in April
What to expect: Crafts and food to welcome the wildflowers back
Who to contact: Winton Chamber of Commerce, (209) 358-5615

Clovis Rodeo
When: Fourth weekend in April
What to expect: Cowboys, cowgirls, broncs, bulls and wild times
Who to contact: Clovis Chamber of Commerce, (209) 299-7273

Cinco de Mayo
When: First weekend in May
What to expect: Celebration of the Americanized Mexican holiday
Who to contact: Delano Chamber of Commerce, (805) 725-2518

Elk Grove Western Festival
When: First weekend in May
What to expect: Crafts, music, horses and hayrides in the park
Who to contact: Elk Grove Chamber of Commerce, (916) 685-3911

Fair Oaks Fiesta
When: First weekend in May
What to expect: All kinds of ethnic foods, games and live music
Who to contact: Fair Oaks Chamber of Commerce, (916) 967-2903

Avenal Oldtimers Days
When: First weekend in May
What to expect: Parade, barbecue and crafts
Who to contact: Avenal Chamber of Commerce, (209) 386-0690

Willows Lamb Derby
When: First Monday through Sunday in May
What to expect: Sheep sheering and sheep dog competitions
Who to contact: Willows Chamber of Commerce, (916) 934-8150

Red Suspenders Days
When: Third Saturday in May
What to expect: Bed races, foot races, firemen's muster, mule show and dance until midnight
Who to contact: Gridley Chamber of Commerce, (916) 846-3142

Horned Toad Derby
When: Memorial Day weekend
What to expect: Wine, food, arts and crafts, music and horned toad races
Who to contact: Coalinga Chamber of Commerce, (209) 935-2948

Davis Street Faire
When: First weekend in June
What to expect: Lots of food of all kind, wine, crafts and music
Who to contact: Davis Chamber of Commerce, (916) 756-5160

Apricot Fiesta
When: First weekend in June
What to expect: Hot air balloons, food, music and apricots galore
Who to contact: Patterson-Westley Chamber of Commerce, (209) 892-2821

Red Bluff Festival '95
When: First Saturday in June
What to expect: Local artists show wood carvings, paintings, jewelry and other crafts
Who to contact: Red Bluff Chamber of Commerce, (916) 665-6225

Tulare Dairy Festival

When: Second weekend in June
What to expect: Milking contests, milk products, food, wine and crafts
Who to contact: Tulare Chamber of Commerce, (209) 686-1547

Los Molinos Luau

When: Second Saturday in June
What to expect: Hawaiian luau with all the food, music and fun in a town on the Sacramento River
Who to contact: Los Molinos Chamber of Commerce, (916) 384-2251

Modesto à la Carte

When: Third weekend in June
What to expect: Wine, food, crafts and music
Who to contact: Modesto Chamber of Commerce, (209) 577-5757

Crawdad Festival

When: Third weekend in June
What to expect: Crawdads cooked-up in lots of ways, wine, more food and music
Who to contact: Isleton Chamber of Commerce, (916) 777-6031

Hilmar Dairy Festival

When: Third Saturday in June
What to expect: Lots of food, cows and cow milking
Who to contact: Hilmar Chamber of Commerce, (209) 668-0719

Valley Heritage Day

When: Fourth of July
What to expect: Lots of home cooking, crafts and music
Who to contact: King City and South Monterey County Chamber of Commerce, (408) 385-3814

Antique & Craft Show

When: Weekend after Fourth of July
What to expect: Antiques, crafts, food and music
Who to contact: Oakdale Chamber of Commerce, (209) 847-2244

Dry Bean Festival
When: First weekend in August
What to expect: Lots of beans and bean-filled foods, more foods, crafts and music
Who to contact: Tracy District Chamber of Commerce, (209) 835-2131

Mountain Festival
When: Third weekend in August
What to expect: Rodeo, western dancing, lots of food, crafts and drink
Who to contact: Tehachapi Chamber of Commerce, (805) 822-4180

Cantaloupe Round-up
When: Fourth weekend in August
What to expect: Food, crafts, music, dancing and cantaloupes
Who to contact: Firebaugh District Chamber of Commerce, (209) 659-3701

Wasco Festival of Roses
When: Weekend after Labor Day
What to expect: Roses, crafts, kids activities and food
Who to contact: Wasco Chamber of Commerce, (805) 758-2746

Kerman Harvest Festival
When: Weekend after Labor Day
What to expect: Local wines, food, crafts and fun
Who to contact: Kerman Chamber of Commerce, (209) 846-6343

Weed's Pasta Cook-Off & Sausage Challenge
When: Second Saturday in September
What to expect: Pasta and sausage to eat, music and crafts to enjoy
Who to contact: Weed Chamber of Commerce, (916) 938-4624

Balloons Over the Valley
When: Second weekend in September
What to expect: Early morning hot air balloon launch, food and crafts
Who to contact: Modesto Convention and Visitors Bureau, (209) 577-5757

Atwater Fall Festival
When: Third weekend in September
What to expect: Lots of music, food, crafts and games
Who to contact: Atwater Chamber of Commerce, (209) 358-4251

Raisin Festival
When: Last weekend in September
What to expect: Lots of raisin-filled foods, crafts, more food and music
Who to contact: Dinuba Chamber of Commerce, (209) 591-2707

Beckwourth Western Days Festival
When: First weekend in October
What to expect: Dress western and enjoy the food, music and crafts
Who to contact: Yuba-Sutter Chamber of Commerce, (916) 743-6501

Renaissance Faire
When: First weekend in October
What to expect: Knights in armor, traditional dances, plays, food and drink
Who to contact: Hanford City Chamber of Commerce, (800) 722-1114

Johnny Appleseed Days
When: First Saturday in October
What to expect: Lots of apple-filled foods, an apple race and crafts booths
Who to contact: Paradise Chamber of Commerce, (916) 877-9356

Riverbank Cheese & Wine Expo
When: Second weekend in October
What to expect: Cheese and wine tasting, crafts and music
Who to contact: Riverbank Chamber of Commerce, (209) 869-4541

Stagecoach Stampede
When: Second weekend in October
What to expect: Food, drink, crafts and a dance
Who to contact: Porterville Chamber of Commerce, (209) 784-7502

Apple Festival
When: Third weekend in October
What to expect: Apple everything, crafts, music and cooking contests
Who to contact: Springville Chamber of Commerce, (209) 539-2312

Almond Blossom Festival
When: Starts Friday, fourth weekend in February
What to expect: Barbecue, crafts and art displays set amidst orchards of
almond blossoms
Who to contact: Ripon Chamber of Commerce, (209) 599-7519

✤ ✤ ✤ ✤

South Coast & San Diego County Leftovers

Olivera Street Mardi Gras
When: Mid-February
What to expect: Party fun and food in Los Angeles' historic area
Who to contact: Olivera Street Merchants, (213) 687-4344

Camellia Festival
When: Last weekend in February
What to expect: Camellia blossom parade floats built by kids
Who to contact: Temple City Chamber of Commerce, (818) 286-3101

San Juan Capistrano Heritage Festival
When: March, date tentative
What to expect: Fair, rodeo, food, arts and crafts
Who to contact: San Juan Capistrano Chamber of Commerce,
(714) 493-4700

Santa Ana Zoo Birthday
When: March 4, 1995
What to expect: Cake, games and lots of fun for kids and adults alike
Who to contact: Santa Ana Zoo, (714) 953-8555

Alhambra Springfest
When: Fourth Saturday in April
What to expect: Lots of food, arts, crafts and live music
Who to contact: Alhambra Chamber of Commerce, (818) 282-8481

California Beach Party
When: Last Saturday in April
What to expect: Beach sand, beach sports, music and food

Who to contact: Ventura Chamber of Commerce, (800) 388-8297

Village Street Faire
When: First Saturday in May
What to expect: International foods, crafts and more
Who to contact: Carlsbad Convention and Visitors Bureau,
    (800) 227-5722

Oxnard Strawberry Festival
When: Third weekend in May
What to expect: Strawberry delights of all sorts, crafts, music and more
Who to contact: Oxnard Greater Chamber of Commerce, (800) 994-4852

Garden Grove Strawberry Festival
When: Memorial Day weekend
What to expect: Strawberries, crafts, a parade and music
Who to contact: Garden Grove Chamber of Commerce, (714) 638-7950

Fiesta de la Artes
When: Memorial Day weekend
What to expect: Big assortment of food, crafts and music
Who to contact: Hermosa Beach Chamber of Commerce, (213) 376-0951

Ojai Music Festival
When: Weekend after Memorial Day
What to expect: Lots of great music of all kinds
Who to contact: Ojai Chamber of Commerce, (805) 646-8126

Julian Heritage Quilt Show
When: June 28 to July 4, 1995
What to expect: Old quilts and new quilts and patterns and supplies for
    all quilt makers
Who to contact: Julian Women's Club, (619) 765-0436

Independence Arts Festival
When: Weekend after Fourth of July
What to expect: Jazz and big band music, food and crafts
Who to contact: Santa Monica Visitor Center, (310) 393-7593

APPENDICES

Malibu Arts Festival
When: Last weekend in July
What to expect: Lots of arts and crafts, food and music
Who to contact: Malibu Chamber of Commerce, (213) 456-9025

Old Spanish Days Fiesta
When: First weekend in August
What to expect: Dancing, arts and crafts, food and music
Who to contact: Santa Barbara Convention and Visitors Bureau,
(800) 927-4688

Venice Summer Arts & Crafts Festival
When: Second Sunday in August
What to expect: Hundreds of crafts booths, food and live music
Who to contact: Venice Chamber of Commerce, (310) 827-2366

Newport Seafest
When: Second Friday through third Sunday in September
What to expect: Seafaring races, surfing and swimming contests, food,
crafts and music
Who to contact: Newport Convention and Visitors Bureau,
(800) 942-6278

Avocado & Wine Festival
When: Second Saturday in September
What to expect: Avocados, wine, food, crafts and music
Who to contact: Fallbrook Chamber of Commerce, (619) 728-5845

Oceanside Harbor Days
When: Third weekend in September
What to expect: Various international foods, seafood, crafts and artists
Who to contact: Oceanside Chamber of Commerce, (619) 721-1101

Costa Mesa Arts on the Green
When: Third weekend in September
What to expect: Music, crafts, food and dancing
Who to contact: Costa Mesa Chamber of Commerce, (714) 574-8780

Bonitafest
When: Last weekend in September
What to expect: Parade, entertainment, crafts, food and dancing
Who to contact: Chula Vista Chamber of Commerce, (619) 420-6603

Oldetime Melodrama & Olio
When: Last four weekends in October
What to expect: Old-time show and scholarship fundraiser at the Julian
    Town Hall
Who to contact: Julian Triangle Club, (619) 765-0761

La Mesa Oktoberfest
When: First weekend in October
What to expect: Great German food, brew and crafts
Who to contact: La Mesa Chamber of Commerce, (619) 456-7700

Maritime Days Festival
When: First weekend in October
What to expect: Seafood, crafts and music
Who to contact: Oxnard Greater Chamber of Commerce, (805) 994-4852

Renaissance Faire
When: Second weekend in October
What to expect: A trip back 300 years to the food, crafts and fun of old
Who to contact: San Marcos Chamber of Commerce, (619) 744-1270

Tustin Tiller Days
When: Second weekend in October
What to expect: International foods, arts, crafts and special games for
    the kids
Who to contact: Tustin Chamber of Commerce, (714) 544-5341

Golden City Days
When: Second weekend in October
What to expect: Music, food, crafts and kids' games
Who to contact: Santa Ana Chamber of Commerce, (714) 541-5353

Boo at the Zoo
When: October 27, 28 & 29, 1995
What to expect: Halloween fun for kids and their parents during this
   weekend at the zoo
Who to contact: Santa Ana Zoo, (714) 953-8555

Inland Empire & Southern Deserts Leftovers

Palm Springs International Film Festival
When: Ten days in January
What to expect: Lots of films, old and new, in a place where the stars
   sometimes vacation
Who to contact: Palm Springs International Film Festival, (619) 322-2930

Ninth Annual Southwest Arts Festival
When: January 21 & 22, 1995
What to expect: Art show for all sorts of art and crafts, with a focus on
   the American Southwest
Who to contact: Indio Chamber of Commerce, (619) 347-0676

Amateur & Pro Snow Ski Competitions
When: January, date not set
What to expect: Great downhill skiing competition
Who to contact: Big Bear Mountain Ski Resort, (909) 585-2519

Italian Festival
When: February 5, 1995
What to expect: Lots of good food for a really good day of eating
Who to contact: Dolly Sinatra Lodge, Desert Hot Springs, (619) 329-4879

Riverside County National Date Festival
When: February 17 to 26, 1995
What to expect: Bring your favorite date, the human kind, to a festival
   celebrating a desert fruit
Who to contact: Desert Expo Center in Indio, (619) 863-8247

Easter Egg Coloring and Hunt
When: Easter weekend
What to expect: Games and an egg hunt designed for kids
Who to contact: Lake Perris State Recreation Area, (909) 657-0676

Colorado River Country Fair
When: Third week in April
What to expect: Animals, food, crafts and fair fun
Who to contact: Blythe Chamber of Commerce, (800) 445-0541

Renaissance Pleasure Faire
When: Weekends beginning the third weekend in April; ending the second weekend in June
What to expect: A trip back to the 16th century, with food and fun
Who to contact: San Bernardino Convention and Visitors Bureau, (800) 669-8336

Desert Dixieland Jazz Festival
When: Last weekend in April to second weekend in May
What to expect: Lots of bands, lots of music, food and fun
Who to contact: Cathedral City Chamber of Commerce, (619) 328-1213

Temecula Balloon & Wine Festival
When: Third weekend in May
What to expect: Hot air balloons, wine, food and crafts
Who to contact: Temecula Chamber of Commerce, (909) 676-5090

Grubstake Days & Rodeo
When: Memorial Day weekend
What to expect: Live music, good food, crafts and fun
Who to contact: Yucca Valley Chamber of Commerce, (619) 365-6323

Fontana Days
When: First weekend in June
What to expect: Music, crafts and food
Who to contact: Fontana Chamber of Commerce, (909) 822-4433

Cherry Festival
When: Second weekend in June
What to expect: Cherries in abundance, more food, music and crafts
Who to contact: Beaumont Chamber of Commerce, (909) 845-9541

Big Bear Valley Clementine Contest
When: July, date not set
What to expect: Country fair, children's events and fun
Who to contact: Old Miners Association, (909) 866-7260

Fourth of July Jamboree
When: Fourth of July
What to expect: Fun contests, food, music and fireworks
Who to contact: Norco Chamber of Commerce, (208) 743-2531

Big Bear Valley Loggers Jubilee
When: July date not set
What to expect: Logging events, a whiskerino contest, crafts and food
Who to contact: Old Miners Association, (909) 866-7260

Chili Cook-off and Fireman's Muster
When: Third weekend in July
What to expect: Firemen games and contests, crafts, music and good food
Who to contact: Redlands Chamber of Commerce, (909) 793-2546

Antelope Valley Fair
When: Fourth weekend in August through Labor Day
What to expect: Fair fun, food, music, parade, carnival and more
Who to contact: Lancaster Chamber of Commerce, (805) 948-4518

Big Bear Valley Chili Cook-Off & Poker Ride
When: August, date not set
What to expect: Good food and a horse race that includes poker hands to win
Who to contact: Old Miner's Association, (909) 866-7260

Gold Rush Days
When: Second weekend in September
What to expect: Lots of music, food, crafts and drink
Who to contact: Mojave Chamber of Commerce, (805) 824-2481

Grape Harvest Festival
When: First Weekend in October
What to expect: Music, food, arts, crafts and wine
Who to contact: Rancho Cucamonga Chamber of Commerce,
(909) 987-1012

Palmdale Fall Festival
When: Second weekend in October
What to expect: Lots of musical fun, artists and their works and food
for all
Who to contact: Palmdale Chamber of Commerce, (805) 273-3232

October Applefest
When: Second weekend in October
What to expect: Lots of apple goodies, apples to buy and apples to pick
Who to contact: Tehachapi Chamber of Commerce, (805) 822-4180

Apple Valley Days
When: Third Saturday in October
What to expect: A rodeo, food and a carnival
Who to contact: Apple Valley Chamber of Commerce, (619) 247-7175

Brawley Cattle Call
When: Second weekend in November
What to expect: A rodeo with food, crafts and music
Who to contact: Brawley Chamber of Commerce, (619) 344-3160

17 Fun Foot Runs & Races

12 Fun Bike Rides & Races

First Time for (Almost) Everything

Bubble or Nothin'
[And A Few Other Odd Contests...]

✤ ✤ ✤ ✤

Index

INDEX

ABOUT THE CALIFORNIA
STATE PARKS FOUNDATION

Walk among the towering and ancient redwood trees; gaze up a 1,200-mile coastline that stretches from Mexico to Oregon; wade through beautiful inland lakes; push onward through the Sierras; revel in the vastness of California's deserts—for over 25 years, the California State Parks Foundation has protected these natural and historic treasures of California.

Now numbering more than 275 State Parks, our California system is truly unique and offers many recreational and educational opportunities for the benefit of all Californians and visitors to this great state.

The mission of the California State Parks Foundation is very straightforward: acquire land and artifacts for our State Parks, protect what needs protecting, and provide funding to the California Department of Parks and Recreation to complete urgently needed projects and programs in our State Park System. The Foundation joins private citizens, corporations and foundations that wish to contribute to the State Park System. This private support makes possible vital projects that benefit all Californians.

We are a public non-profit organization that receives no government funding and is solely dependent upon grants and gifts from private individuals, corporations and foundations, as well as annual contributions from our members.

The State Park System is not frozen in time. New ideas, new lands to incorporate into parks, new demands for buildings and services to help serve tens of millions of visitors—all contribute to a system that grows each year.

You are the owner of the State Park System considered by many to be the finest in the world. The most beautiful areas of California are found in these parks. It should and will last forever. As the guardian of our parks, we can help insure that future with your tax-deductible contribution to the California State Parks Foundation.

Many opportunities exist for interested people and companies to contribute to our State Parks and improve the quality of life here in our California home. Your support is needed. To learn more about how you can help California State Parks and enjoy membership benefits, please write or call:

CALIFORNIA
STATE PARKS
FOUNDATION

The California State Parks Foundation
800 College Avenue, P.O. Box 548
Kentfield, CA 94914
(415) 258-9975

The California State Parks Foundation is an independent membership organization dedicated to protecting and preserving California's State Parks.

Año Nuevo State Reserve: Thousands of northern elephant seals gather in a timeless annual breeding ritual, protected from, and watched over, by thousands of visitors to the San Mateo coast.

Mono Lake Tufa State Reserve: Awesome tufa spires bask under the snow-covered peaks at Mono Lake, feeding grounds for hundreds of thousands of migrating birds in the eastern Sierra.

Hearst Castle State Historic Monument: California's 130-room castle glistens high above the ocean, welcoming a million visitors each year in San Simeon.

Fort Ross State Historic Park: Foundation efforts helped preserve this southernmost outpost of Russian fur traders, first built in 1812, now a popular site for tourists on the Sonoma coast.

State Park Wildlife Reserves: State Parks provide sanctuaries for California's wildlife, including many endangered species.

(Left) Jack London State Historic Park: The great treasures of this author reside in "The House of Happy Walls" on 800 acres in the Valley of the Moon, Sonoma County.